ASSOCIATION
LAW
HANDBOOK

ASSOCIATION LAW HANDBOOK

SECOND EDITION

Jerald A. Jacobs

The Bureau of National Affairs, Inc. • Washington, D.C. 20037

Library of Congress Cataloging-in-Publication Data

Jacobs, Jerald A.
  Association law handbook.

  Bibliography: p.
  Includes index.
  1. Trade and professional associations—
Law and legislation—United States. I. Title.
KF2902.J32 1986   346.73′064   86-18795
ISBN 0-87179-525-6   347.30664

International Standard Book Number: 0-87179-525-6
Printed in the United States of America

FOREWORD

"While our industry and commerce must be based upon incentive to the individual, yet the national interest requires a certain degree of cooperation between individuals in order that we may reduce and eliminate industrial waste, lay the foundation for constant decrease in production and distribution costs, and thereby obtain the fundamental increase in wages and standards of living . . . trade associations have rapidly developed into legitimate and constructive fields of the utmost public interest and have marked a fundamental step in the gradual evolution of our whole economic life."

These words, as contemporary as they sound, were written by my predecessor, Herbert Hoover, as Secretary of Commerce in his foreword to a 1927 Department of Commerce publication on associations.

Trade and professional associations are ruled by laws, as well as by standards of ethics, fairness, equality, and commitment to good citizenship in all of their endeavors. In light of this, associations are legitimate influences on the improvement of our economic life.

The publication of this book on the laws and standards governing trade and professional associations is a milestone in the history of the association movement in the United States. The book will help all who deal with associations to advance the goals of our free enterprise system.

Mr. Jacobs and those who assisted him in his effort are to be congratulated.

Malcolm Baldrige
Secretary of Commerce

INTRODUCTION

This book is a practical guide to the laws that govern trade and professional associations. It is a legal outline for those who work in or with associations. The book provides basic information on how corporate, antitrust and tax laws affect both the formation and the operation of associations.

Throughout this country's history, the contributions made by trade and professional associations to its economy, its government and its society have been enormously important. American citizens, as de Toqueville observed, have always been characterized by their propensity toward forming cooperative organizations. The trade and professional association movement in the United States is the most obvious manifestation of this singular national characteristic. The Constitution contains an implicit protection for forming and operating associations in the First Amendment's "right of the people peaceably to assemble, and to petition the government for redress of grievances." Today's trade and professional association members do indeed "assemble" at conventions, seminars and other meetings; and they "petition" at all levels of government in order to guide and influence government policy and action. Associations also do much more. They are self-governing organizations of member firms or individuals united by their common commitment to lawful joint action. That lawful joint action can include educational activities, statistical programs, research projects, standardization efforts or a host of other endeavors in addition to governmental affairs.

In an age in which men and nations seem more often to obey instincts than laws, government in the United States has nevertheless piled law upon law to guide, control, inhibit, restrict or arrest the actions of all persons and institutions. A full measure of those laws has been made applicable to associations. Laws, regulations and decisions directly affect both the organizing and the managing of every trade or professional association. The ever-growing body of legal directives has made it difficult sometimes to determine what precisely *is* lawful joint action.

This book is a summary of these laws, regulations and decisions which govern trade and professional associations. It is designed to assist executives who *manage* associations by providing a comprehensive overview, and thus an early warning, of issues or areas that pose potential legal dangers. It is intended also to assist attorneys, accountants and others who *advise* associations by providing references, for each subject that is covered in the book, to more extended treatments published elsewhere. The book will even be useful to those who are officers, directors or members of associations and desire a fuller understanding of the legal bases for their organizations' policies and programs.

Winston Churchill once addressed a temperence group and was challenged by a member who accused him of having drunk enough alcohol in his lifetime to fill the meeting room halfway to the ceiling. Churchill responded, "So many things to do; so little time in which to do them. . . ."

This book is ambitious. It summarizes virtually all of the general corporate, antitrust and taxation subjects which can be expected to arise in typical trade or professional associations. Many of the subjects of this book have not been covered elsewhere in the extensive literature on association law. Even for those subjects which have been analyzed in other texts, the treatment here is unique in its plain-English, outline format.

The overriding goal of the author has been to condense a sprawling body of often complicated and occasionally elusive legal principles into a compact handbook that is at once accurate and readable.

With the reader's indulgence, a few cautionary notes are necessary. First, because it is but a summary guide to association law, the book could mislead the unwary. Its outline format does not ordinarily allow for extensive analyses of the complete backgrounds and implications of many association legal requirements. A serious study of any legal issue demands that its history and ramifications be explored fully, for example, by careful review of pertinent court decisions, legislative histories, regulation preambles or interpretive articles. Those who have some special concern or question that is not exhaustively dealt with in this text should, by all means, pursue the extensive references that are given to applicable books, articles, cases, statutes, regulations and other related resources. Such references follow each of the chapters.

It has been said of Eric Severaid that, in an age that rewards (and elects) simplifiers, he is a student of complexity. This book deliberately avoids oversimplification by listing in summary fashion many aspects of the complex legal rules that govern trade and professional associations. In doing so, emphasis is necessarily spread throughout each chapter rather than placed on aspects of the subject most pertinent to particular kinds or sizes of associations. More emphasis, or focus, must be supplied by the conscientious reader in the light of the circumstances of each association that the reader manages, advises or otherwise has interest in.

Next, it must be recognized that sound legal advice requires a thorough understanding of the factual context of any issue or problem that arises for an association. Only then can a reasoned application of law be made to the specific facts upon consideration of the practical problems presented and the legal alternatives available. No book can, by itself, provide sound legal advice, least of all one which is intended only to summarize often lengthy and subtle legal requirements in areas such as antitrust and taxation. Providing legal advice is beyond the scope and purpose of this handbook.

In many areas covered by this book, the law is still emerging and remains subject to interpretation. Whatever authority already exists in those areas is summarized in order to establish a basis for readers' present analyses and future reevaluations as new laws, regulations or decisions provide more definite authority. This handbook is designed to steer the association executive or advisor toward what he should be *thinking about*, not to tell him what he should be *thinking*.

Finally, the author's philosophy is that the nature of trade and professional associations usually demands more conservative approaches to legal problems than are customary for business corporations. This book reflects that philosophy. A business corporation, when faced with interpretive legal ramifications of a particular problem, can evaluate those ramifications and can choose a course in which some minimal legal risks are discounted or even consciously assumed. Associations must ordinarily be more conservative. They have a responsibility to represent their entire trade or profession. They must consider every legal problem in the context of membership relations—perhaps also in the context of public relations or governmental relations. The hardest burden to bear, as Mark Twain said, is that of good example.

In short, the reader is cautioned that this handbook is a summary treatment of association law. It does not provide legal advice. And it reflects a conservative approach to the subject.

A note is in order regarding the Resources sections at the end of each chapter. These sections contain references to books, periodicals, cases, statutes, regulations or other resources which relate to the subjects of their preceding chapters. When citations to legal decisions are given, the order of their listing is the same as that in which the cases were discussed in the text of the chapter. In addition to the chapter references, a bibliographical listing at the end of the book provides more complete information on sources of availability for those books and periodicals most frequently referenced in the text.

The challenge of compacting a large body of law into an accurate but readable outline, in order to maximize its usefulness to association executives and advisors, was awesome. To help meet the challenge, several recognized experts, with vast experience in the association field, agreed to review the text of the First Edition and offer their valuable comments. This book is the product of its author, who is responsible alone for its inevitable errors and omissions. But to the extent that the book fulfills its role as a precise and informative guide to the law of trade and professional associations, these consultants deserve major credit. The author is indebted to each of them for their sage and generous assistance. The experts are Malcolm D. MacArthur, Esq., a partner in the Washington, D.C. law firm of Keller & Heckman, H. Richard Mayberry, Esq., a partner in the Washington, D.C. law firm of Mayberry & Leighton, and Frank B. Reilly, Esq., a partner in the Newark, N.J. law firm of Crummy, Del Deo, Dolan & Purcell.

Samuel B. Shapiro, CAE, deserves special recognition. He inspired the First Edition and reviewed the entire text. He is the retired Executive Director of the Textile Rental Services Association of America. He has also had the honor of serving as the chief elected officer of the American Society of Association Executives. Sam Shapiro is a dean of the modern association executive profession, having assisted in founding the prestigious Certified Association Executive credentialing program and having participated over many years in scores of other research and educational projects that have greatly enhanced the association management profession. He currently provides management consulting services to trade and professional associations through Samuel B. Shapiro Consulting, Inc., in Miami Beach, Florida.

Besides these expert consultants, many other individuals contributed to the creation and production of this book. Numerous professional association executives have planted seeds over the years from which the book grew. Hugh McCahey and Forrest P. Lockwood of the Association Division of the Chamber of Commerce of the United States fertilized and watered the seeds by their kind encouragement and by their assistance in locating published resources. R. William Taylor, CAE, and Elissa M. Myers of the American Society of Association Executives helped with the harvest by arranging with the publisher for ASAE to distribute the book in the association community. Francis Hill Slowinski, Louise R. Goines, and Mary Green Miner, at The Bureau of National Affairs, Inc., brought the harvest to market with their most professional editing and publishing efforts.

Finally, my wife Janice and our children, Peter, Christopher, Elizabeth, Andrew and James (the last two of whom arrived together in this world during final revisions to the First Edition), by their love, understanding and support, contributed to make this book, in a sense, a family project.

Should readers have difficulty in locating referenced materials in the Resources sections, or have questions or comments about the text, the author will attempt to fulfill any reasonable requests for assistance.

Jerald A. Jacobs
Jenner & Block
Washington, D.C.

April 1986

CONTENTS

xiii

I

ASSOCIATION
ADMINISTRATION

Chapter 1

THE IMPORTANCE OF ASSOCIATIONS

Business and professional leaders have long recognized that many of their common business and professional goals can be achieved more quickly and more easily through joint action than through individual action. Associations are joint-action organizations. They are formed to aid members in achieving their common goals while at the same time observing the legal and ethical restraints that a democratic society imposes upon businesses and professions. Associations provide members with tools to more efficiently, more responsibly, and more effectively conduct their businesses or practice their professions. When associations change the quality or conditions of their members for the better, the ramifications are far-reaching. In a broad sense, associations serve to improve the economic and social well-being of the entire nation when they are successful in improving the well-being of their members.

The value of any association to its members is singular and dynamic. The importance of associations in general is concretely demonstrated by a listing of some major activities in which many associations typically engage. These activities were identified in a survey conducted several years ago by the Chamber of Commerce of the United States, and are discussed briefly in the following paragraphs.

SUMMARY

- *Accounting activities* of associations now usually consist of collecting, compiling, and disseminating comprehensive financial data which enable members to measure their own levels of activity against the levels of activity recorded for their entire industry or profession. At one time associations frequently offered more basic accounting education programs with detailed advice and information to assist members in instituting and utilizing simplified modern accounting systems. Today, most association accounting activities begin with a presumption that members have established basic systems and emphasize instead enhancing those systems through the furnishing and explaining of comparative business information. Keeping track of collective financial statements and average business ratios are typical accounting activities of many associations. The legal ramifications of such activities are considered in the Chapter, Statistical Programs.

- *Advertising and Marketing activities* are intended to directly or indirectly promote products and services offered by association members. An association sometimes designs and places media advertising for members' products or services using approaches that avoid differentiation among suppliers. Even more often, association-designed and placed media advertising is used to educate members' customers or clients about the business or profession represented. This activity can create a favorable reception for more direct advertising efforts by members themselves. Besides industry or professional advertising, associations also assist members through market research, development of advertising aids for members' use, promulgation of industry symbols and seals and similar programs.

- *Educational activities* are without any doubt the most extensive and pervasive of all the endeavors of associations. The motivation and goal of education is fundamental to the association movement in the United States. Virtually every association provides frequent opportunities for those with the same business or professional interests to exchange valuable experience and interesting ideas. Members often consider the availability of forums for communications with one another to be the most rewarding service that their association provides. It seems almost universally accepted that informed competitors or colleagues are much preferred over uninformed ones. Thus, associations conduct conventions, seminars and other meetings to assist members in acquiring greater knowledge and understanding of their business or profession. Associations also prepare and distribute educational publications, including newsletters, magazines, journals, books, reports, directories, and manuals that are valuable to those within and outside the businesses or professions they represent. Legal aspects of these are outlined in the Chapter, Publications.

- *Employer-Employee Relations* are fostered through dissemination of information at meetings and in publications concerning personnel wage and hour rules, employment discrimination laws, and worker health and safety requirements. Some associations even serve as joint management bargaining groups for their members. Associations conduct surveys of salaries, fringe benefits, work schedules, productivity, and other labor statistics. They help promote the availability of competent employees by circulating among placement offices career guidance information about the industries or professions they represent, by developing or operating training and educational programs for potential or existing employees of members, and by conducting accreditation and certification activities to assure members and the public that minimum levels of employee competence are attained and retained. Some legal factors concerning these activities are found in the Chapter, Professional Credentialing.

- *Government Relations activities* have become increasingly important for nearly every association, and paramount for some, as governmental review and control is injected further into all aspects of business and professional conduct. Influencing the legislative, administrative, and judicial functions of government; communicating information about governmental initiatives and requirements to members and others; assisting government in taking informed and equitable action on behalf of members and citizens; challenging government when necessary and assisting members in challenging government—these are all common and essential government affairs endeavors of associations today. Government relations activities of associations are the subject of several chapters, including the Chapter, Approaches to Government.

- *Public Relations activities* often interweave advertising and marketing activities as well as government relations activities. Besides actively acquainting users of member products and services with the business or profession they represent, associations typically provide the media and the public with a clearinghouse of information about the industry or profession, make available articulate experts to address in public whatever issues are topical in the business or profession, and, in general, work creatively to assure that the public's impressions of their constituency are appropriate ones.

- *Research projects* are often promoted, administered, financed, or conducted by associations. They can encompass any basic or applied research which might lead to new or better ways to develop or use members' products and services. Association joint research activities today sometimes seek innovative technologies or methodologies for complying with government-mandated safety, health, environmental, or energy-efficiency requirements. The legal issues involved in such undertakings are addressed in the Chapter, Joint Research.

- *Standardization and Simplification activities* are intended to streamline wasteful proliferation of products or processes and to establish criteria for evaluating their facility, durability, and utility. These activities are some of the oldest of any conducted by associations in the United States, dating to the time of the Industrial Revolution. Today, standardization and simplification are as important as ever because of rapid scientific and technological advances which may be utilized more easily or even improved upon by association involvement. Legal considerations appear in the Chapter, Standardization and Simplification.

- *Statistical programs* of associations involve the collection, compilation, and communication of data relating to the businesses and professions of members. Statistical surveys may be conducted on sales, costs, production, profitability, etc. They are often extremely useful adjuncts to association public relations and government relations activities. Through the use of surveys an association can best learn the objective facts about any aspect of its membership when it is expedient to convey accurate, up-to-date information to the public or to government. Legal rules are offered in the Chapter, Statistical Programs.

RESOURCES FOR CHAPTER 1

Books

Association Activities, ASAE, 1972.

Bradley, *The Role of Trade Associations and Professional Business Societies in America*, Penn. State Univ. Press, 1965, page 1.

Gray, "Impact of Nonprofit Organizations" in *Trends in Nonprofit Organizations Law*, 1977, page 1.

Hoover, "Introduction," Jones, *Trade Association Activities*, 1923, page 1.

Kirsh, *Trade Associations in Law and Business*, 1938, page 9.

Principles of Association Management, ASAE and U.S. Chamber, 1975, page 29.

Survey of Association Activities and Business Problems, U.S. Chamber, 1961.

Trade Associations: Their Economic Significance and Legal Status, National Industrial Conference Board, 1925, page 97.

Webster, *The Law of Associations*, Matthew Bender, 1976, page 1.

Chapter 2

KINDS OF ASSOCIATIONS

There are as many kinds of trade and professional associations as there are trades and professions. An association can be categorized quantitatively according to the number of its members, staff, meetings, or publications or the size of its annual budget. It can also be categorized qualitatively according to the type of trade or profession it represents, the geographic area of its membership, or the activities in which it engages. There are trade associations representing manufacturers, distributors, importers, retailers, contractors, subcontractors, service companies, and other delineations in many industries. There are professional associations for virtually every profession. There are chambers of commerce and other business clubs and bureaus which attract members not from any one industry or profession but from all ranks of business people or business companies in a specific geographic area. There are also scientific, educational, and charitable societies, which may differ somewhat from trade and professional associations in their purposes and activities but which also have legal bases in common with associations.

This book refers frequently to "trade and professional associations" or just to "associations." Ordinarily these terms denote traditional trade and professional organizations, but frequently they are used broadly to include groups such as chambers of commerce, scientific, educational, or charitable societies, or business cooperatives.

SUMMARY

- Associations can be classified by size of membership, budget, or staff; alternatively, they can be classified by the type or level of trade or profession represented.

- Trade associations are composed of individuals or firms concerned with a single product or service or those concerned with a number of related products or services.

- Trade associations are composed of manufacturers, distributors, importers, brokers, or retailers of a product or a group of products; they might even have as members individuals or firms concerned with supplying goods or services to a particular industry, those transporting the products of an industry, those using the goods or services of an industry,etc.

- Professional associations are composed of individuals who have acquired knowledge and experience which qualifies them as specialists in performing particular services; occasionally, membership in a professional association is limited to those who have acquired some specified professional credential.

- Trade or professional associations can be "horizontal," servicing one functional level of an industry or profession, or they can be "vertical," serving all functional levels.

- Chambers of commerce and other business clubs and bureaus are composed of individuals or firms engaged in all kinds of business activities in a defined geographical area.

- A scientific, educational, and charitable society is composed of members with interests in whatever kind of science, educational area, or charity is represented by the society.

- Associations might be composed of members from a particular city, state, or region; in some associations, membership is drawn from throughout the nation or the world.

- Associations can be chapters, sections, or affiliates of other associations. Some associations are composed not of individual members but of other associations; these are so-called federations.

RESOURCES FOR CHAPTER 2

Books

Encyclopedia of Associations, Gale Research, 1986.

Hopkins, *The Law of Tax-Exempt Organizations*, Ronald Press, 1979, page 260.

Lamb & Shields, *Trade Association Law and Practice*, Little, Brown, 1971, page 3.

National Trade and Professional Associations of the United States, Columbia Books, 1986.

Oleck, *Non-Profit Corporations, Organizations, and Associations*, Prentice-Hall, 1980, page 74.

Who's Who in Association Management, ASAE, 1986.

Periodicals

"Watch Out, Washington, Here Come the Trade Associations," *National Journal*, June 9, 1979, page 956.

Chapter 3

THE HISTORY OF ASSOCIATIONS

Trade and professional associations have historical roots that are centuries old. The association concept can be traced directly to medieval craft and merchant guilds. Going back even further, ancient cultures in China, Greece, and Rome all had organizations of those in common trades or professions.

In colonial America, the mercantile system inherited from England encouraged substantial cooperation among tradesmen and merchants. The rapid industrialization which followed American independence occasionally required that cooperative trade groups and chambers of commerce be formed to promote favorable business conditions. Of those groups begun in the 1800's, a number have survived and flourished to the present.

Two events in the early part of this century clearly mark the beginning of the modern association movement. First, a widely circulated book was published in 1912 which argued convincingly for the formation of associations. Second, U.S. participation in World War I gave recognition to the fact that united business action was necessary for an effective war effort.

To help cope with the Depression, in the early 1930's the federal government specifically authorized industry self-regulation by nearly a thousand associations under the National Recovery Act. The Act was declared unconstitutional in 1935. Only a few years later the federal government was challenging as anticompetitive the self-regulating activities of some associations despite the fact that those activities had been encouraged previously.

In the last twenty-five years, trade and professional associations have greatly increased in number, stature, and effectiveness. The importance of the association movement to members, government, and society is unquestioned. Associations today are truly "powerful and enlightened members of the community" working for goals common to all citizens, as they were described by de Tocqueville in 1835.

SUMMARY

This list contains some significant dates in the history of trade and professional associations in the United States.

- *1724:* The first enduring American trade association—the Philadelphia House Carpenters—is formed.

- *1743:* The oldest American scientific society—the American Philosophical Society—is formed in Philadelphia by Benjamin Franklin; it has been in continuous existence ever since.

- *1761:* The Boston Society for Encouraging Trade and Commerce is formed to promote better business practices; it is followed by similar groups in New York (1764) and Philadelphia (1768).

- *1762:* An association of New England candlemakers called the Association of Spermaceti Chandlers is organized to conduct broad programs of self-regulation of the candle industry.

- *1776:* Adam Smith's *Wealth of Nations* is published. In the book Smith states: "People of the same trade seldom meet together, even for merriment and diversion, but the conversation ends in some conspiracy against the public or in some contrivance to raise prices."

- *1789:* The Constitution of the United States is adopted; it includes protection for freedom of citizens to associate.

- *1792:* The New York Stock Exchange, still operating today, is started.

- *1835:* Alexis de Tocqueville's *Democracy in America* is published; it includes this passage:
  "Americans of all ages, all conditions, and all dispositions constantly form associations. They have not only commercial and manufacturing compa-

nies, in which all take part, but associations of a thousand other kinds, religious, moral, serious, futile, general or restricted, enormous or diminutive. The Americans make associations to give entertainments, to found seminaries, to build inns, to construct churches, to diffuse books, to send missionaries to the antipodes; in this manner they found hospitals, prisons, and schools. If it is proposed to inculcate some truth or to foster some feeling by the encouragement of a great example, they form a society. Wherever at the head of some new undertaking you see the government in France, or a man of rank in England, in the United States you will be sure to find an association."

- *1861:* An association of Philadelphia shoemakers successfully prosecutes striking journeymen on the basis that a labor strike is a conspiracy in restraint of trade.

- *1890:* Congress enacts the Sherman Act to prohibit agreements in restraint of trade such as price fixing, market allocation, and boycotts.

- *1911:* The U.S. Supreme Court decides the Standard Oil case, declaring that agreements in restraint of trade are illegal only if they violate a "rule of reason."

- *1912:* Arthur J. Eddy's *The New Competition* is published; it advocates the "open-price system" based on the theory that competition would be more effective and there would be less waste if buyers and sellers had complete information about inventories, prices, costs, etc.

- *1913:* Non-profit business associations are specifically accorded federal income-tax-exempt status in the Tariff of 1913 through the efforts of the Chamber of Commerce of the United States.

- *1914:* The Federal Trade Commission Act is passed by Congress to outlaw "unfair methods of competition" and "unfair or deceptive acts or practices."

- *1914:* The Clayton Act is passed to proscribe price discrimination, tying arrangements, and exclusive dealing contracts as well as to impose restrictions on certain mergers.

- *1920:* The American Society of Association Executives is begun.

- *1923:* Secretary of Commerce Herbert Hoover encourages the formation of associations and declares:
  "Trade associations are the safeguards of small business and thus prevent the extinction of competition. . . . With wisdom and devotion, their voluntary forces can accomplish more for our country than any spread of the hand of government."

- *1925:* The U.S. Supreme Court, in the case of *Maple Flooring Mfrs. Assn. v. U.S.,* decides that trade associations may lawfully engage in gathering and disseminating statistical data if certain guidelines are followed.

- *1927:* The Chamber of Commerce of the United States creates a special Association Division.

- *1933:* The National Industrial Recovery Act is passed to encourage industrial self-regulation by associations which formulate Codes of Fair Competition; the Act establishes the National Recovery Administration.

- *1936:* The Robinson-Patman Act is passed; it makes price discrimination and certain allowances illegal.

- *1982:* The U.S. Supreme Court, in the case of *American Society of Mechanical Engineers v. Hydrolevel,* for the first time holds an association liable for antitrust treble damages, based upon anticompetitive conduct of staff and volunteers acting with only the "apparent authority" of the association.

RESOURCES FOR CHAPTER 3

Books

Bradley, *The Role of Trade Associations and Professional Business Societies in America,* Penn. State Univ. Press, 1965, page 17.

Ellis & Noyes, *By the People, A History of Americans as Volunteers,* 1978.

Lamb & Shields, *Trade Association Law and Practice,* Little, Brown, 1971, page 3.

Naylor, "History of Trade Associations in America," Appendix A in Jones, *Trade Association Activities*, 1923, page 301.

Principles of Association Management, ASAE and U.S. Chamber, 1975, page 1.

Stathem & Buek, *Associations and the Tax Laws*, U.S. Chamber 1978, page 1.

Trade Associations: Their Economic Significance and Legal Status, National Industrial Conference Board, 1925, page 7.

Webster, *The Law of Associations*, Matthew Bender, 1976, page 1.1.

Chapter 4

ADVANTAGES OF INCORPORATION

Most associations today elect to become legal corporations either at the time they are organized or at a later time. An association that has become a corporation is an artificial legal entity composed of individual members but considered to have its own existence apart from its members for purposes of organization, operations, liability, longevity, holding property, and so forth.

Incorporation of a nonprofit association has most of the advantages of incorporation of a business enterprise. It eliminates the personal liability of members, establishes continuity, creates psychological stature, and makes available applicable laws and guidelines concerning the formation and administration of the organization.

By comparison, unincorporated associations have no separate existence of their own; but they are treated as if they did when it suits the government to do so. They are not subject to any reliable set of rules for governing unincorporated associations.

Over and above the advantages and disadvantages of incorporation, there are many legal and practical aspects of associations that are unaffected by the legal status of the entity. The taxable or tax-exempt status of an association is unrelated to the fact of incorporation. It depends upon whether the association is organized for profit, the type of revenue received, and the activities engaged in. Nonprofit tax-exempt benefits are granted to qualifying incorporated and unincorporated associations alike. Incorporation has no bearing on the antitrust laws applicable to associations. Violations of the antitrust laws can be alleged against association members and against the association itself regardless of the legal status of the entity. Employment standards, discrimination laws, and requirements concerning withholding of income taxes for employees apply to associations whether incorporated or not. Finally, when state and local taxation is levied upon an association, it is usually unaffected by the group's corporate status.

Those organizing an association or considering incorporating one should attempt to carefully balance the positive points with the negative points of incorporation. Usually the advantages will be more significant than the disadvantages.

SUMMARY

- While there are disadvantages as well as advantages to be considered when deciding whether to incorporate an association, ordinarily the overwhelming advantages will dictate incorporation.

- On the positive side, incorporation protects association members from personal liability for association obligations and from liability if association officers, directors, or staff violate the law in working on behalf of the group. The maximum liability of an incorporated association for contract claims and for personal injury or property damage claims will generally be limited to the amount of the assets of the association.

- An incorporated association has an existence of its own, independent of the terms of office or employment of members, directors, or officers. A corporation theoretically is perpetual although it can be dissolved or its existence can be limited from the outset.

- Protection of the association name may be easier if the group is a corporation. State statutes will likely offer relief to an incorporated or unincorporated group when a new organization seeks to use its name; but an incorporated association, whose name is registered, may find it easier to protect that name from infringement.

- Incorporation is psychologically desirable because individuals and firms are accustomed to dealing with corporations; they tend to regard an incorporated association as more formally structured, more stable, and more businesslike than an unincorporated one.

- An incorporated association can sue and be sued in its corporate name; an unincorporated group usually must go into court or be brought into court in the names of all of its members. Using the names of members could be procedurally cumbersome and could raise public relations or member relations problems.

- An incorporated association can own real estate in its corporate name in most states; an unincorporated group may have to use the names of members or hold the property through trustees.

- All states have laws which give specific guidance for the organization and operation of a corporate entity, including an incorporated association; an unincorporated group may have no more than vague reference or authority for procedures when questions or doubts arise.

- Obtaining insurance, for association professional liability, for example, may be more difficult for an unincorporated association, since in certain circumstances the insurance underwriter may not be able to determine the precise authority for association organization and operation. An incorporated association may not necessarily be more stable than an unincorporated one; but to some it may have the appearance of greater stability.

- Disadvantages of incorporation are primarily related to the moderate expenses involved. Legal fees and filing costs are incurred when incorporating; franchise taxes for corporations are required annually in some states. When an association has offices or does business in states other than the one in which it is incorporated, it must meet and maintain certain standards to qualify for doing business as a corporation in those states. Again, modest expenditures are involved.

- An incorporated association must observe various organizational and operational requirements set up by state law. Also, annual meetings must be held, minutes must be kept, and annual reports must be filed by incorporated organizations in most states. In some instances the requirements are absolute, and in others they apply unless the association provides otherwise in its articles of incorporation or bylaws. The requirements can affect voting, notice of meetings, termination of membership, and other matters.

- If dissolution of an incorporated association becomes necessary or desirable, procedures for dissolution are sometimes complicated and can involve substantial legal expense. An unincorporated association can be dissolved by the will of the membership alone.

RESOURCES FOR CHAPTER 4

Books

Hopkins, *The Law of Tax-Exempt Organizations*, Ronald Press, 1979, page 503.

Lamb & Shields, *Trade Association Law and Practice*, Little, Brown, 1971, page 185.

Lane, "Nonprofit Corporations" in *Legal Handbook for Nonprofit Organizations*, AMACOM, 1980, page 59.

MacArthur, "Should an Association Incorporate?" in *Associations and the Law Book I*, U.S. Chamber, 1967, page 1.

Oleck, *Non-Profit Corporations, Organizations, and Associations*, Prentice-Hall, 1980, page 20.

Webster, *The Law of Associations*, Matthew Bender, 1976, page 2.3.

Webster, Herold, & Dye, *Association Legal Checklist*, U.S. Chamber, 1983, page 3.

Chapter 5

INCORPORATION PROCEDURES

A number of procedural issues must be decided and steps must be taken when an association determines to seek incorporation.

The place of incorporation must be chosen. The individuals who will act as incorporators must be identified. The governing documents of the association must be drafted and adopted. These are the articles of incorporation, bylaws, and, if desired, some other association policy and procedure document. Questions of the association name, purposes, membership, dues, budgets, and other such matters should be settled and articulated in writing at the outset if possible.

In short, at the time of incorporation of an association, a comprehensive plan for what the association will be—and what it will be doing—should be formulated and documented.

SUMMARY

- Those responsible for seeking corporate status for an association should define, at least generally, what the nature and scope of the organization will be, what the group will attempt to accomplish, and the means to be used to reach its goals.

- The place where an association incorporates is usually the state where it has its principal offices; another state or the District of Columbia may be used as the place of incorporation if some compelling reason exists for doing so—for example, where it is desirable to have state laws particularly favorable to the incorporated association or where it is desirable to maintain corporate status in the national capital. But note that some modest additional fees and expenses may be incurred by an association that incorporates in a state other than that in which it has its principal offices.

- Incorporators or promoters, persons who arrange for incorporation of an association and sign the necessary documents, should be chosen. State law may require that there be some minimum number of them. Incorporators or promoters must act in good faith and deal fairly; they must not secretly profit from the incorporation of the association. After incorporation, the association should ratify the acts of the incorporators or promoters.

- For some types of associations, state judicial or administrative approval is necessary before incorporation can become effective; this is particularly so if the association will solicit charitable contributions. If approval is necessary, it should of course be obtained.

- Articles of incorporation must be drafted and filed. They generally accompany and are part of the legal grant of corporate status to an association by the state government. The articles are sometimes known as a "certificate of incorporation" or a corporate "charter."

- Bylaws should be drafted and adopted. Although they are sometimes not strictly required by state law, they are always highly desirable. Bylaws are the main internal rules for association management and government.

- Some larger associations draft and adopt an additional policy and procedure document, known variously as a "manual of policies and procedures," a "policy and procedure statement of the board of directors," or the like. This document is adopted and amended by a simple resolution of the board of directors. It contains the detailed managing and governing positions of the association which do not significantly affect the rights and obligations of members, directors, and officers and thus, need not be included in the articles of incorporation or bylaws.

- At the time of incorporation, an association should prepare the necessary documentation and make a submission to the Internal Revenue Service for a determination

of federal income-tax-exempt status if this status is to
be sought by the organization.

- If the association is going to have offices or carry on
  significant activity in states other than the state of incorporation, registration of the association as a foreign
  corporation in other states may be necessary.

- Incorporation will entail certain association expenses
  such as legal fees, charges for filing the articles of
  incorporation, possible charges for registration in other
  states as a foreign corporation, and so forth.

- At the time of incorporation, the association should
  determine matters such as its name, purpose, membership, activities, dues, budget, reserves, and the like.
  It should also give some thought to who will serve as
  legal counsel.

- Because incorporation of an association is a legal procedure, counsel experienced in association matters
  should be consulted at each step of the incorporation
  process and particularly when association incorporation documents are drafted.

RESOURCES FOR CHAPTER 5

Books

Lamb & Shields, *Trade Association Law and Practice*, Little,
    Brown, 1971, page 185.
Lane, "Nonprofit Corporations" in *Legal Handbook for Non-
    profit Organizations*, AMACOM, 1980, page 59.
Oleck, *Non-Profit Corporations, Organizations, and Associa-
    tions*, Prentice-Hall, 1980, page 327.
Webster, *The Law of Associations*, Matthew Bender, 1976,
    page 2.3.
Webster, Herold, & Dye, *Association Legal Checklist*, U.S.
    Chamber, 1983, pages 3–4.

Periodicals

Webster, "Qualifying to Do Business In Several States," *As-
    sociation Management*, August, 1984, page 65.

Chapter 6

ARTICLES OF INCORPORATION

For an association that is incorporated, the articles of incorporation can be viewed as an agreement between the state which grants incorporated status and the association which holds that status. The articles of incorporation establish the legal basis for an association's separate corporate existence, once, that is, the articles of incorporation have been filed with the proper state office and approved by it and appropriate fees have been paid. The state grants individual legal status to the association in return for its commitment to abide by the rules that the state has established for corporations.

Often the most useful association articles of incorporation are those that are the most concise. State legal requirements for amendment of the articles are sometimes burdensome and time-consuming to fulfill. For example, a vote of a majority or two-thirds of the membership may be required. Amendments will most likely have to be filed and approved by the proper state office just as were the original articles. For these reasons, it is usually desirable to keep an association's articles of incorporation as general as possible while accurately and adequately providing for organization and governing. Detailed provisions can be included in bylaws or in another association policy and procedure document that is more easily amended than the articles of incorporation.

The association should have at least two principal concerns in preparing or revising its articles of incorporation. First, the purposes of the group should be clearly described—this is important for both tax and antitrust reasons. Second, at least minimal guidelines for the organization and governing of the association should be stated in the articles.

An example of association articles of incorporation, written in plain English, is included in the last section of this book.

SUMMARY

- An association's articles of incorporation—alternatively called its certificate of incorporation or corporation charter in some states—give the association its individual, legal corporate status. The document is in effect a contract between the state and the association in which the state provides a separate legal existence for the association in return for its commitment to abide by the state's rules for incorporated associations.

- Complying with state law procedures for amending the articles of incorporation is often a cumbersome process. Therefore, it makes sense for an association's articles to contain accurate but minimal statements of the purposes, powers, and other aspects of the association as required by state laws. Items that are not essential to the articles of incorporation can be included in other governing documents of the association such as the bylaws or a manual of policies and procedures.

- Particular attention should be paid to the statement of purpose in an association's articles of incorporation, since the statement of purpose has ramifications for both the tax-exempt status and the potential antitrust liability of the association.

- Some states have a separate set of laws applicable to articles of incorporation for nonprofit organizations such as associations; in other states, the laws for general business corporations apply to nonprofit groups as well.

- Typical provisions either required absolutely or allowed optionally, depending upon the applicable state laws for association articles of incorporation, include the following:
  —The name of the association
  —The address of the association's principal office
  —The name and address of the legal agent of the association
  —The purposes for the association's formation and existence

—The fact that the association has not been organized for profit, if this is the case

—The anticipated duration of the existence of the association, which is ordinarily indefinite("perpetual") or until terminated

—Whether there will be association bylaws

—General provisions for conducting the internal affairs of the association

—The extent of availability of association membership in general terms

—The geographic area in which the association intends to operate

—A description of the industry, profession, or other segment of business or society represented by the association

—Dues requirements in general terms

—The numbers of directors and officers (or, possibly, the minimum and maximum numbers)

—The names and addresses of initial directors of the association

—The existence of committees

—The holding of meetings

—The expulsion or resignation of members, officers, or directors

—Amendments to the articles of incorporation

—Procedures for termination or dissolution of the association

—Disposition of any remaining assets of the association upon termination or dissolution

—Approval by any state officials that may be required

—The fact (in some states) that previous articles of incorporation have not been filed

—The names, addresses, and (most likely) signatures of individuals acting as sponsors ("incorporators") of the association at the time of its inception and (in some states) the fact that they all meet a minimum-age requirement.

● When completed as required, the articles of incorporation of an association are signed by the sponsors, their signatures are notarized (in some states), and the document containing the articles is submitted with the applicable fee to the state governmental agency (or court in some cases) responsible for approving the granting of corporate status.

- When the agency or court has approved the articles, an official copy is returned to the submitters. An association should maintain in its files several copies of the current articles of incorporation that have been certified as official by the state governmental entity. These are sometimes necessary in dealing with the Internal Revenue Service, in obtaining insurance, and in other endeavors of the association.

RESOURCES FOR CHAPTER 6

Books

Lane, "Nonprofit Corporations" in *Legal Handbook for Nonprofit Organizations*, AMACOM, 1980, page 59.

Oleck, *Non-Profit Corporations, Organizations, and Associations*, Prentice-Hall, 1980, page 327.

Webster, *The Law of Associations*, Matthew Bender, 1976, page 2.3.

Chapter 7

BYLAWS

Bylaws are rules adopted and maintained by an association to define and direct its internal structure and management. Bylaws are subordinate, and complementary, to an association's articles of incorporation. Articles are the primary law of the association. They are best used to establish the general organization and governing of the association needed to achieve corporate existence. Bylaws are the secondary law of the association. They are best used to detail how the association is formed and how it is run.

In most states bylaws are not specifically required for an incorporated or unincorporated association. Even where legally optional, however, most associations elect to have their own set of bylaws because of their usefulness in management operations.

Bylaws may be viewed as constituting the terms of an agreement between an association and its members. The agreement will ordinarily be honored and enforced in a court of law. Bylaws describe the relationships, the rights, and the obligations not only for members of an association but also for directors, officers, and staff. Bylaws can be invaluable in avoiding or resolving differences among those who are part of the association or who deal with it. They are, therefore, well worth the efforts involved in adopting, reviewing, and updating them when necessary.

Sample association bylaws are included in the last section of this book.

SUMMARY

- Bylaws are rules for the internal organizing and governing of an association.

- Bylaws are often not strictly required by state law even for incorporated associations. Nevertheless, it is always highly desirable for an association to adopt and maintain bylaws even where optional under state law.

- Bylaws have advantages for association members, directors, officers, and staff in:
  —Establishing management rules that provide consistency and continuity of operations for the assurance of those both within the association and outside of it
  —Defining relationships between the association and its members and among the members themselves
  —Describing the privileges and duties of those at each functional level of the association
  —Minimizing the likelihood of confusion and disagreement on matters pertaining to association structure and operations.

- Although bylaws are not specifically required in some states, virtually all state incorporation laws refer to bylaws as an appropriate document for stating procedures for membership, meetings, elections, notices, and so forth.

- Obtaining a determination of tax-exempt status would be difficult for an association that had no internal governing document such as bylaws to demonstrate to the Internal Revenue Service under what guidelines the association was organized and operated.

- Association internal governing rules are sometimes called the "Constitution and Bylaws." To avoid confusion, especially for an incorporated association that has another governing document, the articles of incorporation, it is recommended that the internal governing rules be called merely "Bylaws."

- Just as articles of incorporation can be considered an agreement between an association and the state which grants it corporate status, bylaws are in effect the terms of an agreement between the association and those who are its members. The agreement will be enforced by a court in the absence of some overriding public policy in conflict with the bylaws.

- Where there is inconsistency between an association's

articles of incorporation and its bylaws, the articles supersede. In either document, the specific prevails over the general.

- Ordinarily the authority to adopt or amend bylaws rests with the membership. Some states permit delegation of this authority by an association's members to, for example, a board of directors. Since the bylaws are an agreement between the association and its members, it seems best for members not to delegate bylaws approval authority even in states where it is permitted.

- Too frequent amendment of an association's bylaws can be confusing. Amendments should be made only when necessary.

- A consistent and extended association practice or procedure inconsistent with the bylaws may be considered to effectively amend the bylaws, especially when done with the full knowledge, and thus implied consent, of the membership. For this reason, the bylaws should be periodically reviewed and updated to conform to current management rules followed by the association.

- Bylaws provisions are distinct from resolutions of an association's membership or governing board. Bylaws establish continuing, generally applicable policies or procedures basic to the structure or management of the association. Resolutions are for single, temporary, less important, or possibly varying situations and circumstances. Amendments to bylaws generally require advance notice and the following of specific voting procedures by the membership as set out in the bylaws themselves or even in the articles of incorporation. Resolutions generally do not have specific procedures applicable to them other than procedures applicable to all voting in the association.

- In matters in which changes can be anticipated over the life of the association, such as dues structure, number of directors, titles and functions of staff employees, etc., the bylaws should give only general guidance or set minimal requirements. Specific decisions (on these matters) should be left to resolution by the membership or board of directors or should be based on another governing document of the association, such as a manual of policies and procedures.

- Bylaws of an association typically contain matters such as the following:

  —Purposes of the association expressed in greater detail than in the articles of incorporation

  —Membership qualifications, classes, admission procedures, and expulsion or resignation procedures

  —Officers' qualifications, titles, terms of office, time, and manner of election, meetings, powers, duties, and removal procedures

  —Filling of vacancies in officers' or directors' positions

  —Voting by members and directors, including the necessary quorum, number of votes needed to carry an issue, proxy voting, and mail voting

  —Notices, times, places, agendas, and minutes of meetings

  —Property holding and transfer

  —Indemnification of directors and officers

  —Number and use of standing committees

  —Delegation of authority to directors or officers

  —Relationships with other associations such as federations

  —Adoption and use of a seal

  —Bank depository

  —Fiscal year, audits, and financial reports

  —Location of principal and other offices

  —Books, records, and reports

  —Amendment procedures

  —Dissolution procedures

  —Use of funds and disposition of surplus assets or all assets at dissolution

  —Legal compliance including antitrust policy.

- As in the articles of incorporation, the purpose clause in association bylaws is often crucial in antitrust and tax-exemption situations. Its drafting should receive especially close attention.

- Up-to-date copies of association bylaws should be available to all members; copies may even be distributed to members periodically.

- Consistent with the idea that bylaws represent an

agreement between the association and its members,
bylaws should be as simple, concise, and understandable as possible in order to foster members' awareness
of bylaw provisions.

- Well-written bylaws serve many associations as "sell"
documents for new members because they relate important association procedures and present an image
of a professional, business-like, well-managed organization. In addition, legal counsel for existing or prospective association members often reviews the bylaws
to help assess whether the association is mindful of
legal requirements, especially in the area of antitrust
law.

- Drafting and adoption of bylaws and bylaw amendments should be done carefully and thoroughly. The
assistance of legal counsel may be helpful or essential.

RESOURCES FOR CHAPTER 7

Books

Association Bylaws, U.S. Chamber, 1984.

Lamb & Shields, *Trade Association Law and Practice*, Little,
Brown, 1971, page 196.

Oleck, *Non-Profit Corporations, Organizations, and Associations*,
Prentice-Hall, 1980, page 311.

Webster, *The Law of Associations*, Matthew Bender, 1976, pages
2–23.

Webster, "Certificate of Incorporation, Bylaws and Minutes of
Associations: Some Comments" in *Associations and the
Law Book II*, U.S. Chamber, 1968, page 24.

Chapter 8

MANUAL OF POLICIES AND PROCEDURES

Some associations find it efficient to have only the most fundamental and predominent organization and management provisions contained in the articles of incorporation and by-laws or to have them merely summarized in those documents. Where substantial detail and explanation for fundamental and predominant provisions are necessary or desirable, especially in large or complex associations, they can be included in a third document for the administration of the association. The third governing document could take any of several forms— an administrative guide, a compilation of board of directors resolutions, and so forth. Whatever form it takes, this document is an expansion of the terms of formation and operation of the association in accordance with the articles of incorporation and the bylaws.

The manual of policies and procedures is drafted, adopted, and amended typically under the authority of the board of directors rather than that of the full membership. It, therefore, must not derogate or modify the purposes of the association and relationships, rights and obligations of members, directors, officers, and staff.

If the articles of incorporation are viewed as an agreement between the association and the state, and if the bylaws are viewed as an agreement between the association and its membership, this manual of policies and procedures might be viewed as an agreement between the association and its professional management staff. It is really more than that, however. The manual covers basic decisions—for example, broad resolutions—made previously by an association. To a large extent it helps the association avoid "re-inventing the wheel."

Many associations can adequately provide for the government of the organization through well-drafted articles of incorporation and bylaws. If a manual of policies and procedures is considered desirable, this document too should be conscientiously developed and changed when necessary.

SUMMARY

- Many associations, particularly large or complex ones, use a manual of policies and procedures to expand upon the provisions of the articles of incorporation and bylaws in order to avoid having those documents become unwieldy with too many amendments.

- A manual of policies and procedures may also be known as an administrative guide, a compilation of board resolutions on administration, an operations handbook, an office manual, or something similar.

- To be most useful, the manual should be subject only to the approval of the board of directors for adoption or modification.

- The manual should not conflict with the articles of incorporation or bylaws. It also need not repeat the provisions of those governing documents.

- Typical association manuals of policies and procedures may cover these or similar matters:
  —Procedures for operating each of the association's regular activities or programs
  —Detailed statements of pending association policies including those that cover the relationships between the governing board and the staff and between committees and staff
  —Authority of each association staff member
  —Association employee obligations and benefits
  —Specific information on dues structure, including dues amounts, time and method of payment, and procedures to be followed upon nonpayment
  —Fees for association services including member and nonmember fees
  —Legal and procedural guidelines for association sta-

tistical collection programs, standards and certifi-
cation programs, credit reporting, or insurance programs
—Policies regarding association political activity
—Membership application processing
—Maintenance, use, and protection of mailing lists
—Access to, and use of, legal counsel and other association consultants by staff, officers, directors, or
members
—Meetings procedures including notices, agendas, and
minutes
—Office procedures for handling inquiries or requests
from members, directors, or officers
—Operation of committees, committee chairmen responsibilities, lines of reporting by committees, and
assignment of staff to committees
—Association records including document retention,
access by staff, officers, directors, members, and
public or press
—Procedures, deadlines, and responsibilities for producing association publications.

RESOURCES FOR CHAPTER 8

Books

Lamb & Shields, *Trade Association Law and Practice*, Little,
Brown, 1971, page 194.
Policies and Procedures of Associations, ASAE, 1974, 1978.

Chapter 9

ASSOCIATION NAME

The name of an association should accurately and concisely reflect the nature and purposes of the organization. A name should be chosen which protects the good will and reputation of the association and avoids deception or confusion with the name of some other organization. The initials of the association name, its acronym, should also be considered.

Misuse or infringement of an association name can best be avoided through its registration by virtue of state corporation laws or through federal registration of the name as a "service mark." If misuse or infringement occurs, an action based upon common law, or upon the state or federal registration, can be maintained. It is even possible that the federal government might act to stop the misuse of an association's name or infringement upon it if the abuse is so aggravated as to be considered unfair competition.

Legal problems with association names are not common. Practical problems arise more frequently. For example, the name of an association may have to be changed because it no longer reflects the character of the industry or profession it represents.

SUMMARY

- The name of an association above all should reflect the nature and purposes of the group accurately and concisely.

- A name which could cause deception or confusion should be avoided. Do not use a name similar to that of another organization, especially one in a related industry or profession. Naturally, any names with secondary, suggestive, or offensive meanings should also be avoided.

- Consider the initials or acronym of any proposed new or revised association name; if the acronym could create problems, a different name should be chosen. For example, if the new or revised name has an acronym identical or very similar to that of an established association in the same industry or profession, the latter organization may be able to legally force abandonment of the new or revised name. At the very least, the potential confusion is unnecessary and should be avoided.

- The identifying words of an association name may best appear at the beginning of the name. "Widget Manufacturers Association" is easier to find in a telephone book or alphabetical association directory than is "Association of Widget Manufacturers."

- Generally the common law and state and federal statutes will protect any prior user of an organization name against subsequent unauthorized use. Protection will be afforded against use of a confusingly similar name as well as against use of the name itself.

- A state will not grant corporate status to an association if its proposed name conflicts with that of some other existing incorporated association or business. Similarly, an association incorporated elsewhere will not receive permission to carry on activities as a foreign corporation if the name conflicts with that of an existing corporation in the state.

- All states have laws allowing a corporation to bring suit when its name is misused or infringed upon by an individual or another corporation. An incorporated association can take advantage of these laws when necessary.

- Associations, whether incorporated or not, in some circumstances can register their names as "service marks" with the U.S. Patent Office. Registration in this way also facilitates the bringing of a suit to stop misuse or infringement.

- Assistance in stopping misuse or infringement upon an association name may be available from the Federal

Trade Commission or Antitrust Division of the Department of Justice where deception, unfair competition, or another antitrust law violation is involved.

- In most states an incorporated nonprofit association need not use "Incorporated" or "Corporation" in its name as is required of business corporations. States may require that "Association," "Society," or something similar be included in the name of an incorporated nonprofit group to distinguish it from a business corporation.

- State law will typically allow the organization resulting from the merger of two associations to continue to use the name of one of them, although there may sometimes be nonlegal reasons for choosing a completely new name for the resulting organization.

RESOURCES FOR CHAPTER 9

Books

Lamb & Shields, *Trade Association Law and Practice*, Little, Brown, 1971, page 188.

Oleck, *Non-Profit Corporations, Organizations, and Associations*, Prentice-Hall, 1980, page 293.

Webster, *The Law of Associations*, Matthew Bender, 1976, pages 2–13.

Periodicals

Kahoe, "Non-Profit Corporations' Names," *Clev.St.L.Rev.*, 1972, page 114.

Komarow, "Should You Register Your Association Name?," GWSAE *Executive Update*, March, 1985, page 29.

Other Resources

FTC Advisory Opinion 16 C.F.R. Section 15.130 (1967).

Chapter 10

STATEMENT OF PURPOSE

The purposes for which an association has been formed, its raison d'être, should be well thought out and accurately stated in the articles of incorporation, in the bylaws, or, in both. They may also be set out or summarized in submissions to the government, in membership solicitation materials, and in other documents where the aims of the association are pertinent.

The most important statement of the purposes of the association is that given in the articles of incorporation. The stated purposes in the articles may be used in determinations of whether the association is exempt from taxes, whether it can engage in specific activities, whether prospective members desire to join the association, and, occasionally, whether the association may be in violation of the antitrust laws. Other statements of purposes promulgated by the association should be consistent with that in the articles of incorporation, although the others may expand upon or summarize the main statement.

Because of its ramifications, an association's statement of purposes should receive close attention when it is drafted and later when it is referred to.

SUMMARY

- The purposes for which an association exists and operates are stated in the articles of incorporation, bylaws, and possibly elsewhere.

- The stated purposes of the association are sometimes crucial in making such determinations as to whether the association:

  —Can be a nonprofit corporation under state law

—Is exempt from payment of federal or state taxes

—Has interests and activities that are consistent with its purposes

—Can attract individuals or firms desiring to support its objectives by becoming members

—Is organized or operated for purposes which restrain competition.

- Because a statement of purposes can restrict or inhibit an association's operations, the statement is best kept more general than specific.

- When it appears in the articles of incorporation, an association's statement of purposes may be cumbersome to amend; it should be drafted in anticipation of all the forseeable objectives of the association.

- Association purpose statements should not be deceptive, overly vague, inconsistent internally, or in conflict with other association documents describing aims or objectives.

- Purpose statements used by associations have often included these kinds of phrases as examples:

—To promote the interest, welfare, or common good of an industry, a profession, or a group of members

—To deal by lawful means with common problems or concerns

—To foster lawful cooperative action in areas affecting the business or profession of members

—To act as advocate and representative before government bodies

—To establish policies and conduct activities for the advancement of the industry, profession, or membership

—To promote industry products, provide education, foster professional conduct, gather and disseminate information, develop standards, and so forth.

- Certain words may have questionable antitrust implications when used in association purpose statements. They should be avoided completely in any context where their meanings could be misconstrued. The words include:

restrict	eliminate	require	profits
limit	ban	dictate	margins

prohibit	destroy	proscribe	markups
control	boycott	prescribe	production
regulate	fix	prices	market
influence	allocate	fees	customers
	clients	patients	

- An association's statement of purposes should announce the intention of the organization to act consistently with its nonprofit tax-exempt status and to observe the letter and spirit of all applicable laws and regulations including those in antitrust and trade regulation areas.

RESOURCES FOR CHAPTER 10

Books

Lamb & Shields, *Trade Association Law and Practice*, Little, Brown, 1971, page 190.

Oleck, *Non-Profit Corporations, Organizations, and Associations*, Prentice-Hall, 1980, page 216.

Webster, *The Law of Associations*, Matthew Bender, 1976, pages 2–19.

Chapter 11

LEGAL CONTRACTS

The frequent use of legal contracts has become universal in the management of trade and professional associations. Legal contracts, either oral or written, are entered into when an association rents or buys office space, purchases equipment or supplies, arranges for meetings or conventions, and engages in scores of other kinds of routine or extraordinary transactions. Often associations are requested by suppliers of goods or services to become bound by contracts as a condition of doing business. Just as frequently, associations are committed to enforceable terms and conditions of their relationships.

Because the use of contracts is so widespread, one should be familiar with some basic concepts in the laws that determine what constitutes a valid contract and how it may be enforced. Today's contract law is rooted in literally hundreds of years of British and American "common law" (that established by court decisions rather than by legislative fiat) and is further governed in some circumstances by state statutes. The assistance of legal experts is usually essential in drafting and interpreting contracts. Nevertheless, one can make far more efficient use of counsel when one understands some of the basics of contract law. Those basics are explained in this Summary.

SUMMARY

- Contracts are everywhere. Associations enter into legal contracts for all manner of services or products including:
  —Hotels
  —Speakers

41

—Entertainers
—Transportation
—Decorators
—Exhibitors
—Caterers
—Offices
—Furnishings
—Printing
—Supplies
—Computers
—Equipment
—Insurance
—Testing
—Accountants
—Consultants
—Authors
—Attorneys
—Researchers
—Employees
—Executives.

- It is essential to become adept at recognizing contracts. These are some key words and phrases that signal the existence or terms of legal contracts:

  —As agreed
  —We accept
  —You understand that
  —We have a deal
  —Your firm offer
  —Everything is acceptable
  —Unconditional
  —In consideration of
  —We have relied upon
  —Your obligations
  —Our benefit
  —Our assignees.

- A contract is a voluntary understanding between two people or firms which creates a binding relationship between them. As a result of the understanding, each person or firm has obligations and expects something in return.

- Most contracts involve mutual promises to perform actions or deliver products sometime in the future. The promises may be implied by the actions of the parties. It is more than likely that the promises are at least partially expressed, either through oral or written communication.

- There are three essential elements of a legal contract. There must be an offer. There must be acceptance. There must be consideration.

- *Offer.* An offer is a promise conditioned upon something being done by the person promised. The condition may be the performance of an action or a promise to perform an act in the future. To be precise, an offer is a proposal in some definite terms which is communicated to someone else whose manifested acceptance of the terms may result in an agreement. An offer must be distinguished from an invitation to negotiate, which could be withdrawn at any time. But even a valid offer can itself be withdrawn if done through the same channels of communication as those by which it was made. In short, an offer can be withdrawn before it is accepted and no contract will result. Note also that the party making an offer can set some time limit as a condition of acceptance in order for an enforceable contract to ensue.

- *Acceptance.* Mutual assent must be manifested before an offer becomes a contract. Acceptance is an expression of assent to the essential terms of an offer. The assent may be a promise to do what is requested in the offer. It may also take the form of performance of what is requested in the offer. An offer expires either within its own recited time limit or within a reasonable time if none was fixed by the terms of the offer. Generally, one cannot consider silence to be an acceptance.

- The law is flexible about the means or manner of acceptance that can be used in response to an offer. Ordinarily, any reasonable means or manner of making an acceptance will suffice. Unless a specific mode of acceptance is required by the offer, acceptance can be either a promise to perform or it can be performance itself. Only if the offer specifies that "this offer can be accepted only by written confirmation" or the like will the mode of acceptance be restricted.

- Sometimes the recipient of an offer affirms the proposal but makes modifications or additions. If the changes are only minor ones, there is no problem. If the changes are major ones, the acceptance containing them is invalid. No contract results. The rules about new terms contained in an acceptance are somewhat complicated. If an offer states that it can be accepted without modification, that provision will stand. A contract will result only if the acceptance is in the same terms as the offer. Ordinarily, though, the offer does not restrict the scope of the acceptance. When an offer is made and its acceptance contains different or additional terms, the terms of the acceptance may become those of the contract unless they significantly change the offer or unless the one who made the offer rejects the new terms. In short, when an offer does not restrict acceptance to the terms of the offer, new terms in the acceptance become part of the contract unless they are material or they are rejected by the other side.

- To review the situation, new or different terms contained in an acceptance to an offer will ordinarily become part of the contract that results. This is the rule under the Uniform Commercial Code, which is applicable in all states except Louisiana (where only portions of the UCC have been adopted).

- One cannot pick and choose among the terms of an offer. Minor items can be changed or added in one's acceptance. Major items cannot be changed or added.

- *Consideration.* Consideration is anything of value that is exchanged in performing the contract.

- Consideration must be mutual. Both parties must provide something in order for a contract to be valid. There is no requirement that the value of the consideration given by one party be equal to the value of the consideration received by that party. As a general rule the law will hold a party to the deal bargained for, no matter how absurd a value it has.

- Consideration is an element of bargain, doing or agreeing not to do something that one was previously not bound to do or avoid doing except for the contract. Sometimes consideration is spoken of as the detriment to the one making the promise.

- Courts will not inquire into the adequacy of consideration. Consideration does not have to exact any sort of massive detriment making for an equal bargain. The slightest thing may suffice, which is why one often sees the phrase: "For one dollar and other valuable consideration," or something similar.

- When the terms of consideration were never discussed or agreed upon, the entire contract may be avoided by either party. The reason for this outcome is that a proper offer and acceptance as to the essential term of consideration was never made. Courts will sometimes try to imply terms of reasonable consideration where one party has performed obligations under an agreement. There is no guarantee that a court will do this. It is folly to make an agreement without specifying consideration by both parties. Under most circumstances, there is no binding contract.

- The three essential terms of every binding contract, in summary, are offer, acceptance, and consideration. What then is a contract? No single definition works because there are too many exceptions. All of the essential ingredients to a contract may be present but there still may be no contract because promises were induced by fraud. In a utilitarian sense, a contract is anything that a court will enforce as one. It is a bargain. It comes into existence when an offer is accepted by a promise or by performance of what was bargained for. Each side gives something up by way of consideration. In commercial terms, a contract is a binding commitment.

- Even after considering three essential items of every binding legal contract, it is important to know about a few corollary matters. These can affect the existence or operation of a contract.

- *Authority*. Before entering into any contract with anybody to do anything, one should be sure that both sides have actual authority to agree. When dealing with a business firm, one might question whether the individual purporting to represent the business firm actually has authority to do so. Some contracts contain clauses saying that the agreement is not valid until accepted by an officer of the company.

- *Legality.* A contract concerning an illegal subject is void and will not be enforced by courts. Where a contract requires one party to do something that violates the law, the contract raises no binding rights or responsibilities. Contracts which involve the unlawful reproduction of libelous or copyrighted material, for example, may be unenforceable.

- *Jurisdiction.* Local law in the United States may vary on the fine points of contracts. Forty-nine states have adopted the Uniform Commercial Code which has extensive provisions for purchase and sale agreements. Differing versions of the Code have been adopted by some states. Most matters contained in the Uniform Commercial Code can be modified by written agreement of both parties. Ultimately, the interpretation of all contracts is subject to local courts applying local law which may vary considerably from one jurisdiction to another.

- *Assignment.* Often the whole point of entering into a written contract is so that an association can be assured that specific services will be performed for it or products will be supplied to it. If there is any possibility that a firm other than that contracting with an association will fulfill the contract, this factor should not be left in the air. Clauses in a contract either granting or denying the possibility of assignment of rights or obligations should be used.

- *Modification.* Once an offer is accepted, a contract exists. The contract cannot now be modified by one side without the agreement of the other. It is elementary to the idea of a contract being a mutual binding agreement that it takes the concurrence of all parties to modify a contract. Unequivocal acceptance of an unequivocal offer is final, unless both sides agree otherwise.

- What happens to contracts after they are made? Problems arise where one party breaches the contract by either refusing to perform altogether or refusing to perform in accordance with the terms of the contract. Once such a breach has occurred, the party who has performed or is willing to perform the duties under the contract has a potential legal action against the breaching party. A lawsuit can be brought against the breaching party for failure to live up to the terms of the contract.

● In the event that an association becomes involved in a dispute over the terms of a contract, it should keep in mind some guidelines which courts use to interpret and enforce contracts:

—If the contract is in writing the court will always enforce the clear intentions of the parties as set forth in the written words of the contract. This is the most fundamental rule of contract enforcement; and it is applied in every case unless fraud is shown. Even if the parties discussed or agreed upon different terms prior to the signing of the written contract, the court will not admit evidence of such prior agreements where the provisions of the written agreement are clear. This doctrine of excluding prior oral agreements is known as the Parole Evidence Rule. The very existence of the Rule illustrates the overwhelming preference courts have for written agreements.

—If a written contract does not address a particular point, or if the words of the contract are confusing, a court may at its discretion admit evidence from other sources in order to determine what the parties meant. These sources will be used in two situations: where the parties agreed upon terms but did not put the terms in writing, and where the parties simply overlooked certain elements when they negotiated the contract. Thus, a court would admit oral evidence as to the agreed-upon terms or evidence concerning the circumstances surrounding the transaction. Occasionally a court will entertain evidence of an industry's "trade custom." But a trade custom will only be considered in the absence of clear contract terms, when the custom is uniform throughout an industry, and when it can be shown that both parties to the contract actually knew of the custom.

—In the event that the parties enter into a verbal con-

tract without setting the agreement down in writing,
a court will similarly admit evidence from the parties
and other sources to determine the terms of the contract. However, there is a legal doctrine known as
the Statute of Frauds which requires that certain
agreements must be in writing in order to be enforceable. Under the Statute of Frauds, a party may deny
the existence of an oral contract if that party has not
signed a written acknowledgment of the agreement.
The absence of a writing will not change the fact that
an agreement was reached, but it will make the
agreement unenforceable in court. As far as associations are concerned, there are two major types of
agreements which must be in writing in order to be
enforceable: contracts for the sale of goods valued
at more than $500; and contracts which will not be
completed within one year from the date of the contract. The writing requirement of the Statute may be
satisfied by any notation or acknowledgment of the
deal. A signed letter will satisfy the Statute. The
important thing is that the writing, no matter how
insignificant, be signed by the party against whom
enforcement is sought. If there is no signed writing
available to prove the existence of the contract, a
court will be powerless to enforce the agreement.

—Once a breach of contract is established, courts will
attempt to remedy the breach by ordering that money
be paid to the injured party. The money is called
"damages." Courts will not issue injunctions (ordering the breaching party to perform the specified obligations under the contract) if it is possible to
compensate the injured party with an award of damages. Damages may be measured in a number of
ways, but essentially the seller or buyer is entitled
to recover the benefit of the bargain. Both parties are
under a duty to mitigate damages when they are
notified of a breach by the other party.

• Once more, a summary is useful of what is a contract
and how it is enforced. There must be an *offer*—a proposal in defined terms communicated to another. There
must be *acceptance*—specific agreement to the offer.
There must be *consideration*—each side must suffer

some detriment. Other things to be concerned about include *authority* (make sure the person signing has the capacity to do so), *legality* (do not agree to break the law), *jurisdiction* (choose your law), *assignment* (keep it straight who is going to do what), and *modification* (it must be mutually agreed to). The language of contracts should above all be clear and concise. When contracts are clear, courts will enforce them. Courts will not look beyond the language of contracts except to supply missing terms or clarify vague ones. Verbal contracts may not be enforced. Persons who breach contracts will be ordered to pay damages.

● There has been a tendency in recent years to make contracts more readily understandable by non-lawyers. Associations should insist that contracts they enter into are in plain language. No contract is useful if it cannot easily be understood. These replacements for conventional legal rhetoric are suggested:

Eliminate	*Substitute*
hereinbefore	in this agreement
hereinafter	in this agreement
hereof	of this agreement
thereof	of it
witnesseth	DO NOT USE
whereas	since, because
signed and sealed	dated
executed	signed
shall have been	is
provided however	but
enclosed herewith	enclosed
as to	about
as follows	:
each and every	each
paid over	paid
advise	tell
cease	stop
prior to	before
state	say
in order to	to
by means of	by
in the event that	if

Eliminate	*Substitute*
in lieu of	instead of
and/or	DO NOT USE
same	DO NOT USE as a pronoun
to wit	DO NOT USE
unto	to
commence(ment)	begin(ning)
monies	money
with respect to	about
necessity of	need to
this ___ day of ___	on ___
finalize	finish, complete
utilize	use

RESOURCES FOR CHAPTER 11

Periodicals

Jacobs, "What You Need to Know About Legal Contracts," *Association Management*, March, 1984, page 81.

Chapter 12

CONTRACTS WITH ASSOCIATION STAFF

The use of written employment agreements between associations and their executives is becoming commonplace. Surveys show that employment agreements with associations' highest salaried executives may exist in as many as half of all medium-size and larger associations. There is evidence that the prevalence of these employment agreements is increasing.

Association executives derive significant advantages from employment contracts. Among those advantages are the security and the clear specifications of obligations and benefits that contracts afford. There are also significant advantages to the association itself, including the assurance of continuity of management for the association and adequate notice of the departure of the executive.

Many associations use executive employment agreements to detail and memorialize special compensation or benefit arrangements such as deferred compensation or other post-employment plans. Because of the absence of profit motive and shares of stock in nonprofit associations, the methods available for compensating association executives are more limited than the methods available for compensating executives in business corporations. Careful planning is necessary to assure that the association executive receives compensation and benefits in a scheme that is mutually acceptable and is likely to further the long-term goals of both the association and the executive.

SUMMARY

- Written employment agreements between associations and their executives are now common, especially for principal executives. Written agreements in abbreviated form are sometimes even used for nonclerical association employees other than principal executives.

- Whether an association executive should have a written employment agreement ought to depend upon assessments of advantages and disadvantages to the association and to the executive.

- The decision whether or not to have an association executive contract should not depend upon the prevalence of employment contracts within the trade or profession represented by the association. This is because association management is a singular profession and should be viewed as such by the association's governing body.

- An association seeking to attract an outstanding new executive or to assure the continued services of a valued manager already employed is often the most inclined to offer a written employment agreement.

- As in any legal relationship, the existence of a clearly written agreement between two parties tends to foster better understanding between them and to minimize the possibility of eventual disagreement over subjects in the agreement.

- One commentator has been quoted as outlining these pros and cons for association executive employment contracts:

Advantages

—Contracts help insure stability, which is especially important with respect to principal association executives.
—A contract serves as a quality control mechanism for association programs and policies by clearly placing responsibility for them with the executive.
—Contracts establish criteria, procedures, and timetables for reviewing and evaluating the performance of association executives.
—Contracts minimize misunderstandings that can arise from unwritten agreements.
—Contracts enhance the images of associations by

demonstrating their progressive attitudes and commitment to assuring the highest level of professional management.

—Contracts help associations attract and retain the most qualified and successful executives.

Disadvantages

—Contracts can be misused by dictatorial or arbitrary executives.

—Contracts inhibit the possibility of changing executives, since the individual who is right for the association today may not be right for it later on.

- Some examples of provisions which are typically covered in written employment agreements between associations and their principal executives include:

    —Names, addresses, descriptions of the parties (i.e., "Widget Manufacturers Association of Washington, D.C., a District of Columbia Nonprofit Corporation and John Doe, of New York, N.Y.")

    —A statement that the agreement is based upon mutual consideration and that both parties acknowledge receipt of consideration

    —An indication of the type of association involved (i.e., "a trade association whose members are manufacturers of widgets"

    —The title of the position for which the executive is being retained

    —The term of the agreement including designation of the starting date for the executive

    —The general or specific duties of the executive (such as representing the association and its members before the industry, the government, and the public; hiring and firing of other employees of the association; or general administrative and financial management)

    —Stipulation that the executive will devote his full efforts and time to the position

    —A reasonably limited proscription against the executive later taking a position with a competitive association or firm (the extent to which the law will recognize and allow enforcement of these kinds of

restrictive provisions, if at all, depends upon laws and decisions in each state; the more restrictive the provision, the less likely it will be honored)
—Any benefits available to the executive such as relocation expenses, travel and entertainment expenses, vacations, sick leave, life/health/accident insurance, dues for membership in professional societies, etc.
—Provisions for termination, including the right of termination by the association without notice in circumstances of gross negligence or dishonesty by the executive, the period and method of notice of termination by the association or the executive in other circumstances, and the effects upon the agreement in the event of illness or death of the executive
—The results for the executive in the event of merger or consolidation of the association
—Indemnification of the executive by the association to the extent allowed by state law
—Renewal provisions
—Non-assignability of the rights and obligations of the executive and the association
—Provisions for arbitration of differences
—Relinquishment by the executive of all rights or claims in files, records, publications, technical or marketing information, or other documents or information developed during the employment and agreement by the executive not to remove association documents from the control of the association during or after employment
—Specification of which state's laws govern interpretation of the agreement
—Signatures and dates of signing.

• Many forms of compensation and benefits besides salary payments might be agreed upon between associations and their executives. Even smaller associations can take advantage of a wide range of methods of compensating their principal executives. Beyond salary, there are the possibilities of using bonuses, deferred compensation plans, pension plans, savings plans, medical and hospitalization plans, life insurance, disability plans, continuing education benefits, business travel and entertainment allowances, business auto-mobiles, club dues, professional association member-ships, professional liability insurance, low-interest loans, prepaid legal expenses, and so forth. All of these compensation opportunities have their own sets of le-gal and financial considerations. None should be in-stituted without the advice of experienced professional advisors such as attorneys or accountants for the as-sociations contemplating them. Qualified pension plans, for example, must meet the extensive requirements of the Internal Revenue Service and the principles of the Employee Retirement Income Security Act (ERISA). Business automobiles, a frequently offered perquisite, may be subject to special treatment for associations and executives to the extent they are used for incidental personal transportation (which may include driving to and from work, in many circumstances). Of particular concern is the extent to which any of the compensation methods will result in taxable income to the executive.

- Some associations provide their principal executives with deferred compensation plans. The plans may be included in the provisions of an executive employment agreement or in a separate agreement. Typical provi-sions of deferred compensation plans include the fol-lowing:

  —Provision is made for payment of periodic fixed amounts to the executive over a period of years or during his lifetime after leaving the employ of the association.
  —Payments are sometimes designated to go to the spouse of the executive or to some other designee in the event of the executive's death.
  —To be entitled to the deferred compensation pay-ments, the executive is ordinarily required to comply with the provisions of the employment agreement during the employment term with the association and possibly to comply with some additional require-ments after leaving the association, such as furnish-ing consulting services or to abstain from working with competitive associations or firms.
  —An association may finance a deferred compensation plan for its executive through payments to a deferred

compensation fund to which the executive does not have access before leaving the association. It is extremely important that the executive not share in any aspects of ownership in the plan or its tax-deferment feature might be defeated. Money for payments by the association to the deferred compensation fund may come from regular association income, investments, insurance policies, and so forth.

- Associations and their executives must comply with many other complicated and subtle provisions to insure that deferred compensation plans are consistent with tax and other laws and in particular to assure that payments to deferred compensation funds are not considered ordinary income until actually received. Over the years legislative changes and Internal Revenue Service positions have limited or eliminated certain kinds or aspects of deferred compensation plans whose provisions have not been formally approved in advance by IRS. No association should consider a deferred compensation plan without the advice and assistance of expert advisors.

- Because nonprofit, tax-exempt associations have neither shares of stock nor profit motives, benefits based on stock and profitability are not available to executives. Consequently, many associations provide more liberal pension plans and other benefits than are provided by business entities.

- Many associations do have employee pension plans. These should be carefully reviewed each year by tax or pension counsel to assure compliance with the Employee Retirement Income Security Act and all other applicable laws and regulations. This is especially important since several new laws that affect employee benefit plans have been passed in recent years.

- Associations which have comprehensive written agreements with their highest paid executives sometimes also have abbreviated written agreements with other nonclerical employees. Provisions of these agreements may include:

   —The names, addresses, and descriptions of the parties

—A statement that the employee will adequately and faithfully perform the duties of employment

—A statement of the amount, time, method of payment, and review of compensation

—The requirement that the employee will devote full time to the employment and accept no outside or additional work

—Provisions for termination, including notice of termination

—Provisions barring conflict of interest by the employee

—Provisions reasonably prohibiting the employee from working for a competitive association or firm or from removing association records, files, publications, technical information, or other documents or information upon termination.

RESOURCES FOR CHAPTER 12

Books

Boehret, Brandenburg, Kempler & Altman, "Deferral of Federal Income Tax on Association Executives' Non-Qualified Deferred Compensation Arrangements" in *Association Issues*, Jacobs, Editor, ASAE, 1983, page 35.

Gilchrist, "Association-Sponsored Pension and Profit-Sharing Plans" in *Associations and the Law Book III*, U.S. Chamber, 1969, page 64.

Paul & Severin, "Fringe Benefits" in *Managing Membership Societies*, Grief, Editor, ASAE, 1979, page 57.

Reilly, "Executive Deferred Compensation Revisited Under ERISA" in *Associations and the Law Book VII*, U.S. Chamber, 1976, page 51.

Reilly, "Private Employee Retirement Plans to Undergo Major Revision" in *Associations and the Law Book VI*, U.S. Chamber, 1975, page 73.

Reilly, "Status of Deferred Compensation Agreements for Association Executives" in *Associations and the Law Book VI*, U.S. Chamber, 1975, page 82.

Ryan & Meldrin, "Avoid the Pitfalls in Setting Up Your Staff Pension Plan" in *Guidelines for Effective Association Insurance Programs*, ASAE, 1979, page 79.

Shapiro, *Financial Incentives for Association Executives: The Theory*, ASAE Foundation, 1983.

Webster, *The Law of Associations*, Matthew Bender, 1976, page 4-1.

Webster, Boehret, Panaro, & Hazard, *Financial Incentives for Association Executives: The Practice*, ASAE Foundation, 1984.

Periodicals

Anderson, "Perks: An Important Part of an Association Executive's Compensation," GWSAE *Executive Update*, May, 1985, at 67.

Anderson, "A 401(k) Plan—Is It for Your Association?," GWSAE *Executive Update*, January, 1985, page 28.

Anderson, "Negotiating an Employment Contract," GWSAE *Executive Update*, September, 1984, page 34.

"Bob Statham's List of Over 150 Fringe Benefits for Organization, Institution, & Association Executives," *Association Trends*, January 6, 1984, page 8.

Bryant & Schwartz, "Deciding to Sign on the Dotted Line," *Association Management*, March 1985, page 119.

Fellows, "What Are the Terms of Your Agreement?," *Association Trends*, October 5, 1984.

Fontana, "Looking at the Executives Employment Contract From Both Directions—Employer & Employee," *Association Trends*, August 14, 1981, page 8.

"The Pros and Cons of an Employment Contract for the Chief Staff Executive," *Leadership*, November, 1979, pages 59 and 64.

Webster, "The Advantages of Having an Employment Contract," *Association Management*, September, 1977, page 20.

Webster, "Honoring Employees With Tax-Free Money," *Association Management*, March, 1986, page 53.

Webster, "Protecting Executive Compensation," *Association Management*, December, 1985, page 49.

Webster, "Setting Up a Deferred Compensation Plan," *Association Management*, March, 1984, page 49.

Webster, "When Should an Association Executive Defer Compensation?," *Association Management*, March, 1983, page 39.

Chapter 13

TERMINATING EMPLOYEES

There was a time when an association's executive management could "fire" or terminate another employee whose performance was inadequate without any real concern of legal liability, assuming the terminated employee was not protected by a contract of employment. Employees were considered under the law to be employed "at will," i.e., at the complete discretion of the employer. The employment "at will" principle still governs most employment situations. However, courts in many states have begun to recognize an employee's "right to employment" in some situations and, in those situations, to penalize employers for the "wrongful discharge" of the employee.

The prudent association executive who makes employee termination decisions or reviews termination recommendations must become sensitive to the potential liability lurking beneath many time-honored reasons for terminating employees. For example, some stated explanations for termination, such as "he's a troublemaker," "she was insubordinate," or "his attendance has been lousy," cannot safely be taken at face value, for any of these reasons may be shorthand for "retaliation" which the emerging law of wrongful discharge prohibits.

The "troublemaker" might have just complained to his supervisor or a public authority about some perceived violation of law. The "insubordination" might have been a refusal to perform a work assignment felt to be illegal or unethical. The "non-attendance" might have been occasioned by a workplace injury for which the employee has filed, or is preparing to file, a workers' compensation claim. In each case, the applicable state law may forbid termination in retaliation for "whistleblowing," for refusing to participate in a violation of law, or for exercising the right to file a workers' compensation claim. Despite the stated explanation for the termination, a judge or jury sympathetic to the "underdog" employee may determine what is considered to be the real reason for the termination.

59

In addition, and related to the emerging law of wrongful discharge, associations should be particularly sensitive to terminations of employees known or suspected to be involved in substance abuse, i.e., alcoholism, drug dependency, etc. Human compassion as well as potential legal liability dictate that employees with substance abuse problems be given special attention before termination.

This Summary addresses both wrongful discharge liability and management of employees with substance abuse problems.

SUMMARY

- Courts in many states have created "public policy" exceptions to the centuries-old employment rule that an employee not covered by a contract lawfully could be terminated for any reason whatsoever or for no reason at all. Among the various rationales for creating this exception to the "employment at will" doctrine are these:

  —One public policy exception protects the employee who is terminated in retaliation for performing some public obligation, such as performing jury duty or disclosing corporate or organizational wrongdoing. In addition to the many courts that have protected whistleblowers by judicial decision, the legislatures in several states have enacted whistleblower protection statutes applicable to the private sector.

  —Another public policy exception protects the employee who is terminated for refusing to perform an illegal, or in some cases even an unethical, act.

  —Still another exception covers termination in retaliation for an employee's exercise of a legal right, such as the filing of a workers' compensation claim or (increasingly) the refusal to take a polygraph test. In one case, a federal appeals court held unlawful a private employer's termination of an employee in retaliation for his opposing the employer's political stand regarding new state legislation important to the employer.

- Because many reasons for dismissing employees may (even subconsciously) mask unlawful, retaliatory motivations, association employers are well advised to carefully consider the reasons for termination. It is not enough, however, for the responsible association executive to be satisfied that the recommending supervisor is not trying to punish the employee for some legally protected activity. The association executive must also be sensitive to appearances and think of a potential jury's perception of the true reason for termination if the termination were challenged. Accordingly, timing is critical. If, for example, an employee whose performance is genuinely inadequate is terminated just after returning from jury service or a work-related injury, it may be impossible to persuade a jury of the real reason for the termination.

- Other circumstances that can make it difficult to overcome an inference of illegal retaliation include the presence of extraneous material in the employee's personnel file, a paucity of documentation of the employee's performance deficiencies, sugar-coated "morale-building" performance evaluations, "loose-lipped" supervisors, and the inclusion of unsupportable grounds in the termination letter.

- Association employers may find it worthwhile to take special preventive measures. To minimize whistle-blower exposure, an association might profitably establish and publicize an internal complaint procedure that employees must use to register complaints about wrongdoing by association officers, directors, members, executives, or fellow employees. Employees should be encouraged to use the procedure and be advised that no retaliation will befall them for using it; and the association should then dutifully investigate and respond to employee complaints.

- Exposure to wrongful discharge liability at the hands of employees who refuse to carry out work assignments for legal or ethical reasons can be reduced in similar fashion. The careful association employer should prescribe a procedure for supervisors to follow when employees object on principle to work directives. The procedure should include these elements:

—Requiring the employee to articulate the particulars of his or her objection to the assignment;

—Investigating the validity of the objection, modifying the assignment if the objection appears valid, and explaining to the employee why the objection is invalid if the association concludes that it is ill-founded;

—Consulting with legal counsel if it appears that the employee might not accept and comply with the routine resolution of the objection.

- If an association employer does not want to permit the spectre of a wrongful discharge suit by a malingerer who happens to claim an employment accident or illness to forestall termination for absenteeism, one possible tactic is to institute a strict attendance policy and apply it unvaryingly to absences caused by work-related and non-work-related disabilities alike. Although the validity of such a policy may depend upon the particulars of the pertinent state workers' compensation act, the policy will likely refute any claim that an employee was singled out for termination because of the filing, or intention to file, a workers' compensation claim.

- If an association employer needs an incentive to institute protective measures, it should consider the legal remedies available to "victims" of wrongful discharge. Except where a state statute provides a more limited remedy, most courts that have entertained lawsuits based upon wrongful discharge claims have also decided that wrongful discharge actions deserve the same kind of remedies as personal injury actions. Thus, typically, juries will be instructed to award not only lost wages and benefits but also possibly compensatory and punitive damages. In some cases, the compensatory and punitive damages have dwarfed the lost wages and have registered in six or even seven figures.

- The workplace abuse of alcohol and/or drugs is an increasing concern for many association employers. Yet various federal and state laws which protect the mentally and physically handicapped impact upon association employers' responses to this trend. Some basic guidelines can help minimize the risk that an association will incur legal exposure in the process of resolving these problems.

- The association executive should at all times keep the focus on the employee's job performance and the workplace impact of the problem, rather than disciplining an employee simply because of alcohol or drug dependency. Discipline or discharge because an employee is "an alcoholic" or "a drug user" is viewed by many courts and government agencies as discrimination based on "handicap," and thus, potentially illegal. In contrast, discipline for unsatisfactory attendance, substandard job performance, or having prohibited substances on company property are all generally regarded as proper employer concerns. For this reason, throughout the process of dealing with a problem employee, the association executive should address the work-related *symptoms* of the problem rather than its medical or social causes.

- When a problem arises, the association executive should move promptly to confront and resolve it. Confronting the employee is usually distasteful, and many employers avoid the inevitable by hoping that the problem will solve itself. Not only does that infrequently happen, but delay can cause more serious disruption to the organization. When the problem gets so obvious that the association executive cannot ignore it any longer, association leaders, members, and other association personnel are by then invariably well aware of the situation. The executive is then faced with the dilemma of either moving hastily to "root out the problem," which may create legal exposure, or else taking the additional time required to move carefully toward a resolution during which time the association may well suffer further.

- When the problem is identified and the employee has been confronted, the association executive should spell out clear and specific expectations for required performance levels, as well as definite (and relatively prompt) timetables within which those expectations must be met. Typically, the employee will deny that he or she has an alcohol or drug problem, and it generally is not profitable to debate that. Instead, the expectations should be put in terms of "behavior modification" by requiring correction of the unacceptable systems (e.g., "the two-hour lunches and the Monday morning absenteeism must stop"). If the necessary correction is not promptly forthcoming, the association executive should provide continual and candid follow-up, with escalating warnings regarding the seriousness of the problem and the consequences if it is not corrected. If the problem is serious enough to lead to discharge, the employee should be told that bluntly, and told that discharge will in fact occur unless the behavior is modified. The literature on the subject indicates that many alcoholics and drug abusers will not consider changing their behavior until they face an immediate and substantial trauma (e.g., loss of job, divorce, imprisonment). Thus, as a last resort before discharge, some association executives will suspend an employee for several months without pay to emphasize the ultimate seriousness of the situation.

- The association executive should consider urging the employee to seek professional counseling or medical assistance, such as Alcoholics Anonymous. Although this tends to be effective only when the employee acknowledges the problem, some association executives require such outside treatment as a condition of continued employment.

- Every step of the process—from management conversations and counseling, through warning and discipline, to discharge—should be thoroughly documented, with copies provided to the employee. "Building a record" is invaluable if discharge results and the employer defends its decision in a legal action. Also, thorough documentation supplied to the employee can serve to emphasize the seriousness of the situation and the probable consequences and shake the employee out of any self-delusion.

- It is, finally, important that drug and alcohol problems be handled with substantial consistency. As an example, abruptly firing a female secretary for using drugs during breaks while overlooking alcohol abuse by a senior male manager could expose the organization to liability for sex discrimination. Identical treatment is sometimes impossible, as individual cases will differ;

but general uniformity is essential if the association employer is to avoid the risk of legal exposure.

RESOURCES FOR CHAPTER 13

Periodicals

Webster, "Caution: Fire With Care," *Association Management*, September, 1985, page 59.

Chapter 14

ASSOCIATION FINANCES

Although association finances do not ordinarily present legal problems other than in the area of taxation and tax exemption, there are some general legal considerations involved in association budgets and dues.

Budgets should be adequate to provide for all of the activities that members consider necessary. The nature of budgeted income and expenditures should be such that questions are not raised about federal tax status if the association is exempt. To preserve tax-exempt status, budgets should not provide for too large an accumulation of surplus. These and other tax issues are considered in greater detail in later chapters.

Association dues must not be used as a mechanism for arbitrarily restricting membership. Also, dues-collection activities can raise legal concerns in some circumstances. Finally, there can sometimes be a serious question whether dues or assessments contributed on a voluntary basis by association members, rather than those required of members, can be deducted by the members as business expenses for federal income tax purposes.

Information about the finances of their association should be provided to members in understandable form and at reasonably frequent intervals. Some associations provide summary financial information to members on a quarterly schedule. Audited reports on association finances should be available annually if possible.

SUMMARY

- General legal considerations that could be raised about association finances relate to association budgeting for operations and dues required of members.

- Budgeted income and expenditures should be consistent with the regulations and guidelines covering federal income-tax exemption for organizations. It should be kept in mind that if the proportion of income unrelated to the purposes for which the association received or maintains its tax-exempt status is too large, the association's tax-exempt status could be jeopardized.

- The association budget should not result in too large an accumulation of surplus or tax-exempt status may also be jeopardized. The accumulation of surplus equal to no more than one or two times an association's total annual budget has been recommended by commentators as ordinarily acceptable unless there are special circumstances. The Internal Revenue Service has not established any rule on the subject. A few examples of factors which might justify accumulating a particularly large surplus include:
  —The necessity to provide for some extraordinary potential for liability such as that resulting from the cancellation of a major association meeting or that from a research project with possible high risk.
  —The accumulation of funds over a period of years for some association project or goal which will require major expenditures, such as a large increase in association staff or purchase of an association headquarters building or computer equipment.
  —A history of financial difficulties or fluctuations in the association which accumulated surplus funds could mitigate if the conditions were to occur again.

- Member dues should be levied only after obtaining the required approval, as stipulated in the bylaws or other governing documents of the association.

- Once dues are established, their imposition in effect forms separate, binding contracts between the association and each of its members. Members delinquent in payment of dues can be held liable to the association under these contracts.

- Association dues may be in flat amounts for all members or may be in varying amounts, depending, for example, upon the amount of a member's gross sales, payroll, or employee hours, number of establishments, number of years in a profession or business, units of production.

- Where dues are based upon the sales or production of member firms, dues categories should be established to correspond to broad categories of gross sales or production amounts. This is also true when dues are based upon other factors whose specification and disclosure should remain confidential.

- Where dues categories are used, members may be asked to verify in writing that they are paying dues in the proper categories. Members suspected of paying dues in the wrong categories can be pursued but should not be made the subject of public investigations or discussions in the association, activities which could be considered libelous.

- Some associations have begun assessing interest if dues payments are made after the required date. Before proceeding to levy interest charges, association legal counsel should be asked to review any state laws regarding interest payments that might be applicable. Especially if the membership of the association includes individuals rather than businesses, federal requirements for disclosure of finance charges may also have to be followed.

- Where varying dues amounts apply, maximum and minimum dues amounts may be imposed to avoid too great a disparity between dues of the largest and smallest members, which could result in financial dominance by large members, payments of insignificant amounts by small members, and other problems.

- Dues or initiation fees should not be set so arbitrarily that they become instruments for restricting membership, excluding competitors from the association, or otherwise preventing firms from receiving benefits of membership.

- Initiation fees should be avoided unless they are nominal and reflect actual costs of administration or services for new members. Otherwise, again, they might be challenged as intended to arbitrarily restrict membership.

- Dues for associate or supplier members, such as those who provide goods or services to regular members, can be higher or lower than dues for regular members.

- Dues and assessments that are required to be paid as a condition of association membership are tax deductible to members as business expenses, according to IRS regulations. On the other hand, dues or assessments voluntarily paid or contributed by members may not always be deductible by them as business expenses. To be deductible, members must be able to show that the voluntarily remitted amounts are made with the expectation of business benefit commensurate with the payments. Caution is warranted in this area in which the tax laws have not yet been well developed. Particular care should be taken to avoid giving members the expectation that their voluntary payments or contributions are automatically tax deductible.

RESOURCES FOR CHAPTER 14

Books

Association Dues Structures: Theory and Practice, ASAE, 1969.

Gross & Warshauer, *Financial and Accounting Guide for Nonprofit Organizations*, Ronald Press, 1983.

Lamb & Shields, *Trade Association Law and Practice*, Little, Brown, 1971, page 198.

Olsen, "Accounting" in *Managing Membership Societies*, Grief, Editor, ASAE, 1979, page 99.

Principles of Association Management, ASAE and U.S. Chamber, 1975, page 305.

Webster, *The Law of Associations*, Matthew Bender, 1976, page 18.1.

Webster, Herold, & Dye, *Association Legal Checklist*, U.S. Chamber, 1983, page 5.

Cases

Associated Press v. United States, 326 U.S. 1 (1945). Setting of prohibitive expenses for association participation.

Robert Montgomery v. United States, 63 Ct.Cl. 588, 6 AFTR 6787
(1927). Deductibility as business expenses of voluntary dues
or assessments to associations.

Regulations

IRS Regulations. Sections 1.162-20 and 1.162-15(b).

Chapter 15

ASSOCIATION RECORD RETENTION

Associations routinely maintain many kinds of files and records covering membership, finances, programs, personnel, and many other subjects. What documents should be kept and for how long are questions often considered by associations. Various federal or state laws often require association files and records to be maintained for stipulated periods. While it is important, especially for tax purposes, to carefully consider document retention and storage, the expenses of retaining files and records increase with increased costs of paper, file cabinets, rent, and clerical assistance. Practical reasons therefore dictate that associations maintain documents only for as long as absolutely necessary. In short, there are substantial legal and practical reasons for every association to establish and follow a clear record-retention program that details what is to be kept as well as time periods for the retaining and purging of each kind of association file and record.

Obviously, all association records cannot and should not be purged periodically. Certain categories of documents have long-term usefulness. A few categories should never be destroyed. Together with the practical reasons for not retaining association records and files beyond the time useful or necessary one must consider federal and state laws which *require* the maintaining of some items, often for stipulated periods.

State nonprofit incorporation laws sometimes dictate that particular records be made and kept by organizations subject to those laws. All associations must heed federal and state taxation and employment law requirements for maintaining documentation in those areas.

A well-planned and carefully followed association record-retention program will insure that out-of-date and unused information will not be kept around to clutter the association's offices and other record storage areas. Equally important, adherence to the program will ensure that current and useful

71

information—as well as that which is legally required—will not be destroyed.

SUMMARY

- Determining which association files and records shall be routinely maintained—and for how long—involves a consideration of both practical and legal implications. Opening, using, and storing files consumes valuable association resources. To retain documents beyond their periods of usefulness runs certain risks should an antitrust or other investigation be brought against an association. State and federal laws dictate the maintaining of files and records in some subject areas. Any association document-retention policy or program must begin with a cataloging of these items which the organization is required by law to retain.

- State corporation laws applicable to incorporated associations often stipulate that certain documentation be made and kept. Ohio, for example, has this provision: "Each corporation shall keep correct and complete books and records of account, together with minutes of the proceedings of its incorporators, members, trustees, and committees of the trustees or members."

- While prescribing that such documentation as financial records, minutes, or lists of members' names and addresses be kept, state corporation laws on record retention typically do not indicate how long to keep the specified documents. In the absence of state agency or court decisions interpreting the laws, associations must assume that at least the specified documents are to be retained indefinitely.

- Even more specific requirements for association record retention emanate from tax and employment laws both at the federal and state levels.

- The Internal Revenue Code specifically requires organizations that have federal income-tax-exempt status to maintain records and to make them available for inspection by IRS agents, for example, in an audit. Records held for IRS purposes to detail receipts and disbursements, gross income, unrelated business income, exempt association activities, and other books and records must be available for IRS inspection as long as the IRS can levy tax assessments against the association. The IRS can always challenge a tax return filed within three years of the challenge. The period for challenge is six years if a major error in stating gross income is made; it is unlimited if the IRS claims that a tax return is false or fraudulent or if no return at all was filed. Accordingly, the following specific recommendations can be made:

—Retain permanently articles of incorporation, other organizing and governing documents, the IRS tax exemption determination letter, minute books, and bank statements.

—Retain for at least seven years all cancelled checks and other supporting documentation for income and expenses. Exempt organizations that fail to maintain adequate records to substantiate annual informational returns, IRS Form 990, can lose their tax-exempt status. National associations are also required to retain records relating to their chapters if the chapters hold federal income tax exemption under a group exemption obtained by the national association.

• As with all employers, associations must retain records concerning employees' wages and taxes withheld from wages, unemployment tax records, and records of Social Security taxes for periods of four years from either the due date of the tax or the date of payment.

• The Labor Department requires that several types of employment records be retained as specified under the Fair Labor Standards Act. Some large associations may also be required to maintain specified records under the Age Discrimination Act of 1967. Finally, unless an association has fewer than seven employees and has had no death or serious occupational accident, certain record-keeping requirements must be met to comply with the Occupational Safety and Health Act.

• Beyond federal and state statutory requirements there

are other legal reasons for which material should be
retained. Association contracts, insurance policies,
deeds, leases, trademark or patent registration certif-
icates, and similar documents should be maintained
while they are in effect and for a period of time after
they expire in order to protect the rights of the association under the documents. Claims based on these
kinds of documents made after a certain number of
years specified in applicable state statutes of limitation will very likely be barred.

- In the antitrust area, once an association has any
knowledge of an investigation by the federal or state
governments in which antitrust law violations are being
considered, great caution should be exercised before
any association files or records are destroyed lest the
association be accused of obstruction of justice. For
federal antitrust investigations, serious penalties could
apply:
  —In Department of Justice criminal antitrust investigations where evidence is typically gathered by grand
  jury subpoena, separate federal criminal laws prohibit attempts to obstruct or impede the investigations by, for example, intentional destruction of
  documents covered by the grand jury subpoenas.
  —In Department of Justice civil antitrust investigations
  where information is typically gathered by civil investigative demands, intentional destruction of documents covered by the demands is also a separate
  criminal offense.
  —In Federal Trade Commission investigations where
  information is typically gathered by subpoena, it is
  likely that intentional destruction of materials sought
  by the FTC would constitute a separate violation of
  the Federal Trade Commission Act, for which criminal penalties can be applied.
- Even where there is no specific penalty provision applicable to the destruction of materials, it is clear that
adverse legal inferences can be drawn in any litigation
where it can be shown that an association failed to
maintain, or will fully purged pertinent files and records.
- Assuming that retention of particular association doc-

uments is not required by law, the mere possibility of perusal of those files and records by others in an antitrust challenge suggests that an association not retain them beyond the periods of their usefulness or necessity. The antitrust laws, and especially their interpretation by agencies and courts, are subtle and changing. It is unwise to facilitate a scenario in which a memorandum drafted for an association today, for example, might be construed by those seeking to find fault with the association or interpreted under the antitrust laws as they might exist 30 or 40 years from now. No organization can protect itself completely against the possibility of receiving or disseminating some document that is written in haste or without clear understanding of its legal implications. While the document may be innocuous, it could be interpreted out of context. Similarly, a document that is most appropriate today could seem prejudicial in other times, especially when reviewed by a government or private-sector antagonist. A systematic document-retention—and document-destruction—program is the best protection.

- Every association should develop and follow a record-retention program to assure that necessary files and records are retained and unnecessary ones are systematically removed and destroyed.

- The association record-retention program should specify the periods of time for holding specified categories of files and records.

- The record-retention program should be routinely followed; exceptions should be made only for good reason and upon the authority of senior association staff.

- The retention program should include those categories of documents in which records are retained for legal reasons; the program may also give periods of time for keeping records where no legal reasons dictate retention.

RESOURCES FOR CHAPTER 15

Books

Fellman, "Affirmative Record Maintenance of Minutes, Memoranda, and Notes" in *Associations and the Law Book VII*, U.S. Chamber, 1976, page 17.

Jacobs, "The Ounce of Prevention: An Antitrust Compliance Program of Associations" in *Associations and the Law Book V*, U.S. Chamber, 1973, page 22.

Lenehan, "Association Records: Retain or Destroy?" in *Associations and the Law Book IX*, U.S. Chamber, 1979, page 1.

Oleck, *Non-Profit Corporations, Organizations, and Associations*, Prentice-Hall, 1980, page 374.

Webster, Herold, & Dye, *Association Legal Checklist*, U.S. Chamber, 1983, pages 9–10.

Periodicals

Beckstrom, "Destruction of Documents with Federal Antitrust Significance," *NW. L. Rev.*, 1966, page 687.

Webster, "Pointers for Maintaining Association Tax Records," *Association Management*, February, 1978, page 18.

Statutes

Ohio Rev. Code Sec. 1702.15(1955).

Chapter 16

MEMBERS' ACCESS TO
ASSOCIATION RECORDS

The right to inspect or copy association records can be requested in several kinds of situations. The Federal Trade Commission, the Antitrust Division of the Department of Justice or some other federal or state agency might informally request or even subpoena association records in the course of a government investigation or in preparation for a trial. Nongovernment parties might request or subpoena association records in the course of a private lawsuit. Members or nonmembers might request access to association records in circumstances not involving litigation. The members could be dissidents, for example. The nonmembers could be those who claim that some association records (such as membership lists) bestow competitive advantage and should be available to them.

Government access to association records in antitrust investigations is addressed elsewhere in this book. Availability of association services, publications, and records to nonmembers is also covered elsewhere. The following is a summary of state law requirements concerning members' access to association records in circumstances where the association would prefer not to disclose the records.

SUMMARY

- Access by members to association records is frequently guaranteed by the requirements of state corporation laws and decisions interpreting those laws. That the members requesting association records are dissidents will ordinarily not prohibit them from inspecting and copying material such as membership lists, minutes of meetings, or dues payments.

- In some states the right of access by members to association records is explicitly stated by statute. Where this is not the case, state laws that give shareholders access to business records of corporations may be applied analogously to nonprofit corporations when members of the latter seek organization records.

- State laws or decisions on access by members to association records typically require that members' requests for access be for proper purposes and be reasonably defined.

- Even where members may desire to alter the association's leadership or structure, their requests will be considered proper so long as they are acting in good faith and have the best interests of the entire association in mind.

- Under some decisions, however, where the members may desire to set up a competitive association or otherwise undermine or subvert the association, a proper purpose may not exist.

- Even if there are valid reasons for access to association records, members' requests must reasonably define which records are sought. Some state laws are explicit as to what records must be given to members; if laws are not explicit, a general test of reasonableness would be applied by a reviewing court.

- Some states specify which records must be shown to members upon request. For example, associations incorporated in the District of Columbia must permit members to inspect books and records of account, minutes, and lists of voting members. Generally, state laws include the following among records that must be shown upon request:

  —Minutes of board of directors meetings
  —Minutes of committee meetings
  —Membership lists
  —Financial records.

- Members' requests for association records which officers or staff have any reason to question should be the subject of review under applicable state laws or decisions.

RESOURCES FOR CHAPTER 16

Periodicals

Webster, "What You Should Know About Members' Rights to Association Records," *Association Management*, April, 1977, page 24.

Statutes

D.C. Code Sec. 29-1026(1973).

Cases

Crouse v. Rogers Park Apartments, 343 Ill. App. 319, 99 N.E. 2d 404 (1951). Common law right of stockholder to view corporate records.
Davids v. Sillcox, 66 N.Y.S. 2d 508 (1946). Examination of motives before disclosing corporate information.
Application of Santuccio, 334 N.Y.S. 2d (1972). Attempt to view nonprofit organizations' records.
Application of Atwater, 85 N.Y.S. 2d 738 (1948). Overbroad request for association information.

Chapter 17

LIABILITY OF OFFICERS AND DIRECTORS

Officers and directors of an association ordinarily serve voluntarily without pay. They accept the positions, whether received by election or appointment, because of their interest in the trade or profession represented by the association and because of their desire to see that trade or profession enlightened and advanced. Despite the generosity they display in accepting the positions and agreeing to serve, association officers and directors should be aware that there is at least a possibility of personal liability stemming from their activities on behalf of the association. The successful assertion of personal liability against association officers and directors is rare. But its consequences are drastic enough that associations should consider apprising officers and directors of the possibility and taking steps to guard against it.

The basic rule of liability for business corporations has long been that, so long as an officer or director exercises ordinary diligence and care, no personal liability will arise, even when actions or decisions made in poor judgment cause damage or injury. Good faith is the principal test of ordinary diligence and care. This business corporation rule will ordinarily hold true for officers and directors of associations as well; but the unique exposure of associations to potential antitrust and other problems justifies special caution.

Officers or directors may knowingly perform or approve association activities which are beyond the association's appropriate sphere of authority. In the course of association work, they may intentionally cause injury or damage to persons or property. Officers or directors may even commit or facilitate acts while representing the association which violate antitrust or other laws. In any of these cases, they could be held personally liable.

There are steps that can be taken to minimize the exposure of officers and directors to personal liability. If allowed by the appropriate state laws, associations may indemnify their of-

80

ficers and directors against liability incurred from their activities or decisions on behalf of the association. Associations may even provide insurance for this purpose. Association professional liability insurance is the subject of the next chapter in this book.

SUMMARY

- Association officers and directors, even though they serve voluntarily and without pay, may be exposed in some circumstances to personal criminal or civil liability for acts they perform on behalf of the association.

- Ordinarily, an association officer or director who acts in good faith—using ordinary diligence and care—will not be found liable. Even incompetence or bad judgment will not generally be enough upon which to make a case for liability against an officer or director. Bad faith or fraud are tests for liability.

- In general, an honest office or director who uses reasonable discretion has no personal liability for the association's debts or obligations.

- Officers and directors are ordinarily entitled to rely upon the advice and opinion of credentialed experts such as accountants and attorneys.

- Officers and directors involved in association activities obviously beyond the corporate power and authority of the association could be subject to personal civil liability. Even approving such activities could have the same result if the approval is given with full knowledge of the nature of an activity and the fact that it is outside of the power and authority of the association. Officers and directors are held to the standard of a theoretical "reasonable and prudent man" in determining whether or not they are liable in these circumstances.

- Activities of officers and directors which intentionally cause injury or damage to persons or property (which in the law are called "torts") could give rise to personal liability even though the activities were carried on at the behest of the association. The association may also be separately liable for torts committed by its officers and directors. There was once a prevalent legal doctrine of immunity from tort liability for nonprofit groups; it is now nearly extinct.

- Injury or damage to persons or property which might be committed by officers or directors in the course of association activities may result in the following complaints, including among others:
  —Negligence
  —Slander
  —Interference with contract rights

- Officers and directors are not liable for the torts of association employees unless the officers or directors participated in the activities personally. They are also not liable for any acts of other officers or directors committed before they began serving.

- An association can itself be responsible for criminal activity, for example, when it is held to violate the antitrust laws. Association officers and directors who participate in or knowingly approve criminal activities, such as those involving antitrust violations, can also be personally liable. They are not likely to be liable for criminal acts of others such as association employees unless the officers and directors were themselves involved in the criminal acts. But officer or director involvement in association activities that are proven to be in violation of the criminal antitrust laws against, say, price fixing surely can, and very likely will, result in personal criminal liability for the individual participants to the extent that fines or jail terms are imposed. Extreme vigilance is justified here.

- In the landmark 1982 *Hydrolevel* case in the Supreme Court, an association was itself held liable for treble damages resulting from the anticompetitive interpretation of one of its product standards. The interpretation was made by the association's lower staff in concert with subcommittee volunteers. They only appeared to be acting on behalf of the association, which did not know about the interpretation, did not approve of it, and did not benefit from it. *Hydrolevel* establishes the new antitrust principle of association liability for antitrust violations of anyone acting with the apparent authority of the association.

• Officers and directors usually are not liable for the performance of contracts entered into by the association unless fraud is involved.

• State statutes or the association's own articles of incorporation and bylaws frequently define the duties of officers and directors. To knowingly and willfully fail in those duties could give rise to claims of personal liability. Once again, however, mere incompetence or bad judgment (as distinguished from bad faith) are not enough on which to base personal liability.

• A 1974 federal court case interpreted the duty and responsibility of directors of a charitable organization, a hospital formed under the District of Columbia nonprofit corporation laws, and held that a director would be in default if:

—While assigned to a particular committee of the board having general financial or investment responsibility, he had failed to use "due diligence in supervising" the actions of the officers, employees or outside experts to whom the day-to-day decision-making responsibility had been delegated.

—He had knowingly permitted the hospital to enter into business transactions with organizations in which he had a substantial interest or principal position without having made a prior full disclosure of the nature of his interest to the board or other persons charged with approving the transaction.

—Except as required by the preceding paragraph, he actively participated in or voted in favor of a decision by the board or any committee or subcommittee to transact business with himself or any organization in which he had a substantial interest or position.

—"He otherwise failed to perform his duties honestly, in good faith, and with a reasonable amount of diligence and care."

These criteria could well serve for trade and professional association officers and directors seeking guidelines on their measure of duty and responsibility.

- Association officers and directors can help protect
  against the possibility of claims for personal liability
  by:
  - —Attending association meetings and reading asso-
    ciation publications and correspondence carefully to
    keep fully aware of all association policies and ac-
    tivities
  - —Reviewing from time to time all association articles
    of incorporation, bylaws, and other governing doc-
    uments
  - —Avoiding completely any conflicts of interest in deal-
    ing with the association and disclosing fully any po-
    tential conflicts
  - —Insisting that meeting minutes accurately reflect any
    comments or votes in opposition to matters acted upon
    at meetings
  - —Requesting that a legal opinion be obtained on any
    matter that has unclear legal ramifications
  - —Obtaining and carefully reviewing both audited and
    unaudited periodic financial reports of the associa-
    tion.

- The laws in many states allow nonprofit corporations
  to indemnify their officers and directors against claims
  made against them if the claims are based upon officers' or directors' activities on behalf of the associations except in criminal situations or those involving
  gross negligence or fraud.

- Indemnification of officers and directors, where the law
  permits, should be stated in the association bylaws.

- In many states nonprofit corporations can purchase officer and director liability insurance to protect themselves if they are required to pay claims or defend officers
  and directors which they have indemnified. Some policies, which are now usually called "Association
  Professional Liability Insurance" when the policies have
  been tailored to the special circumstances of associations, protect the association and the officers, directors,
  staff, and others, even in the absence of indemnification provisions adopted by the insured association.

- Because of the potential for personal liability on the
  part of officers and directors, association policies and

activities should be continuously monitored by experienced legal counsel to help assure that no bases for such liability arise.

RESOURCES FOR CHAPTER 17

Books

Gross & Warshauer, "Responsibilities of Treasurers and Chief Financial Officers" in *Financial and Accounting Guide for Nonprofit Organizations*, Ronald Press, 1983, page 3.

Herold, "Antitrust, Trade Regulation, and Other Nontax Aspects of Association Activities" in *Managing Membership Societies*, Grief, Editor, ASAE, 1979, page 128.

Oleck, *Non-Profit Corporations, Organizations, and Associations*, Prentice-Hall, 1980, page 581.

Owen, "Liability of Association Officers and Directors" in *Associations and the Law Book V*, U.S. Chamber, 1973, page 59.

Webster, *The Law of Associations*, Matthew Bender, 1976, pages 2–75.

Webster, Herold, & Dye, *Association Legal Checklist*, U.S. Chamber, 1983, page 8.

Periodicals

Herold, "Your Legal Responsibilities as a Member of the Board," *Association Management*, December, 1982, page A27.

Howe, "Association Liability for Affiliates, Subsidiaries, and Chapters: Who's in Charge? Who's Responsible?," *Association Counsel*, Jacobs, Editor, CNA Insurance, Winter, 1985.

Jacobs, "Association Liability," *Association & Society Manager*, February/March, 1979, page 35.

Jacobs, "Association Subsidiaries and the Law," *Association Digest*, January/February and March/April, 1986, page 27.

Jacobs, "Is Your Association Liable?," *Association Management*, January, 1985, page 67.

Owen & Hart, "What Association Boards Should Know About Liability," *Legal Times of Washington*, December 10, 1979, page 23.

MacArthur, "Know Your Legal Responsibilities," *Leadership*, 1986, page 55.

MacArthur, "What Are Your Legal Responsibilities?," *Leadership*, 1986, page 55.

Webster, "For What Activities Can Your Officers and Directors Be Held Liable?," *Association Management*, October, 1983, page 53.

Webster, "Staying Out of Court," *Association Management*, May, 1985, page 49.

Webster, "When Can a National Association Be Held Liable for Its Chapters?," *Association Management*, August, 1983.

Webster, "Take Care in Organizing Local Chapters," *Association Management*, October, 1985, page 57.

Webster, "Your Legal Responsibilities as an Association Director," *Leadership*, May, 1979, page 47.

Cases

Stern v. Lucy Webb Hayes National Training School for Deaconesses & Missionaries, 381 F. Supp. 1003 (D. D.C. 1974). Responsibilities of nonprofit organization governing boards.

Hydrolevel Corp. v. ASME, Inc., 456 U.S. 556 (1982). Association held liable for antitrust violations of volunteer members acting with the apparent authority of the association.

Chapter 18

ASSOCIATION PROFESSIONAL LIABILITY INSURANCE

An association officer or director usually regards the election or appointment to his position as an honor as well as a duty to the trade or profession represented by the association. He is aware of his responsibilities to the association and to the industry or profession. He is often not as well aware of the legal responsibility that may accompany the position and of the potential, although it is remote, for personal liability.

Nearly every area of association activity can become the basis of some sort of claim by a firm or individual which considers itself damaged or injured by association activity or the individuals responsible for it. Even if the claim is ultimately proved groundless, the cost of defending against the claim can be enormous, especially if the claim involves alleged violations of the antitrust laws or trade regulations.

To encourage the best people to accept positions as officers or directors, many associations purchase insurance to cover officer and director liability. In recent years several insurance firms have issued policies specifically tailored to the needs of the trade and professional association community; the policies are generally designated "Association Professional Liability Insurance." This insurance is designed to pay for claims and defend against them when the claims assert liability on the part of association officers and directors acting on behalf of the association.

Virtually all kinds of liability insurance policies have detailed limitations and qualifications. Association professional liability policies are often very limited and qualified. They can vary widely among different insurance carriers. They often protect the association and its staff as well as its officers and directors. Before purchasing this type of insurance, a careful analysis should be made of the coverage afforded under the policies being considered, and a thorough comparison should be made of those coverages against the applicable premiums for each policy. In particular, the antitrust coverage should be closely analyzed, since antitrust indemnification and defense is often the overriding reason for purchasing association insurance in the first place.

SUMMARY

- Association officers and directors are exposed to potential personal liability in several ways. Even the best of intentions may sometimes be insufficient to protect against some entity or individual asserting claims or filing actions alleging personal liability on the part of those who oversee the policies and activities of the association. While the likelihood of eventual success in such claims or actions is remote in the absence of bad faith or fraud by the officers or directors, still, a defense must be made against them when they are asserted.

- Associations should consider indemnifying their officers and directors against personal liability for their good faith actions on behalf of the association and funding the indemnification by purchasing liability insurance. Some types of officer and director liability insurance policies depend upon the existence of indemnification provisions by the association. Others do not.

- Liability insurance that protects association officers and directors is written by several carriers and varies widely in coverages, terms, exclusions, conditions, limitations, definitions, deductibles, premiums, and endorsements. Before purchasing the insurance, several policies should be analyzed and compared.

- The insurance usually covers errors and omissions by officers and directors acting on behalf of the association. It provides payment for damages and costs of defense in claims against these individuals. Policies frequently exclude from this coverage such matters as the following:

—Liability resulting from fraud or dishonesty, unjust enrichment, and gross negligence

—Personal injury and property claims

—Fines imposed by law

—Claims based on activities which occurred before the insurance was purchased

—Deductible or retention amounts payable by the insured association.

- Some kinds of these association liability insurance policies exclude coverage for antitrust claims either entirely or when the antitrust liability exceeds some specified amount. Occasionally such claims are excluded only if the insured loses the antitrust claim (in which case the money spent by the insurance company in defending the individuals must be paid back). Because of the potential that many association activities have for raising antitrust claims, associations should seriously consider if there is any significant value to policies which exclude antitrust coverage in whole or in part. Where coverage only applies if one wins an antitrust claim, the results upon settlement should be set out clearly. This is because the time and expense ordinarily required to bring an antitrust claim to final judgment are so substantial that the majority of cases are settled, not clearly won or lost.

- Some policies provide coverage not only for payment of claims in matters involving officers and directors but also in those involving the association itself or the association staff. These "association professional liability" policies are designed especially for associations and offer significant advantages over policies that merely cover officers and directors.

- Most of these kinds of association liability insurance policies exclude coverage for bodily injury and property damage claims, since they are assumed to be covered in the association's basic comprehensive general liability policy (which may cover liability for accidents in the association's offices and the like). However, many comprehensive general liability policies exclude coverage for "professional liability" or other remote or derived bodily injury or property damage claims. Increasingly, associations are receiving claims for

damages alleged to have resulted from too-lax asso-
ciation-issued product standards or certification, from
inaccurate association-promulgated advice on technical or medical issues, or from the association's failure
to correct or warn the public of a hazard. Insurance
policies should be reviewed very carefully to see if
these kinds of claims are covered.

• A few carriers of association liability insurance may
be willing to negotiate and change by endorsement the
coverages, terms, or other provisions in their standard
policies. An association should not assume that this—
or any—insurance is only available on a take-it-or-
leave-it basis.

• Association officer and director or professional liability
insurance can be an extremely complicated subject; the
assistance of knowledgeable consultants is ordinarily
essential to obtain the broadest possible coverage for
the association at the lowest possible premiums.

RESOURCES FOR CHAPTER 18

Books

Herold, "Antitrust, Trade Regulation, and Other Nontax Aspects of Association Activities" in *Managing Membership
Societies*, Grief, Editor, ASAE, 1979, page 128.
Jacobs, "Liability Insurance for Association Officers and Di-
rectors" in *Associations and the Law Book VI*, U.S. Cham-
ber, 1975, page 50.
Pariso, "Liability Insurance Checklist for Your Association,"
page 84, and Webster, "How to Insure Against the Personal
Liability of Officers and Members," page 54, in *Guidelines
for Effective Association Insurance Programs*, ASAE, 1979.
Webster, Herold, & Dye, *Association Legal Checklist*, U.S.
Chamber, 1983, page 8.

Periodicals

Armstrong, "Professional Liability vs. D and O Insurance: Which
Is Better for Your Organization?," *Association Management*, March, 1980, page 79.

Fierstein, "Protect Your Directors, Officers From Liability," *Association Management*, January, 1983, page 75.

Gorham, "Providing a Safe Harbor in a Litigation Storm," *Association & Society Manager*, August/September, 1981, page 27.

Harper, "Liability Insurance: Changing Policies to Meet a Growing Need," *Association & Society Manager*, October/November, 1984, page 15.

Jacobs, "Association Liability," *Association & Society Manager*, February/March, 1979, page 35.

Jacobs, "Is Your Association Liable?," *Association Management*, January, 1985, page 67.

Owen & Hart, "The Changing Scope of Association Professional Liability Insurance," *Association Letter*, August, 1979, page 3.

Chapter 19

ARRANGING FOR PROFESSIONAL SERVICES

Nearly all associations regularly obtain the advice and assistance of outside professionals. Accounting, advertising, audio-visual, data processing, insurance, investing, graphic design, legal, lobbying, mailing, management consulting, public relations, research, and travel consulting services tailored to the needs of associations are widely available. Relationships between associations and outside providers of professional services often have developed over long periods and are based upon familiarity and mutual trust. It may be felt that these relationships do not require formal written agreements. On the other hand, sometimes circumstances warrant at least a simple agreement or letter confirming the generalities of a continuing arrangement between the association and outside professionals. This may be the case when the relationship is just being formed, when there is a substantial amount of money involved, or when the relationship involves complicated obligations. The principles discussed elsewhere in this book of choosing and working with association legal counsel may be applied analogously to continuing association relationships with other outside professional providers of services.

Where the relationship between an association and an outside provider of services is not expected to be continuous or other factors indicate that clarification of the terms of the relationship is desirable, a written contract should be entered into. For example, for a special report on the future of the industry or profession represented by the association, a statistical survey of the members of the association or a technical or scientific research project on some matter affecting association members, it may be prudent to retain by agreement the services of consultants, researchers, writers, or other experts. Special projects are more likely to be completed satisfactorily if the association and the outside experts agree in advance upon the details of the project. It should be recognized that there are advantages to both sides in having a written contract. Later misunderstandings that could result in embarrassment, mistake, additional expense, or unfortunate ill-feelings can be avoided when the specifics have been negotiated and confirmed in an agreement.

SUMMARY

- Associations frequently retain outside professionals to provide services in areas where the association needs staff support, expert advice, or technical assistance.

- Whether or not the outside professional services are to be secured by written agreement is usually determined by the nature of the relationship between the association and the professionals, the length of time for which the relationship is expected to continue, and the amount and kind of services to be performed.

- As a rule, it is desirable for both sides to have a written agreement when the outside professional services are to be performed in connection with some special association project or activity.

- An agreement for outside services of professionals in connection with a particular project may include:
  —A description of the project
  —The specific work to be performed by the professionals
  —The time within which the work of the professionals is to be completed, either for the whole project or for identified phases of it
  —The amount, time, and method of payment to the professionals for their services
  —Whether out-of-pocket expenses of the professionals are to be paid by the association; if so, the details and any limitations on expenses
  —An indication of whether the professionals are to be considered independent contractors or employees of the association
  —Specification of the ownership rights of any report,

information, or expertise developed in the course of
the project, including copyrights, trademarks, and
patent rights
—Designation of which association members or staff
persons are responsible for supervising the project,
assisting the professionals, assessing whether their
work is satisfactory, and approving payments to the
professionals
—Provisions regarding any corollary or successive
projects related to the original one.

RESOURCES FOR CHAPTER 19

Books

Inglis, "Advisors—When and How to Use Them" in *Managing
Membership Societies*, Grief, Editor, ASAE, 1979, page 147.
Oleck, *Non-Profit Corporations, Organizations, and Associa-
tions*, Prentice-Hall, 1980, page 674.
Smith, "Contracting for Special Reports" in *Associations and
the Law Book II*, U.S. Chamber, 1968, page 40.

Periodicals

Chipps, "Association Consultants: Expert Advice for a Price,"
Association Management, December, 1981, page 117.
Dalton, "How to Select and Use a Consultant," *Association
Management*, January, 1975, page 72.

Chapter 20

ASSOCIATION MANAGEMENT
FIRMS

It is not uncommon for an association to agree to share the services of its paid executive and administrative staff with another association or with several others. The staff becomes responsible for the management of two or more groups. The concept was once called "multiple management" but is now more often called simply "association management." Sharing of staffs is most logical where an association cannot afford the size or type of staff considered necessary or desirable. This may be because the association represents a relatively small trade or profession or only a segment of one. It may also be because the association has only recently been formed. But a relatively small budget is not the only factor which encourages associations to share the services of staffs. Association management is sometimes attractive to several associations representing interests in the same industry or profession or otherwise connected or involved with one another. Occasionally associations with budgets that could easily support large individual staffs find that through association management they can be more efficient in their operations and more effective in their activities.

Unique legal problems suggested by the concept and practice of association management are few. Generally, they involve the relationship among the associations that are sharing staffs with one another or the relationship between each association and its shared staff.

SUMMARY

- Association management is often attractive to the small- to medium-sized associations or to associations which

find it beneficial or expedient to share their executive
and administrative staffs with one another for any reason.

- Firms or individuals managing more than one association—association management firms—have few
  special concerns in legal areas of exempt organization
  taxation as well as antitrust and trade regulation.

- Association management firms must keep the financial
  assets and records of one association separate from
  the financial assets and records of other associations
  which they manage. Internal Revenue Service letters
  regarding exempt status, tax reports or returns, audi-
  tors' letters, bank accounts, investments, and all other
  books and records should be maintained separately for
  each association.

- Association management firms must be particularly
  careful to keep their own financial assets and records
  separate from those of the associations which they
  manage. A management firm, whether a proprietor-
  ship, a partnership, or a corporation, will ordinarily be
  operated for profit. To confuse or combine the assets
  or records of the management firm with those of the
  associations could conceivably jeopardize the tax-exempt status of the associations. It could also raise questions concerning the legality and ethics of the
  arrangements between the managers and the associations.

- Association management firms have no unique exposure to antitrust or conflict-of-interest problems. But
  like all association executives, they should be aware
  of the possibility that antitrust situations or conflict-of-
  interest issues could arise if:

  —Two or more associations are managed together where
    one association's members' products or services are
    in competition with those of another association's
    members.
  —Two or more associations are managed together where

one association's members are suppliers to, or customers of, the members of another association, or

—Two or more associations are managed together and information that is private to one association is intentionally or inadvertently given by their executive to the other association(s).

- Like all associations, those using association management firms generally retain independent legal counsel to assist and advise in the general legal, antitrust, and tax-exemption aspects of association policies and programs as well as to assist in government relations activities when necessary.

- Just as there are significant benefits to be derived from a written contract between an association and its directly employed executive, the association using a management firm is well advised to negotiate and execute a written contract with its association management firm. Some matters which can be included in the contract are:

  —The identification and nature of the association (i.e., nonprofit, tax-exempt corporation) and the association management firm (i.e., business corporation)
  —The term of the contract and rights of cancellation
  —The fee to be paid by the association to the association management firm, as well as the time and method of payment
  —The extent to which the fee covers salaries, office expenses, travel expenses, insurance, rent, publication expenses, and other disbursement items
  —The approximate amounts of time which each staff person will spend on matters involving the association (i.e., the full time of one secretary, one half the time of of one professional association manager, etc.)
  —Prohibition of conflicts of interest with other associations managed by the association management firm
  —Stipulation of what records, publications, research materials, and the like are to remain the property of the association
  —Any other matters detailing the rights and respon-

sibilities of the association and the association management firm.

RESOURCES FOR CHAPTER 20

Books

Lamb & Shields, *Trade Association Law and Practice*, Little, Brown, 1971, page 226.

Chapter 21

LEGAL COUNSEL

All associations adopt policies or engage in activities which can have legal implications of one sort or another. The implications may sometimes be immediately apparent or may come to light only after it is too late to change the policies or discontinue the activities. Associations retain counsel primarily to spotlight the legal implications of their policies and activities and to advise on how to proceed without legal entanglements.

Legal counsel for associations can provide guidance on strict antitrust and trade regulation compliance, can help procure and assure maintenance of tax-exempt status, can keep up with and affect the direction of legislative and administrative decisions important to the association and its members, and can give objective advice on various association positions and programs.

The criteria for selecting counsel vary somewhat with the nature of the association and its needs for legal assistance. In all circumstances, it is competence that should be the principle requisite of association counsel. Legal competence is a function of integrity, industry, knowledge, and experience. In addition, counsel must be an individual who can relate personally and work productively with association staff on day-to-day matters and with association officers, directors, and members at their meetings and on special projects. If an association has had legal problems with a certain branch of government or in a specialized area of law, it would be helpful for legal counsel to have some familiarity with the government branch or legal specialty. It would also be particularly beneficial if counsel happened to represent other associations whose problems and concerns sometimes duplicated one another's without, at the same time, raising conflicts of interest.

Association representation is a highly unique specialty of law practice not familiar to most attorneys, even those experienced in business-corporation representation. Associations often encounter singular legal, antitrust, and taxation issues, as is evident from a perusal of any of the summaries in this book. Legal counsel who specialize in association representation can invariably advise upon these issues more effectively and efficiently. Association law specialists are practicing in most major cities, especially in Washington, New York, and Chicago.

A final important criterion is cost. Counsel chosen by an association must be someone whose fees for services are within the limits of the anticipated budget of the group, although it must be recognized that good legal representation is rarely inexpensive except when viewed against results achieved or problems avoided. For example, how does one cope with government regulation? Each year, it becomes increasingly difficult for associations and their members to influence, understand, and comply with the myriad laws and regulations that issue from state and federal government. Association legal counsel can be the key to successful dealings with government, and, consequently, a significant investment for the advice of experienced counsel can actually constitute a savings.

SUMMARY

- Because nearly all association policies or activities may have direct or indirect legal implications, it is essential for associations to have access to the services of competent legal counsel.

- Legal counsel may be retained to advise concerning a special association legal problem or to continuously monitor all policies and activities of the association for possible general antitrust, tax-exemption, or other legal implications.

- Some areas in which association legal counsel can be used to work mainly with persons or agencies outside the association are:
  —Representation in litigation and in government or private inquiries which could lead to litigation. Rep-

resentation by counsel in lawsuits or investigations is usually essential rather than discretionary.

—Development and supervision of antitrust compliance. Review of association documents, programs, and positions; participation at association meetings; and frequent communications with association staff by legal counsel familiar with antitrust issues are among the best ways to avoid lengthy and costly problems in antitrust and trade regulation areas.

—Obtaining and maintaining tax-exempt status. Review of existing policies and activities and continuous monitoring of new positions or endeavors by association counsel can assure that federal income-tax-exempt status is continued and taxes on occasional unrelated business activities of associations are avoided or minimized.

—Participation in legislative activities. Lobbying and other legislative activities of associations at the federal and local levels can be enhanced by efforts of legal counsel in drafting bills, writing or presenting testimony, and otherwise assisting the organization in having its views recognized by legislatures.

—Participation in administrative government activities. Counsel can help assure that legislation is implemented by government agencies and commissioners in ways that are acceptable or even favorable to associations and their members, can maintain liaison with important government staff people—particularly with an agency or department legal staff—and can assist in digesting and reporting information to association members concerning complicated regulatory matters.

● Some types of assistance which association legal counsel can provide mainly within the association are:

—Initial and periodic review to assure that association organization and management documents, publications, reports, meeting agenda and minutes, and other documents issued by the association comply with legal requirements.

—Consultation and reporting on legal and governmental issues that arise at membership, board of directors, and possibly other meetings of the asso-

ciation and review and approval of the minutes of
meetings. A major purpose of this activity is to demonstrate to participants the association's unequivocal commitment to legal compliance.

—Objective, critical review of association issues by
someone outside the staff or membership. Advice of
counsel in both legal and nonlegal matters is often
sought by associations for its disinterested point of
view.

—Participation in convention and seminar presentations. Association counsel can provide valuable information on subjects in which counsel has experience
or expertise.

—Protection against liability. Counsel can play a major role in assuring that potential liability for the acts
and decisions of officers and directors is completely
avoided.

• Legal counsel for an association is ultimately responsible to the board of directors or other chief governing
body of the association in most instances; but for convenience and efficiency of association management,
usually counsel is immediately responsible to the chief
staff executive of the association. Counsel should work
with and report to the executive in all association matters. Only when such things as negotiation of an employment agreement for the executive or conflicts
between staff and the board are involved should counsel bypass the association executive and report directly
to the governing board.

• Selection of association counsel is usually the decision
of the governing board based upon recommendations
from:

—The chief staff executive of the association
—An ad hoc selection committee formed for this pur-
pose
—Both the executive and the committee.

• Many associations with larger budgets employ legal
counsel as in-house staff attorneys. Ordinarily, some
efficiencies and conveniences can be achieved in this
way if the association's needs for legal services are
sufficient to justify the significant salary, benefits, and

other attendant office expenses required to maintain legal professionals on staff. It is unlikely for one individual, or sometimes for even several, to have the knowledge and experience necessary to deal expertly with all of the legal and governmental issues faced by larger associations—issues of general corporate law, litigation, antitrust law and trade regulation, federal income-tax-exemption, legislative and administrative governmental issues, etc. Therefore, even associations that employ in-house legal counsel frequently also look to outside counsel for representation in areas where specialized knowledge or experience is needed.

- An association may seek outside legal counsel whose offices are located near the association's own main office for convenience in travel and communications. It is often not essential, however, for counsel to be located near an association's headquarters. Much association business with legal counsel is conducted by telephone or mail. Some attorneys now communicate with clients by telex, mailgram, telecopier, and communicating word processor or computer. Many associations headquartered elsewhere retain legal counsel in Washington, D.C., in order to have continuous representation at the scene of federal government affairs. Other reasons might compel the use of legal counsel located in New York, Chicago, or another city even though an association's headquarters are elsewhere.

- Careful consideration should be given to actual or potential conflicts of interest that may exist if the outside lawyer or law firm representing an association also represents another association with adverse or potentially adverse interests or if the lawyer or law firm representing an association also represents individuals or companies with interests adverse or potentially adverse to one or more of the association's members. Courts have determined that, for conflict of interest considerations, the members of a client association may themselves be considered, in effect, clients of the association's lawyer or law firm if, for example, confidential information about the members has been gained in representing the association. Obviously, the integrity demonstrated by an association attorney in ad-

dressing directly and assessing fairly the issue of
conflicts or potential conflicts of interest should be an
important consideration for the association in its evaluation of that attorney.

- There are three typical methods for an association to
  compensate outside legal counsel:

  —*Straight retainer basis:* The association pays legal
  counsel a fixed amount each month, quarter, or year
  to cover all anticipated routine legal services during
  the period of the retainer. This allows the association
  to budget its total legal expenses for a coming period. If sometimes results in the association paying
  either too much when legal activity is low during a
  certain period or too little when legal activity is high.
  For this reason, from time to time the retainer should
  be adjusted to reflect actual services, including exceptions for litigation or work on other extraordinary
  legal or governmental matters that may arise.

  —*Retainer plus override basis:* The association pays
  legal counsel a fixed amount each month, quarter,
  or year to cover specified routine legal activities that
  can reasonably be anticipated. When the level of
  legal activities exceeds that covered by the retainer,
  the association pays for the excess on an hourly basis. This method guarantees the availability of counsel at anticipated fee amounts for most activities but
  fairly compensates for unanticipated activities.

  —*Straight hourly fee basis:* The association pays legal
  counsel only for each hour or fraction of an hour spent
  on association activities. This is certainly the most
  accurate and objective method of compensating
  counsel. It is easily the best for singular projects for
  which counsel is called in from time to time. A straight
  hourly basis may be most satisfactory for long-term,
  comprehensive legal advice and representation if
  counsel assists in budgeting for projected legal expenses and shares some responsibility with association management for assuring to the extent possible
  that the budget is not exceeded. The straight hourly
  basis is perhaps the most prevalent method used to
  compensate attorneys.

- Legal counsel for trade or professional associations can

play extremely important and beneficial roles in advancing the interests of the associations and their members while minimizing adverse consequences in legal and governmental endeavors. Counsel should be chosen first of all on the basis of competence—integrity, industry, knowledge, and experience. Ability to deal openly with personalities and creatively with issues in and around the association should also be seriously evaluated. Finally, expenses of representation must be carefully weighed against benefits anticipated; neither associations nor counsel should shrink from frank discussions of financial matters. In the end, the more time and effort an association invests in the selection of legal counsel, and the budgeting of legal expenses, the better will be the results.

RESOURCES FOR CHAPTER 21

Books

Counihan, "The Selection and Compensation of Association Legal Counsel" in *Associations and the Law Book II*, U.S. Chamber, 1968, page 22.

Fellman, "Major Compensation Methods for Legal Counsel" in *Association and Law Book V*, U.S. Chamber, 1973, page 1.

Fellman & Contney, "How to Hire and Fire Attorneys and Keep Under Budget" in *ASAE 3rd Annual Management Conference Proceedings*, 1985, page 254.

Fellman & Herold, "Making the Best Use of Legal Counsel" in *Associations and the Law Book IX*, U.S. Chamber, 1979, page 11.

Lamb, "What Trade Association Counsel Expects of Company Counsel" in *Associations and the Law Book I*, U.S. Chamber, 1967, page 6.

Lamb & Shields, *Trade Association Law and Practice*, Little, Brown, 1971, page 229.

MacArthur, *Associations and the Antitrust Laws*, U.S. Chamber, 1984, page 80.

Principles of Association Management, ASAE and U.S. Chamber, 1975, page 167.

Webster, "Legal Counsel: Relationship With and Duties to Associations and Association Executives" in *Associations and the Law Book III*, U.S. Chamber, 1969, page 19.

Webster & Herold, *Antitrust Guide for Association Executives*, ASAE, 1979, page 137.

Webster, Herold, & Dye, *Association Legal Checklist*, U.S. Chamber, 1983, page 12.

Periodicals

Auerbach, "Why Your Association Needs Legal Counsel," *Association Management*, March, 1983, page 93.

Bistline, "Lawyers and Their Fees: How to Manage Both," *Association Management*, October, 1981, page 89.

Dunkelberger, "The Lawyer's Role in Advising the Trade Association," *Antitrust Bulletin*, 1965, page 583.

Webster, "How to Buy . . . Legal Services for Your Association," *Association Management*, April, 1981, page 115.

Webster, "What Your Legal Advisor Should Do for You," *Association Management*, November, 1972, page 24.

Cases

Glueck v. Jonathan Logan, Inc., 653 F.2d 746 (2d Cir. 1981). A law firm that represents an association in joint management bargaining with a union is barred by conflict of interest from representing an individual client in a wrongful discharge suit against an association member company unrelated to union representation.

Westinghouse v. Kerr-McGee Corp., 580 F.2d 1311 (7th Cir.) cert. denied, 439 U.S. 955 (1978). Conflict arose in law firm representation against association member because law firm acquired confidential information about the member in representing the association.

II

ASSOCIATION
ACTIVITIES

Chapter 22

MEETING PROCEDURES

Associations typically hold numerous meetings throughout the year for members, committees, subcommittees, directors, or officers. The meetings may be routinely scheduled each year or may be called for special purposes. Meetings provide opportunities for direct communication among participants. Informative programs are presented; association business is conducted; policies are formulated and activities planned or reviewed. Because they are attended by competitors joined to promote common goals of an industry or profession, association meetings are forums where antitrust violations could occur, inadvertently or not. Conscientious antitrust compliance and fairness to participants demand that association meetings be conducted properly. Meeting procedures should be carefully established and rigidly adhered to.

SUMMARY

- Association meetings should be held only when there are appropriate, substantive matters to be discussed.

- Attendance and participation at meetings must be voluntary.

- Advance written notice should be given to those who will participate. The notice should indicate the time and place of the meeting and include the proposed agenda.

- Only legitimate subjects for association discussions or activities should be included in meeting agendas.

- Agenda items should be specific and detailed. There should be no vague or unexplained references to subjects like "marketing" or "standards" which might later give rise to questions about their appropriateness if reviewed by those unfamiliar with what was intended to have occurred at a meeting. Prices should never be discussed.

- Meeting agendas should be reviewed by association legal counsel before they are distributed if they include items with potentially sensitive legal implications.

- Meeting discussions should closely follow the agenda. At the beginning of a meeting the chair generally asks if there are additional items for consideration. Subjects raised at meetings which are not on the agenda should be held for consideration at a subsequent meeting if time does not permit their being considered when first raised. No one should be permitted to distribute documents at an association meeting which have been not been reviewed first by association staff or counsel.

- Parliamentary rules should be followed at association meetings.

- Accurate minutes should be kept.

- Ordinarily, tape recordings or stenographic transcripts should not be made of discussions at association meetings; if recordings or transcripts are made to assist in writing minutes, they should not be retained after the minutes are written.

- Many associations require that legal counsel attend certain kinds of association meetings routinely. Attendance of counsel may be especially important at membership meetings, board meetings, and meetings of officers; attendance at other meetings often depends upon whether matters with legal implications will be discussed.

- Attendance at association meetings may be limited to members where only internal association affairs are discussed.

- Nonmembers must be allowed to attend and participate in those association meetings where matters are discussed which might offer competitive benefit to participants. Nonmember attendance at these meetings need not be solicited or promoted by the association, and nonmembers may be charged more for their participation than is charged to members where meeting costs are borne in part by members' dues. Where space limitations prevent the attendance of nonmembers at these meetings, a transcript or record of the meeting should be made available to nonmembers upon request.

- No secret, informal, "ad hoc," or "rump session" association meetings should be held at any time or for any purpose.

RESOURCES FOR CHAPTER 22

Books

Hills, *Managing Corporate Meetings, A Legal and Procedural Guide*, Ronald Press, 1976.

Lamb & Shields, *Trade Association Law and Practice*, Little, Brown, 1971, page 231.

MacArthur, *Associations and the Antitrust Laws*, U.S. Chamber, 1984, page 78.

Oleck, *Non-Profit Corporations, Organizations, and Associations*, Prentice-Hall, 1980, page 581.

Webster, *The Law of Associations*, Matthew Bender, 1976, pages 2–66.

Periodicals

Webster, "When Should a Lawyer Be Present at Association Meetings," *Association Management*, November, 1979, page 16.

Chapter 23

MINUTES OF MEETINGS

The minutes of an association meeting are a permanent record of what occurred at the meeting, and provide an account of the meeting for members who could not attend. Minutes are useful as guidelines for association staff; they make it possible to determine precisely what disposition was made of a matter at some previous meeting.

Association meeting minutes are more than a convenient record. They are a necessary legal document. In many states, the law requires that minutes be kept of board of directors, membership, and other meetings if the association is incorporated. Courts and agencies have in past instances carefully studied the texts of meeting minutes when association policies or programs were challenged for tax or antitrust reasons. Written minutes of meetings have sometimes been given greater credibility than the later recollections of persons who attended the meetings. Those who draft minutes should do so with the realization that the minutes might one day be examined in an investigation of the association or used in litigation involving the organization. It is essential that they accurately reflect what has occurred at an association meeting and that they be written so as not to raise questions later about the propriety of what occurred. Meeting minutes can be of significant benefit to associations if they are written as affirmative legal compliance documents. For example, minutes can verify that the legal implications of a questioned policy or activity were recognized, addressed by counsel, and only then adopted at an association meeting. If written properly, minutes can be the best evidence of conscientious legal compliance by the association.

SUMMARY

- Complete and accurate minutes should be kept of each association meeting, whether it is a meeting of the membership, of the board of directors, or of a committee.

- Minutes should be a record of what was considered and accomplished at a meeting, not a record of each statement that was made by those attending.

- Minutes should indicate the place, date, and time of the meeting. They should contain the statement that notice of the meeting was given to those entitled to receive notice or that notice was waived by those entitled to it. The names of those attending the meeting should be listed—the names of those absent may be listed as well—and it should be noted whether the required quorum was present.

- There should be a statement that the minutes of the previous meeting had been distributed and were approved either as written or as changed; all changes to the minutes of the previous meeting should be set out.

- Minutes should follow a standard format; numbered sections and paragraphs should be used in minutes for ease of future reference.

- Minutes should describe each motion, report, or communication made at the meeting, as well as naming the person making the motion, report, or communication and noting the action of the participants in response to each. The number of votes for or against an action should be recorded in the minutes.

- Actions of individuals which were made on behalf of all those attending a meeting and which were made since the last meeting may be ratified at the meeting and recorded in the minutes.

- Written contracts—leases, insurance policies, employment, retainer, consulting, and research agreements—may be approved at the meeting and recorded in the minutes. Copies of these may be attached to the minutes as exhibits.

- The ultimate legal importance of association meeting minutes can be substantial if antitrust, tax, or other

legal issues regarding meeting discussions or resolutions are raised in litigation or some other context. In
several antitrust cases, for example, later recollections
of those who attended meetings were disregarded or
discounted in the face of minutes in conflict with those
recollections.

- Whenever appropriate, minutes should include self-
serving statements about the procedures used by the
association to assure legal compliance.

- If a question as to the propriety of an association matter
is raised at a meeting, the minutes should reflect the
question, state that the matter was submitted for review by legal counsel, give the opinion of counsel, and
indicate whether the opinion was followed.

- To help avoid later complications, many associations
routinely ask legal counsel to review, approve, and
sign meeting minutes.

- Early drafts of minutes, and notes used to make them,
should not be retained in association files once the
final draft of the minutes is prepared and distributed.

- Copies of the minutes should be distributed to those
who attended the meeting and should be retained in
the files of the association.

RESOURCES FOR CHAPTER 23

Books

Fellman, "Affirmative Record Maintenance of Minutes, Memoranda and Notes," *Associations and the Law Book VII*,
U.S. Chamber, 1976, page 17.

Lamb & Shields, *Trade Association Law and Practice*, Little,
Brown, 1971, page 237.

Oleck, *Non-Profit Corporations, Organizations, and Associations*, Prentice-Hall, 1980, page 374.

Owen, "How to Keep Proper Minutes," *Associations and the
Law Book IV*, U.S. Chamber, 1971, page 55.

Webster, *The Law of Associations*, Matthew Bender, 1976, pages
2–71.

Webster, Herold, & Dye, *Association Legal Checklist*, U.S.
Chamber, 1983, pages 6–7.

Periodicals

Anderson, "Meeting Minutes: Failure to Keep Them Properly
Can Result in Association Liability," GWSAE *Executive
Update*, August, 1984, page 18.
"Meeting Minutes: What They Should Contain," *Leadership*,
May, 1979, page 59.
Webster, "Keeping Board Meetings Legal," *Association Man-
agement*, April, 1984, page 49.

Cases

C.H. Musselman Co., 51 F.T.C. 224 (1954), 52 F.T.C. 1068 (1956).
Evidentiary value of written records in antitrust case.
United States v. United States Gypsum Co., 333 U.S. 364 (1948).
Evidentiary value of written records in antitrust case.

Chapter 24

PARLIAMENTARY PROCEDURE

Proper use of parliamentary rules at association meetings assures that the viewpoints of all participants are voiced, that the meetings proceed in an orderly fashion, and that delays are minimized. The accepted authority on parliamentary rules, *Robert's Rules of Order*, is lengthy and complicated. For most association meetings, it is sufficient if only the basics are understood and followed. One matter is considered at a time. Motions can be amended. They are seconded and voted upon. Some motions take precedence over others. Effective use of the rules benefits all participants; abuse of the rules can be a hindrance. Ultimately, the common sense and fairness of the association officer or committee chairman presiding at a meeting will most likely result in the orderly and productive conduct of association business.

SUMMARY

- Parliamentary rules should be followed at association meetings.

- Individuals presiding at meetings should be familiar with at least the basic parliamentary rules.

- Only one subject matter at a time comes before a meeting.

- All business is brought before the meeting as a motion, a report, or a communication.

- A motion is made by one participant and seconded by another after recognition from the chair.

- The individual who makes a motion begins the discussion of it and, once finished, does not speak again until all others have been heard.

- The chairman may ask the group if it is ready to vote the question and, if so, may then put the motion to a vote. Alternatively, a motion to close debate may be made, seconded, and voted upon; if that vote is affirmative, then a vote is taken on the main motion.

- Amendments directly related to the main motion are made, seconded, and voted upon before a vote on the main motion. No more than one amendment of an amendment (known as a second degree amendment) can be pending at one time without a vote.

- "Privileged" motions take precedence over any pending main motion, cannot be discussed, and, once seconded, must be voted upon at once. These are motions:

  —To set a time for adjournment
  —To adjourn
  —To hold a recess
  —To raise a question of privilege
  —To call for orders of the day.

- "Incidental" motions arise out of main motions and relate to procedures. They give way to privileged motions but to no others. The chair decides points of order and procedural questions or inquiries. Participants vote upon and do not debate appeals from decisions of the chair, objections to consideration of matters, questions on methods of voting, or motions to suspend the rules (which require two-thirds vote).

- "Subsidiary" motions give way only to privileged or incidental motions. They must be decided before returning to the main motion. They are motions:

  —To lay on the table (not debatable)
  —To close debate
  —To limit or extend debate
  —To postpone a motion to a certain time
  —To refer a matter elsewhere
  —To amend a motion
  —To postpone a matter indefinitely.

- A motion to reconsider is made where the number or sentiment of meeting participants has changed. It can only be made by one who voted in the majority the first time a matter was considered. If the motion to recon-

sider is seconded and passed, the original matter is
again discussed and voted upon.

RESOURCES FOR CHAPTER 24

Books

Oleck, *Non-Profit Corporations, Organizations, and Associations*, Prentice-Hall, 1980, page 1152.
Owen, "Parliamentary Procedure for Associations," *Associations and the Law Book VII*, U.S. Chamber, 1976, page 46.
Renkes, "Parliamentary Law Trends in Nonprofit Organizations" in *Trends in Nonprofit Organizations Law*, American
Law Institute, 1977, page 105.
Robert, *Robert's Rules of Order*, 1st ed., Bell Publishing Co.,
1876.

Periodicals

Bliss, "The Meeting Will Now Come to Order . . . Or Will It?,"
Association Management, April, 1982, page 71.

Chapter 25

ARRANGING FOR MEETING FACILITIES

Methods of making arrangements for meetings, seminars, and conventions at hotels, conference centers, or other facilities vary widely from one association to another and from one meeting facility to another. Small meetings obviously require fewer arrangements than large meetings. Meetings combined with trade shows, tours, or other activities are naturally more complicated in their arrangements. The following Summary concerns itself only with certain legal aspects of preparing for meetings.

Arrangements for meeting facilities should always be made or confirmed in writing. This should be done in such a way that a binding contract exists between the association and the meeting facility management. Mere oral contracts for meeting facilities may not be enforceable. They should be avoided.

Meeting cancellation insurance and insurance for liability arising from meetings should be considered.

SUMMARY

- Arrangements for meeting facilities should be made sufficiently in advance of meeting dates to assure the availability of adequate facilities and to allow time to communicate and confirm the arrangements in writing.

- Arrangements for meeting facilities are ordinarily negotiated by telephone or in person; they should always be made the subject of a subsequent written confirmation between the association and the facility management.

- Oral contracts for arrangements for meeting facilities

can give rise to misunderstandings, may not always be legally enforceable, and should be avoided.

- A written agreement as to arrangements for meeting facilities can be in a formal contract or merely in an informal contract effected by means of an exchange of correspondence between an association and a meeting facility.

- For an exchange of correspondence to become a binding, enforceable contract between an association and a meeting facility, there must at least be a clear offer and acceptance of the specific terms of the arrangements. Typically, the arrangements are discussed and negotiated by phone or in person. The association or the meeting facility then confirms the arrangements by letter. The recipient of the letter should acknowledge and assent to those stipulated arrangements; if the recipient makes changes, they should be agreed to in writing by whomever made the original proposal.

- Note that there are many subtleties and nuances to contract law. State statutes and decisions differ on fine points. By all means, associations should consult with their legal counsel for assistance in effecting valid, binding contracts for meeting facilities.

- The association should make certain that the representative of the meeting facility has authority to make a written agreement concerning the arrangements.

- Once a written agreement is made, it should not be changed except by further written agreement of both the association and the meeting facility management.

- Some hotels or meeting facilities insist upon the use of a standard form contract to book longer meetings. These form contracts are usually drawn primarily for the protection of the meeting facility. They should be particularly well scrutinized by an association and its legal counsel before the association signs. The association should not feel apprehension or reluctance about negotiating changes in a form contract offered by a meeting facility.

- Written agreements about arrangements for meeting

facilities may contain specific terms for any aspects of
the meetings or the facilities, including:
—Meeting dates
—Anticipated participants and spouses
—Estimated numbers and types of rooms needed
—Prices of rooms
—Assurance of lowest room prices available to any
 guests at the time of the meeting
—Holding of rooms for late arrivals
—Cut-off date after which specific number of rooms
 will be guaranteed by the association
—"Escape" clause allowing the association to cancel
 well before stipulated dates without any obligation
—Arrangements for association approval of suite re-
 quests by meeting attendees
—Arrangements for earlier check-ins or stay-overs at
 reduced rates
—Promotion and publicity of meetings
—Firm or estimated prices for functions (with or with-
 out escalation clauses as meeting dates approach)
—Local taxes
—Gratuities
—Use of master charge account
—Payment terms for associations
—Deposits by meeting participants
—Use of credit cards and check cashing by meeting
 participants
—Transportation to and from airports to meeting fa-
 cilities
—Local transportation during the meetings
—Complimentary rooms and association staff offices
 at meeting facility
—Conferences between association and facility staffs
 before the meetings
—Daily conferences with facility staffs during meet-
 ings
—Availability of additional meeting facility personnel
 at registration, check-out, restaurants and cocktail
 lounges, etc.
—Availability and full functioning of all regular food,
 entertainment, recreation, and transportation facilities for association members

—Procedures and payments if association members are "walked", i.e., denied accommodations despite confirmed or guaranteed reservations

—Numbers and types of meeting rooms

—Exhibit space

—Registration space

—Audio-visual equipment and facilities

—Meeting room sound, lighting, heating and air-conditioning as well as availability of meeting facility staff to adjust these when necessary

—Use of outside services by association

—Entertainment

—Food and beverage service

—Labor costs

—Security service

—Fire drills for employees

—Fire protection equipment

—Frequency with which facility is patrolled

—Kinds of locks on doors

—Cancellation because of strike, natural disaster, failure of mass transportation, and so forth

—Specific improvements at facility guaranteed before the meetings

—Assignability of contract for meeting facilities if management or ownership of facilities changes before meeting dates

—Maintenance by meeting facility of adequate liability insurance

—Stipulated damages for failure of meeting facility to provide agreed-upon rooms or other agreed-upon services

—Final occupancy report for the association after the meetings.

• Insurance is available to cover expenses and lost revenue resulting from cancellation of major meetings, including conventions, trade shows, and exhibits. A major meeting usually represents an enormous investment for an association, especially if a trade show or exhibit is included; it also represents one of the major revenue sources for most associations. Such calamities as a strike, fire, roof-collapse, disease outbreak, or breakdown of heating or air conditioning can force last-minute cancellation or curtailment. Insurers are willing to indemnify against expenses and lost revenue from cancellation of a meeting or from continuation of it under adverse circumstances. This insurance should certainly be considered.

- The holding of major meetings can give rise to special kinds and extraordinary amounts of potential liability for the association sponsor of the meeting. Coverage for this extra liability in an association's comprehensive general liability insurance policy may be insufficient. Consideration should be given to special high-policy-limit umbrella insurance for major meetings. Often the cost of this insurance can be shared with, or borne by, the meeting facility as an element of negotiations for the meeting.

RESOURCES FOR CHAPTER 25

Books

Howe, "Cooperative Buying, Employment Contracts, Publications, Hotel and Exhibit Contracts: The Law of Associations" in *Trade and Professional Associations*, Hammond, Editor, Practising Law Institute, 1977, page 31.

Principles of Association Management, ASAE and U.S Chamber, 1975, page 209.

Webster, *The Law of Associations*, Matthew Bender, 1976, page 3-1.

Webster, Herold, & Dye, *Association Legal Checklist*, U.S. Chamber, 1983, page 11.

Periodicals

Anderson, "Legal Pointers for Convention and Meeting Planners," GWSAE *Executive Update*, August, 1985, page 27.

Bartow, "Pointers for Negotiating with Hotels," *Association Management*, December, 1979, page 46.

Block, "Risk Management for Meetings and Conventions," GWSAE *Executive Update*, February, 1984, page 28.

"How to Buy . . . Hotel Rooms for Your Convention," *Association Management*, September, 1982, page 91.

Stratton, "Negotiating Contracts with Convention Centers: Don't Overlook the 'Little Extras'," *Association Management*, February, 1979, page 38.

Webster, "A Good Hotel–Association Relationship Requires Good Faith, Good Contract," *Association Management*, January, 1983, page 33.

Chapter 26

ARRANGEMENTS WITH TRADE SHOW EXHIBITORS

Trade shows or exhibits are frequently sponsored by associations and held in connection with major association meetings or even as separate events. They serve the useful and appropriate function of educating members or the public about new products and services available. Trade shows and exhibits can be simple, amounting to a few table-top displays of literature on products or services aimed at members attending an association meeting and laid out near the meeting facilities; or they can be elaborate, with many booths occupying one or more exhibition halls and staffed by marketing and technical personnel demonstrating working models of products and explaining services aimed both at the general public and association members.

In past years, there were potentially serious federal tax concerns for tax-exempt associations which received revenue from the sponsorship of trade shows or exhibitions where sales were made by exhibitors. Provisions of the Tax Reform Act of 1976 relieved these concerns for trade or professional associations but the provisions do not apply to charitable, educational, or scientific associations, as is discussed elsewhere in this book.

Managing a trade show or exhibition of any size requires careful consideration of the needs of exhibitors, attendees, exhibition facility management, and providers of supplementary exhibit services. Since the show or exhibition is usually held in connection with an association meeting, additional coordination of schedules is necessary.

General problems that sometimes arise from trade shows or exhibitions generally concern the relationship between the sponsoring association and the exhibition facility or between the association and an exhibitor. Making arrangements with the exhibition facility is in many ways similar to making arrangements with a meeting facility. Arranging for meeting facilities has been considered in the preceding chapter of this

125

book. The following Summary primarily concerns arrangements between sponsoring associations and exhibitors.

SUMMARY

- Trade shows or exhibits are an important activity for many associations. They are singularly effective in providing immediate and realistic demonstrations for members or the public of new or improved products and services.

- The association's role in sponsoring a trade show or exhibit is to make arrangements for adequate space for anticipated exhibitors, solicit and arrange for exhibitors, and manage such related concerns as publicity, ticketing, association meetings, or seminars held concurrently with the trade show or exhibition.

- Associations which sponsor trade shows or exhibitions should pay careful attention to arrangements made with exhibitors, since legal problems can occasionally arise in this area. First of all, solicitations for potential exhibitors should be undertaken with due regard for potential problems.

- The right to display at trade shows or exhibitions should be made available to sponsoring association members and nonmembers alike, since exhibition privileges can ordinarily be considered an area of competitive advantage in commerce. To discriminate against nonmembers by preventing or impeding their ability to display goods or services could give rise to an antitrust challenge against the sponsoring association.

- Courts and federal antitrust agencies can be expected to insist upon compliance with a general rule that there be equal opportunity for all competitors to obtain exhibit space from a sponsoring association on equal, nondiscriminatory terms. A 1962 case brought by the Department of Justice against an association of winter sports representatives ended in a consent decree requiring such a rule; a 1975 Federal Trade Commission case also supports the principle.

- Nonmembers need not be solicited to exhibit and can be charged more than members for exhibit space where association members' dues are used to directly or indirectly defray costs of the show or exhibition. The nonmember premium must bear a reasonable relationship to those dues contributions.

- Other than where the charging of premiums for exhibition space used by nonmembers can be justified, there should be no discrimination against nonmembers, such as allowing them to reserve space only if there is space available after members' reservations have been made or restricting them to particular areas or types of space.

- A written contract form should be used by sponsoring associations to make arrangements with exhibitors for display space. Oral agreements may not always be binding or enforceable against exhibitors who cancel at the last minute, cause damage or injury, or otherwise violate arrangements or rules established by the sponsoring association.

- Written contracts covering arrangements for trade show or exhibition space may include specific terms for such items as:
  —Exhibition dates
  —Price for the exhibition space and terms for payment
  —Cut-off dates after which space reserved must be partially or fully paid to assure that the space will be held
  —Responsibility for promotion and publicity for the exhibition and the extent of these activities
  —Provisions for collecting local taxes from exhibitors where they are applicable
  —Location of each exhibitor's space, including attachment of a floor plan designating the location
  —Provisions for changing the location of exhibitor's space if necessary (possibly only upon prior approval by the exhibitor)
  —Indication of any competitor exhibitors from whose display space it is desirable to be separated
  —Availability of food or beverage service, lounge areas,

registration or reception areas, restroom facilities, and so forth

—Availability of commercial police

—Cancellation because of strikes, natural disaster, or failure of mass transportation

—Assignability of contract for exhibit space if exhibitor ownership changes or for other reasons

—Availability and designation of suppliers of supplementary exhibition services, including skilled and unskilled labor, drayage contractor, booth contractor, sign contractor, decorator, audio-visual equipment, telephone service, or photographer

—Existence of any particular labor union requirements

—Existence of any local laws on hours of operation, alcoholic beverages, or fire prevention

—Restrictions on exhibiting or promoting exhibits outside the trade show or exhibition area

—Restrictions against excessive noise, heat, light, or pollution emanating from exhibits

—Time after which shipments of display materials may arrive and time before which they must be removed

—Times when exhibition area will be available for inspection, set up, display, and dismantling

—Exact name, title, firm, address, and phone number of exhibitor representative and indication that the representative has the authority of the firm to enter into the contract

—Restrictions as to the type of products or services for which displays will be allowed

—Indication of the type of products or services of the particular exhibitor

—Designation of material to be printed in any exhibits list or on standard display signs or maps

—Limitation of liability on the part of the sponsoring association, for example, for injuries to employees or exhibitors or their suppliers

—Requirement that the exhibitor provide insurance for display materials

—Provisions for sharing of exhibit space

—Restrictions on certain sales activities such as delivering goods or receiving payment at the trade show or exhibition

—Provisions for written cancellation of reservations for exhibit space

—Provisions for free or discount tickets or registrations for entry to the trade show or exhibition by personnel, particular customers, or other individuals designated by the exhibitor

—Provisions for amendment to the contract only upon written consent of both the sponsoring association and the exhibitor.

RESOURCES FOR CHAPTER 26

Books

Herold, "Association Services for Non-Members" in *Associations and the Law Book IX*, U.S. Chamber, 1979, page 37.

Howe, "Cooperative Buying, Employment Contracts, Publications, Hotel and Exhibit Contracts; The Law of Associations" in *Trade and Professional Associations*, Hammond, Editor, Practising Law Institute, 1977, page 33.

Principles of Association Management, ASAE and U.S. Chamber, 1975, page 217.

Webster, *The Law of Associations*, Matthew Bender, 1976, pages 3–4.

Periodicals

Webster, "Watch How You Restrict Exhibitors at Your Trade Shows," *Association Management*, October, 1980, page 55.

Jacobs, "Trade Show Restrictions and Antitrust Liability," *Association Counsel*, CNA Insurance, Spring, 1986.

Cases

United States v. Western Winter Sports Representatives Assn., Inc., (1962) Trade Reg. Rep. (CCH) para. 70,418 (N.D. Cal. 1962). Participation of nonmembers in trade show.

National Assn. of Women's and Children's Apparel Salesmen, Inc., v. F.T.C., 479 F.2d 139 (5th Cir. 1973). Participation of nonmembers in trade show.

United States v. Material Handling Institute, Inc., (1973) Trade
Reg. Rep. (CCH) para. 74,362 (W.D. Pa. 1973). Consent decree requiring availability of trade show participation to
foreign manufacturers and goods.

Gamco, Inc. v. Providence Fruit and Produce Building, 194 F.2d
484 (1st Cir. 1952). Requires reasonable selection criteria
in deciding whether to permit the lease of a stall in a
market building.

Interface Group v. Gordon Publications, Inc., 562 F. Supp. 1235
(D. Mass. 1983). Computer trade show did not violate the
antitrust laws by refusing to permit distribution of a commercial firm's newsletter at the show because the show
was not an "essential facility," i.e., there are other computer trade shows available to the newsletter firm.

*Family Boating Center, Inc. v. Washington Area Marine Deal-
er's Assn., Inc.*, (1982-1) Trade Reg. Rep. (CCH) para. 64,592
(D. D.C. 1982). No violation of antitrust laws for refusal to
lease trade show exhibit space because other similar shows
were available to the plaintiff.

*Claudia Designs, Inc. v. American Fashion Home Serving
Council, Inc.*, (1972) Trade Reg. Rep. (CCH) para. 72,907
(S.D. N.Y. 1972). Refusal to enjoin denial of trade show
participation.

Chapter 27

PUBLICATIONS

Association publications are important means of communication with members and others. Publications by associations typically include newsletters, magazines, directories, manuals, and reports. They may be written or edited by association members, staff, or consultants. The association responsible for producing and distributing publications should be familiar with some legal implications of publishing activities.

Publications of associations can raise questions of copyright law, libel, or invasion of privacy. A recent major revision of federal copyright laws deserves close attention. Fundamental federal income tax exemption issues can arise from publishing activities, especially if they become dominant activities of the association or generate significant advertising revenue. These tax implications are addressed elsewhere in this book. Problems might also concern endorsements, mailing lists, and availability of publications to nonmembers.

SUMMARY

- Legal issues raised by association publications include those dealing with copyrights, libel, invasion of privacy, taxation, endorsements, mailing lists, and availability to nonmembers.

- A copyright is the legal protection afforded an original work set out in some tangible form. It can apply to association newsletters, magazines, books, directories, catalogs, compilations, reports, films, tapes, etc.

- A new federal copyright law became effective on January 1, 1978, and made several important changes in the law enacted in 1909.

- Owners' rights in all copyrightable works—on paper, film and audio, or visual tape—are protected from the time the works are created, even if they have not yet been published or produced. The copyright owner holds the exclusive right to reproduce, adopt, publish, perform, or display the work subject to copyright. The owner can transfer all or part of those rights. The rights can also be inherited. Copyright protection extends for the author's lifetime plus another 50 years if the author is an individual. If the copyright owner is a corporation, such as an association, the protection extends for 100 years from the time of the creation of the work or 75 years from its publication, whichever ends earliest.

- Copyright for any work made for hire, such an an article by an association employee produced for its newsletter, is presumed to be owned by the employer—here the association. This arrangement can be changed, however, by written agreement between the employer and the employee.

- Outside contributions by nonemployees to an association publication, whether solicited or unsolicited, do not have any work-for-hire presumption attached to them. The association ordinarily receives only the right to publish these contributions as part of the work for which they were submitted (for example, the association's newsletter or magazine). Any other rights for use of the contributions must be separately arranged.

- In effect, the independent author of the work (unless it was done "for hire") has a bundle of rights, all of which are not automatically transferred when one is. The lesson for associations is to try to anticipate all possible uses for submitted contributions (original publication in a newsletter, reprint in a compilation or book, use by members, etc.) and make written agreements with the original copyright owners that will cover all of those possible uses.

- An exception to the copyright owner's protections exists for limited use of works, such as excerpts in reviews or articles. Congress authorized the exception to facilitate "purposes such as criticism, comment, news reporting, teaching, scholarship or research." This *fair*

use exception is determined by considering the following statutory factors:

—The purpose and character of use (is it commercial
or for nonprofit educational use?)

—The nature of the copyrighted work

—The amount and substantiality of the portion used,
and

—The effect of the use on the potential market for or
value of the copyrighted work.

These factors are intentionally vague. Ultimately, overall fairness must dictate whether the *fair use* exception
is applicable.

- Association publications should ordinarily be published with a copyright notice—the word "Copyright,"
the abbreviation "Copr.," or the symbol © followed by
the date of first publication and the name of the copyright owner. It should be placed where it gives reasonable notice, for example, on the masthead of a
periodical or at the bottom of the first page of a newsletter. An extra measure of warning may be afforded
by the additional sentence following the actual copyright notice: "All rights reserved." Because copyright
protection is now subject to certain presumptions, associations which do not want to claim any copyright
protection for particular publications in order to encourage readers to duplicate or re-use them should indicate that fact explicitly with a statement such as "No
copyright claimed" or "Not copyrighted."

- Certain errors or omissions in providing a copyright
notice are exonerated by the federal law if made by
the copyright owner.

- Registration of a copyright with the Copyright Office
of the Library of Congress is not essential to obtain
protection for the copyright owner. However, registration is recommended because it *is* essential for maintaining an action for infringement and provides benefits
in recovering damages which relate to the time of registration.

- Form TX, available from the Copyright Office, is used
to register a copyright. It may be filed by:

—The author of the work

—The "copyright claimant," defined as a person or organization that has obtained all rights to the work, including the right to claim legal title to the copyright in an application for copyright registration

—The owner of an exclusive right—someone who has received from the owner a limited right, such as the right to publish the work in a periodical, or

—A duly authorized agent—a person who is acting on behalf of someone in one of the above categories.

A copyright registration fee of $10 should be sent with form TX plus two copies of the work.

- Especially because the first major overhaul of the federal copyright laws in seventy years is relatively recent, associations should be guided closely by legal counsel familiar with the laws. This is necessary both to assure protection for copyrights owned by associations and to assure that copyrights owned by others are not violated.

- Libelous statements in association publications must be carefully avoided; they may subject the association to major damage suits by persons who consider themselves to have been defamed.

- Associations must particularly avoid any statements declaring persons to be dishonest, fraudulent, or immoral, since no specific damages need be proven to recover in court for these kinds of statements.

- Statements which might be considered libelous should not be used in publications unless the association can prove from clear evidence that the statements are true; truth is a defense to a claim of libel.

- Associations should be sure that they have provided for protection against the payment of libel claims either in their comprehensive general liability insurance policies, through directors' and officers' liability insurance, or through association professional liability insurance.

- Association publications must not include names or pictures which invade rights of privacy of individuals.

- Names or pictures should not be used to advertise or

promote products or services without obtaining permission from the individuals.

- Names or pictures should not be used in any discrediting or embarrassing way without obtaining permission from the individuals.

- Associations should ordinarily refrain from endorsing products or services in their publications; endorsements could raise tax problems or subject associations to liability claims if the products or services are not effective or result in injuries (see chapter on Product Liability).

- Associations should respect the ownership rights that others may have in mailing lists; written permission to use mailing lists should be obtained in advance from the owners of the lists; if a mailing list has copyright protection, permission must be obtained from the owner of the copyright.

- Associations should protect the ownership rights in their own mailing lists; lists should have copyright notice and registration where circumstances permit.

- Association publications which have information of competitive value should be made available when requested to persons or firms that are not association members; the availability of publications to nonmembers need not be promoted; nonmembers may be charged more for association publications than members when members' dues subsidize part of the expense of the publications.

RESOURCES FOR CHAPTER 27

Books

Althen, "Legal Considerations for Association Periodicals and Other Publications" in *Associations and the Law Book VIII*, U.S. Chamber, 1978, page 1.

Association Publishing Procedures, ASAE, 1978.

Howe, "Cooperative Buying, Employment Contracts, Publications, Hotel and Exhibit Contracts; The Law of Associations" in *Trade and Professional Associations*, Hammond, Editor, Practising Law Institute, 1977, page 28.

Mossinghoff & Lehman, *Trademark & Copyright Infringement*, Harcourt, Brace, 1985.

Owen & Bearden, "The New Copyright Law—One Year After," *Associations and the Law Book IX*, U.S. Chamber, 1979, page 21.

Principles of Association Management, ASAE and U.S. Chamber, 1975, page 189.

Smith, "Some Legal Aspects of Association Publications" in *Associations and the Law Book VIII*, U.S. Chamber, 1978, page 1.

Periodicals

Bistline, "A Guide to Understanding the New Copyright Law," *Association Management*, July, 1978, page 35.

Bistline, "Before You Make Your Next Photocopy: What You Should Know About the New Copyright Law," *Association Management*, September, 1978, page 77.

Hogan, "How New Copyright Law Affects Associations," *Association Management*, February, 1977, page 55.

Hogan & Hogan, "What You Should Know About Recent Libel Law Cases," *Association Management*, July, 1976, page 42.

MacArthur, "Copyright Revision Act of 1976," *Association Letter*, July, 1977, page 2.

Webster, "Trademarks and Copyrights: What Can You Register?," *Association Management*, February, 1982, page 51.

Statutes

The Copyright Act, 17 U.S.C. Sections 101–810 (1977).

Chapter 28

PRODUCT LIABILITY

Lawsuits by consumers seeking damages resulting from defective products were relatively uncommon ten or fifteen years ago. Within the past few years, the rate at which these lawsuits are filed has exceeded several hundred thousand annually.

The reasons for the product liability claim explosion are not entirely clear. Greater consumer awareness and assertiveness provides one explanation. Another is the increasing hospitality that courts have given to product suits. Perhaps most important of all, many states now recognize one form or other of the legal doctrine of strict liability—consumer plaintiffs are allowed to receive damages without having to prove that the supplier defendants were negligent in designing, making, selling, or installing the product.

Associations do not ordinarily make or sell products. Their direct exposure to product liability is therefore minimal. But associations do sometimes have programs for testing, certifying, endorsing, or guaranteeing products. Product liability claims against associations have sometimes been successful when such programs exist. In addition, many associations have among their membership firms that are acutely concerned about product liability. These associations are disseminating information about the problem, advocating legislation to ameliorate it, assisting in product liability insurance matters, and otherwise acting on behalf of their members.

The Product Liability Risk Retention Act, passed in 1981, also provides the opportunity for associations to establish group insurance cooperatives; the Act is considered in the next chapter of this book.

SUMMARY

- Consumer actions for damages claimed to have resulted from defective products are becoming an increasing concern of associations and their members.

- Associations are not usually directly vulnerable to product liability suits because they do not make or sell products.

- Associations which do occasionally sell or give away products can purchase product liability insurance to indemnify against potential liability from the use of the products. Insurance coverage for these "incidental products" is usually not expensive and can often be added to the associations' general liability insurance policies.

- Other than for "incidental" products sold or given away by associations, by far the greatest potential for claims is in association testing, certification, endorsement, or guarantee programs. Claimants might say they were encouraged to use certain defective products because of these association activities. If the association was lax or negligent in its testing, certifying, etc., it could be held liable.

- Product liability cases are much more infrequent against associations which certify products than against firms which make or sell them. To prove a case against a manufacturer or supplier of a product, the claimant has to show:
  —That the seller is engaged in the business of selling the product
  —That the product is expected to, and does, reach the user or consumer without substantial change in its condition
  —That the product is defective so as to have caused physical harm to the consumer or his property.
  To prove a case against an association certifier of a product, on the other hand, the claimant has to show:
  —That the association failed to exercise reasonable care in ascertaining the accuracy of the information or the manner in which the information was communicated

—That the consumer actually relied on the information given

—That the consumer suffered physical injury as a result.

- Associations which certify, test, endorse, or guarantee products must exercise reasonable care in examining and assessing the products. Where a defect which causes damages could not reasonably be discovered, the association will not be liable for resulting damage according to the decisions so far issued.

- To minimize exposure to product liability suits, associations which certify, test, endorse, or guarantee products should:

  —Be sure that products *actually are* carefully evaluated before they are certified, endorsed, or guaranteed.

  —Make certain that objective experts conduct any tests, assessments, or evaluations using fair or recognized procedures.

  —Carefully choose whatever terms are used in certifying, endorsing, or guaranteeing products; the more specific the terms, the more likely it is that a consumer can show that the terms were relied upon.

- Associations without formal certification-type programs should guard against inadvertently endorsing or promoting products or services in publications or at meetings; merely allowing manufacturers or suppliers to advertise or exhibit products or services will not ordinarily constitute an endorsement. (Note the cases listed in the Resources section at the end of this chapter.)

- Associations of members experiencing serious product liability problems should consider joint industry action to help alleviate the problems. Some possibilities are:

  —Educational programs to assist firms in *risk control*—safe product design, manufacture, distribution, and installation

  —Educational programs to assist firms in *risk transfer*—obtaining adequate product liability insurance

  —Collecting and disseminating specific information on subjects and dispositions of previous and pending

product liability claims (published in such a way as
to minimize exposure to potential claimants)
—Obtaining and disseminating information on the
availability of product liability insurance and the
interpretation of terms, conditions, exclusions, deductibles, and endorsements contained in typical
policies of members
—Organizing to share the cost of defense of a particular
product liability suit where the outcome of the suit
will clearly have effects on other firms
—Organizing joint legal defense efforts where several
association members have pending product liability
cases including sharing of motions and briefs, information on expert defense witnesses, and experiences with various defense settlement and trial
strategies
—Arranging for group product liability insurance coverage, possibly by setting up a captive insurance
firm to underwrite the insurance where association
members' interest and capitalization are adequate
for such a major project.

RESOURCES FOR CHAPTER 28

Books

Brown, "How to Set Up an Association Captive Insurance Company," page 28, Feder, "How One Association Set Up a
Successful Member-Owned Insurance Firm," page 26,
Skinner, "How One Association Formed a Successful In-
surance Company for Members," page 23, Stratton, "The
Slow Road to Product Liability Reform," page 45, Tooze,
"How to Help Your Members Avoid (and Defend) Product
Liability Suits," page 40, Wilson, "Product Liability: A Re-
view of the Options Available to Associations," page 37
in *Guidelines for Effective Association Insurance Pro-
grams*, ASAE, 1979.
Interagency Task Force on Product Liability, Final Report, U.S.
Dept. Commerce, 1977.
Jacobs, "Association Exposure in Product Liability Suits" in
Associations and the Law Book VII, U.S. Chamber, 1976,
page 32.

Owen, "Insuring Difficult Risks—Safety Groups, Captives, Off-Shore Insurance and Self-Insurance" in *Associations and the Law Book IX*, U.S. Chamber, 1979, page 40.

Product Liability: A Candid Assessment, Research Institute of America, 1977.

Webster & Matternas, *How to Form and Operate an Association Captive Insurance Company*, ASAE, 1982.

Periodicals

Bessy, "Association Captive Provides Members With Afford-able Liability Insurance," *Association & Society Manager*, January, 1983, page 51.

Gorham, "Success With a Captive," *Association & Society Manager*, February/March, 1983, page 25.

Harper, "Setting Up a Captive: Pro and Con," *Association & Society Manager*, August/September, 1984, page 29.

Lehtronen, "Control Insurance Dollars With a Captive," *Association Management*, August, 1984, page 161.

"Liability of Certifiers of Products for Personal Injuries to the User or Consumer," Cornell L. Rev., 1979, page 132.

Schotland & Rhyne, "Product Liability Implications of Trade Association Activities," *Journal of Products Liability*, Pergamon Press, 1984, page 215.

Singer, "Stemming the Cost of Product Liability Insurance," *National Journal*, June 9, 1979, page 951.

Stern, "What Risk Management Can Do for Professional Society Members," *Association Management*, December, 1982, page 76.

Webster, "Forty Questions to Ask (and Have Answered) About Captive Insurance Firms," *Association Management*, July, 1980, page 31.

Cases

Hanberry v. Hearst Corp., 81 Cal.App.2d 680; 39 ALR 3rd 173 (Ct.App. 1969). Rejection by court of strict liability theory against firm issuing Good Housekeeping Seal of Approval to a shoe that was slippery.

Kasel v. Remington Arms Co., 24 Cal.App.3rd 771,101 Cal.Rprt. 314 (Ct.App. 1972). Reconsideration of rejection of strict liability theory in *Hanberry* where Mexican affiliate made exploding shell.

Collins v. American Optometric Assn., 693 F.2d 636 (7th Cir. 1982). Individual claimed injured by inadequate diagnoses by optometrists sued association for its pronouncements about the qualifications of optometrists; suit was dismissed for lack of proof that individual first saw and relied upon the association's pronouncements.

Chapter 29

RISK RETENTION GROUPS

The Product Liability Risk Retention Act is designed to aid businesses which cannot afford the increasing cost of product liability insurance by permitting product manufacturers, distributors, and sellers to self-insure through insurance cooperatives called "risk retention groups," or to purchase insurance on a group basis at more favorable rates. Group participants will be able to spread and assume all, or any portion, of their product liability risk exposure.

The Act provides smaller companies with the ability to decide what level of asset protection they want. It further allows them to deal competitively by buying the support services they need from insurance carriers. Services could include loss control, claims and administration, investment management, and accounting services.

Attractive alternatives to the present product liability insurance system are provided to risk retention or purchasing groups by this Act. It is anticipated that associations comprised of those engaged in product manufacture, distribution, or sales will become the primary organizers and administrators of those groups. Associations should therefore carefully consider the formation and maintenance of risk retention or purchasing groups.

SUMMARY

- The Product Liability Risk Retention Act addresses the high cost of product liability insurance by permitting product manufacturers, distributors, and sellers to self-insure through insurance cooperatives known as "risk retention groups," or to purchase group insurance favorably; it is intended that associations take the lead in organizing and operating risk retention groups.

- A risk retention group can be incorporated or formed in any state. It should then be chartered as an insurance company in a state with favorable insurance laws. The laws of the chartering state, not those of the incorporating state, govern the organization and operation of the risk retention group.

- Presently, only Bermuda, the Cayman Islands, and a few states have favorable insurance laws allowing the formation of risk retention groups. It is necessary for those groups chartering in the two offshore jurisdictions to meet the minimum capitalization requirements of at least one state.

- Once the risk retention group is incorporated and chartered, it can operate and do business in any state in which it is registered. Registration requires filing duplicative copies of the group's charter and bylaws. Each state may have additional requirements but, under the Act, such requirements cannot be burdensome.

- Associations are ideal as vehicles to use in locating and organizing potential members of a risk retention or purchasing group. Members of associations often have similar liability insurance needs and could most easily organize a group under the new law.

- Certain insurance companies offer risk retention group support services such as loss control, claims administration, investment management, and accounting services.

- Risk retention and purchasing groups could enable members to spend substantially less than what the market otherwise charges for product liability coverage.

- A "risk retention group" is any corporation or limited liability association taxed as a corporation or insurance company, formed under the laws of any state, Bermuda, or the Cayman Islands:

  —which is organized for the purpose of, and has as its primary activity, assuming and spreading product and completed operations liability insurance coverage among its members

—which is chartered under the laws of any state, or prior to January 1, 1985, under the laws of Bermuda or the Cayman Islands

—which does not exclude persons from membership in the group solely to provide its members with a competitive advantage over those persons; such exclusion would be actionable under federal or state antitrust laws as an act of boycott

—which is composed of members principally engaged in the "manufacture, design, importation, distribution, packaging, labeling, lease or sale of a product."

• A risk retention group can be incorporated in one state and chartered in another state. For the purpose of the Act, the jurisdiction in which the group is chartered as an insurer can apply all of its insurance laws concerning the organization and operation of the company to the group.

• A "purchasing group" is any group which has as one of its purposes the purchase of product or completed operations liability insurance on a group basis.

• "Product liability" is defined as liability for damages due to personal injury, death, emotional harm, consequential, economic, or property damage.

• "Completed operations liability" includes liability arising from the installation, maintenance, or repair of any product at premises which are not owned or controlled by any person who performs the work.

• The Act preempts state law to the extent that such law would prohibit or regulate the formation or operation of a risk retention group other than by and under the laws of the chartering state. This eliminates the need for a risk retention group to comply with numerous nonchartering state statutes. Nonchartering states may impose premium taxes and other taxes on risk retention groups in the same manner as they tax other insurance companies.

• Persons injured within a state are accorded the same rights regarding settlement practices against a risk retention group as they would have against a licensed insurer.

- A risk retention group is required to submit to its state insurance authority any special reports or information required of licensed insurers in the state concerning liability losses and expenses.

- A state may require risk retention groups to register with and designate the state insurance commissioner as its agent for the purpose of receiving service of legal process and other documents.

- If the insurance commissioner in any state in which the group is doing business has reason to believe that the risk retention group is in a financially impaired condition and the insurance commissioner in the chartering state has not begun an examination of the group, the group must submit to an examination by the state insurance commissioner where it is doing business.

- The Act should not be interpreted to provide any immunity from, or defense to, any action under the federal antitrust laws for any risk retention group or group member. Activities of the groups are subject to the same antitrust principles developed by the courts to govern association activities.

- A purchasing group is exempt from any state law which prohibits the establishment of a purchasing group, which makes it unlawful for an insurer to provide insurance to a purchasing group, or which discriminates against such a group or its members.

- The federal securities laws are generally inapplicable to risk retention groups.

- The Act rejects any federal role in forming or regulating risk retention groups.

RESOURCES FOR CHAPTER 29

Periodicals

Wilson, "What It Means for Associations," *Association Management*, January, 1982, page 51.

Statutes

Product Liability Risk Retention Act, 15 U.S.C. Section 3901.

Chapter 30

JOINT EMPLOYER COLLECTIVE BARGAINING

Many trade associations participate in collective bargaining on behalf of their employer members. A 1972 survey by the American Society of Association Executives showed that 44 percent of respondent national and state trade associations engaged in some form of employer-employee relations. Of those, 20 percent engaged in collective bargaining. As would be expected, association bargaining efforts ordinarily have been on a multiemployer basis. Members benefit from the greater efficiency, and possibly greater bargaining leverage, that association multiemployer bargaining affords. In such situations, the association's role is usually to act as the principal bargaining agent in dealing with the unions representing employees of the association's members. Negotiation and administration of the collective bargaining agreement are the responsibility of either the national association or its local chapter, depending upon the geographic scope of the labor contract involved. The association bargaining agent may or may not sign the contract. If the association does sign the contract, it may be as a party or merely as a nonparty observer.

Multiemployer bargaining is used in many industries. A 1978 survey found that 42 percent of major collective bargaining agreements (those covering 1,000 or more employees) were multiemployer in nature; those agreements covered many millions of employees. Industries where this approach is common include those such as the garment industry, where there are numerous employers with small work forces, and those such as transportation, longshoring, and building construction, where it is common for workers to change employers on a daily or weekly basis. Employers have found it desirable to bargain on a group basis through employer associations in order to match the increase in union strength which has arisen since passage of the National Labor Relations Act in 1935. The prevalence of multiemployer bargaining may have decreased recently in fields such as construction, as employers have

147

substantially reduced their use of union labor in order to become more competitive with nonunion contractors and sub-contractors.

Various federal and state labor, civil rights, antitrust, and other laws have been invoked to challenge the conduct of trade associations that participate in collective bargaining, usually on a multiemployer basis. With respect to labor, civil rights, and other laws relating to employment, a key factor is often whether the association has acted as an "employer" or agent of an employer as defined in those laws (which ordinarily hinge "employer" status upon participation in hiring, advancement, or firing). However, some laws that apply to association multiemployer bargaining do not depend upon "employer" status—the prime example is the Sherman Antitrust Act.

Litigation arises very frequently from collective bargaining activities. Usually the collective bargaining, and likewise the litigation, do not involve associations. Even when associations are participants in collective bargaining, litigation seems most often to be directed at other participants in the bargaining process, such as labor unions or individual employers that are subject to multiemployer labor contracts. In addition, the financial responsibilities for past violations of applicable laws most frequently are held to fall upon those other parties, rather than a participant association or its officials. Nevertheless, if only because of the very high incidence of collective bargaining litigation, associations have been the subjects of major and minor reported lawsuits arising from bargaining. It is clear from the suits that associations and their directors, officers, members, and staff face substantial risk of claims and potential liability under labor, civil rights, antitrust, and other laws.

SUMMARY

- The National Labor Relations Act, enacted in 1935, prohibits employer discrimination against employees because of union activity and employer refusal to bargain with properly authorized collective bargaining agents of employees. Congress has enacted two major amendments to the NLRA. The first is the 1947 Taft-Hartley Act; the second is the 1959 Landrum-Griffin Act. In addition to forbidding specific unfair union practices, these statutes added various independent reporting and enforcement provisions to federal labor laws. Trade associations engaged in multiemployer or other collective bargaining activities are subject to the requirements of these laws where their activities bring them within the statutory definition of "employer" or when they assist member employers in specified ways.

• The NLRA empowers the National Labor Relations Board to prevent any "person" from engaging in any "unfair labor practice" that affects interstate commerce.

• As broadly defined in the Act, the term "person" includes individuals, associations, or corporations. The NLRB has the authority to enter an order to prevent any "person" from committing an unfair labor practice. The term "employer" includes "any person acting as an agent of an employer, directly or indirectly."

• Associations involved directly or indirectly in collective bargaining or employment activity may be subject to NLRA requirements under this definition on one of two bases. One is that the association's activities and conduct are such that it is, in effect, an employer, jointly liable with its company members. A court once found, for example, that a nonprofit association and its member clubs that operate soccer teams are joint "employers" of the players on each team. On a second basis, an employer association is clearly an agent of each employer member where it negotiates or administers a collective bargaining agreement with a labor organization on behalf of the members.

• Association involvement in collective bargaining activities, such as negotiation and administration, is often sufficient to trigger NLRA requirements against the association or its individual leaders:
  —An association of construction contractors was cited under the Act for its unlawful refusal to furnish a full membership roster to unions
  —A soccer league commissioner was held responsible as the league's agent under the Act.

- The practical aspects of enforcement actions against associations and their officials include various elements. On the positive side is the relatively small number of actions in the past that have been brought against associations or their officials. Relief is usually limited to enjoining the improper practices, rather than seeking financial remedies, such as backpay. On the negative side are such factors as the potentially heavy litigation costs and the substantial financial burden that may arise in the unlikely event that backpay and other financial remedies are ordered. Another negative factor is that associations often bring cases on behalf of their members that may involve substantial counterclaim litigation. For example, there is a case that was decided by the Supreme Court adversely to the association after a film producers' association and television network filed an unfair labor practice charge against a union.

- The Taft-Hartley Act places restrictions on those involved in collective bargaining. It restricts financial transactions, such as payment or lending of money by an employer or its agent to employees, representatives, or labor organizations. In one case, an association fell within the restrictions on employers where members used it to carry out business functions. Willful violations of this requirement are criminal misdemeanors.

- Another section of Taft-Hartley authorizes suits for damages and other relief for violations that occur during collective bargaining by a union with employers whose activities affect commerce. This provision specifies that employers are bound by the acts of their agents. Several decisions have allowed associations that conducted bargaining and signed agreements to bring actions on behalf of their members. At least one decision has permitted a union to maintain a counterclaim, based on the conduct of a member of a group, against the association that executed a labor contract for the group.

- The Landrum-Griffith Act originally covered disclosure of welfare and pension plans. Those disclosure requirements were later incorporated into the Employee Retirement Income Security Act of 1974. What remains of Landrum-Griffith deals with various reporting, disclosure, and other public information provisions; several of them may apply to associations that are involved in collective bargaining or related labor activity:

—Employers and employer associations must report certain payments to unions, employees (other than for wages), and labor relations consultants, as well as for labor relations information

—Another type of triggering conduct occurs when an association is involved in activity on behalf of an employer to "persuade" employees as to their organizing and collective bargaining rights. For example, an association was held to have engaged in persuader activity where its executive spoke to employees of three of its 800 member firms.

• Beyond the federal labor laws, association involvement in multiemployer collective bargaining activity on behalf of its members may give rise to actions based upon alleged employment discrimination for violation of various federal civil rights laws. Actions seeking damages and injunctive relief for violations of these statutes are often directed at unions, employers, or both. An association that exercises control over access to jobs can come within the definition of "employer" and be subject to civil rights challenges.

• Various federal statutes prohibit employment discrimination on certain grounds. These bases, which vary from one statute to another, include discrimination against any individual on account of race, color, religion, sex, age, or national origin. The law recognizes several major categories of discrimination, with disparate legal treatment as to prohibited grounds of discrimination, present continuation of past discrimination, policies or practices that have a disparate impact not justified by business necessity, and failure to make reasonable accommodation to an employee's religious practices or handicap.

• Some of the most complex questions involving an association's role in multiemployer joint collective bargaining arise in the antitrust context. Multiemployer associations have been targets of antitrust lawsuits filed by unions, nonmember companies, and even other

associations. Antitrust litigation has frequently been
more appealing to union or other plaintiffs than cases
premised on labor relations law because of the greater
potential antitrust recoveries. Successful parties involved in actions premised on the Sherman Act can
obtain three times the amount of damages they have
suffered as well as attorneys' fees and costs. The in-
terrelationship between labor relations law and antitrust is one that raises problems of vast complexity.
Thus far there has been no satisfactory accommodation
between antitrust and labor laws in a collective bargaining context.

- Two types of antitrust exemptions, statutory and nonstatutory, apply to collective bargaining activities. The
statutory exemption arises from the Clayton Act and
the Norris-LaGuardia Act. Provisions in these laws
generally limit the use of injunctive relief against specified labor activities and exempt many aspects of labor
union operations. Federal courts have also created a
nonstatutory exemption for collective bargaining
agreements that would otherwise be restraints of trade
under the antitrust laws. The Supreme Court has recognized that most labor activities have some impact
on prices and competition; but the Court has ruled that,
for example, labor union organizing efforts are exempt
from the antitrust laws because they are not mainly
directed toward curtailing price competition in the
commercial market for the employer's goods. As a result, collective bargaining provisions that involve or
are intimately related to mandatory bargaining subjects under the NLRA of direct union concern ordinarily
fall within the nonstatutory antitrust exemption. However, for the nonstatutory exemption to be effective, the
collective bargaining agreement must not impair the
ability of the parties to contract freely with third parties; and the provision in question must advance a proper
labor goal and must not restrain trade more than necessary to reach that goal.

- Many decisions have upheld, under antitrust challenge, the propriety of collective bargaining activities
by an association or its members after analyzing the
market impact. On the other hand, some decisions have

found antitrust violations after analyzing the competitive impact of collective bargaining agreements. In the 1975 *Connell* case, the Supreme Court held that an agreement that limited subcontracting to union contractors was an unfair labor practice under the NLRA and not immune from antitrust liability.

- There are several limitations that bear upon the issue of potential association antitrust liability from multiemployer collective bargaining activity:
  - —The Supreme Court has limited the ability of unions to file antitrust treble damage claims against associations and their employer members; in a 1983 case, the Court ruled that a union was not injured by violation of the antitrust laws and lacked standing to sue as a result of the employer association's alleged antiunion coercion of employers.
  - —Some courts have also imposed limits on the ability of employers and their associations to sue for alleged injuries as a result of labor-area antitrust violations.
  - —Employment practices that purportedly violate fair employment laws may not be sustained under the antitrust laws because of alleged unlawful boycotts of minority employees. The scope of liability is a subject that needs to be examined on the basis of specific actions. Even where conduct in a collective bargaining setting is outside the labor exemption and is subject to the antitrust laws, the Norris-LaGuardia Act mandates that there be "clear proof of actual participation in or actual authorization . . . or ratification . . . " of the improper acts before a union, employer or individual can be found liable for the conduct of other persons.
  - —Antitrust pitfalls may arise in counterclaims to suits brought by an association engaged in collective bargaining.
  - —Certain industries are subject to special antitrust requirements. This is the case with collective bargaining affecting maritime shipping and professional baseball (but not other professional sports), for example.
- Various statutes of general applicability may pertain to an association's multiemployer joint collective bar-

gaining efforts. The nature of an association's activities in negotiating or administering aspects of a bargaining contract that deal with covered benefits, such as retirement, health, etc., will determine the extent to which ERISA's substantive or disclosure requirements apply to its conduct.

● In conclusion, it is clear that trade association involvement in joint employer collective bargaining on behalf of employer members is a legal minefield that must be approached and traversed, if necessary, with the greatest of caution.

RESOURCES FOR CHAPTER 30

Statutes

National Labor Relations Act ("NLRA"), 29 U.S.C. 151.
Labor Management Relations Act ("Taft-Hartley"), 29 U.S.C. 141.
Labor-Management Reporting and Disclosure Act ("Landrum-Griffith"), 29 U.S.C. 153.
Employee Retirement Income Security Act of 1974 ("ERISA"), 29 U.S.C. 10001.
Norris-LaGuardia Act, 29 U.S.C. 101.

Cases

North American Soccer League v. NLRB, 613 F.2d 1379 (5th Cir.), cert. denied, 449 U.S. 899 (1980). Court upholds finding that association of soccer clubs is an "employer" under the NLRA.
NLRB v. Assoc. Gen. Contractors of Calif., 633 F.2d 766 (9th Cir. 1980), cert. denied, 452 U.S. 915 (1981). Association responsible for unfair labor practice by refusal to furnish full membership roster to union.
American Broadcasting Cos. v. Writers Guild, 437 U.S. 411 (1978). Supreme Court case involving counterclaim after a film producers' association and several television networks filed an unfair labor practice suit against a union.
U.S. v. Donovan, 339 F.2d 404 (7th Cir. 1964), cert. denied, 380

U.S. 975 (1965). Association is an "employer" where members carry out business functions.

Donovan v. Master Printers Assn., 532 F. Supp. 1140 (N.D. Ill. 1981), *aff'd*, 699 F.2d 370 (7th Cir. 1983), *cert. denied*, 104 S.Ct. 703 (1984). An association was held to be an "employer" in "persuading" employees in their organizing and bargaining rights where association executives talked to several employees.

Connell Construction Co. v. Plumbers Local No. 100, 421 U.S. 616, 622 (1975). Agreement limiting subcontracting to union contractors was not immune from antitrust challenge, according to the Supreme Court.

Apex Hosiery Co. v. Leader, 310 U.S. 469 (1940). Original Supreme Court decision creating a nonstatutory antitrust exemption for certain collective bargaining agreements.

Associated General Contractors of Calif., Inc. v. California State Council of Carpenters, 74 L.Ed.2d 723 (1983). Association's alleged antiunion coercion of employers did not injure union, which also lacked standing for antitrust challenge.

Chapter 31

ASSOCIATION POLITICAL ACTION COMMITTEES

Federal laws passed since 1971 have outlined the nature and extent of allowable association participation in the federal election process. One method provided in the laws is through association sponsorship of political action committees (PACs) to solicit funds and make contributions to candidates for federal office.

Although political action committees have existed for years, it has only been since 1971, when the first of a series of new federal election laws was passed that there has been a proliferation of association-related PACs. In federal elections after 1971, association PACs showed signs of political strength that led opponents to push for provisions, passed in 1976, that limit the ability of these PACs to solicit and expend money on federal election campaigns.

Nevertheless, political action committees remain legitimate and effective vehicles through which associations channel their members' campaign contributions to candidates for federal office who are most sympathetic with objectives of the associations.

The Federal Election Campaign Act of 1971 and amendments to it in 1974, 1976, and 1979 sanction the formation of PACs by corporations, including incorporated associations, and allow the corporations to pay the costs of organizing, operating, and soliciting contributions to the PACs. There need not be any anxiety about their fundamental legality. Associations that have formed PACs or are considering doing so need only be concerned about knowing and following the laws and regulations applicable to political action committees.

Political action committees are effective in advancing the interests of associations. They can be a useful complement to—but not a substitute for—long-term federal government affairs programs of associations that include lobbying, political education, publications, and other activities.

The following chapters provide associations with some

156

basic guidelines for the establishment and operation of PACs. The guidelines cover only federal-level PACs; associations interested in PACs that support local or state-level candidates should consult local and state laws and regulations.

These guidelines concerning federal-level PACs provide only a first step toward a comprehensive understanding of the requirements of the Federal Election Campaign Act, Federal Election Commission, and Internal Revenue Service regulations and other authorities such as government advisory opinions and publications. The requirements are complex and are subject to updated interpretations. Any association contemplating the formation of a PAC or already operating one should be closely advised by legal counsel familiar with this specialized area.

SUMMARY

- Association PACs are clearly legitimate if they are formed and operated according to the federal requirements. PACs can be one of the most effective means for association participation in federal elections.

- Federal legislation, agency regulations, and advisory opinions establish detailed guidelines for the establishment and administration of PACs.

- Early legislation in this area, beginning in 1907, prohibited corporations and unions from making political contributions. The few PACs formed under early legislation were therefore kept administratively separate from any corporations or unions.

- The Federal Election Campaign Act of 1971 for the first time sanctioned the use of corporate funds to institute and maintain political action committees.

- The Federal Election Campaign Amendments of 1974 clarified that government contractors, like other corporations, may use their funds to organize and operate PACs. It became legitimate for corporations, including incorporated associations, to set up and operate, with their own funds, political action committees to channel campaign contributions from employees, members, and shareholders to federal candidates. The 1974 amendments also established the Federal Election Commission and provided for public financing of presidential campaigns.

- When the constitutionality of the 1974 amendments was challenged in *Buckley v. Valeo*, the U.S. Supreme Court affirmed some parts of the amendments and required changes in other parts. Provisions regarding corporate and association political action committees were not affected.

- Changes in the federal election laws required by the Supreme Court in the *Buckley* case were incorporated by Congress in the Federal Election Campaign Amendments of 1976. While spelling out some of the rights and responsibilities of association PACs, Congress also imposed additional limitations upon PAC solicitations and expenditures.

- Certain technical changes in the law were made in the Federal Election Campaign Act Amendments of 1979. General reporting obligations were reduced; but of significance to association PACs, the law was clarified that the name of the sponsoring entity must be included in the official name of the PAC.

- The purpose of the FEC regulations for PACs is to interpret the federal laws for those who must comply with them.

- It remains illegal today for incorporated associations to use their own funds for contributions to federal candidates. However, association funds may be used to establish and administer PACs that solicit political campaign contributions from association members and direct the funds to candidates. The only qualifications on this use of funds are those provided in federal election and tax laws.

- Some reasons for forming an association PAC are:
  —To direct campaign funds to candidates for federal office
  —To assist in effectively presenting positions on leg-

islative matters important to the association, by aiding the campaigns of candidates who support the
passage of that legislation

—To counterbalance the influence of campaign funding and lobby groups already taking strong positions
on federal legislative matters

—To give notice that an association is interested in
affecting the governmental process generally or with
respect to specific issues

—To take advantage of higher limits on PAC contributions to candidates than are permitted individual
contributors

—To provide a convenient and direct way for association members to support election campaigns—with
significant tax advantages

—To involve association members actively in the political process.

- A number of association PACs have been successful in
meeting their goals for receipt of PAC contributions and
in reinforcing their overall government affairs efforts
by making expenditures to candidates sympathetic with
the associations' legislative positions. They often cite
similar reasons for their success:

—Conscientious attempts to establish and administer
the PACs in full compliance with all applicable rules,
so that association members who become PAC contributors can be assured of the legitimacy of the endeavor

—Consistent professional efforts toward effective fundraising through direct mail, presentations at meetings, and personal contact with association members—designed to achieve realistic long-term goals
for the desired level of PAC financial activity

—Reliance, in soliciting for PAC contributions, upon
the substantial federal income tax advantages available to contributors

—Systematic distribution of PAC contributions to candidates to further the legislative aims of the associations by supporting candidates who support the
associations' objectives, regardless of party affiliations, and

160 ASSOCIATION LAW HANDBOOK

—Pacing of the PAC's activities to ensure that momentum is carried from election years through nonelection years.

• Associations that have PACs or that intend to form PACs must closely observe applicable federal laws and regulations. Criminal and civil sanctions can be levied for violations.

RESOURCES FOR CHAPTER 31

Books

Campaign Guide for Corporations and Labor Organizations, Federal Election Commission, 1984.

Combs & Herold, "How to Form and Operate Political Action Committees" in *Associations and the Law Book VI,* U.S. Chamber, 1975, page 17.

Dye & Herold, "Association PACs and the 1976 Amendments" in *Associations and the Law Book VIII,* U.S. Chamber, 1978, page 57.

Federal Election Campaign Financing Guide, Commerce Clearing House.

Federal Taxation of Political Activities, Arthur Anderson & Co., 1980.

Fraser/Associates, *Business' Political Awakening: PAC Overview,* 1979.

Guidelines for Corporate PACs, U.S. Chamber, 1977.

Herold, "Antitrust, Trade Regulation, and Other Nontax Aspects of Association Activities" in *Managing Membership Societies,* Greif, Editor, ASAE, 1979, page 131.

Jacobs, "The Law of Lobbying" in *ASAE 3rd Annual Management Conference Proceedings,* 1985, page 330.

Klein, "Political Expenditures," 231-2d *Tax Management,* The Bureau of National Affairs, Inc., 19____.

Ryan, "Forming an Association PAC: Why and When?" in *Associations and the Law Book VIII,* U.S. Chamber, 1978, page 64.

Schwarz & Nielsen, Editors, *The Corporation in Politics, PACs, Lobbying Laws and Public Affairs,* Practising Law Institute, 1983.

"The Trade Association" in *The Corporation in Politics*, Practising Law Institute, 1980, page 185.

Webster, *Political Action Committees, A Guide to Association Involvement in the Political Press*, ASAE, 1979.

Webster, Herold, & Dye, *Association Legal Checklist*, U.S. Chamber, 1983, pages 13–14.

Whelan & Johnson, Editors, *Campaign Finance, Ethics and Lobby Law, Blue Book, 1984–85*, Council of State Governments, 1984.

Periodicals

Alexander, "Business and Labor in Politics," *Financing the 1976 Elections*, 1979, page 533.

Alexander, "How New Campaign Laws Affect Associations," *Association Management*, October, 1972, page 107.

Bauer, "Federal Election Laws Today," *Association Management*, February, 1982, page 97.

Boggs & Stevens, "Keeping Up With the PACs: The Frontrunners of Campaign Finance," *District Lawyer*, December/January, 1979, page 20.

Combs & Herold, "Political Action Committees: The Handling of Contributions and Disclosure Requirements," *Association Letter*, October, 1973, page 5.

Combs & Herold, "Political Action Committees: Implications of Federal Tax Laws and IRS Regulations," *Association Letter*, November, 1973, page 9.

Combs & Herold, "Political Action Committees: Some Statutory Provisions on Corporate Political Activities as They Restrict Associations," *Association Letter*, March, 1978, page 16.

Combs & Herold, "Political Action Committees: Their Place and Function in the Business Community," *Association Letter*, July, 1973, page 1.

Eddingger & Brightup, "Association PACs: Major Players in the Political Arena," *Association Special Report*, U.S. Chamber, August, 1982.

Elliott, "You Can't Judge PACs by the Numbers Alone," *Association Management*, October, 1980, page 167.

Fisher, "How to Start a National Association Political Action Committee," *Association Management*, June, 1981, page 67.

Godown, "Political Action: What You Can and Can't Do," *Association Management*, December, 1976, page 76.

Hahn, "Give Away Your PAC Dollars Systematically," *Association Management*, September, 1980, page 83.

Hucker, "Congress Fine Tunes Campaign Law," *Congressional Quarterly*, January 5, 1980, page 31.

Jacobs, "Guidelines for Association Political Action Committees," *Association Letter*, June, 1979, page 2.

Malbin, "Corporate PAC-backers Chart a Trail Through Congress," *National Journal*, March 10, 1976, page 470.

Mayberry, "In-Kind and Independent PAC Activities—Money Isn't Everything," *Association Letter*, January, 1980, page 3.

Parkinson, "Congress Considers Changes in PAC Operation," *Association Management*, September, 1979, page 73.

Parkinson, "Political Action Committees: Is the PAC Parade Passing You By?," *Association Management*, May, 1979, page 29.

Porter, "Put the Myths about PACs to Rest," *Association Management*, July, 1982, page 35.

Stratton, "The ABCs of the FEC: How the Federal Election Commission Regulates the Political Process," *Association Management*, June, 1979, page 57.

Vandergrift, "Trade Association PACs Still Have Influence," *Legal Times of Washington*, February 5, 1979, page 15.

Walters, "PACs: Do They Buy Votes or Support a Point of View?," *Association Management*, July, 1983, page 51.

Webster, "Campaign Contributions, Know Your Limits," *Association Management*, January, 1980, page 16.

Webster, "Legal: How Federal Election Amendments Affect Political Action Committees," *Association Management*, September, 1976, page 20.

Webster, "Operating Your Political Committee," *Association Management*, October, 1972, page 110.

Cases

Buckley v. Valeo, 424 U.S. 1 (1976). Constitutionality of federal election laws.

First National Bank of Boston v. Bellotti, 435 U.S. 765 (1978). Corporate political expenditures.

Statutes and Regulations

Federal Election Campaign Act Amendments of 1979, 2 U.S.C. Sections 431–455 (1980).
Federal Election Regulations, 11 C.F.R. Parts 100–115 (1985).

Other Resources

Legislative History of the Federal Election Campaign Act Amendments of 1976 (1977).
FEC Advisory Opinion 1975-23. Permissibility of corporate PAC concept.
Federal Election Commission, *Record* (published monthly).
Federal Election Commission, *Trade Associations* (brochure).

Chapter 32

PAC BYLAWS

Most every association PAC prefers to promulgate some governing document that can be referred to for authority in its structure and operations. This Summary concerns such a document, the PAC's bylaws.

Sample association PAC bylaws are included in the last section of this book.

SUMMARY

- Although not strictly required by federal laws or regulations, an association is well advised to adopt some governing document—most often called bylaws—that explains the organization and management of its PAC.

- Some association PACs also develop an administrative manual to give detailed guidelines to the PAC's officers and staff about solicitations, contributions, expenditures, reports, record-keeping, and other operational matters.

- The bylaws of an association PAC often include such provisions as:
  —the name of the PAC and the identity of the association and any other political committee to which it is related
  —The structure of the PAC as a voluntary, nonprofit political committee composed of individual noncorporate members (if the PAC has members) who might be described, for example, as those who are interested in the purposes of the PAC and who are contributing to it
  —The general purposes of the PAC (e.g., to solicit and receive funds and to make contributions to those po-

litical candidates or committees who have demonstrated understanding of, and interest in, the views of the PAC); the specific purpose, as required by the tax laws, should also be included (see "PAC Organization")

—The authority of the PAC to solicit and receive funds and make political campaign contributions according to procedures set out in the bylaws and administrative manual (if one has been developed) and consistent with federal election campaign laws and regulations

—The composition and responsibilities of any governing board the PAC may establish—including, for example, the number of board representatives, whether they are elected or appointed, length of terms, and provisions for voting

—The number, statement of election or appointment, terms, duties, and authority of the officers of the PAC—including a chairman, treasurer, vice chairman, and assistant treasurer

—Requirements for meetings of the PAC members (if any), governing board, or officers and

—Provisions for amendment of the bylaws.

• Association PAC bylaws can be distributed to association members when their contributions are solicited by the PAC to acquaint them with its structure and purposes.

RESOURCES FOR CHAPTER 32

Books

Federal Election Campaign Financing Guide, Commerce Clearing House.

Guidelines for Corporate PACs, U.S. Chamber, 1977, Chapter 1.

Jacobs, "The Law of Lobbying" in *ASAE 3rd Annual Management Conference Proceedings*, 1985, page 330.

Webster, *Political Action Committees, A Guide to Association Involvement in the Political Process*, ASAE, 1979, page 4.

Periodicals

Jacobs, "Guidelines for Association Political Action Committees," *Association Letter*, June, 1979, page 3.

Chapter 33

PAC ORGANIZATION

The organization of an association PAC that will support candidates for election to federal office is dictated in many ways by stringent federal election laws. In order to maintain tax-exempt status and to achieve tax benefits for contributors, the association PAC must observe even further federal requirements. Here is a summary of some that pertain to organization.

SUMMARY

- Organization of association PACs is subject to several considerations dictated by federal laws, regulations, and FEC interpretations

- The official name of the PAC must include the full name of the association sponsoring it. That full name must be included in the FEC statement of organization, on all reports, and as part of any legal notices required on solicitations. FEC has advised that an abbreviated name for the PAC can be used on letterhead and checks of the PAC. For example: The National Widget Association (NWA) should name its PAC the National Widget Association Political Action Committee. On letter head or checks it may use a recognizable abbreviation such as NWA PAC. It may not be satisfactory to name or call its PAC the Good Government Fund or Widget PAC.

- The law requires a PAC to be registered within 10 days following its formation. The registration is on a government form and must include:

    —The name, address, and type of political committee involved

166

—The names, addresses, and relationship of any connected organizations or affiliated committees

—The name, address, and position of the custodian of the books and accounts of the committee

—The name and address of the treasurer of the committee

—A listing of all banks, safety deposit boxes, or other depositories used by the committee.

- In most instances, the PAC's registration is filed with the Federal Election Commission. But, it is filed with the Secretary of the Senate if only candidates for the U.S. Senate are supported or with the Clerk of the House if only candidates for the U.S. House of Representatives are supported.

- The registration statement must be amended within 10 days whenever information given previously has changed. Thus, for example, whenever a new treasurer is appointed, amendment of the registration is necessary.

- Upon registration, the PAC will receive an identification number, which must be used on all filings.

- Copies of the PAC's registration must be sent to the secretary of state (or other designated official) in states where the PAC supports candidates for election or makes expenditures for candidates for president or vice president.

- If it is intended that support will be given to state candidates as well as federal candidates, it may be desirable to establish separate federal-level and state-level PACs and to register them individually. Exclusively state-level PACs may be subject to different rules and do not have to be registered with the federal government.

- Association PACs need not be incorporated. In fact, federal law prohibits campaign contributions by corporations. FEC regulations do permit PACs to incorporate, but for liability purposes only. Notwithstanding this incorporation, however, treasurers of PACs remain personally responsible for their duties under the law.

- The PAC must be organized and operated exclusively

to further the nomination or election of candidates for public office. This exclusive purpose is required by the tax laws for PAC contributors to be eligible for personal income tax credits. IRS requires that a PAC not engage in any general political, educational, or legislative activities if it intends its contributors to receive tax benefits. If the association establishing the PAC engages in political activities other than furthering the nomination or election of candidates, it should conduct these activities outside the PAC to avoid jeopardizing tax benefits for PAC contributors.

- For the PAC to gain and maintain tax-exempt status, a different IRS test is applied. The PAC must be organized and operated primarily to accept contributions and make expenditures intended to influence the selection, nomination, election, or appointment of individuals for public office. When a PAC meets this test, revenue received in the form of contributions is clearly exempt from federal income tax. The Internal Revenue Code and regulations for "political committees" detail what other kinds of PAC income qualify as "exempt function income" to avoid federal taxation. Interest received by a PAC on its deposited funds, for example, would not be exempt from taxation but would be subject to a $100 specific deduction.

- A PAC must have a treasurer in office whenever funds are received or disbursed. The bylaws and registration statement should provide for an assistant treasurer to serve if the treasurer is not available.

- Association funds may be used to pay for PAC administrative and solicitation costs. Association funds cannot be used as contributions to the PAC or to candidates through the PAC. Examples of PAC administrative costs that can be paid from association funds—thereby maximizing the amount of PAC funds that can be used to make expenditures to political candidates—include:
  —Printing, mailing, and other expenses for PAC solicitations
  —Salaries of PAC employees or association employees assigned to PAC administrative activities
  —Rent and other expenses of maintaining PAC offices

—Fees of attorneys, accountants, political consultants, direct mail consultants, or other professional advisers to the PAC.

- The IRS has advised that a corporation's costs in forming and administering its PAC are nondeductible expenditures. The IRS ruled that PAC administrative expenditures allow for participation in political campaigns or grass roots lobbying efforts, and consequently are nondeductible. The IRS has not specifically addressed this matter as it applies to trade or professional association PACs, but associations should be aware of the trend towards disallowing such deductions. The major concern for association members is whether the portion of their membership dues that is used by the association to administer a PAC is tax deductible. Under the'IRS ruling, it is possible that association membership dues used to pay *substantial* administrative and solicitation costs for their political action committees may be viewed as nondeductible expenses. Whether IRS would view membership dues used to make *de minimus* PAC administration expenditures as nondeductible is unlikely and likely not a cause for association concern.

- It is clear that executives of an association's member companies may contribute their time to the operation of the PAC. However, the IRS has advised that corporations must allocate a portion of their employees' salaries as nondeductible expenses when those employees devote their time to the operation of the PAC. Such time was considered by IRS to be an indirect expense related to grass roots lobbying and, hence, nondeductible. In the specific case addressed by IRS, the corporation's employees worked on the PAC as part of their employment for the corporation. If employees of association member companies were to *volunteer* their time to the PAC, nondeductibility issues may not arise. Nevertheless, associations must be aware of this IRS position and take cognizance of the IRS trend toward disallowing deductions.

RESOURCES FOR CHAPTER 33

Books

Campaign Guide for Corporations and Labor Organizations,
    Federal Election Commission, 1984.
Federal Election Campaign Financing Guide, Commerce Clear-
    ing House.
Guidelines for Corporate PACs, U.S. Chamber, 1977, Chapters
    1, 2, 5, and 9.
Jacobs, "The Law of Lobbying" in *ASAE 3rd Annual Manage-
    ment Conference Proceedings,* 1985, page 330.
Webster, *Political Action Committees, A Guide to Association
    Involvement in the Political Process,* ASAE, 1979.

Periodicals

Bruce, "Taxing of Political Organizations, Candidates, Con-
    tributors," *A.B.A.J.* 1976, page 123.
Greenberger, "The Tax Treatment of Political Action Commit-
    tees," *Practical Accountant,* 1976, page 55.
Mayberry, "The IRS Goes After Soft-Money Political Dona-
    tions," *Association Management,* August, 1985, page 139.
Streng, "The Federal Tax Treatment of Political Contributions
    and Political Organizations," *Tax Lawyer,* 1975, page 139.

Statutes and Regulations

Federal Election Campaign Act Amendments of 1979, 2 U.S.C.
    Sections 432, 433.
Internal Revenue Code, Sections 41, 527.
Federal Election Regulations, 11 C.F.R. Section 102 (1985); 11
    C.F.R. Section 114.1(b) (1985).

Other Resources

FEC Advisory Opinion 1980-10. Name of a PAC.
FEC Advisory Opinion 1980-23. Name of a PAC.
FEC Advisory Opinion 1980-59. Corporate member contribution
    to PAC to defray administration and solicitation costs.
IRS Technical Advice Memoranda 8202019 and 8202021 (1982).

Chapter 34

PAC SOLICITATIONS

The federal election laws stipulate certain restrictions on the ability of association PACs to solicit campaign contribution funds. Perhaps the most notorious and most onerous is the administrative requirement that executives and stockholders of association corporate member firms may only be solicited after the corporate member firms have given their approval. This and other provisions regarding PAC solicitations are included in the following Summary.

SUMMARY

- A PAC may not solicit or accept contributions from any corporation.
- The rules for association PAC solicitations are complicated. In essence, an association PAC may solicit contributions:
    - —from specified corporate member individuals—executive and administrative personnel, stockholders and their families—after receiving advance approval from the member corporation
    - —From the association's noncorporate members (including partnerships) and their families, without restriction
    - —From specified association executive and administrative personnel and their families, without restrictions—but from its other employees only twice a year.
- An association must obtain advance approval from a corporate member before contributions to the PAC may be solicited from executive and administrative personnel, stockholders, or their families of the member corporation. Contributions may not be solicited from any

other corporate member employees. Federal law requires that the approval be "separate and specific."
FEC regulations require that the approval be in writing.

- Each member corporation can give approval for solicitation by only one federal-level, association-related
PAC for each calendar year. But, an approval specified
as applicable for a future year can be requested by the
association and provided by the member corporation.
The separate corporate member approval for each future year need not be on a separate document. The
request for approval is sent to the corporate member
representative with whom the association normally
deals. The association can note in this request that it
intends to limit any solicitation (such as, perhaps, to
only executive and administrative personnel or even
just to one or more named individuals). Approval for
solicitation by additional state- or local-level PACs may
be granted (where permission is required) if allowed
by state or local law.

- A separately incorporated subsidiary, branch, division, or affiliate of a corporation can approve solicitations by one trade association PAC for each year if
the separately incorporated entity is itself a member
of the association.

- Whether an association member is a "corporation"—
and thus subject to the advance approval requirement—is determined by state law. FEC has determined
that a municipal corporation is subject to the rules for
other corporate members of associations.

- FEC has taken the position that certain "indicia" of
membership are required before an association may
consider a firm eligible to be solicited (upon advance
written approval). Merely "associating" with a soliciting organization is insufficient, according to a court
decision on the matter. FEC has advised an association
that it *may not* solicit from its associate members where
those members "do not have the right to vote at any
meeting or have any voice in the association or any
control over its officers."

- The advance approval is required even before solicitation of an association's officers and board members if they are corporate member individuals.

- In seeking advance approval for PAC solicitation from an association corporate member, one copy of sample solicitation materials may be mailed or given to the corporate member representative with whom the association normally deals.

- An association may publish a form for obtaining solicitation approval from corporate member representatives in a newsletter or other association publication; but the wording of the form must make clear that it is a request for approval to solicit rather than a solicitation itself.

- Since prior, not simultaneous, approval is required, solicitation in newsletters or other association publications reaching corporate member individuals who have not given written approval is prohibited. FEC has taken a restrictive position that articles about a PAC which might provoke an individual to make an unsolicited contribution are to be viewed as actual solicitations. FEC has allowed PAC solicitations in association publications where the number and percentages of corporate member personnel whose companies had not approved solicitations were relatively incidental (1,000 persons, 3 percent of circulation in one case; 3,217 persons, .16 percent of circulation in another case) and the solicitations stated that contributions from nonapproved individuals would be returned to the contributors. An association must approach PAC articles in newsletters with caution lest the articles be considered by the FEC as solicitations.

- Once advance approval is received, the PAC may solicit contributions from executive or administrative personnel, stockholders (or their families) of the association member corporation as often as is desired and whether or not the corporation has set up its own corporate PAC. A corporate PAC can solicit corporate employees even though the corporation has given solicitation approval to an association PAC. The corporation, in its approval, may limit the manner and frequency of association PAC solicitations. Corporate approval can be withdrawn at any time.

- If a parent corporation is a member of the association but a subsidiary is not—or vice versa—only the corporate individuals of the member entity (parent or subsidiary) may, with prior approval, be solicited.

- Advance approval is not necessary for PAC solicitations made to individual association members who are not employees or stockholders of a member corporation, as well as to family members of those individual association members.

- Solicitations for PAC contributions may be made to the association's own administrative or executive employees (or their families); but solicitations to other nonexecutive association employees may be made only twice a year by letter mailed to the employees at home. These solicitations must be made in such a way that the association and the PAC remain unaware of who makes single contributions of $50 or less, multiple contributions totaling $200 or less, or no contribution at all.

- An association PAC may not solicit contributions from its corporate member's PAC unless the two are affiliated.

- The PAC must keep records of all association members who have approved solicitations or who do not require advance approval for solicitation (if any). The advance approval documents must be kept by the PAC for three years after the year for which the approval applies.

- FEC has said that a solicitation occurs if the association or PAC publicizes the right of individuals to contribute, provides information on how to contribute, or encourages support for the PAC such as, for example, by congratulating those who have contributed. FEC has said that a solicitation does not occur if the association merely requests solicitation approval from a corporate member, provides factual or statistical or historical information about the PAC, or explains the laws that apply to the PAC.

- Mail solicitations may be addressed only to individuals from whom advance approval has been obtained or from whom approval is unnecessary because they are noncorporate members. Subject to the advance approval requirement, there is no prohibition against including solicitation materials with other routine association mailings.

- Oral solicitations and distribution of solicitation materials at association seminars, meetings, or conventions attended by corporate member executives or stockholders may be made only if the association PAC has received advance approval for solicitation from the corporate members in attendance. However, the FEC has stated that an association may maintain a PAC booth at meetings attended by association corporate member individuals to make solicitations and receive contributions under certain conditions. Some suggested procedures for these PAC booths are:

—The PAC booth should be staffed by personnel familiar with the laws and regulations.

—References to the PAC booth should be avoided in premeeting publicity by the association; during the meeting, no announcements should be made about the existence of the PAC booth or its location.

—Simple signs directing meeting delegates to the PAC booth and a simple sign at the booth are acceptable.

—There should be a sign at the booth informing contributors of the solicitation restrictions.

—Any meeting delegate inquiring at the booth can be offered a PAC brochure explaining its purposes and outlining the advance approval requirement for executives of association corporate members.

—Written advance approval for solicitation of association corporation member executives should be accepted only from authorized corporate officers; a list of those approved for solicitation should be maintained.

—Solicitations for contributions to the PAC should only be made to meeting delegates who are with association corporate members that have given advance approval for the solicitation of individuals; likewise contributions should only be accepted from those individuals.

- Solicitation for contributions to the association PAC may not be secured by force or threat of discrimination or reprisal or as a condition of membership.

- Whether they are made by mail or at association meetings, solicitations for contributions to an association PAC must clearly state the political purpose of the PAC.

- Solicitations must include a statement to the effect that those solicited may decline to contribute to the PAC without fear of reprisal by the association or by their employer.

- Written solicitations for contributions to an association PAC need not include the statements that the solicitations are paid for by the association PAC and are not authorized by any candidate or candidate's committee because the solicitations are not made to the general public.

- Solicitations for contributions may include a statement to the effect that no corporate funds will be accepted by the association PAC.

- Solicitations for contributions to the PAC may include information on the tax advantages of contributions (i.e., a tax credit up to $50, $100 on a joint return, is available for one-half of the amount of a contribution to the PAC).

- Solicitations may include the fact that single contributions to the PAC of more than $50 or multiple contributions exceeding $200 by law must be reported to the government in detail.

- The FEC has advised that associations may place a voluntary check-off designation for a PAC contribution on its dues statements as long as no corporate PAC contributions are solicited and no portion of the dues is used as a contribution. A suggested PAC contribution amount, but not a minimum amount, may also be used if it is made clear that one may contribute more or less than the suggested amount.

RESOURCES FOR CHAPTER 34

Books

Boggs & Boyce, "Legislation/Regulations Affecting PACs" in *Association Issues*, Jacobs, Editor, ASAE, 1983, page 77.
Campaign Guide for Corporations and Labor Organizations, Federal Election Committee, 1984.

Federal Election Campaign Financing Guide, Commerce Clearing House.

Goldberg, "Solicitation of Funds by Association PACS" in *Association and the Law Book IX*, U.S. Chamber, 1979, page 72.

Guidelines for Corporate PACs, U.S. Chamber, 1977, Chapter 3.

Jacobs, "The Law of Lobbying," in *ASAE 3rd Annual Management Conference Proceedings*, 1985, page 330.

Webster, *Political Action Committees, A Guide to Association Involvement in the Political Process*, ASAE, 1979, page 5.

Periodicals

Jacobs, "Guidelines for Association Political Action Committees," *Association Letter*, June, 1979, page 5.

Mayberry, "PAC Booths at Annual Meetings," *Association Letter*, August, 1979, page 1.

Statutes and Regulations

Federal Election Campaign Act Amendments of 1979, 2 U.S.C. Section 441b(b) (4) (D) (Cum. Supp. 1980).

Federal Election Regulations, 11 C.F.R. Section 114.8 (1980).

Cases

Bread Political Action Committee v. Federal Election Commission, 591 F.2d (7th Cir. 1979). Propriety of fundraising cocktail party.

National Chamber Alliance for Politics v. Federal Election Commission, Civil Action No. 78-1333 (D.D.C. 1978), *appeal docketed*, No. 79-1027 (D.C. Cir. Nov. 29, 1978). Propriety of solicitation restrictions.

Federal Election Commission v. National Right to Work Committee, No. 77-125 (D.D.C. 1980).

Other Resources

FEC Advisory Opinion 1976-27. Actions constituting solicitation.

FEC Advisory Opinion 1977-67. Determining who is a "member."

FEC Advisory Opinion 1978-83. Solicitation at convention booth.

FEC Advisory Opinion 1978-18. Distribution of voting records.

FEC Advisory Opinion 1978-97. Solicitation in association publication.

FEC Advisory Opinion 1981-7. Solicitation in association publication.

FEC Advisory Opinion 1981-41. Advance approval request form in association publication.

FEC Advisory Opinion 1982-11. Association dues check-off program with suggested contribution amount.

FEC Advisory Opinion 1982-26. Municipal corporation association members.

FEC Advisory Opinion 1984-61. Separate corporate solicitation approvals for future years need not be separate documents.

Chapter 35

PAC RECEIPTS AND EXPENDITURES

As with other administrative functions of association PACs, federal law lays down requirements for how PACs handle money that they receive from contributors, as well as money that they give to candidates for federal elective office. Of particular importance is observance of spending limits imposed by law on individual contributions (such as to an association PAC) and on PAC contributions (to candidates). How the funds are handled also can affect tax aspects of PACs. Here are some summary guidelines.

SUMMARY

- An association PAC may not accept cash contributions of more than $100 from any individual. Some PACs discourage all cash contributions because checks provide a better record of contributions.

- No contribution from any corporation may be accepted by a PAC. If it is unclear whether a contribution is personal or corporate, that fact must be determined before accepting it. Contributions to PACs from national banks, government contractors, and federally incorporated firms are also prohibited.

- As noted earlier, an association can pay for administrative expenses of a PAC. FEC has permitted a corporate association member to give the association funds for PAC administrative expenses and to donate merchandise for PAC fundraising. Gifts or raffle prizes supplied by an association to encourage PAC contributions are permitted, but costs of the gifts or prizes that exceed

179

one-third of the resulting PAC contributions must be reimbursed to the association. Tax issues for the PAC and any contributing corporation should be carefully reviewed.

- An association PAC may not accept a contribution from an individual who is not a U.S. citizen. This is true even if the contributor is a foreign member of the association related to the PAC. The PAC may not accept a contribution that is made in the name of another individual or corporation.

- Special rules are applicable to "earmarked" contributions, i.e., those designated to be given by the association PAC to a particular candidate or campaign committee:
  —The intended recipient must be informed of earmarked contributions made through the PAC when the contribution is passed on to the recipient.
  —The intended recipient must be given any earmarked contributions made through the PAC within ten days of when the PAC receives them, together with the identity of the sources of the earmarked contributions.
  —Earmarked contributions must be described by the PAC separately in its regular reports to the government.

- A PAC may not accept contributions in excess of $5,000 per year from any individual.

- Individuals may contribute no more than $25,000 in a calendar year in total political contributions to all recipient candidates, national parties, and political action committees.

- All contributions received and accepted by an association PAC must be deposited in the PAC checking account. All expenditures made by the PAC, other than petty cash amounts, must be disbursed from that account.

- A receipt for contributions to an association PAC—in the form of a thank-you letter, certificate of recognition, or any other written document—is appropriate and may be necessary for the contributor to receive tax credit benefits. The Internal Revenue Service will ordinarily accept an individual's canceled check as evidence of a PAC contribution qualifying for the tax credit benefit. But, IRS reserves the right to require the individual to produce additional documentation on the nature and purposes of the PAC and the contribution. Therefore, it may be desirable for a PAC to provide a receipt stating:

—The name of the PAC and the fact that it supported candidates for federal office in the applicable year
—The amount and date of the contribution
—The name of the contributor
—The signature of an authorized PAC agent.

- An association PAC may contribute no more than $1,000 to any one candidate in any election for federal office (primary and general elections are counted separately).

- The $1,000 limit for PAC contributions to individual candidates is increased to $5,000 per election when the PAC qualifies as a "multi-candidate committee" by (1) being registered for at least six months, (2) receiving contributions for federal elections from at least 50 individuals, and (3) making expenditures to five or more federal candidates.

- An association PAC that is a multi-candidate committee may give no more than $15,000 in a calendar year to a national political party.

- An association PAC may give no more than $5,000 in a calendar year to another political committee, such as a corporate or association-related political action committee (but note the proscription against PAC solicitations to other unaffiliated, member PACs).

- PACs of "affiliated" associations must combine their expenditures for purposes of the expenditure limits. FEC regulations consider state and local entities of a trade or professional association to be "affiliated."

- No contribution may be accepted nor expenditure made by an association PAC without the authorization of its treasurer. However, the treasurer may delegate (orally or in writing) to another authority to make expenditures.

- There are no requirements that PAC expenditures be bi-partisan or otherwise balanced among candidates of differing political philosophies or persuasions.

- For PAC contributors to be eligible for personal income tax credits, the PAC must be operated exclusively to further the nomination or election of candidates. This precludes spending PAC money on general political, educational, or legislative activities. Whether it precludes spending PAC money on administrative expenses, solicitation expenses, etc., is not resolved by IRS regulations.

- For contributors to receive tax benefits, the PAC must support at least one candidate during the year of its contributions. For a contributor of earmarked funds, the designated candidate must be supported by the PAC during the year of the contribution. Unspent contributions may be retained by the PAC to support candidates in future elections, but must be spent "within a reasonable period of time," according to IRS regulations.

- Special rules apply to "in kind" contributions of other than funds and to "independent" expenditures made to further a candidacy but without authorization by the candidate.

RESOURCES FOR CHAPTER 35

Books

Boggs & Boyce, "Legislation/Regulations Affecting PACs" in *Association Issues*, Jacobs, Editor, ASAE, 1983, page 77.

Campaign Guide for Corporations and Labor Organizations, Federal Election Commission, 1984.

Federal Election Campaign Financing Guide, Commerce Clearing House.

Guidelines for Corporate PACs, U.S. Chamber, 1977, Chapter 2.

Jacobs, "The Law of Lobbying" in *ASAE 3rd Annual Management Conference Proceedings*, 1985, page 330.

Webster, *Political Action Committees, A Guide to Association Involvement in the Political Process*, ASAE, 1979, page 9.

Periodicals

Glen, "How to Get Around the Campaign Spending Limits,"
    National Journal, June 23, 1979, page 1044.
Jacobs, "Guidelines for Association Political Action Commit-
    tees," *Association Letter*, June, 1979, page 6.

Statutes and Regulations

Internal Revenue Code of 1954, 26 U.S.C. Section 41.
Federal Election Campaign Act Amendments of 1979, 2 U.S.C.
    Section 441a (Cum. Supp. 1980).
Federal Election Regulations, 11 C.F.R. 110 (1980).
Internal Revenue Service Regulations, 26 C.F.R. Sections 1.41-
    1, 1.41-2 and 1.41-3 (1985).

Other Resources

FEC Advisory Opinion 1982-36. Corporate contributions to de-
    fray PAC administrative costs.

Chapter 36

PAC REPORTING AND RECORDKEEPING

Federal election laws and tax laws provide for certain reporting and recordkeeping by association political action committees. This Summary outlines the reporting and record-keeping provisions.

SUMMARY

- The treasurer of an association PAC is required by law to keep records of contributions received and expenditures made. The treasurer is also responsible for signing and filing reports accurately and on time. FEC specifies that a PAC treasurer must use "best efforts" to carry out the recordkeeping and reporting obligations.

- For each contribution received, records must be kept of:
  —The name and mailing address of each contributor from whom contributions totaling more than $50 are received in a year
  —The name, mailing address, occupation, and employer's name for each contributor from whom contributions totaling more than $200 are received in a year
  —The date and the amount received.

- Association PACs may not solicit funds from other kinds of PACs or campaign committees; but if such funds are received unsolicited, records must be kept of the amount, date, and name and address of the contributing entity.

184

- Records should be kept of transfers from affiliated PACs by amount, date, and name and address of the PAC.

- For every disbursement of any kind, the PAC must keep records which identify at least:
  —The name and address of the individual to whom it is made
  —The date and amount
  —The purpose of the disbursement.

- For each campaign expenditure made, records must be kept of:
  —The name and address of the individual to whom it is made
  —The date and the amount
  —The name of the candidate (if the expenditure was made on behalf of a candidate)
  —The office sought by the candidate
  —The election for which the disbursement is made.

- For campaign expenditures in amounts of more than $200 for whomever receives the expenditure, the PAC's treasurer must obtain and retain a "receipted bill," which may be a check or invoice.

- PAC records must be kept for at least three years.

- Records are not required to be kept by the PAC of administrative expenses paid by a related association, although sound financial management would suggest that such records be kept by the PAC or by the association.

- The PAC is required to file periodic financial reports with the FEC or with the Secretary of the Senate or Clerk of the House (if only candidates for senator or representative, respectively, are supported).

- The PAC may file semiannual reports during nonelection years and quarterly reports in election years or, alternatively, it may file monthly reports for each year regardless of whether an election is being held.

- Semiannual reports in nonelection years must be filed by July 31 and January 31. Quarterly reports in election years are due on April 15, July 15, October 15, and January 31. A quarterly report is waived if a pre-election report is due 5–15 days after the end of the quarter.

- In addition to the quarterly reports, these reports must also be filed:

  —A pre-election report, due the 12th day before a primary or general election if previously unreported expenditures have been made

  —A post-general-election report, due the 30th day after a general election and complete as of the 20th day after the election.

- The PAC filing monthly instead of semiannually and quarterly must file within 20 days after the end of the month. In lieu of the November and December reports in an election year, the PAC must file a 12 day pre-election report, a 30 day post-general-election report, and a year-end report which is due on January 31 for the preceding year.

- A PAC may change its filing schedule, such as from monthly to semiannually in a nonelection year, only once per year by notification to FEC with any report.

- Reports must be made by an association PAC on the appropriate forms. They must contain cumulative information on all contributions received and expenditures made by the PAC. Specifically, the reports must disclose:

  —Cash on hand at the beginning of the reporting period

  —The name, mailing address, occupation, name of employer, date, and amount for each contribution received from contributors who gave the PAC more than $200 in the current calendar year

  —The total contributions received by the PAC in the reporting period, other than those listed separately

  —The name, address, date, and amount of each expenditure made to a candidate or PAC of more than $200 in the current calendar year

  —The total expenditures made by the PAC in the reporting period and the calendar year

  —Other information—such as loans, debts, ticket sales, investment income, contributions, or expenditures of goods or services—where applicable.

- Copies of the reports must be furnished to those secretaries of state (or other designated officials) who have received the PAC's registration and amendments.

• In addition to the election campaign reports, an association PAC may be required to file a report with the Internal Revenue Service for years in which it has had taxable income. Contributions received by the PAC are not considered taxable income nor are other types of "exempt function income." However, the tax laws and IRS rules do require that reports be filed and taxes be paid on revenue that is not considered "exempt function income." This is a subject that deserves close attention by the association PAC's professional legal or accounting advisors.

RESOURCES FOR CHAPTER 36

Books

Boggs & Boyce, "Federal Regulation of Lobbying" in *Association Issues*, Jacobs, Editor, ASAE, 1983, page 85.
Campaign Guide for Corporations and Labor Organizations, Federal Election Committee, 1984.
Federal Election Campaign Financing Guide, Commerce Clearing House.
Guidelines for Corporate PACs, U.S. Chamber, 1977, Chapters 2, 3.
Jacobs, "The Law of Lobbying" in *ASAE 3rd Annual Management Conference Proceedings*, 1985, page 330.
Jacobs, "Guidelines for Association PACs" in *Political Action for Business: The PAC Handbook*, Fraser/Associates, 1981, page 134.
Nesbitt, "PAC Accounting Guidelines" in *Political Action for Business: The PAC Handbook*, Fraser/Associates, 1981, page 263.
Webster, "Political Action Committees" in *A Guide to Association Involvement in the Political Process*, ASAE, 1979, pages 11, 14.

Periodicals

Jacobs, "Guidelines for Association Political Action Committees," *Association Letter*, June, 1979, page 7.

Statutes and Regulations

Federal Election Campaign Act Amendments of 1979, 2 U.S.C.
    Section 434.
Federal Election Regulations, 11 C.F.R. Parts 102 and 104 (1985).

Chapter 37

INDEPENDENT EXPENDITURES

Association political action committees (but not incorporated trade and professional associations themselves) may support candidates for federal office by making independent expenditures on behalf of the candidates. Independent expenditures may be made without limit since they do not count against the contribution limits for PACs established by the Federal Election Campaign Act. This Summary explains the term "independent expenditure" and the reporting and other requirements related to independent expenditures.

SUMMARY

- An "independent expenditure" is an expenditure for communications expressly advocating the election or defeat of a clearly identified federal candidate which is not made with the cooperation or consent of, or in consultation with, or at the request or suggestion of, any candidate or any agent or authorized committe of a candidate.
  - —A "clearly identified candidate" is one whose name, photograph, or drawing appears or whose identity is apparent by unambiguous reference.
  - —"Agent" means any person who has actual oral or written authority, either express or implied, to make or to authorize the making of expenditures on behalf of a candidate; or it means any person who has been placed in a position within the campaign organization where it would reasonably appear that in the ordinary course of campaign-related activities the person may authorize expenditures.
- When an expenditure is made other than under the

specific circumstances described above, it results in an "in kind contribution" rather than an "independent expenditure" and therefore counts against the PAC's contribution limits.

—Any expenditure made in cooperation, consultation, or in concert with the candidate (or agent), or as a result of the candidate's request or suggestion, is considered an in-kind contribution, not an independent expenditure. When, however, an association PAC merely requests and receives from a candidate Federal Election Commission guidelines on independent expenditures, the PAC is not considered to have coordinated, cooperated, or consulted with the candidate.

—Any expenditure to finance the dissemination or republication of a broadcast or other campaign materials prepared by a candidate (or the candidate's campaign) is considered an in-kind contribution, not an independent expenditure.

—An expenditure made on behalf of a federal candidate but directed by a current or former officer or employee of that candidate's committee, or by a person who has received compensation or reimbursement from the campaign, is presumed not to be independent.

• For example, assume an association PAC not previously involved in the campaign of U.S. Senate candidate Smith purchases a newspaper advertisement supporting Smith without ever contacting the candidate or any of Smith's campaign staff. The purchase is considered an independent expenditure. Assume, however, before purchasing the ad, a representative of the association PAC asks candidate Smith or Smith's campaign staff how the PAC may help the campaign or when Smith wants a newspaper ad to appear. The PAC makes an in-kind contribution. Or, if the PAC buys a campaign advertisement using text actually prepared by Smith's campaign staff, the PAC makes an in-kind contribution to the candidate. (An in-kind contribution, when combined with all other contributions from the same PAC, accumulates against the PAC's expenditure limits).

- Any independent expenditure must include a clear and conspicuous public notice in the printed material or during the broadcast. The notice must:

  —State that the communication is not authorized by the candidate or the candidate's authorized committee; and

  —Identify the name of the person or committee, in this case the association PAC, that financed the expenditure.

- An association PAC registered with the Federal Election Commission must itemize each independent expenditure it makes exceeding $200 at the end of any reporting period in which the expenditure is made. In addition, the total of all independent expenditures of $200 or less must be reported but not itemized.

- Any independent expenditure of $1,000 or more made between 2 and 20 days before an election must be reported within 24 hours to the FEC, the Secretary of the Senate, or the Clerk of the House, as appropriate. An association PAC must disclose a last-minute independent expenditure a second time with its next scheduled report. The PAC may, if it wishes, note that the expenditure was previously reported.

- Itemized reports on independent expenditures must include:

  —A certification, under penalty of perjury, that the expenditure meets the standard of "independence."

  —The date, amount, and purpose of the expenditure (i.e., a brief description of why the disbursement was made) and it must indicate whether the expenditure is in support of or in opposition to the candidate(s). Note that when an independent expenditure is made on behalf of more than one clearly identified candidate, the expenditure must be allocated among the candidates in proportion to the benefit they are expected to receive.

  —The name and address of the candidate(s) and the office sought.

  —The name and address of the person to whom the expenditure was made.

  —The name, mailing address, occupation, and name

of the employer of each person who contributes more than $200 to the association PAC that makes the expenditure.

RESOURCES FOR CHAPTER 37

Periodicals

Independent Expenditures, Federal Election Commission, 1982.

Statutes and Regulations

Federal Election Campaign Act, 2 U.S.C. Section 431.
FEC Regulations, 11 C.F.R. Sections 100, 104, and 109.

Chapter 38

POLITICAL COMMUNICATIONS

The Federal Election Campaign Act prohibits corporations, including incorporated trade and professional associations, from using their corporate treasury funds to make contributions or expenditures in connection with federal elections. However, incorporated associations may participate in the federal election process by using their treasury funds to make communications, both partisan and nonpartisan, under specified circumstances. This Summary, which applies only to federal election activity, describes the rules for different kinds of communications made by incorporated trade or professional associations.

SUMMARY

- An incorporated trade or professional association may use its corporate treasury funds to make partisan communications. However, partisan communications must be directed only to the association's "restricted class." Partisan communications, although they may advocate a federal candidate's election or defeat, do not have to include the notice required for advocacy communications directed to the general public (i.e., ". . . paid for by . . .").

- The "restricted class" to which the association may direct partisan communications includes:
  —Noncorporate members of the association and their families
  —Executive and administrative personnel of the association and their families
  —Individual representatives of the association's cor-

porate members—those with whom the association normally conducts its business.

- The association may produce and distribute publications of a partisan nature to its "restricted class." The material must convey the views of the association and may not simply be a republication of candidate-prepared material. However, an association, in expressing its own views, may use brief quotations from speeches or other candidate-prepared material.

- The association may set up a phone bank to urge its "restricted class" to register to vote and to vote for particular candidates.

- The association may allow candidates, their representatives, or representatives of a political party to address the "restricted class" at a meeting, convention, or other function of the association. The association may express its support of the candidate or party, and the speaker may request contributions to the candidate's campaign or party. Certain individuals outside the "restricted class" may be present—specifically, employees who administer the meeting (other than executive and administrative personnel who are already included in the "restricted class"), news media representatives, and limited invited guests and observers (such as speakers or recipients of awards).

- The association may conduct partisan voter registration and get-out-the-vote drives aimed only at its "restricted class." The drive may be partisan in that members of the "restricted class" may be urged to register with a particular party or to vote for a particular candidate. The drive may include transporting voters to the polls, although voter assistance may not be withheld on a partisan basis.

- The association may endorse a candidate and communicate the endorsement to its "restricted class." The association can announce the endorsement through a press release, assuming that the release is distributed only to the association's regular press contacts.

- An association must report the costs of communications which expressly advocate the election or defeat of clearly identified federal candidates if the cost aggregate over

$2,000 per election. Communications primarily devoted to subjects other than candidate advocacy are not reportable. Note that the $2,000 threshold applies separately to a parent association and to each subordinate under the parent.

- If a communication advocates the election of more than one candidate, the association should allocate the cost between the candidates according to the benefit derived. Note, however, that the entire cost of the communication, rather than the allocated costs per candidate, applies to the $2,000 reporting threshold.

- Costs for partisan communications by associations are reported to the Federal Election Commission on FEC Form 7 or in a letter to the FEC containing the information required on the form.

- In addition to making partisan communications, incorporated trade and professional associations may use their corporate treasury funds for nonpartisan communications. In most cases, these communications may be directed to the general public. Note that nonpartisan communications are limited to specific types of communications. Moreover, the association must comply with the particular rules that apply to each kind of nonpartisan communication activity. However, no reporting is required.

- The association may permit candidates, their representatives, or party representatives to address the association's "restricted class," as well as other employees and their families, at a meeting, convention, or other function of the association. Although the speaker may advocate the candidacy or party of an individual candidate, the association must ensure the nonpartisan nature of this activity by:
  —Providing an opportunity for other speakers
  —Avoiding solicitations and endorsements.

- The rules of the FEC for providing opportunities for others when the association permits a nonpartisan address at a meeting, convention, or other function of the association are these:
  —If a U.S. House or Senate candidate or the candidate's representative addresses the association's "restricted

class" and other employees, the association must give
the same opportunity to all candidates for the same
seat, if they request it.

—If a Presidential or Vice Presidential candidate or the
candidate's representative addresses the association's "restricted class" and other employees, the association must give the same opportunity, if requested,
to all candidates for that office who are seeking a
major party's nomination or who are on the general
election ballot in enough states to win a majority of
electoral votes.

—If a party representative makes an appearance, the
association must give the same opportunity, if requested, to all political parties which had a candidate on the ballot in the previous general election or
which anticipate having a candidate on the ballot in
the next general election. Note that the above rules
apply only to appearances in connection with a federal election. The requirements do not apply when
the association requests an incumbent, who may also
be a federal candidate, to appear in the capacity of
an office holder at a public meeting sponsored by
the association. If the discussion is limited to issues
of concern to the association or its industry or profession, such as pending legislation, and avoids any
reference to campaign activity, the association may
finance the meeting without triggering the "equal
opportunity to appear" requirement.

- The association may not, in conjunction with a nonpartisan appearance, either endorse a candidate or party
or solicit contributions on their behalf.

- The association may prepare and distribute to the general public voting records of members of Congress, provided the activity is not undertaken to influence federal
elections. The association may publish a factual record
on an incumbent's votes on legislative measures and
may score or index an incumbent's votes on specific
issues. The indexes or scores, however, must be based
on actual votes. The publication may include the association's name, acronym, or logo, or otherwise identify the association as the sponsor.

- The association may prepare and distribute to the gen-

eral public nonpartisan voter guides describing candidates' positions on issues. A voter guide consists of
questions posed to candidates concerning their positions on campaign issues and the candidates' responses to those questions. The association may also
ask each candidate to provide biographical information for inclusion in the voter guide, such as education,
employment background, offices held and community
involvement; the association may limit the number of
words per submission for biographical material. The
voter guide may include the association's name, acronym, or logo, or may otherwise identify the sponsor.

- In determining whether a voter guide is nonpartisan,
  the Federal Election Commission may consider the following factors, among others:
  —Whether the questions are directed to all Congressional candidates running for a particular seat, giving the candidates equal time to respond; and, in the
  case of Presidential and Vice Presidential candidates, whether the association directs questions to
  major party candidates or to those appearing on the
  general election ballot in enough states to win a majority of electoral votes.
  —Whether the voter guides reprint verbatim the responses of each candidate without any change or
  additional comment. The association may, however,
  limit the length of the candidates' responses when
  questionnaires are sent to participants. If a candidate exceeds the word limit, the association may
  print the response in its entirety or delete the part of
  the response which exceeds the limit.
  —Whether the wording of the questions is unbiased
  and does not favor any position on the issues covered.
  —Whether the voter guide excludes any editorial position on the issues and does not support or oppose
  any candidates or political party.
  —Whether the voter guide is made available to the
  general public in the geographic area in which the
  association normally operates.

- An incorporated trade or professional association may
  also distribute voter guides obtained from a "nonpar-

tisan, tax-exempt organization," i.e., one exempt from federal income taxation as a charitable, educational, or scientific organization (tax-exempt under Section 501(c) (3) of the Internal Revenue Code), or as an affinity organization (under Section 501(c) (4) of the Code) if the "nonpartisan, tax-exempt organization" does not support, endorse, or oppose candidates or political parties. Alternatively the "nonpartisan, tax-exempt organization" itself may distribute its own voter guide. In either situation, the voter guide, while not subject to the above guidelines, may not favor one candidate or party over another.

- The association may distribute to the general public (or reprint in whole and then distribute) registration and voter information prepared by election officials. The information may include, for example, instructional materials or registration-by-mail forms. The association may set up a table or rack on its own premises for distributing official voter information to the public; and the association's employees or members may help distribute materials. Distribution, however, must be carried out in a nonpartisan manner; the association may not endorse or support a candidate or party in connection with the distribution.

- An association may donate funds to state and local election administrators to help defray the costs of printing and distributing official registration and voting information and forms.

- An association may also purchase nonpartisan voter registration and get-out-the-vote advertisements directed to the general public (e.g., "Please Register to Vote"). The association may disseminate the message through posters, billboards, broadcasting media, newspapers, newsletters, brochures, or similar means of communication. In determining whether such ads are nonpartisan, the Federal Election Commission may consider the following factors:
  —Whether the scope of the ad is limited to urging the

public to register and vote and describing the time
and place of registration and voting.
—Whether the ad either names all candidates for a
particular office, without favoritism, or makes no
mention of any candidate.
—Whether the ad excludes any mention of political
party other than to identify the party affiliation of
each candidate listed.

- The association may jointly sponsor a nonpartisan voter
registration or get-out-the-vote drive with a "nonpartisan, tax-exempt organization" or with a state or local
agency responsible for administering elections. The
drive may include personal services, such as transporting voters to the polls, but they must be made available without regard to a voter's political preference.
Moreover, the election agency or "nonpartisan, tax-exempt organization" must itself conduct the activities,
i.e., participate in the administration of the drive. The
association may, however, donate funds for the drive
to the election agency or "nonpartisan, tax-exempt organization"; it may also make available its facilities
and employees or members for drive activities. Voter
drive materials prepared for distribution to the general
public must include the full name of all sponsors. Note
that a "nonpartisan, tax-exempt organization" may
conduct a nonpartisan voter registration or get-out-the-
vote drive on its own, without a co-sponsor.

- The association may donate corporate treasury funds
to a "nonpartisan, tax-exempt organization" to stage
nonpartisan, public debates between candidates.
Moreover, a bona fide broadcaster, newspaper, magazine, or other periodical publication (whether or not
incorporated) may itself stage nonpartisan candidate
debates.

- All partisan and nonpartisan political communications
by associations can potentially raise questions of taxation for the associations that conduct, sponsor, or support the communications. These tax ramifications are

assessed under the Internal Revenue Code and the regulations of the Internal Revenue Service, not those of
the Federal Election Commission. They should be thoroughly considered by associations before conducting,
sponsoring, or supporting political communications.

RESOURCES FOR CHAPTER 38

Periodicals

Corporate/Labor Communications, Federal Election Commission, 1984.

Regulations

FEC Regulations, 11 C.F.R. Sections 100, 104, and 114.

Chapter 39

HONORARIA

Associations often seek the participation of federal officials to appear or speak at conventions, conferences, or other association meetings; likewise associations often solicit the submission of articles by federal officials for publication in magazines, newsletters, or other association journals. The expertise and experience of an important federal official can greatly enhance an association meeting or publication; and so the association is generally·quite willing to pay an honorarium to the official in return for the efforts expended. Honoraria paid by associations to federal officials in return for appearances, speeches, or articles are legal; and they have become common and accepted. They are specifically provided for, and limited by, federal laws and regulations. This Summary concerns those provisions and limitations on honoraria.

SUMMARY

- An honorarium is the payment of money or anything else of value to an elected or appointed officer or employee of the federal government in return for an appearance, speech, or article by the official.

- Honoraria can be paid directly to the official by an incorporated association from its general funds (they are not considered political campaign contributions which corporations are prohibited from making). Honoraria may be used by the recipient federal official without restriction, although receipt of honoraria is subject to various limitations and reporting requirements applicable to the official. They are also includable in the official's taxable income and tax deductible for the official if given to charity.

- "Honoraria" does not include:
  - —Reasonable travel and subsistence expenses for the federal official, a spouse, or an aide
  - —Fees or commissions paid to an agent of the official
  - —Books
  - —Awards made in recognition of religious, educational, scientific, or civil achievement by the official
  - —Gifts
  - —Stipends or payment for the services of the official on a continuing basis
  - —Campaign contributions.

- No elected or appointed officer or employee of the federal government, including a member of Congress, may accept an honorarium in excess of $2,000.

- An honorarium is considered to be "accepted" when the official has actual or constructive receipt of it, has exercised dominion and control over it, and determines its subsequent use.

- Members of the House of Representatives may not receive total outside earned income, including honoraria, each year in excess of 30 percent of their Congressional salary; an honorarium is prohibited by the House rules if it is in excess of the usual and customary value of the services provided (i.e., the appearance, speech, or article).

- Members of the Senate are limited to maximum total honoraria each year of 40 percent of their Congressional salary.

- The official may designate a charitable organization to receive the payment, and it will then not be considered an "honorarium." At least the House of Representatives, however, will still require the member to report such designations to charities, although they will not count against the annual limit on outside earned income. A former requirement that the official provide a list of five or more charities, from which the organization making the honorarium must choose one, has been eliminated.

- Several Federal Election Commission advisory opinions have addressed honoraria:

—Payment of an honorarium and related expenses for an appearance, speech, or article is not a prohibited corporate political campaign contribution.

—The expense of providing a corporate aircraft to transport a federal official to an appearance or speech is not a campaign contribution.

—An honorarium could become a campaign contribution if there is an indication by the organization providing the honorarium of any purpose to influence a campaign for federal elective office.

—Payments received as honoraria can become campaign contributions if they are turned over to a candidate's campaign committee.

• Associations that pay honoraria to federal officials may be required in some circumstances to file with the Internal Revenue Service a Form 1099, which is used generally to report payments to independent contractors or others who receive income payments from the associations, when those payments exceed $600 annually. Penalties apply for failure to file Form 1099.

RESOURCES FOR CHAPTER 39

Books

Jacobs, "The Law of Lobbying" in *ASAE 3rd Annual Management Conference Proceedings*, 1985, page 330.

Statutes and Regulations

Federal Election Campaign Act, 2 U.S.C. 441i.
Federal Election Regulations, 11 C.F.R. 110.12.

Chapter 40

LOBBYING REGISTRATION

The Federal Regulation of Lobbying Act of 1946 requires that individuals and organizations that engage in lobbying at the federal level must register in advance and must file quarterly reports on their lobbying activities.

Federal court decisions have significantly narrowed the scope of who must register and report and of what activities constitute "lobbying" that triggers the registration and reporting requirements.

The federal lobbying regulation requirements are not burdensome. There have been many calls for increased federal lobbying regulation from members of Congress and from groups that consider the present requirements inadequate to permit detailed monitoring of lobbying activities.

Especially since the present law is relatively easy to comply with, associations that engage in any federal-level lobbying should be sure to pay careful attention to the requirements of the law and to comply scrupulously with those requirements. Substantial penalties can be levied against those who violate the law.

SUMMARY

- The Federal Regulation of Lobbying Act of 1946 requires public registration of "any person" whose "principal purpose" is to: (1) "aid . . . the passage or defeat of any legislation" or (2) "influence, directly or indirectly, the passage or defeat of any legislation by the Congress . . . ."

    —"Person" is defined as an individual, partnership, committee, association, corporation, and any other organization or group of persons.

—"Legislation" is defined as bills, resolutions, amendments, nominations, and other matters pending or proposed in either the Senate or the House of Representatives, and includes any other matter which may be the subject of action by either house.

—Exempted are: persons testifying before committees; public officials acting in their official capacity; members of the press while engaged in their regular business activity; and practices and activities regulated by another law, the Federal Corrupt Practices Act.

—The Act only applies to federal-level lobbying.

- The Supreme Court decision in *United States v. Harriss* limited the Act's registration requirement to those persons who have solicited, collected, or received contributions, the principal purpose of which is to influence the passage or defeat of legislation through "direct" lobbying communications with members of Congress. Many "lobbying" activities are not required to be reported, such as:

—Lobbying committee staff or the personal staff of members

—Efforts by trade or professional associations to encourage their members to "lobby" or influence the Congress

—Cooperative efforts between government contractors and federal agencies to influence the passage or defeat of legislation.

- Who are "persons" engaged in lobbying? Although court interpretations of the Act have been very few, they have made clear that only persons who have primarily solicited, collected, or received money or other things of value for lobbying purposes must register as lobbyists, even though the Act requires registration without regard to any payments.

—In the *Slaughter* case, persons assisting a witness in the preparation of testimony for a Congressional hearing were found not required to register under the Act.

—In the *U.S. Savings & Loan League* case, a person who agreed to lobby for pay, and then received partial payment but failed to register, did not violate

the Act since he had done nothing to influence legislation.

—Associations are covered by the Act's definition of
"person" if the associations employ persons to lobby
and gather legislative information of interest to association members.

- Registration is required only if one has solicited, collected, or received money for lobbying activities, and
the principal purpose of the contribution is to influence
legislation. According to the *Harriss* case, registration
is required only if a "substantial part" of activities is
directed to influence legislation through direct communication with Congress

- Another result of the *Harriss* case is that the Act covers
only activities which are "lobbying in its commonly
accepted sense—direct communications with Members of Congress on pending or proposed legislation
. . . ." Persons or organizations must register only if
they exert "direct" pressure themselves, "through their
hirelings or through an artificially stimulated letter
campaign . . . ."

  —"Direct" lobbying includes letters to, or conversations with, members of Congress about legislation;
communications with a member's staff or a committee staff are not considered "direct" lobbying.

  —Periodic inquiries on the status of legislation, and
"grass-roots" legislative programs in which letters
are sent to other organizations or members of the
public requesting that they write their legislators to
support certain legislation, are not considered "direct" lobbying.

- One must file with the Secretary of the Senate and the
Clerk of the House of Representatives before any lobbying activities commence. The registration form requires the registrant to state:

  —Its name, business address, and nature of business
  —The employer's name and address
  —The duration of employment
  —The nature and amount of anticipated expenses and
the rate of compensation
  —Who will pay the amount

—The general legislative interests of the registrant

—Specific legislative interests and positions

—Any publications to be distributed in connection with these legislative interests, plus their description, quantities distributed, date of distribution, and printer's name.

- Every quarter, a registered lobbyist must file detailed reports if, in that quarter, the lobbyist has received any contributions or expended any money principally to influence or accomplish the passage or defeat of legislation. The report requires disclosure of the names and addresses of those making contributions of $500 or more, but the amounts of their contributions need not be disclosed. Ten dollars is the threshold for reporting. Receipt of any money, loans, dues, assessments, and gifts of anything of value, must be listed.

- Any person who violates the Act may be convicted of a misdemeanor and fined not more than $5,000 or imprisoned for up to 12 months, or both. Further, for a period of three years from the date of conviction, the person is prohibited from engaging in lobbying on legislation or from appearing before a Congressional committee to discuss legislation. A willful violation of the Act constitutes a felony punishable by a $10,000 fine, or imprisonment for up to five years, or both.

RESOURCES FOR CHAPTER 40

Books

Boggs & Boyce, "Federal Regulation of Lobbying" in *Association Issues*, Jacobs, Editor, ASAE, 1983, page 85.

Jacobs, "The Law of Lobbying" in *ASAE 3rd Annual Management Conference Proceedings*, 1985, page 330.

Smith, "Associations and the Federal Regulation of Lobbying Act" in *Associations and the Law Book IV*, U.S. Chamber, 1971, page 1.

Webster & Krebs, *Associations & Lobbying Regulation*, U.S. Chamber, 1983.

Periodicals

Jacobs, "Federal Regulation of Lobbying Act," *Association Trends*, October 4, 1985, page 5.

Cases

United States v. Harriss, 347 U.S. 612 (1954). Applicability of federal lobbying registration and reporting.
United States v. Slaughter, 89 F. Supp. 876 (D. D.C. 1950). Applicability of federal lobbying registration and reporting.
United States v. U.S. Savings & Loan League, 9 F.R.D. 450 (D. D.C. 1949). Applicability of federal lobbying registration and reporting.

Statutes

Federal Regulation of Lobbying Act, 2 U.S.C. Sections 261–70.

Other Resources

Clerk of the House of Representatives, Federal Regulation of Lobbying Act, Outline of Instructions for Filing Reports (1967).

Chapter 41

LOBBYING AND FEDERAL CONTRACTS OR GRANTS

Most trade and professional associations are unaware of, and unaffected by, the complex area of federal contract and grant laws and regulations. This area only deserves an association's attention if the association happens to receive federal contract funds, for example to conduct testing or research, or if it receives federal grant funds, for example to develop educational programming or materials.

In the early 1980s, the federal government became concerned that some nonprofit social reform organizations were utilizing federal contract or grant money to conduct lobbying before Congress or at the federal agencies. The government's response was a directive issued by the Office of Management and Budget which applied the longstanding ban on the use of federal contract or grant funds for lobbying to the situation of nonprofit organizations, including associations.

This Summary concerns the OMB directive.

SUMMARY

- After a long and controversial proceeding, the Office of Management and Budget published in 1984 the final revision of its OMB Circular A-122 which describes what are not allowable as lobbying costs to nonprofit organizations such as associations that are federal contractors or recipients of federal grants.

- The Circular essentially implements a longtime statutory prohibition against the use of federal contract or grant funds to pay expenses of lobbying.

- OMB A-122 prohibits nonprofit organizations that receive federal contract or grant money from declaring certain lobbying expenses as costs reimbursable to the organizations by the federal government under the contracts or grants. The prohibited lobbying activities for which costs are not allowable include:

—Federal, state, or local electioneering and support of such entities as campaign organizations and political action committees

—Most direct lobbying of Congress and, with some exceptions, state legislatures, to influence legislation

—Lobbying of the federal Executive Branch in connection with decisions to sign or veto legislation

—Efforts to utilize state or local officials to lobby Congress or state legislatures

—Grass-roots lobbying concerning either federal or state legislation

—Legislative liaison activities in support of unallowable lobbying activities.

- A number of kinds of lobbying costs, however, are allowable under OMB A-122:

    —Lobbying at the local level

    —Lobbying to influence state legislation in order to directly reduce the cost of performing the contract or grant or to avoid impairing the organization's authority to do so

    —Lobbying in the form of technical and factual presentations to Congress or state legislatures at their request

    —Contacts with federal Executive Branch officials other than lobbying for the veto or signing of enrolled bills

    —Lobbying on regulatory actions.

- OMB A-122 makes unallowable as costs for nonprofit federal contractors or grant recipients only the allocable portion of costs attributed to lobbying; it also permits employees of nonprofit federal contractors or grant recipients to avoid time logs or calendars to determine allocation of costs if the organizations certify that less than 25 percent of the time of these employees is spent in the lobbying activities for which costs are not allowable.

- The standard penalty for violating OMB Circular A-122

is recovery of the misspent money by the federal government agency involved. In cases of serious abuse, however, the federal grant or contract may be suspended or terminated, or the nonprofit organization recipient may be barred from receiving further federal grants or contracts for a specified period.

RESOURCES FOR CHAPTER 41

Books

Jacobs, "The Law of Lobbying" in *ASAE 3rd Annual Management Conference Proceedings*, 1985, at page 330.

Periodicals

Webster, "OMB Release Final Version of OMB A-122," *Association Management*, February, 1984, at page 51.

Other Resources

OMB Circular A-122, 49 *Federal Register* 18259, April 27, 1984.

III

ASSOCIATION ANTITRUST

Chapter 42

DISCUSSIONS AT MEETINGS

Discussions at association meetings often cover broad ranges of issues pertinent to the interests or concerns of participants. As a general rule, discussions can address any subject without raising antitrust concerns if the discussions are kept scrupulously free of even the suggestion of private regulation of an industry or profession. Participants should be aware that opinions expressed or conclusions reached at association meetings can never be binding upon them. The opinions or conclusions are no more than informative presentations upon which participants may act as each considers appropriate. A participant should always have the right to object to the discussion of any subject which might present legal problems. The advice of legal counsel can then be obtained. Some subjects clearly are not appropriate for discussion; others very likely are appropriate. A few of each are listed here.

A number of association policies or programs that might be discussed at association meetings raise issues of antitrust and trade regulation that are most complex and have long series of court and agency decisions and opinions relating to them. These areas include membership restrictions, categories, and termination; membership services to nonmembers; trade show restrictions; business or professional codes; statistical programs; price activities; cost programs; standardization and simplification; product certification; professional restrictions and credentialing; joint research; credit reporting; group buying and selling; and others. Each of these has a separate summary on antitrust implications in succeeding chapters in this book.

SUMMARY

- Participants at association meetings, whether they be meetings of the membership, the governing board, of-

215

ficers, committees, or subcommittees, must be made aware that discussions of certain subjects raise grave antitrust dangers and therefore must be avoided.

- From a negative point of view, and in very general terms, there must be no discussions at association meetings that may in any way tend to:
  —Raise, lower, or stabilize prices or fees
  —Regulate production levels or schedules
  —Affect the availability of product or services
  —Affect allocation of markets, territories, customers, or patients
  —Encourage boycotts of products or services
  —Foster unfair practices involving advertising, merchandising, standardization, certification, or accreditation
  —Encourage anyone to refrain from competing
  —Limit or exclude anyone from manufacture, sale, or practice
  —Result in illegal brokerage or rebates
  —Affect improper reciprocity in dealing.

- A publication by the American Society of Association Executives lists the following topics of discussion which must be avoided at association meetings:
  —Current or future prices (great care must be taken in discussing past prices)
  —What constitutes a "fair" profit level
  —Possible increases or decreases in prices
  —Standardization or stabilization of prices
  —Pricing procedures
  —Cash discounts
  —Credit terms
  —Control of sales
  —Allocation of markets
  —Refusal to deal with a corporation because of its pricing or distribution practices
  —Whether or not the pricing practices of any industry member are unethical or constitute an unfair trade practice.

- Another commentator on antitrust compliance suggests a list of subjects that should ordinarily be avoided in discussions with competitors, e.g., at association meetings, lest an understanding or agreement on the subjects, express or implied, be effected and subsequently challenged:

—Prices
—Costs
—Profits
—Product or service offerings
—Terms or conditions of sale
—Deliveries
—Production facilities or capacity
—Production or sales volume
—Market share
—Decisions to quote or not to quote
—Customer or supplier classification, allocation, or selection
—Sales territories
—Distribution methods or channels.

● From a positive point of view, ordinarily there can be appropriate discussions at association meetings that have as a purpose or result:

—Reporting on general industry or profession economic trends
—Describing advances or problems in relevant technology or research
—Demonstrating methods by which an individual or firm can become more profitable by acquiring better knowledge of its own costs
—Summarizing effective methods of purchasing, manufacturing, and marketing
—Educating about various aspects of the science and art of management
—Considering industry or profession relations with local, state, or federal governments
—Reporting on experiences and developments in employment relations
—Relating efforts toward improvement of products
—Developing ways to respond individually to "consumerists" and "environmentalists"
—Effecting energy usage and supply.

● These very general lists of appropriate and inappropriate discussion goals or subjects are far from exhaustive or unequivocal. An area quite appropriate for discussion can be rendered inappropriate by an improper approach to it. The lists are illustrative only.

● If any area of association legal concerns justifies constant and intense monitoring by legal counsel experienced in antitrust implications of association policies and programs, it is the area of meeting discussions. The ramifications of antitrust laws and trade regulations are subtle and dynamic. They are not necessarily avoided merely by avoiding discussions in areas indicated in this Summary. By all means, associations should seek expert advice on the appropriateness of meeting discussions whenever questions are raised.

RESOURCES FOR CHAPTER 42

Books

Lamb & Shields, *Trade Association Law and Practice*, Little, Brown, 1971, page 232.

MacArthur, *Associations and the Antitrust Laws*, U.S. Chamber, 1984, page 78.

MacArthur, "An Antitrust Guide for Association Members" in *Associations and the Law Book IX*, U.S. Chamber, 1979, page 62.

MacArthur, "Dangers in Discussing Prices at Association Meetings" in *Associations and the Law Book III*, U.S. Chamber, 1969, page 46.

Menzines & Fellman, *Antitrust Guide for Association Members*, ASAE.

Periodicals

"National Institute on Preventive Antitrust," *ABA Antitrust L.J.*, 1980, page 265.

Rich, "The Conduct of Trade Association Meetings," *Brooklyn L. Rev.*, Winter, 1980, page 181.

Other Resources

FTC Advisory Opinions 16 C.F.R. Sections 15.85 (1966), .137 (1967), .199 (1968), .281 (1968), and .407 (1970).

Chapter 43

MEMBERSHIP RESTRICTIONS

Almost every association seeks to attract as members the greatest number of businesses or practitioners in the trade or profession represented by it. To obtain broad participation is beneficial to an association because it maximizes revenues and minimizes the share of expenses borne by each member. It assures an association access to a cross-section of firms or individuals in the trade or profession and to a sufficient number of interested and active participants in the association's affairs. It allows the association to approach government entities and other organizations as a true spokesman for the trade or profession. Thus, the advantages of wide representation by an association are manifest. Any policy to arbitrarily or unnecessarily limit association membership seems ill-advised and can be suspect.

There can be serious legal problems for an association which unreasonably restricts membership. Associations exist to provide information and services which enable firms to do business more successfully and enable practitioners to be more proficient in their professions. Because belonging to an association is beneficial, competitors of the association's members may be placed at an unfair disadvantage if denied access to the information and services received by the members. A significant impairment of the ability to even one nonmember to compete with those who are members of an association could be a violation of the antitrust laws.

Obviously, there must be some limits or restrictions on the availability of association membership. Without any curbs, an organization might grow too large to be functional. Limitations as to the type of business or profession from which members are drawn or as to the geographic area from which members are drawn are necessary and can be imposed if done so in ways that are not unreasonable.

The first problem of association membership is to delineate membership requirements so as to assure that they are not unfairly restrictive. Beyond membership definitions there

are other potential problem areas such as membership clas-
sifications, expulsion from membership, and availability of
association member services to nonmembers. These areas are
discussed in succeeding chapters.

SUMMARY

- Association membership is ordinarily a *privilege* which
  may be granted or denied if done so on reasonable
  grounds; but association membership may sometimes
  become a *right* when denial of it would result in a
  serious economic disadvantage to outsiders.

- Members derive commercial and professional benefits
  from associations; to restrict from membership one who
  is part of the trade or profession represented by the
  association may deprive him of the ability to compete
  on an equal basis with association members and, thus,
  may violate the antitrust laws.

- The greater the competitive advantage derived from
  association membership, the more likely it is that exclusion of a competitor from membership will be considered an unreasonable restraint of trade in violation
  of the antitrust laws.

- Associations ordinarily may restrict membership to
  persons or firms engaged in the same kind of trade or
  profession (e.g., the widget industry).

- Associations ordinarily may restrict membership to those
  engaged in a particular functional level within the trade
  or profession (e.g., widget distributors).

- Associations ordinarily may restrict membership to those
  engaged in a trade or business within some recognized
  geographic boundaries (e.g., widget dealers of Minnesota).

- Associations ordinarily may restrict membership to those
  willing to adhere to a reasonable code, business or
  professional, and able to promptly pay dues.

- Additional qualifications for association membership

may or may not be reasonable restrictions depending upon whether they arbitrarily exclude bona fide persons or firms in direct competition with members. Types of membership qualifications which must be assessed on this basis include:

—Requirements that members meet some minimum size in terms of sales, employees, production, etc.
—Stipulations of minimum percentage amounts of total business or practice of members that must be engaged in the trade or profession represented by the association (e.g., at least 80 percent of firm sales must be in widget manufacturing)
—Requirements for minimum numbers of years in which members must have engaged in the trade or practiced in the profession represented by the association
—Requisite educational background or achievement of certification, accreditation, or other private or governmental credentialing
—Arrangements in which association membership is available only to those belonging to another organization (e.g., members of the local association chapter must belong to the national or vice versa)
—Requirements that members must manufacture goods in the United States.

• Restrictions on association membership because of race, religion, or sex are ordinarily not permissible; the same is true of restrictions based merely on unpopular business or professional views or practices of applicants (e.g., "price discounting").

• Examples of restrictions which have been prohibited in particular factual situations of decided or settled cases (listed under Resources) include:

—Allowing existing members to block or "blackball" prospective members of a news-gathering association arbitrarily or to prohibit dissemination of association newsgathering services to nonmembers
—Limiting membership in a florists telegraph association to only one florist in each city, excluding from membership any florist that is a member of a competing association and barring members from dealing with nonmember florist groups

—Limiting membership in a florists telegraph association to those not also engaged in any unrelated
business endeavors

—Drawing geographical boundary lines for membership on a local tobacco board in order to specifically
exclude an unwelcome competitor

—Granting members of a cooperative trailer rental association the right to be exclusive members within
their areas of operation

—Restricting participation in an association's bowling
tournament to those who have bowled at members'
establishments; note that, in another situation, a
professional golfers association was allowed to restrict participation in its golf tournaments to members and approved players

—Arbitrarily eliminating physicians from medical association membership where only members have
hospital use privileges

—Requiring that members of a fireplace accessories
association maintain a certain substantial dollar
amount of stock in trade and refrain from selling
through nonmember dealers.

● An important case for federated associations involved
an antitrust challenge by several dentists against a
local dental society, a state dental society, and a national dental society all of which required that, to join
any one of the groups, a dentist must also belong to
the other two of the three groups. The court examined
the reasonableness of the challenged "tie-in" between
membership in one component of the federation and
membership in the other two components; it concluded
that there was no monopoly or other illegal restraint
of trade and relied upon several important factors in
the case:

—It was not necessary to belong to any of federated
groups in order to practice dentistry.

—A large minority (25%) of the dentists in the local area
did not belong to the groups.

—Nonmembers could purchase services or products
sponsored by any of the three component groups.

—A referral service maintained by the local dental society was not a major factor for the practices of any

of the challenging dentists (*Boddicker* listed in Resources).

- Another important case on association membership restrictions involved requirements for participation in a real estate multiple listing service which were challenged by the federal government as excessive and unjustifiable. The multiple listing service required that each applicant (1) be a real estate broker licensed by the state, (2) have a favorable credit report and business reputation, (3) maintain an active real estate office open during customary business hours, and (4) pay a $1000 fee. The appellate court refused to hold restrictions (2) through (4) illegal on their face but held instead that they were apparently unreasonable, and therefore likely illegal under the Sherman Act. The case was sent back to the lower court for a final decision. The appellate court offered the following rules for examining the reasonableness of association membership restrictions:

  —"The more directly the association is involved in its member's business, the more likely it is that exclusion from membership will produce concrete anti-competitive effects."
  —The greater the economic power possessed by an association "to shape and influence the economic environment of the particular field involved," the greater the antitrust dangers from exclusionary membership policies.
  —Restrictive membership rules "must be shown to be justified by the legitimate competitive needs of the association."
  —"The requirements of the rules themselves must be reasonably necessary to the accomplishment of the legitimate goals and narrowly tailored to that end."
  —"Where (an association) seeks to establish the reasonable necessity of membership criteria regulating areas already generally covered by state regulation, it must make a showing either that the legitimate needs of the (association) require protection in excess of that provided by the state or that the state does not adequately enforce its own regulations."
  —"Subjective membership criteria are generally not

narrowly tailored to accomplish any legitimate goal of an association." (*Realty Multi-List* listed in Resources).

- An official of the Department of Justice has capsulized the antitrust principles of association membership restrictions as follows:

  —Membership rules may not seek to intentionally exclude competitors from access to the competitively significant benefits of membership. To do so is *per se* unlawful.

  —Membership rules that are designed to enhance the operation of industry markets should be reasonably related to the legitimate *procompetitive* purposes of the association. Rules should not attempt to exclude new members for reasons other than the enhancement of competition or market efficiency.

  —Rules that seek to further legitimate competitive ends must not be drawn overly broad, eliminating more competitors than necessary to accomplish their legitimate procompetitive ends.

  —Rules that restrict the participation of members in other competing groups or in other procompetitive activities also may not withstand antitrust scrutiny. They may well be broader than necessary to serve any legitimate competitive interest of the association.

  —Membership fees charged to new members which are excessive and do not represent a fair share of costs may unreasonably exclude competition without furthering a competitive need of the association.

  —Rules which require evidence of the bona fides and competitive capabilities of new members will be acceptable only if they are narrowly drawn to ensure that (1) these factors are measured by objective criteria and (2) they address the actual competitive needs of the association and do not exclude more members than necessary to achieve this narrowly drawn competitive end.

  —Membership rules must not restrict the ability of members to compete in ways that are not related to the legitimate goals of the association. For example, they should not restrict the hours of a member's business, nor should they restrict a member's ability to expand into new markets or new industries. (Remarks of R. Favretto listed in Resources).

RESOURCES FOR CHAPTER 43

Books

Althen, "Antitrust Laws and the Interrelated Membership Requirements of National, State and Local Associations" in *Associations and the Law Book VI*, U.S. Chamber, 1975, page 1.

Combs & Herold, "Antitrust Implications of Membership Requirements" in *Associations and the Law Book VII*, U.S. Chamber, 1976, page 6.

Hammond, "Antitrust Problems of Associations" in *Trade and Professional Associations*, Hammond, Editor, Practising Law Institute, 1977, page 204.

Herold, "Antitrust Implications of Refusing Membership to Foreign Competitors" in *Associations and the Law Book V*, U.S. Chamber, 1973, page 16.

Lamb, "Legal Aspects of Denying Association Membership" in *Associations and the Law Book I*, U.S. Chamber, 1967, page 4.

Lamb & Shields, *Trade Association Law and Practice*, Little, Brown, 1971, page 201.

MacArthur, *Associations and the Antitrust Laws*, U.S. Chamber, 1984, page 36.

Olson, "Trade Associations and Other Associations of Competitors," Chapter 7 of *Antitrust Advisor* 3rd Edition, Hills, Editor, Shepard's/McGraw-Hill, 1971, age 495.

Webster, *The Law of Associations*, Matthew Bender, 1976, pages 2–51.

Webster & Herold, *Antitrust Guide for Association Executives*, ASAE, 1979, page 37.

Webster, Herold, & Dye, *Association Legal Checklist*, U.S. Chamber, 1983, pages 20-22.

Periodicals

Althen, "The Lessons of *Boddicker v. Arizona State Dental Association, "Association Letter*, October, 1980, page 3.

Anderson, "Legal Guidelines Affecting Association Membership," GWSAE *Executive Update,* January, 1986, page 25.

Anderson, "Your Association Membership Requirements—Will They Withstand FTC Scrutiny?," GWSAE *Executive Update,* April, 1984, page 17.

Bodner, "Antitrust Restrictions on Trade Association Membership and Participation: Recent Developments," *N.Y.L.S.L. Rev.* 1979, page 907.

Bodner, "Antitrust Restrictions on Trade Association Membership and Participation," *A.B.A.J.,* 1968, page 555.

Fellman & Hart, "Restrictions on Membership and Advertising May Cause Antitrust Problems," *Association Management,* August, 1978, page 88.

Haddock, "The Right of Trade Associations to Deny Membership and to Expel Members," *Antitrust Bull.,* 1968, page 555.

Herold, "What Can an Association Do to Meet Foreign Competition?," *Antitrust Bull.,* 1973, page 181.

Howe, "A Different Sort of Reference Check: Does Your Association Require Provision of Information in Accepting Members?," *Association Trends,* March 14, 1986, page 8.

"Judicial Intervention in Admission Decisions of Private Professional Associations," *U. Chicago L. Rev.,* Summer, 1982, page 840.

Webster, "Can You Bar Foreign Members from Membership?," *Association Management,* January, 1984, page 47.

Cases

Associated Press v. United States, 362 U.S. 1 (1945). Existing members "blackballing" prospective members.

United States v. Florists' Telegraph Delivery Assn., (1956) Trade Reg. Rep. (CCH) para. 68,367 (E.D. Mich. 1956). Limiting members to one per city.

United States v. Florists' Transworld Delivery Assn., (1969) Trade Reg. Rep. (CCH) para. 72,717 (E.D. Mich. 1969). Membership exclusion because of other business affiliations.

American Federation of Tobacco Growers v. Neal, 183 F.2d 869 (4th Cir. 1950). Arbitrary geographic boundary for membership.

United States v. Nationwide Trailer Rental System, 156 F. Supp. 800 (D. Kan. 1956). Assignment of exclusive memberships by geographic areas.

Washington State Bowling Proprietors' Assn., Inc. v. Pacific Lanes, Inc., 356 F.2d 371 (9th Cir. 1966). Tournament participation denied to patrons of nonmembers.

Deesen v. Professional Golfers' Assn. of America, 358 F.2d 165 (9th Cir. 1966), *cert. denied*, 385 U.S. 846 (1966). Limitation of tournament participants to association members.

Falcone v. Middlesex County Medical Society, 170 A.2d 791 (N.J. 1961). Arbitrary medical society membership denial.

Montague & Co. v. Lowry, 193 U.S. 38 (1904). Minimum inventory requirement as prerequisite to membership.

Grillo v. Board of Realtors, 219 A.2d 635 (N.J. Super. 1966). Access to multiple listing service tied to membership.

Marjorie Webster Jr. College v. Middle States Assn. of Colleges & Secondary Schools, 302 F. Supp. 459 (D. D.C. 1969), *rev'd.*, 432 F. 2d 650 (D.C. Cir. 1970). Denial of membership because school is proprietary rather than non-profit.

Silver v. New York Stock Exchange, 373 U.S. 341 (1963). Denial of membership as boycott; need for fair procedures.

United States v. Material Handling Institute, (1973) Trade Reg. Rep. (CCH) para. 74,362 (W.D. Pa. 1973). Exclusion of foreign competitors.

Boddicker v. Arizona State Dental Assn., 549 F.2d 626 (9th Cir. 1977), *cert. denied*, 434 U.S. 825 (1978). Challenge to conditioning membership in one association upon membership in another.

Other Resources

FTC Advisory Opinions 16 C.F.R. Sections 15.64 (1966), .335 (1976), .336 (1969), .488 (1974), and (uncodified) to National Electronics Service Dealers Assn., Inc. (1974).

Chapter 44

MEMBERSHIP CLASSES
AND SECTIONS

Associations frequently separate their membership into several classes in order to distinguish varying rights and obligations of different types of members. Likewise, associations frequently separate their membership into several sections in order to facilitate communication and activity among members whose specific concerns are not shared by all members of the association.

Examples of *classes* of association membership include regular, associate, technical, and so forth. Typically, additional classes of membership are established when those most directly involved find that they can benefit from participation of others involved only indirectly or in a different way. In a trade association, manufacturers may want to attract suppliers to the manufacturers. In a professional association, graduate licensed professionals may want to attract students or assistants to the professionals.

Examples of *sections* of association members include research, labor relations, education, etc. Typically, associations divide their membership into different sections when all members have common interests in some aspects of what the association represents or is doing—communications, government affairs, or whatever—but some segments of the membership have additional interests in matters relating more specifically to them. Thus, an association of manufacturers might have sections dealing with each type of product made by member firms. A professional association might have sections dealing with specialities within the profession.

Legal issues concerning classes and sections of membership include restrictiveness of classes, roles of supplier and foreign members, and relationships of sections to their association.

SUMMARY

- Associations often have different classes of members for groups which join the association in different ways, for different reasons, or from different functional levels of an industry or profession. Regular, full, or sustaining members are distinguished from other kinds such as associates, supplier, honorary, professional, technician, student, retired, provisional, domestic, foreign, manufacturer, distributor, retailer, assistant, trade press, firm, and individual.

- Suppliers of goods or services to regular association members should be admitted to membership in a class only where they can make significant contributions beyond merely promoting and selling their products and services. Where suppliers are interested in furthering an industry or profession by sponsoring education and research efforts, public relations drives, legislative and other governmental activities, their participation by way of a separate membership class could be most beneficial.

- Some potential for antitrust difficulties exists inevitably whenever sellers and customers belong to an association together. In such circumstances, particularly rigorous policies and procedures should be established to minimize the likelihood of illegal discussions or activities involving prices or terms of sale, boycotting of suppliers, allocations of markets or customers, and other dangerous areas (see consent decree cases listed in Resources).

- Classes of membership in associations may be established for foreign members where they can benefit from participation and contribute at the same time. Where foreign individuals or firms are operating in the United States in direct competition with domestic firms, it may be necessary or desirable to admit them on the same basis as regular members rather than in separate classes.

- Associations often have different sections for members who have different or more intense interests beyond the general interests common to all members. Sections may be formed, for example, in areas or with denominations such as technical, research, statistical, labor relations, occupational safety, educational, public relations, or traffic.

- In one recent antitrust challenge, against a professional association of dental specialists that limited the association's highest membership category to those who practice exclusively in the specialty, and brought by a dental specialist who practiced in that specialty and in others as well, the dental specialist claimed that denial of membership in the highest category of the association resulted in a loss of referrals from other dentists who use the association's membership directory to make referrals. The federal appellate court ordered that there be consideration of whether (1) the limitation has a pro-competitive effect, (2) it increases the quality of patient care, and (3) it is the least restrictive means to achieve the ends sought by the association.

- Sections of associations might have separate programs and activities, separate boards, separately assigned association staff, and other aspects of autonomy. If they remain without separate legal identities such as through incorporation, the rights and liabilities of the sections will ordinarily be attributed to the main association itself. For this reason, the relationship between the association and each of its sections should be clearly set out in the association bylaws, in a charter for the sections or in some other document. Aspects of the relationship which may be covered in such a document include:

  —General and specific authority of the association over the sections
  —Membership in the sections
  —Sources, control, use, and depository or section finances
  —Association staff assignments and assistance to the sections
  —Election or appointment of leadership for the sections
  —Activities and programs of the sections.

RESOURCES FOR CHAPTER 44

Books

Lamb & Shields, *Trade Association Law and Practice*, Little, Brown, 1971, page 218.

Periodicals

Howe, "A Different Sort of Reference Check: Does Your Association Require Provision of Information in Accepting Members?," *Association Trends*, March 14, 1986, page 8.

Webster, "International, State, and Local Chapters" in *Managing Membership Societies*, ASAE, 1979, page 71.

Cases

United States v. National Audio-Visual Assn., Inc., (1977) Trade Reg. Rep. (CCH) para. 68,833 (E.D. Va. 1977). Customers urging suppliers not to deal with nonmembers.

United States v. Allied Florists Assn. of Ill., (1952–1953 Transfer Binder) Trade Reg. Rep. (CCH) para 67,433 (N.D. Ill. 1953). Customers urging suppliers not to deal with nonmembers.

United States v. United Fruit Co., (1958) Trade Reg. Rep. (CCH) para. 68,941 (E.D. La. 1958). Suppliers urging customers against certain dealings.

United States v. Republic Steel Corp., (1952–1953 Transfer Binder) Trade Reg. Rep. (CCH) para. 67,510 (N.D. Ohio 1953). Suppliers urging customers against certain dealings.

Kreuzer v. American Academy of Periodontology, (1984) Trade Reg. Rep. (CCH) para. 66,029 (D.C. Cir. 1984).

Other Resources

FTC Advisory Opinion 16 C.F.R. Section 15.336 (1969).

Chapter 45

MEMBERSHIP TERMINATION

Termination of association membership most often occurs on the initiative of a member who no longer is part of the industry or profession represented by the association or, for whatever other reasons, no longer values membership in the association and stops paying dues. Voluntary termination in this way presents few legal problems other than the right of the association to collect any unpaid dues and the right of the former member to a share in association property.

Likewise, there are few legal problems when the association on its own initiative terminates the membership of a member for failure to comply with basic administrative requirements such as payment of dues.

Beyond these routine situations, involuntary termination of association membership nearly always raises questions of anticompetitive motives and restraint of trade. The antitrust laws may be violated when association membership offers an economic advantage, and a member is expelled for violating arbitrary ethical, social, or economic rules or customs of the association or its other members.

In the same way that restrictions on joining associations can be challenged when they arbitrarily exclude from membership those who could derive benefit from the associations and are in competition with members, expulsion of members can also be challenged on similar antitrust grounds.

Before expelling any members against their wishes, an association must be certain that the reasons for expulsion are legitimate and not anticompetitive. The association must also follow several procedural steps to assure that the members have adequate notice of the charges and reasonable opportunity to refute them.

In short, expulsion of members almost always involves sensitive legal issues; it is a matter for which the advice of legal counsel is essential.

SUMMARY

- Termination of association membership most often occurs at the request of the member; since association membership is not compulsory, resignations must be accepted.

- Members who resign from an association while owing dues have legally enforceable obligations to the association. This is true for all payments that become due before resignation even when the association requires dues to be paid in advance for a future period such as the upcoming year. As a practical matter, the association may decide not to sue upon these obligations and to reach a satisfactory settlement with the former member in the hope that the member might someday rejoin.

- Generally, a member's right to the property of a voluntary, nonprofit association, whether incorporated or not, ends when the member leaves the association, whether voluntarily or involuntarily. This is provided by law in some states; it may be made clear in the association's bylaws, if desired. An exception may exist when an association is about to dissolve and the property of the association is to be distributed to members. In this circumstance, it may be fair to set aside *pro rata* shares of the association's property for those whose membership was terminated just before dissolution. Of course, for tax-exemption reasons in most associations it is provided that any remaining property at dissolution is distributed not to members but to some other exempt organization. In those cases, property rights of members are not a consideration.

- Termination of association membership involuntarily—expulsion—may occur without any particular legal consequences when the reason for termination is simply nonpayment of dues, withdrawal from the industry or profession, loss of required government licensing, or failure to comply with other reasonable association rules which are unrelated to competition among members.

- Involuntary termination may raise serious potential

antitrust problems when the reason for expulsion is the failure of a member to comply with association-promulgated business or professional codes, ethics requirements, or other arbitrary conditions imposed by the association or by other members.

- Just as qualified participants in a trade or profession cannot arbitrarily be deprived of association membership when they first apply, they cannot be arbitrarily stripped of membership if they are in competition with other members and obtain significant business or professional benefits from the association.

- The greater the economic benefit one derives from the association, the more likely it is that expulsion based upon inappropriate or unreasonable criteria could be found to be anticompetitive and in restraint of trade.

- To assure that no member is expelled from an association arbitrarily, certain procedural safegaurds must be used (except, perhaps, in instances such as termination for nonpayment of dues):

  —Requirements for maintaining association membership must be reasonably related to the proper purposes of the association and must not have primarily anticompetitive effects.
  —Requirements for maintaining membership must be clearly explained in some document given to all members (this may be the association bylaws).
  —Any board or committee considering expulsion of a member must do so only upon the basis of criteria explained in that document.
  —Formal procedures for receiving and acting upon requests for expulsion should be established and adhered to strictly.
  —A member facing expulsion should be given a written notice which includes a description of the charges.
  —There should be an opportunity for the member to appear in person or to be represented by someone before the board or committee considering expulsion so that a response may be made to charges; or, at the discretion of the member, there should be an opportunity to respond to the charges in writing.
  —In cases where a committee considers and recom-

mends expulsion, there should be an opportunity of
appeal to the board of directors or highest governing
board.

—If it was the board of directors that originally considered and decided upon the expulsion, it may provide additional legal defense safegaurds to offer an
appeal to some special body established for that purpose (perhaps an *ad hoc* appeals board comprised
of distinguished members of the industry or profession, past chief elected officers of the association,
etc.).

- In a recent United States Supreme Court decision, at
issue was the expulsion of a firm from a stationery
buying cooperative association with apparently no due
process provided to the expelled firm. The Court said
that the lack of due process in making the expulsion
was not, in itself, enough to warrant review of the expulsion in an antitrust challenge under the rigorous
per se test (in which the motives of the association
would not be considered as mitigating the potential
violation); rather, according to the Court, the reasonableness test would still be used (the expulsion would
be found to violate the antitrust laws only if it was
unreasonable). The Court said one must look to whether
the cooperative association possessed market power
or exclusive access to an element essential for competition in the stationery business in this area.

RESOURCES FOR CHAPTER 45

Books

Johnson, "Legal Aspects of Terminating Association Membership" in *Associations and the Law Book III*, U.S. Chamber,
1969, page 24.

Lamb & Shields, *Trade Association Law and Practice*, Little,
Brown, 1971, page 219.

MacArthur, *Associations and the Antitrust Laws*, U.S. Chamber, 1984, page 36.

Webster & Herold, *Antitrust Guide for Association Executives*,
ASAE, 1977, page 44.

Periodicals

"Exclusion from Private Associations," *Yale L.J.*, 1965, page 1313.

Howe, "A Different Sort of Reference Check: Does Your Association Require Provision of Information in Accepting Members?," *Association Trends*, March 14, 1986, page 8.

"Judicial Review of Expulsion Actions in Voluntary Associations," *Washburn L.J.*, 1966, page 160.

Cases

Silver v. New York Stock Exchange, 373 U.S. 341 (1973). Lack of fair procedures.

McCreery Angus Farms v. American Angus Assn., 379 F. Supp. 1008 (S.D. Ill. 1974), *aff'd*, 506 F.2d 1404 (7th Cir. 1974). Lack of fair procedures.

United States v. Southern Wholesale Grocers' Assn., 207 F. Supp. 434 (N.D. Ala. 1913). Appropriate grounds for expulsion when membership definitional requirements not met.

Northwest Wholesale Stationers, Inc. v. Pacific Stationery & Printing Co., (1985-1) Trade Reg. Rep. (CCH) para. 66,640 (S.Ct. 1985). Expulsion from buying cooperative association.

Other Resources

FTC Advisory Opinion 16 C.F.R. Section 15.488 (1974).

Chapter 46

MEMBERSHIP SERVICES TO NONMEMBERS

Every association strives to develop and furnish services which members consider necessary or desirable in their businesses or professions. An association that can offer basic, valuable membership services has the greatest chance of retaining existing members and attracting new ones. Ideally, the association hopes to provide educational publications or statistical studies, meeting or seminar participation, liaison with federal or local government, and other valuable services which cannot be obtained elsewhere. Among the most accurate measures of the success of any association are the quality and importance of its membership services.

With this in mind, it often comes as a surprise to associations to learn that many membership services must be made available even to nonmembers when there are requests to do so. As disconcerting as this tenet may be, the reasons for it are simple.

Just as association membership itself may not be denied to those who compete with association members and could receive economic benefit from membership, so also association membership services cannot be denied to those who choose not to join. To do either might be considered anticompetitive or in restraint of trade.

Association services need not be advertised or promoted to nonmembers. Nonmembers may be charged more than members for requested services to the extent that association dues income helps support those services. In a few instances, like statistical studies, it may be possible to restrict receipt of the results of an association service only to those (members or nonmembers) who chose to participate in the first place. But these qualifications do not dilute the basic principle—association services which involve significant competitive or economic advantage must be available to members and nonmembers alike.

SUMMARY

- In the same way that association membership must be available to those who would be competitively harmed if denied membership, services of an association must be available to those who would be competitively harmed if denied the services because they are not members.

- The only "exclusive membership services" of an association should be those which cannot be considered to confer important competitive or economic benefit (attendance at association business meetings, for example).

- The greater the competitive advantage derived from an association service, the more likely it is that refusing to furnish the service to nonmembers will be considered an unreasonable restraint of trade in violation of the antitrust laws.

- The theory of the requirement is that it would be unfair to tie together the obtaining of some isolated association service to the obtaining of all association services by requiring that membership be an absolute prerequisite. Antitrust cases have frequently held these "tying arrangements" to be illegal.

- The requirement is also supported by the fact that a tax-exempt association enjoys that status because it exists to benefit an entire industry or profession. To restrict association services to members alone might jeopardize tax-exempt status. In a case involving the Glass Container Industry Research Corporation, it was held that the organization was not entitled to exempt status because it did not make its research available to nonmembers.

- Membership services do not have to be advertised or promoted to nonmembers.

- Nonmembers may be charged more than members are charged for association services to take into account the fact that the nonmembers pay no dues. Nonmember charges should be reasonably related to the extent to which dues income supports the services being sought.

Nonmember charges for services should not be so high as to effectively compel joining the association; this, it could be argued, might violate the principle of availability of membership services to nonmembers.

- Participation at association meetings should be available to nonmembers where the subjects of the meetings go beyond mere internal association business and cover subjects that confer significant economic or business information of competitive value. If space limitations prohibit participation by nonmembers, tapes or transcripts of the meetings should be available to them upon request.

- In research, testing, consultant, and other association projects which do not involve participation by individuals or firms but do involve competitive advantages for those who receive the results, results should be available to nonmembers. In two antitrust cases involving automobile pollution control research and railroad car coupling research, court orders prohibited restrictions on publicizing the results of the research to nonparticipants.

- Programs for the favorable purchasing of insurance, supplies, travel arrangements, or other goods or services, to the extent they offer important economic or business benefits of competitive value, should also be available to nonmembers.

- In statistical studies, certification programs, credit reporting programs, research, testing, consultant, and other projects which involve active participation by individuals or firms, such as the submission of data, results should be available as follows:

  —The association member who participates in the project should have access to its results.
  —The nonmember should be allowed to participate and have access to the results, but may be charged a higher fee than is charged to members.
  —The association member who does not participate may be denied access to the results of the project.
  —The nonmember who does not participate in the project, but had an opportunity to do so, may also be denied access to the results of the project.

—Suppliers and customers of those who participate in the project may also be entitled to its results according to some decided antitrust cases. (*Sugar Institute* and *Tag Manufacturers*, listed in Resources).

—Rental of booth space at association sponsored trade shows is one service that seems clearly to offer a significant competitive benefit. Booth space should be available to members and nonmembers alike on a first-come, first-serve basis with no particular booths reserved for members only (*Western Winter Sports Representatives* and *Women's and Children's Apparel Salesmen* cases in Resources).

—Requests from nonmembers can be viewed positively rather than negatively—once the service is furnished, a vigorous appeal can be made for the nonmember to join.

—To avoid completely any problems of restricting services to members, some associations have promulgated the policy of making all of their business, professional, educational and similar services available to members and nonmembers alike, although at higher rates for the nonmembers.

RESOURCES FOR CHAPTER 46

Books

Herold, "Antitrust, Trade Regulation, and Other Nontax Aspects of Association Activities" in *Managing Membership Societies*, Grief, Editor, ASAE, 1979, page 123.

Herold, "Association Services for Non-Members" in *Associations and the Law Book IX*, U.S. Chamber, 1979, page 34.

Hopkins, *The Law of Tax-Exempt Organizations*, Ronald Press, 1979, page 269.

MacArthur, *Associations and the Antitrust Laws*, U.S. Chamber, 1984, page 36.

Webster & Herold, *Antitrust Guide for Association Executives*, ASAE, 1979, page 127.

Webster, Herold, & Dye, *Association Legal Checklist*, U.S. Chamber, 1983, pages 35–37.

Periodicals

Fellman, "What Services Must a Trade Association Render to Nonmembers?," *Antitrust Bull.*, 1973, page 167.

Herold, "Association Services: Can You Legally Say No to Non-Members?" *Association Management*, February, 1983, page 71.

Cases

United States v. Associated Press, 326 U.S. 1 (1946). Access to wire service denied to nonmembers.

International Salt Co. v. United States, 332 U.S. 392 (1947). Illegal tying of one product to another.

IBM v. United States, 298 U.S. 131 (1936). Illegal tying of one product to another.

Glass Container Industry Research Corp. v. United States, 70-1 U.S.T.C. 9214 (W.D. Pa. 1970). Tax exempt status denied organization whose research not available to nonmembers.

United States v. Automobile Manufacturers Assn., (1969) Trade Reg. Rep. (CCH) para. 72,907 (S.D. Cal. 1969). Prohibition on restricting publicity about association research.

United States v. National Malleable & Steel Castings Co., (1957) Trade Reg. Rep. (CCH) para. 68,890 (N.D. Ohio 1957). Disclosure required of joint research project results.

Sugar Institute, Inc. v. United States, 297 U.S. 553 (1936). Dissemination of statistical data to customers by placing it in a central depository.

Tag Mfrs. Institute v. FTC, 174 F.2d 452 (1st Cir. 1949). Dissemination of statistical data to customers through news media.

United States v. Western Winter Sports Representatives Assn., Inc., (1962) Trade Reg. Rep. (CCH) para. 70,418 (N.D. Cal. 1962). Nonmember participation at trade shows.

National Assn. of Women's & Children's Apparel Salesmen, Inc. v. FTC, 479 F.2d 139 (5th Cir. 1973). Nonmember participation at trade shows.

Other Resources

FTC Advisory Opinion 16 C.F.R. Section 15.457 (1973).

Chapter 47

BUSINESS OR PROFESSIONAL CODES AND SELF-REGULATION

It is a rare trade or professional association that has not at some time in its history adopted a business or professional code, code of ethics, or other guide to conduct or practices in the industry or profession. A 1979 survey showed that 41 percent of associations polled had these codes. Business or professional codes request or require members to adhere to minimum standards set out for honest and reasonable practices and policies. Association codes serve the lofty purpose of pointing out to members what is considered fair dealing and what is not. To the extent that sanctions are applied against members who violate association codes, they serve as the means for "self-regulation" of industries or professions. Associations have promulgated codes or directives for self-regulation of many aspects of the industries or professions they represent such as advertising practices, dealings with customers or patients, etc.

Self-regulation is a desirable goal often pursued vigorously by associations in these times of increasing external regulation by federal and local governments. Through self-regulation, associations hope to avoid or diminish increased regulation by government with its attendant costs and confusion in interpretation, misunderstandings in application, and frequently unfavorable publicity.

Self-regulation of business or professional conduct through association-promulgated codes has been broadly endorsed in principle by courts and administrative officials. At the same time, association programs for self-regulation have sometimes been declared illegal in circumstances where they have appeared to restrain competition in ways that were otherwise in violation of the antitrust laws.

Association business or professional codes, codes of ethics, or other conduct and practices guides will likely raise no problems unless their provisions are manifestations of separate illegal agreements among members or unless restrictive enforcement procedures are provided. Associations must be certain that their codes are not memorializations of illegal agreements. When compliance with code provisions is enforced by sanctions, care must be taken to assure that imposition of the sanctions does not have anticompetitive effects. In addition, enforcement of association self-regulation codes, even when enforcement is not anticompetitive, must be carried out in accordance with specific procedures to assure proper notice and a fair hearing for alleged offenders.

SUMMARY

- Associations frequently promulgate business or professional codes, codes of ethics, or other guidelines which specify practices or policies of members that are commonly recognized and accepted to be illegal.

- Typical association codes or guidelines might include general provisions on subjects such as:
  —Honest and fair business or professional dealings with customers, clients, or patients
  —Acceptable levels of safety, efficacy, or cleanliness of products, services, or facilities
  —Nondeceptive advertising and promotion of products or services
  —Maintenance of qualified personnel, performance of competent services, furnishing of quality products
  —Desirability of adequate experience or education for individuals serving in the business or profession
  —Promotion of practices or policies which reflect favorably upon the industry or profession.

- Association codes might include specific provisions on subjects which historically have been of particular concern to members.

- Care should be taken to assure that association codes have not been used to advise or remind of some separate agreement among members to act in violation of the antitrust laws.

- Where sanctions or penalties are applicable to violations of association business or professional codes, codes of ethics, or other conduct or practices guides, antitrust dangers may exist. In general, efforts at self-regulation, however laudible their intent, will not escape antitrust scrutiny if they coincidentally result in illegal restraint of trade (see *Professional Engineers, Sugar Institute* and *Fashion Originators* cases in Resources).

- Expulsion of a member for violation of the association's code may be anticompetitive and illegal where membership in the association confers significant business or professional benefits.

- Imposition of fines on members for violations of association codes or temporary deprivation of benefits which do not confer competitive advantages may be reasonable in certain circumstances. (See FTC Advisory Opinion No. 128 in Resources).

- Any sanctions for violations of association codes or guides must be assessed as to their possible anticompetitive *effects* regardless of their good intentions. Legal case situations in which it was determined that imposition of various sanctions was contrary to the antitrust laws include:
  —A professional engineers' association whose code prohibited competitive bidding of members
  —A sugar industry association whose code of ethics prohibited members from granting secret price rebates
  —A women's apparel manufacturing association whose code prohibited members from dealing with retailers that handled "pirated" fashion styles.

- The professional engineers situation is especially noteworthy because it resulted in a clear statement from the United States Supreme Court of the antitrust dangers of code of ethics provisions. The professional engineers association had argued that the public and the profession are best served by a code of ethics ban on competitive bidding for engineering work. Competitive bidding, they said, would lead to assignment of engineering work on the basis of price rather than quality and might result in unsafe buildings, bridges, and other structures. The Supreme Court disagreed and held that the obvious anticompetitive effects of the bidding ban violate the antitrust laws. (*National Society of Professional Engineers*).

- In another landmark association code of ethics decision against the American Medical Association, the Federal Trade Commission had found general prohibitions on physician advertising imposed by professional codes of national and local medical societies to be in violation of the antitrust laws, although FTC made clear in its order that it remains appropriate for professional groups to ban false or deceptive advertising. The FTC decision was affirmed with certain modifications by a federal appellate court despite the arguments of the AMA that it had long ago removed the advertising prohibition provisions from its code and that the FTC lacked authority over the association. The United States Supreme Court, by an equally divided Court and without issuing an opinion, let the appellate court ruling stand that affirmed the FTC order against AMA.

- An earlier United States Supreme Court case, decided on constitutional grounds rather than antitrust grounds, had determined that bar association disciplinary rules against advertising by lawyers were illegal. (*Bates*). The Supreme Court had already determined that a local bar association's minimum fee schedule enforced by a state bar association violates the antitrust laws and is not protected by any "learned profession" or "state action" exemptions from those laws. (*Goldfarb*).

- An extremely important development is an advisory opinion issued by the Federal Trade Commission which, for the first time, approves in its entirety a comprehensive association code of professional conduct. The code applies to eye surgeons who belong to the American Academy of Ophthalmology. Although the FTC advisory opinion does not set any precedent, and does not apply to any other association's enforced code of conduct, it nevertheless does provide the first look at how FTC applies its views regarding association codes in an actual situation, rather than just in speeches and articles. One significant aspect of this FTC-approved code is that it largely avoids addressing issues of professional fees or reimbursement; but the code does cover in detail such subjects as:

—Responsibilities of eye surgeons in performing experimental or investigational procedures

—Responsibilities regarding colleagues who are impaired in their professional abilities such as by age or substance abuse

—Circumstances of delegation of professional authority for patient care

—Circumstances of requisite post-surgical follow-up care

—Banning of false and deceptive communications to the public, with the terms "false and deceptive" described at length as to specific situations.

- The FTC advisory opinion on the eye surgeons' code of professional conduct also reviews the extensive procedures employed in administering and enforcing the code, including such sanctions as reprimand, suspension, or termination from membership in the association and, significantly, referral by the association of the entire investigational file in the code enforcement proceeding to a court or government agency conducting its own adjudication or investigation of the conduct of the sanctioned member.

- The FTC advisory opinion on the eye surgeon code contains, in addition, numerous conditions, qualifications, and warnings as to how the association could, in administering or enforcing the code, still violate the FTC's antitrust or consumer protection proscriptions; these should be heeded carefully by any association planning or conducting a business or professional code effort.

- Association code, bylaw, or resolution provisions regulating conduct by members have been alleged as antitrust violations in cases or federal antitrust agency advisories when they have:

—Required suppliers to give firm price quotations
—Suggested fair profit levels
—Set prices for returned products
—Prohibited price advertising
—Prohibited advertising

—Prohibited competitive bidding
—Prohibited proposals to clients of others
—Required uniform terms and conditions of sale or credit
—Suggested the use of specific raw materials
—Prohibited overcharging and short-weighing
—Prohibited dual distribution as manufacturers and distributors or retailers
—Encouraged boycotting of prepaid service plans
—Encouraged boycotting of nonmembers.

- Administration of reasonable and nonrestrictive sanctions for violations of association codes or guides must be fair and impartial. Procedures should include:

  —A written notice to the member of the alleged violation, the proposed sanction, and the right to comment or hearing
  —A hearing on the matter, if requested, at which the member may present views personally or through a representative such as a lawyer
  —The right to appeal an adverse decision to some higher authority such as the association board of directors or other governing board, or *ad hoc* appeals board established for that purpose.

- Because of the possible antitrust pitfalls, associations should include legal counsel in any activities which involve writing, modifying, interpreting, or enforcing association self-regulation codes.

RESOURCES FOR CHAPTER 47

Books

Chalk, Frankel, & Chafer, *AAAS Professional Ethics Project: Professional Ethics Activities in the Scientific and Engineering Societies*, American Association for the Advancement of Science, 1980.
Fellman, "Industry Self-Regulation: Dream, Reality or Necessity?" in *Associations and the Law Book II*, U.S. Chamber, 1971, page 24.

Frey, "Commercial Codes of Ethics: Where Do They Stand?" in *Associations and the Law Book V*, U.S. Chamber, 1973, page 9.

Hammond, "Antitrust Problems of Associations" in *Trade and Professional Associations*, Hammond, Editor, Practising Law Institute, 1977, page 211.

Harris & Kintner, "Industry Self-Regulation: An Interim Report" in *Associations and the Law Book II*, U.S. Chamber, 1968, page 18.

Horn, *On Professions, Professionals, and Professional Ethics*, Am. Inst. Prop. & Liab. Underwriters, 1978.

Jacobs, "Introduction," page 1, D. Miller, "Maximizing the Benefits of Self-Regulation," page 6, Ginsberg, "Administration Efforts to Enhance the Opportunities for Self-Regulation," page 14, Havighurst, "Remarks," page 24, N. Offen, "The Direct Selling Association's Consumer Protection Code of Ethics," page 33, Bomba, "Remarks," page 46, Tankersley, "Remarks," page 53, Holding, "A Window of Opportunity," page 62, Dinkins, "The Role of Self-Regulation in Regulatory Reform," page 68, in *White House Conference on Association Self-Regulation*, Jacobs, Moderator, ASAE, 1984.

Kintner, "Industry Codes of Ethics" in *Associations and the Law Book I*, U.S. Chamber, 1967, page 47.

La Barbera, *Advertising Self-Regulation: Trade Association Adoptions and Resistance*, New York University, Graduate School of Business Administration, February, 1981.

Lad, *Policy-Making Between Business and Government: A Conceptual Synthesis of Industry Self-Regulation and a Case Study Analysis of the Direct Selling Association Code of Conduct*, Boston University School of Management, 1985.

Lamb & Shields, *Trade Association Law and Practice*, Little, Brown, 1971, page 145.

MacArthur, *Associations and the Antitrust Laws*, U.S. Chamber, 1984, page 59.

Michaelson & Dowling, "Business and Professional Codes," in *Association Issues*, Jacobs, Editor, ASAE, 1983, page 71.

Opinion Research Corporation, *Codes of Ethics in Corporations and Trade Associations and the Teaching of Ethics in Graduate Business Schools*, Ethics Resource Center, 1979.

Opinion Research Corporation, *Implementation and Enforcement of Codes of Ethics in Corporations and Associations*, Ethics Resource Center, 1980.

Pollard & Leibenluft, *Antitrust and the Health Professions: Policy Planning Issues Paper*, Federal Trade Commission, July, 1981.

Shields, "Industry Self-Regulation: Does Silver Have an Afterglow?" *Associations and the Law Book IV*, U.S. Chamber, 1971, page 20.

Webster, *The Law of Associations*, Matthew Bender, 1976, page 2.

Webster & Herold, *Antitrust Guide for Association Executives*, ASAE, 1979, page 111.

Webster, Herold, & Dye, *Association Legal Checklist*, U.S. Chamber, 1983, pages 29–31.

Periodicals

Anderson, "Justice Department Refuses to Approve Association Code of Ethics," GWSAE *Executive Update*, November, 1984, page 18.

Baram, Sandberg, Dufault, & McAllister, "Managing Risks to Health, Safety and Environment by the Use of Alternatives to Regulation," *New England Law Review*, 1981, page 657.

Bierig, "What Ever Happened to Professional Self-Regulation?," *American Bar Association Journal*, May 1983, page 616.

Bowman, "The Management of Ethics: Codes of Conduct in Organizations," *Public Personnel Management Journal*, 1981, page 59.

Braemer, "Disciplinary Procedures for Trade and Professional Associations," *Bus. Law.*, 1968, page 959.

Braithwaite, "Enforced Self-Regulation: A New Strategy for Corporate Crime Control," *Michigan Law Review*, June, 1982, page 1466.

Brebbia, "Joint Legislative Activities and Codes of Ethics," *Antitrust Bull.*, 1973, page 221.

Butz, "The Government's Role in Industry Self-Regulation," *Antitrust Bull.*, 1965, page 555.

Garvin, "Can Industry Self-Regulation Work?," *California Management Review*, Summer, 1983, page 37.

Garvin, "Deregulating and Self-Regulating," *Wharton Magazine*, Spring 1981, page 57.

Gupta & Lad, "Industry Self-Regulation: An Economic, Organizational, and Political Analysis," *Academy of Management Review*, July 1983, page 416.

Halverson, "Expanded Roles for Trade Associations," *Antitrust Bull.*, 1973, page 221.

Harris, "Structuring a Workable Business Code of Ethics," *University of Florida Law Review*, 1978, page 310.

Herold, "Codes of Ethics and Other Industry Self-Regulation Plans Covered by Attorney Expert," *Association Trends*, March 15, 1985, page 5.

Jacobs, "Self-Regulation by Associations in the Year 2000," *Vanguard*, ASAE, November/December, 1983, page 4.

Kanwit, "When Should Professional Associations Be Liable for Antitrust Violations?," *Chicago Bar Record*, November–December, 1977, page 14.

Krumm & Greenhill, "The Extent of Industry Self-Regulation Through Trade Association Codes of Ethics," *The Antitrust Bulletin*, March, 1972, page 379.

La Barbera, "The Diffusion of Trade Association Advertising Self-Regulation," *Journal of Marketing*, Winter, 1983, page 58.

Lane, "Trade and Professional Associations: Ethics and Standards," *ABA Antitrust L.J.*, 1977, page 653.

MacArthur, "Impact of Antitrust Laws on Professional Societies," *Association Management*, April, 1978, page 42.

Miron, "Trade Association Codes of Ethical Conduct," *ABA Antitrust Section*, 1965, page 163.

Patterson, "The Function of a Code of Legal Ethics," *University of Miami Law Review*, 1981, page 695.

Ring, "The Role of Trade Associations in Industry Self-Regulation," *ABA Antitrust Section*, 1965, page 142.

Rockefeller, "Industry Efforts At Self-Regulation," *Antitrust Bull.*, 1965, page 555.

Snapper, "Whether Professional Associations May Enforce Professional Codes," *Business & Professional Ethics Journal*, Winter, 1984, page 43.

Taylor, "Rule of Reason Cases Since *National Society of Professional Engineers*," *Antitrust Law Journal*, 1982, page 185.

"The Antitrust Liability of Professional Associations After *Goldfarb:* Reformulating the Learned Professions Exemption in the Lower Courts," *Duke Law Journal*, 1977, page 1047.

Walters, "Can An Association Uphold a Code of Ethics in the Eighties?," October, 1983, page 62.

Weiss, "Social Regulation of Business Activity: Reforming the Corporate Governance System to Resolve an Institutional Impasse," *UCLA Law Review*, February, 1981, page 343.

Cases

National Society of Professional Engineers v. United States, 435 U.S. 679 (1978). Code of ethics prohibited competitive bidding by engineers.

Sugar Institute v. United States, 297 U.S. 553 (1936). Code of ethics adopted to end secret price concessions elicited by customers' misrepresentations.

Fashion Originators' Guild of America v. FTC, 312 U.S. 457 (1974). Code of ethics adopted to end sales to merchants who handled copies of patented styles.

American Medical Assn., FTC Docket No. 9064 (October 12, 1979), *aff'd mod.*, 638 F.2d 443, (2d Cir. 1980); *aff'd by equally divided court*, 455 U.S. 679 (1982). Ethical restraints on physician advertising.

Bates v. State Bar of Arizona, 433 U.S. 350 (1977). Bar association prohibition of attorney advertising.

Goldfarb v. Virginia State Bar, 421 U.S. 773 (1975). Bar association minimum fee schedule.

Mardirosian v. American Institute of Architects, 474 F. Supp. 628 (D. D.C. 1979). Ban on architects seeking commissions where others have been selected.

Other Resources

FTC Advisory Opinions 16 C.F.R. Sections 15.15 (1966), .55 (1966), .59 (1966), .64 (1966), .80 (1966), .97a (1966), .115 (1967), .119 (1967), .128 (1967), .133 (1967), .246 (1968), .249 (1968), .268 (1968), .281 (1968), .287 (1968), .329 (1969), .332 (1976), .373 (1969), (uncodified) to Wire Institute (1978), and (uncodified) to American Academy of Ophthalmology (1983).

R. Favretto, *Competition and Professional Ethics*, Speech before American Society of Civil Engineers, Oct. 17, 1978.

L. Costillo, Speech before Houston Bar Association Corporation Counsel Section, March 19, 1980.

Chapter 48

STATISTICAL PROGRAMS

Every firm can benefit from access to statistical data on sales, costs, labor rates, and other economic and business factors about its industry. To some extent, practicing professionals can also benefit from receiving statistical information about the business aspects of their practices. Statistical programs are designed to survey and report on business conditions and provide the means for measuring one's own performance against the norms of competitors in an industry or profession. For many firms, statistical reports issued by their associations are considered indispensible tools for maximizing productivity, efficiency, and profitability.

To be useful, business statistics must be as extensive, accurate, and as current as practicable. Whether gross figures or average figures are surveyed and reported, it is most desirable for them to be drawn from as large a number of firms as possible. In some instances, general business statistics developed by government agencies and circulated to association members can be helpful. More often, the associations themselves are best situated and equipped to accumulate pertinent and specific data on their industries or professions and to periodically report the data in ways most understandable by members and useful to them. Association statistical programs represent one of the few areas of association activity for which a rather large and surprisingly consistent body of law is available to provide guidelines for what procedures are appropriate and what are not. Courts and government agencies have on numerous occasions declared association statistical activities to be, in theory, entirely legal and beneficial. In a number of specific instances, however, they have found association statistical activities to be, in practice, contrary to the antitrust laws.

This Summary provides general rules for the establishment and administration of association statistical programs. Succeeding summaries in this book deal more specifically with association price activities and cost accounting where statistical surveys and reports may be incidentally involved.

Sample guidelines for association statistical programs are included in the last section of this book.

SUMMARY

- Association statistical programs involve the collection and dissemination of business information considered useful by members. Statistics can be used by an association member to keep abreast of conditions and trends and to compare the firm's performance with the average performance of competing firms.

- The basic legality of statistical programs conducted by associations was first affirmed in a 1925 Supreme Court case which held that "persons who unite in gathering and disseminating information . . . in statistical reports on industry . . . are not engaged in unlawful conspiracies" necessarily (*Maple Flooring*). This principle has been reaffirmed in several more recent Supreme Court cases and in speeches and opinions by officials of the federal antitrust enforcement agencies.

- Association statistical programs have been condemned by courts and federal agencies where their establishment or operation was found to be a functional component of some plan to restrain trade by fixing prices, regulating production, allocating markets, or the like.

- From the numerous court decisions and agency pronouncements on association statistical programs a series of guidelines can be derived which, if observed, will help assure that a specific program will not be challenged on antitrust grounds. The guidelines are not mandatory, inflexible requirements. Some could probably be ignored in circumstances where other appropriate safeguards were provided. By contrast, even a statistical program following all of the guidelines could be used for anticompetitive ends by ill-motivated but resourceful conspirators. Even though they are not ironclad, these guidelines should be observed wher-

ever possible since each responds to some aspect of
actual statistical programs which has been cited as
objectionable by a court or agency:

—Participation in the statistical program must be voluntary; no direct or indirect coercion should be applied to force, require, or intimidate association
members or nonmembers into participation. By the
same token, there should be no enforcement of the
accuracy of responses to the program such as by
required audits of participants.

—The purpose of the program should be promulgated
and understood by all as the collection and furnishing of specific useful business information rather than
the effecting of any agreement or understanding with
respect to business activities. Only business information directly pertinent to participants' legitimate
business interests should be involved.

—Information received and published should be historical rather than projected; only past transactions
or figures should be used. The less current the information, the less likely that it can be used as the
basis for an illegal agreement or understanding.

—The confidentiality of information supplied by each
participant must be maintained; only composite or
average figures should be used in statistical reports;
no average or composite should be used where less
than three or four individual component figures are
available lest one participant be able to extrapolate
information on the other or others.

—Data supplied by individual participants should not
be shown to any other participants for any reason.
In order to maintain confidentiality, it may be necessary to send it to some third party such as an accounting or research organization. It may be also
desirable to remove information identifying participants upon receipt of data and to encode it before it
is utilized.

—Published association statistical reports should not
contain comments upon the information contained in
the reports that could in any way be interpreted as
an exhortation to participants that they take some
joint or concerted action in response to the informa-

tion. Similarly, discussion and analysis of the information at association meetings should be approached with caution, or better still, avoided completely.

—Results of association statistical programs must be available to nonmembers, including customers and suppliers of members, whenever they have a legitimate business need to receive the results. Nonmembers can be charged higher prices than those charged to members to reflect association membership funds that contributed to financing the statistical programs. The nonmember prices should not be so high that they are tantamount to compelling membership. Results of association statistical programs can be denied to members and nonmembers who are eligible to participate in the programs but chose not to; however, this restriction should not be applied to deny the results to members or nonmembers with a legitimate business need to receive the results but who were not eligible to participate.

—Unless retention of the information is considered particularly important for some purposes, individual submissions by participants in association statistical programs should be returned or discarded as soon as they have been used to make composite or average computations in order to avoid release in some subsequent government or private investigation or suit of data that participants may consider confidential.

—Statistical programs ordinarily should not include price information except under compelling circumstances. Price reporting may be undertaken under strict rules listed elsewhere in this book, but it must be understood that no legal safeguards can absolutely protect association-published price information from being used for illegal purposes.

RESOURCES FOR CHAPTER 48

Books

Fellman & Zeronda, "Statistical Compilations, Credit Reporting, Standards and Advertising—The Legal Implications of Basic Association Activities" in *Trade and Professional Associations*, Hammond, Editor, Practising Law Institute, 1977, page 147.

Herold, "Antitrust, Trade Regulation and Other Nontax Aspects of Association Activities" in *Managing Membership Societies*, Grief, Editor, ASAE, 1979, page 123.

Lamb & Shields, *Trade Association Law and Practice*, Little, Brown, 1971, page 34.

MacArthur, *Associations and the Antitrust Laws*, U.S. Chamber, 1984, page 44.

Olverson, "Statistical Reporting Programs and the Antitrust Laws" in *Associations and the Law Book I*, U.S. Chamber, 1967, page 29.

Principles of Association Management, ASAE and U.S. Chamber, 1975, page 357.

Webster, *The Law of Associations*, Matthew Bender, 1976, page 8-1.

Webster & Herold, *Antitrust Guide for Association Executives*, ASAE, 1979, page 58.

Webster, Herold, & Dye, *Association Legal Checklist*, U.S. Chamber, 1983, pages 23–25.

Periodicals

Fellman, "You Can't Completely Protect Confidential Survey Data, But You Can Try," *Association Management*, September, 1981, page 67.

Fellman, "Can Associations Develop Adequate Statistics and Participate Fully in Standard Making Procedures on an Industry Basis Without Antitrust Liability?," *Antitrust Bull.*, 1974, page 723.

"Guidelines for Data Dissemination Through Trade Associations," *Washburn L.J.*, 1970, page 93.

Herold, "Be Aware of Antitrust Risks in Statistical Reporting and Standard-Setting Programs," *Association Management*, September, 1977, page 85.

MacNee, "The FTC and Trade Association Statistics," *Antitrust Bull.*, 1962, page 753.

Miron, "Antitrust Implications of the Exchange of Business Information," *Antitrust Bull.*, 1965, page 485.

Webster, "Guidelines for Association Statistical Programs," *Association Management*, January, 1975, page 20.

Cases

Maple Flooring Manufacturers Assn. v. United States, 268 U.S.
563 (1925). Statistical program following certain guidelines
does not violate antitrust laws.

American Column & Lumber Co. v. United States, 257 U.S. 377
(1921). Comprehensive statistical and business information exchange program evidenced agreement to restrain
competition.

United States v. American Linseed Oil Co., 262 U.S. 371 (1923).
Statistical program with penalties and audits for noncompliance restrained competition among sellers.

Cement Manufacturers Protective Assn. v. United States, 268
U.S. 588 (1925). Statistical program meeting guidelines not
in violation.

Sugar Institute v. United States, 297 U.S. 553 (1936). Price reporting program with coercion and secrecy of results condemned.

Other Resources

FTC Advisory Opinions 16 C.F.R. Sections 15.162 (1968), .205
(1968), .303 (1968), .345 (1969), .359 (1969), .432 (1973), .486
(1974), .487 (1974; and (uncodified) to Business and Institutional Furniture Manufacturers Assn. (1978) and Independent Wire Producers Assn. (1978).

Chapter 49

PRICES AND FEES OF MEMBERS

The subject of members' prices and fees deserves to command far greater attention and concern from an antitrust viewpoint than any other. A thorough understanding and serious respect for the implications of this subject are essential for association members, committee chairmen, directors, officers, staff, and counsel. The subject raises the highest imaginable danger from a legal point of view—the real consequences of misapprehending its dangers may include huge fines or damages, extended jail sentences, or even forced disbanding of the association. The consequences even of mere allegations of wrongdoing with respect to the subject usually include major commitments of time and money in defending against the allegations as well as serious adverse publicity to the association and its industry or profession which are claimed to be illegally involved.

The cautious association has a simple approach to the subject of prices and fees of members. It tolerates no activities or policies relating to prices or fees in any way. It allows no communications, written or oral, about them. It establishes an affirmative association antitrust compliance program, the emphasis of which is on avoidance of even the potential for price-fixing or fee-setting situations. This conservative approach to the subject of members' prices and fees is not legally required. There are some limited areas of association endeavor where members' price or fee matters can be involved, such as in surveys of past prices or fees, if adequate precautions are taken to avoid antitrust problems. But some risks inherent in any association policy or activity relating to prices or fees may never be entirely eliminated. The risks can be minimized. Close scrutiny and vigilance against impropriety is crucial.

The legal or illegal spectre raised by association involvement in the subject of prices or fees of members is that of price-fixing and fee-setting. These are *per se* violations of the antitrust laws. This means that those accused of the violations

258

are not allowed even to attempt to explain the reasonableness
and good intentions of their involvement. Alleged price-fixing
and fee-setting violations comprise the major area of antitrust
enforcement by the government and by private litigants in
class actions. The incidence of antitrust enforcement of price-
fixing or fee-setting prohibitions is particularly high in antitrust cases brought against associations and their members.
As indicated, the penalties for adverse judgments related to
these violations are extremely severe.

This Summary includes some fundamental information on
what constitutes price-fixing or fee-setting and how some variations of it can occur in an association. It lists the elements
of legally acceptable reports on average past prices and covers
some more recent trends in association activities concerning
professional fees.

SUMMARY

- Activities involving prices or fees are far and away the
  ones most often complained of in antitrust allegations
  against associations; the subject of members' prices or
  fees constitutes the single most dangerous subject from
  a legal point of view that associations can ever address.

- Association members are in competition with one another. They have the competitor's natural instinct to
  know about prevailing prices or fees and to discuss
  factors within and outside the business or profession
  which affect prices and fees. These instincts must be
  suppressed to avoid the possibility of serious antitrust
  violations. All antitrust allegations concerning prices
  and fees are serious ones.

- Price-fixing (or fee-setting) is an expansive and evolving legal concept that can include virtually any agreement or understanding, whether express or implied,
  that has the effect of raising, lowering, or stablizing
  prices. Courts have condemned nearly any program or

activity which tends to significantly diminish the independent establishment of prices by individual competitors as required by the antitrust laws. Nearly any joint tampering with prices or price structure is unlawful. Price-fixing may occur even if terms and conditions of sale other than price are agreed upon. It may occur between direct competitors or between suppliers and customers. It may occur between bidders on government or private contracts. It may be manifest by competitors changing prices concurrently if any assent has been made between them concerning the changes.

- Price-fixing (or fee-setting) is a *per se* antitrust violation. No excuses can be advanced by those charged with price-fixing to show that it was reasonable under the circumstances.

- Conviction in a government criminal action for price-fixing or fee-setting can result in criminal fines of up to $1,000,000 for corporations or up to $100,000 and three years of imprisonment for individuals. Injured customers or competitors, sometimes representing a large class of plaintiffs, can bring civil actions to recover damages resulting from price-fixing. The law provides that these damages, when proven, are automatically multiplied by three. They are called "treble damages."

- The following are some examples of activities by competitors, often in an association setting, which have been condemned as illegal price-fixing in decided antitrust cases or antitrust settlements:
    —Agreement by members to adhere to prices published by the association (even though many members failed to live up to the agreement)
    —Agreement within an association to publish price lists, even when accompanied by no agreement to adhere to them
    —Use of an association to advertise goods or services of members where the association exercises authority in establishing prices or fees advertised
    —Reciprocal exchange by competitors of information on actual prices recently charged or quoted to identified customers
    —Circulation by an association of lists of minimum

prices to avoid violation of state laws prohibiting sales below cost
—Association discussions of recommended percentage increases in prices
—Agreements within an association to refrain from giving discounts, premiums, trading stamps, etc.
—Recommended limitations by associations on warranty terms, credit terms, or other terms of sale
—Exchange of information at association meetings on current or future prices as part of an agreement to adjust them
—Agreements to submit deliberately high bids in order to assure that the lower bid of a certain competitor will be acceptable
—Agreements within an association on what rate competitors will be willing to pay for an expense item which is a significant component of price.

- Written communications by an association or discussions before, during, or after an association meeting that relate to prices or fees are too risky to be tolerated. Even if no agreement results, one might be inferred later. Steps should routinely be taken to help assure that the association does not become involved in price-fixing or fee-setting:

—Association staff, officers, directors, and members should periodically be advised by legal counsel on the antitrust prohibitions against price-fixing and fee-setting.
—Meeting announcements, agendas, minutes, or reports should never include references to prices and price discussions (or fees and fee discussions) and, where possible, should be reviewed in advance by counsel.
—Legal counsel should attend any association meeting where the subject could relate even remotely to prices or fees.
—If a discussion of prices or fees occurs at a meeting where counsel is not in attendance, association staff or any member should terminate the discussion immediately; if they are unsuccessful, they should terminate the meeting.
—The advice of legal counsel should be sought on any

association activity or policy which relates to prices or fees of members.

- Whether an association is named by the government or by private litigants in price-fixing or fee-setting allegations, and whether the claims against the association are sustained, will largely depend upon the extent of the involvement of the association's representatives—staff, officers, directors, and members—in the matters complained of.

- If the associations' representatives actively encouraged illegal price or fee activities, or even knew of the activities and took no steps to curtail them, it is possible that the association itself could be held responsible.

- Mere membership in an association charged with price-fixing or fee-setting is insufficient grounds to hold a member also responsible unless the member knowingly, intentionally, and actively participated.

- Price or fee reporting programs carried on by associations can be legally dangerous because of the nature of the information being collected and disseminated. The nature of the industry or profession from which data are received and to which they are sent is also an important consideration. Oligopolistic situations, for example, lend themselves more readily to joint action based on data received than do situations in which there are many competitors. Price or fee reporting programs are not themselves illegal if appropriate guidelines are strictly followed in their administration. The guidelines will help reduce the legal risks of price or fee reporting programs but will not necessarily eliminate the risks because the association can never be completely certain that the uses made of the reported information are not subject to challenge. Here are the guidelines:

  —Only gross sales or average prices or fees should be reported.
  —Individual sellers/buyers or transactions should never be reported or identifiable from the report.
  —Only past information should be collected and disseminated; the more recent the information is, and

the more frequently it is reported, the greater the legal danger.

—A program should not include the discretion by participants or those administering the program to establish subjectively "consensus" prices or fees based upon interpretations or experience as well as reported data.

—There should be no agreement or even encouragement to adhere to the information reported or to use it in any way.

—The program should be voluntary.

—There should be no discussion of the information in writing or at meetings.

—Reports should be available to sellers, buyers, and nonmembers.

• Beyond these simplistic rules are other considerations that must be addressed in analyzing any association price or fee reporting system. The concept of price-fixing or fee-setting is a most subtle and dynamic one as evaluated in specific factual situations by federal antitrust enforcement agencies, by private antitrust claimants, and, ultimately, by the courts. An association must attempt a similar evaluation based on announced government positions and decided court cases before it can assume that its price or fee reporting program is safe from successful challenge. For example, any concept of "consensus pricing" suggests price-fixing. After discussing association programs that he termed "consensus pricing" (see the *New York Coffee and Sugar Exchange* consent order case in Resources), a government antitrust enforcement official suggested in a 1980 speech some considerations of how his agency evaluates these consensus price reporting programs operated by associations:

—"The general rule" applied "to the the majority of consensus price development schemes is that . . . these schemes are usually unlawful and probably criminal."

—The agency "will almost never accept as legitimate any consensus price scheme involving predictive prices or price trending."

—"Lack of agreement among industry members about how to use the consensus price data will not shield the activity from criminal antitrust prosecution."

—Assuming a good intent, "the best reason for the circulation of current price information is a market structure that requires such information if it is to function competitively."

—"Even if the intent is good and the market conditions are right," the agency "will still sue if the price information system being used can be made substantially less likely to lead to anticompetitive results."

—The agency "is substantially less likely to take action if the information scheme involves only historic, statistically objective, composite price information." (Remarks of R. Favretto listed in Resources).

- Professional associations and their members do not have any special exemption from the antitrust laws (see *Goldfarb* case). Some antitrust cases or antitrust settlements have prohibited the following fee activities of professional associations:

  —Establishment or enforcement of recommended or minimum fees for services (*Goldfarb*)

  —Establishment of a relative value scale to list professional services and their degree of relative skill or time required for performance which, by the application of a dollar conversion factor, could be used as a fee schedule (see several FTC Consent Orders prohibiting relative value scale *but* a Justice Department case in which the court finds no violation from use of relative value scale)

  —Prohibition or discouragement by an association of advertising professional services (FTC order, sustained by the courts, against medical association)

  —Prohibition or discouragement by an association of competitive bidding by professionals (engineers' association case).

- It is obvious that price and fee policies or activities of associations raise the greatest of all antitrust dangers. The advice of knowledgable experts in these areas is essential to conscientious association compliance.

RESOURCES FOR CHAPTER 49

Books

Carretta, "Price Reporting as an Activity of Associations" in *Associations and the Law Book I*, U.S. Chamber, 1967, page 33.

Herold, "Antitrust, Trade Regulation, and Other Nontax Aspects of Association Activities" in *Managing Membership Societies*, Grief, Editor, ASAE, 1979, page 123.

Lamb & Shields, *Trade Association Law and Practice*, Little, Brown, 1971, page 54.

MacArthur, *Associations and the Antitrust Laws*, U.S. Chamber, 1984, page 28.

MacArthur, "Dangers in Discussing Prices at Association Meetings" in *Associations and the Law Book III*, U.S. Chamber, 1969, page 46.

Shields, "Association Membership as Evidence of Conspiracy" in *Associations and the Law Book VII*, U.S. Chamber, 1976, page 77.

Webster, *The Law of Associations*, Matthew Bender, 1976, page 9-9.

Webster & Herold, *Antitrust Guide for Association Executives*, ASAE, 1979, page 49.

Periodicals

"Antitrust Implications of the Exchange of Price Information Among Competitors: The Container Case," *Mich. L. Rev.*, 1970, page 720.

"Antitrust: Agreement to Exchange Price Information Violates Sherman Act," *Minn. L. Rev.*, 1969, page 206.

Clabault, "Practicalities in Competitors Exchanging Price Information," *Antitrust Bull.*, 1967, page 49.

"The Creation of a Separate Rule of Reason: Antitrust Liability for the Exchange of Price Information Among Competitors," *Duke, L.J.*, 1979, page 1004.

Galgay, "Antitrust Considerations in the Exchange of Price Information Among Competitors," *Antitrust Bull.*, 1963, page 617.

Senner, "Dissemination of Price Information," *ABA Antitrust L.J.*, 1977, page 664.

Cases

American Column & Lumber Co. v. United States, 257 U.S. 377 (1921). Price information exchange.

United States v. American Linseed Oil Co., 262 U.S. 371 (1923). Price information exchange.

Maple Flooring Manufacturers Assn. v. United States, 268 U.S. 563 (1925). Price information exchange.

Cement Manufacturers Protective Assn. v. United States, 268 U.S. 588 (1925). Price information exchange.

United States v. Sugar Institute, Inc., 297 U.S. 593 (1936). Price information exchange.

United States v. Socony-Vacuum Oil Co., 310 U.S. 150 (1940). Price information exchange.

FTC v. Cement Institute, 333 U.S. 683 (1948). Price information exchange.

United States v. Container Corp. of America, 393 U.S. 333 (1969). Price information exchange.

United States v. United States Gypsum Co., 438 U.S. 422 (1978). Price information exchange.

United States v. Nationwide Trailer Rental System, Inc., 156 F. Supp. 800 (D. Kan.), aff'd. mem., 355 U.S. 10 (1957). Association price-fixing challenge.

Northern California Pharmaceutical Assn. v. United States, 306 F.2d 379 (9th Cir. 1962), cert. denied, 370 U.S. 862 (1962). Association price-fixing challenge.

Plymouth Dealers Assn. of Northern California v. United States, 279 F.2d 128 (9th Cir. 1960). Association price-fixing challenge.

United States v. Society of Independent Gasoline Marketers of America, (1980-I Transfer Binder) Trade Reg. Rep. (CCH) para. 63,097 (4th Cir. 1979). Association price-fixing challenge.

United States v. New York Coffee & Sugar Exchange, (1979-I Transfer Binder) Trade Reg. Rep. (CCH) para. 62,665 (S.D.N.Y. 1979). Consensus price development.

In the Matter of Chain Institute, Inc., FTC Docket No. 4878, (1957) Trade Reg. Rep. (CCH) para. 68,757. Association price activities.

United States v. Garage Door Manufacturers Assn., (1973) Trade Reg. Rep. (CCH) para. 74,657 (E.D.Pa. 1973). Association price activities.

Goldfarb v. Virginia State Bar, 421 U.S. 773 (1975). Bar association minimum fee schedule.

United States v. American Society of Anesthesiologists, Inc., 473 F. Supp. 147 (S.D.N.Y. 1979). Relative value scale found legal.

The American Academy of Orthopedic Surgeons, 88 F.T.C. 968 (1976). Agreement to abandon relative value scale.

California Medical Assn., 93 F.T.C. 519 (1979). Agreement to abandon relative value scale.

American Medical Assn., FTC Docket No. 9064 (Oct. 12, 1979), *aff'd mod.*, 638 F.2d 443 (2nd Cir. 1980), *aff'd by equally divided court*, 455 U.S. 676 (1982). Order against ethical bans on physician advertising.

National Society of Professional Engineers v. United States, 435 U.S. 679 (1978). Illegality of ethical ban on competitive bidding.

Other Resources

FTC Advisory Opinions 16 C.F.R. Sections 15.15 (1966), .97 (1966), .115 (1967), .137 (1967), .158 (1968), .199 (1968), .200 (1968), .201 (1968), .246 (1968), .257 (1968), .268 (1968), .273 (1968), .281 (1968), .395 (1969), and (uncodified) to Beauty and Barber Supply Institute (1974).

R. Favretto, "Trade Associations and the Development of consensus or Average Price Information—An Antitrust Perspective," Speech before Bar Association of the District of Columbia, February 18, 1980.

E. Johnson, "Exchanges of Price-Affecting Information as 'Facilitating Practices'—An FTC View," Speech before Bar Association of the District of Columbia, February 28, 1980.

Chapter 50

COST PROGRAMS

From their earliest days, a primary endeavor of associations has been to provide useful business information and assistance to their members. At one time, many businesses were operated by persons unsophisticated in even the rudiments of accounting, economics, management, or marketing. Associations helped meet the need for education in these areas by developing business programs specifically tailored to the industries they represented. Today, while the programs are somewhat more advanced to reflect the generally higher level of business knowledge attained by members, associations still are active in their business education efforts. A major aspect of these efforts involves costs of doing business.

Two types of cost programs have regularly been carried on by associations. The first is an association uniform accounting system whose purpose is to help members, especially members that are small businesses, understand and utilize sound cost accounting as a routine procedure. Uniform accounting systems are ordinarily developed by accounting experts retained by the association who specifically address the singular cost accounting circumstances common to members of the association. Generally, publications and seminars are offered periodically to educate interested members in the implementation and use of the association's uniform cost-accounting system. The system may be updated every few years to reflect new or different aspects of typical cost factors of members. The second type of association cost program is a cost survey. This is a species of the statistical studies considered elsewhere in this book. In a cost survey, members are asked to voluntarily report itemized costs of doing business—material costs, sales costs, labor costs, financing costs, administrative costs, etc. Reports received from members are averaged by cost item and the averages are published. The average costs by themselves are considered helpful by members for comparing their own costs of doing business against industry norms. In addition, many associations publish the average costs as ratios which show the relationships between costs and other financial data. These ratio studies are particularly helpful to members as a means of business analysis and planning.

Both uniform cost-accounting systems and cost surveys have been given careful antitrust scrutiny in the courts and federal agencies. Both kinds of programs can be conducted legally; but both can be abused for illegal purposes. As with other association business or statistical programs, care must be taken to assure that cost programs are not conducive to price-fixing or other antitrust violations.

SUMMARY

- Associations conduct two types of cost accounting programs to assist members in identifying and evaluating their costs of doing business:
  - —Uniform cost-accounting systems tailored to the needs of typical association members and available to be put in place in members' businesses
  - —Cost surveys in which associations accumulate cost information from members, develop averages or ratios from the information, and publish it for members to use in comparing their own costs against industry norms.

- Uniform cost-accounting systems are not as prevalent as in years past when association members were less sophisticated in business matters, but they are still occasionally developed and utilized. Several cases have found antitrust violations inherent in the systems or relating to them when:
  - —Standard costs were published by a federation of printing industry associations which suggested prices to be used by members and included a uniform percentage of costs to be included as a mark-up in determining selling prices.
  - —Average costs were published in a manual by a uniform exchange with a specific profit allowance and

members of the exchange were required to use the published figure.

—Average costs were compiled by a state candy manufacturers association to assist members in complying with prohibitions against sales below cost but which resulted in price-fixing.

- Cost surveys conducted by associations, in which members report their itemized costs which are then averaged and published, should follow the general rules for association statistical studies. They can be summarized as follows:

—Voluntary participation
—Legitimate purpose
—Past data only
—Confidentiality of individual data
—Submission of data to third party
—No comments or discussion of data
—Availability of results to nonmembers
—Return or discarding of individual data
—No current or future price information
—Review by legal counsel.

RESOURCES FOR CHAPTER 50

BOOKS

Lamb & Shields, *Trade Association Law and Practice*, Little, Brown, 1971, page 114.

Principles of Association Management, ASAE and U.S. Chamber, 1975, page 357.

MacArthur, *Associations and the Antitrust Laws*, U.S. Chamber, 1984, page 28.

Webster & Herold, *Antitrust Guide for Association Executives*, ASAE, 1979, page 58.

Periodicals

Jacobs, "Association Surveys of Members' Costs of Doing Business," *Association & Society Manager*, April/May, 1980, page 75.

Velvel, "Legality Under the Antitrust Laws of Wage Statistics

Compiled by Professional Associations," *Catholic U.L. Rev.*, 1978, page 729.

Cases

Maple Flooring Assn. v. United States, 268 U.S. 563 (1925). Legality of average cost data exchanges.

United Typothetae of America, 6 F.T.C. 345 (1923). Elements of legality and illegality in comprehensive cost accounting and statistical information program in printing industry.

Vitrified China Assn., 49 F.T.C. 1571 (1953). Average cost study by association not illegal.

Uniform Manufacturers Exchange, Inc., 35 F.T.C. 472 (1942). Order against association price activities permitted activities in uniform cost accounting and statistical exchanges.

Western Confectioners Assn., Inc., 34 F.T.C. 1431 (1942). Association average cost study used to assist members in complying with California ban on sales below cost.

United States v. National Container Corp., (1940–1943 Transfer Binder) Trade Reg. Rep. (CCH) para. 56,028 (S.D.N.Y. 1940). Consent decree permitting extensive cost activities.

Other Resources

FTC Advisory Opinions 16 C.F.R. Sections 15.162 (1968), .345 (1969), .359 (1969), and (uncodified) to Independent Wire Producers Assn. (1978).

Chapter 51

STANDARDIZATION AND SIMPLIFICATION

Standardization and simplification efforts of associations are, along with statistical programs, among the most important and beneficial activities that associations undertake. Standardization involves the establishment of models or criteria with which the attributes of products or services can be compared. Simplication involves the reduction of many types or variations of products or services by designating a lesser number of those that are most common and available. Although the two efforts produce different results, standardization and simplification programs have similar legal and practical implications and so are often considered together.

Association standards programs are extremely widespread. At least four hundred associations have developed their own voluntary product or service standards that are included among the over twenty thousand standards estimated to be in existence. The continued popularity of association standards programs—which have flourished from the very beginning of associations in the United States—is no doubt attributable to the fact that standards can be highly beneficial to members of an industry and to their customers alike.

Industry members realize greater efficiency and interchangeability from standards; customers obtain a means to measure the value of what they buy. Even the government benefits from privately developed voluntary product and service standards. Regulatory or procurement agencies frequently adopt previously developed voluntary standards as mandatory government requirements when needs arise to control an industry's products or services. In this way, the agencies may assure safety to consumers or workers or may assure quality or consistency of government purchases.

As with other association programs, the basic legality of standards-making activities is clear. Association standards programs have been commented upon favorably by courts and administrative officials periodically for over half a century.

Yet, standards can also be used for illegal purposes such as to create artificial barriers to entry into markets, to restrict competition among the parties setting the standards, to discriminate against particular competitors, or to mislead customers. Clearly, a major danger to be avoided in association standard-setting is the tendency for standard products or services to become subject to standard pricing.

Standards have an immense capacity to do public good; they also have a capacity to do public harm. If conducted fairly and with due regard for the potential antitrust pitfalls, association standardization and simplification activities can be among the most important activites ever engaged in jointly by competitors.

One of the most important Supreme Court decisions ever for associations, the *Hydrolevel* case, involved the anticompetitive interpretation of a product standard by a professional association of engineers. The case and its ramifications are considered in the next chapter.

SUMMARY

- Association standardization and simplification activities are among the most common and most beneficial activities carried on by associations.

- Standardization of products or services involves the development and specification of such things as reasonable:

    —Definitions, terminology, symbols, or abbreviations
    —Criteria for design, materials, performance, or procedures
    —Methods of testing, rating, or analysis
    —Concepts of size, weight, or volume
    —Techniques of practice, safety, health, or construction.

- Simplification involves the identification of aspects of products and services that have the greatest demand or utility and excluding those that are less popular and efficacious by designation of particular types, sizes, or grades.

- In standardization, the focus is upon products or services most desirable and worthy of continuation; in simplification the focus is upon products or services least desirable and, therefore, eligible to be eliminated. Despite the differing results sought from the two activities, both have similar legal ramifications.

- Benefits from association standardization efforts are realized by producers and suppliers in an industry as well as by customers and users of their products or services. For producers and suppliers, standardization:
  —Allows for interchangeability of parts or items supplied to or by the industry
  —Channels technological improvement into coherent and consistent directions
  —Produces efficiency by limiting the product or service lines offered, thereby reducing costs of manufacturing, warehousing, marketing, etc.
  —Provides the measure for quality, safety, or performance with which to rate production, make advertising claims, etc.
  For customers and users, standardization:
  —Facilitates performance and price comparisons between similar products and services
  —Provides an assurance of minimum levels of quality, safety, or performance
  —Limits the number of items or services that must be purchased in some circumstances
  —Generally serves as a shorthand mechanism for communications between suppliers and customers.

- There are two principal kinds of standards for products—design standards and performance standards. The former prescribe materials and dimensions of productions while the latter prescribe levels of operation or capacities to be achieved. When it is possible to shape standards either for design or performance, the latter are preferable because they allow more easily for technical innovation and improvement of products.

- Standards are developed privately by organizations such as associations, in which case they are usually voluntary standards. Standards are often developed by governmental agencies, in which case they are often mandatory standards incorporated into regulations. Privately developed voluntary standards are generally preferable because:

—They can ordinarily be developed or revised more easily, more quickly, and more inexpensively.

—They can be developed primarily by those most knowledgable about the subject of the standardization efforts.

—Government standards, even when first promulgated with government assistance as voluntary ones, have the greatest tendency to be made into mandatory government regulations with applicable fines and other penalties for noncompliance.

—They can be developed and administered by utilizing existing, experienced organizations rather than by creating new tax-supported agencies or expanding existing ones.

—They can be developed with a view toward all the implications of standardizing a product or service rather than from the limited purview of a particular governmental agency charged, for example, only with worker safety concerns or governmental procurement concerns.

• The federal government, in promulgating a policy on participation and use of voluntary standards, said this: "When properly conducted, standardization can increase productivity and efficiency in industry, expand opportunities for international trade, conserve resources, and improve health and safety. It also must be recognized, however, that these activites, if improperly conducted, could suppress free and fair competition, impede innovation and technical progress, exclude safer and less expensive products, or otherwise adversely affect trade, commerce, health, or safety." (*OMB Circular*)

• The basic legality of standardization has been affirmed by numerous court decisions and antitrust agency pronouncements where the benefits to both producers and consumers have been pointed out.

• Standardization efforts by associations have been con-

sidered illegal in decided or settled cases when they
have been part of alleged antitrust law violations in
conspiracies to fix prices, exclude competitors, or control production, as in circumstances of:

—An association of macaroni manufacturers which
promulgated a standard altering the recipe for macaroni to reduce the content of one ingredient when
that ingredient had become scarce in order to avoid
price competition among the manufacturers for the
available supply of the ingredient
—Associations of manufacturers which set standards
prohibiting the sale of noncomplying products in order to avoid price competition from these poor quality
and, thus, less expensive products
—An association of pencil manufacturers which developed standards to limit styles, grades, and qualities of pencils as part of a price-fixing conspiracy
—An association of mechanical engineers whose lower
staff and volunteer members incorrectly interpreted
its standard for safety devices for boilers to exclude
an innovative product, even though the association
itself and its leadership were not aware of the incorrect interpretation, did not approve of it, and did
not benefit from it (the *Hydrolevel* case, discussed at
length in a separate chapter).

• Countering these cases of alleged antitrust illegality
are several others where courts considered the reasonableness of challenged standards activities and found
the activities not to be reprehensible where:

—A court rejected a claim that a requirement for fire
alarms to sound for at least three minutes was unreasonable since it considered that the requirement
was not a mandatory one, not against public policy,
and not arbitrarily developed.
—A court refused to hold against an association which
had failed to update its standard for plywood to include a demonstrably equal but noncomplying new
plywood product because the court found no intent
to restrain trade in the association's failure to act.
—A court did not find unreasonable two allegedly anticompetitive actions of an association of domestic
cement asbestos pipe manufacturers in persuading

other organizations to accept standards requiring that certain testing be performed in the United States.

- There are some general rules for association standardization programs which federal antitrust enforcement agencies have declared they will use to determine if the programs are anticompetitive. The rules are derived from decided or settled cases or from antitrust enforcement agency pronouncements. It should be noted that the inadequacy of an association standards program with respect to one or some of the rules does not necessarily render the program illegal. Absent a situation involving price-fixing, boycotts, or other antitrust violations (which courts in some cases have considered antitrust violations without examining any alleged reasonableness of the schemes), each standards program will ordinarily be decided on the reasonableness of its own facts. But the converse does apply; compliance with all of the rules would likely assure that a standardization program would pass antitrust scrutiny:

  —Standardization programs must not be used as devices for fixing prices or otherwise lessening competition.
  —Standardization programs must not have the effect of boycotting or excluding competitors.
  —Standardization programs must not have the effect of withholding or controlling production.
  —Design, specification, or construction standards should not be used except in exceptional circumstances and never when performance standards can be developed.
  —Initial formulation of a proposed standard should involve as many interested parties as is feasible. This includes manufacturers, distributors, service representatives, consumers, etc.
  —Once the proposed standard has been formulated, it should be given the widest possible circulation among persons affected by its provisions, particularly those classes mentioned above.
  —Care should be taken that all comments on a proposed standard are considered and proper weight given to them.

—It is incumbent upon any association sponsoring, adopting, administering, interpreting, or enforcing standards to insure that its standards reflect existing technology and are kept current and adequately upgraded to allow for technological innovation.

—Fees charged in connection with participation in a standardization program must be reasonable as related to the direct and indirect costs involved.

—Membership in groups or organizations sponsoring, promulgating, or administering standardization programs must be open to all competitors.

—Due process must be accorded all parties interested in or affected by a standardization program including suppliers, manufacturers, distributors, customers, and users; due process includes, but is not limited to, the conduct of timely hearings with prompt decisions on claims respecting standards.

—Standards programs, unless otherwise clearly required, for example, by considerations of safety, should not be used to reduce, restrict, or limit in any manner, the kinds, quantities, sizes, styles, or qualities of products.

—The exercise of the responsibility of validating any proposed standard should include a determination by a laboratory or other appropriate entity independent of those immediately affected by the proposed standard that the criteria set forth in such standard are meaningful and relevant.

—Representations made by standards organizations with respect to testing procedures must be truthful.

—In cases involving a challenge to standards, the burden of proof respecting reasonableness is upon those who develop and enforce the standards.

—All standards must be voluntary.

—Standards should not involve business practices or contract terms—for example, for freight, credit, etc.— between sellers and buyers.

• Underscoring these general rules derived from antitrust considerations is the need for due process and other basic considerations that, at one time, were to be used by the federal government in deciding whether to list voluntary standard-making organizations. Inclusion of an organization in this listing was proposed to be a trigger in allowing federal executive and administrative employees to participate in the activities of the organization and would also allow federal procurement agencies to rely upon standards issued by the organization. The criteria were once published by the Office of Federal Procurement Policy of the Office of Management and Budget. They were later withdrawn, and they no longer represent the requirements of the federal government for standards-making programs in which government personnel may participate and which can be referred to in government purchasing decisions. Nevertheless, these *withdrawn* OMB procedural criteria are useful as an indication of what some in the government would have expected as minimal requirements for government-sanctioned standards programs. They are as follows:

"The due process and other basic criteria to be adhered to by listed voluntary standards bodies are as follows:

"(1) That public notice of meetings and other standards activities is provided in an appropriate and timely fashion; and, to invite broadly-based representation, through media which are designed to reach those persons reasonably expected to have an interested in the subject. Interested persons may include, for example, consumers; small business concerns; manufacturers; labor; suppliers; distributors; industrial, institutional and other users; environmental and conservation groups; and State and local procurement and code officials. Such notices should include a clear and meaningful description of the purpose of the meeting or other proposed activity;

"(2) That public notice is given in an appropriate and timely fashion of the initiation, final review, and adoption or approval of new and revised voluntary standards, and the proposed withdrawal of such standards, through media characterized in paragraph (1). Such notice must clearly describe the purpose and scope of the relevant standards;

"(3) That meetings are open and that participation in standards activities is available to interested persons. Unreasonable restrictions on membership in standards-developing groups by means of professional or technical qualifications, trade requirements, unreasonable fees, or other such restrictions must be avoided;

"(4) That decisions reached by voluntary standards bodies in their standards activities represent substantial agreement, after a concerted effort to resolve objections, and that such agreements are reached by the participants in accordance with the published procedures of the voluntary standards body and the judgment of the official(s) duly appointed by the voluntary standards body. Such agreements imply more than a simple majority but not necessarily unanimity;

"(5) That prompt consideration is given to the expressed views and concerns of all interested parties including proposals made for new or revised standards;

"(6) That adequate and impartial mechanisms for handling substantive and procedural complaints and appeals are in force for use by interested parties;

"(7) That appropriate records, sufficient to review and understand what transpired, are maintained of formal discussions, decisions, standards drafts, technical or other rationale for critical requirements of standards, complaints/appeals and their resolution, meeting minutes and balloting results; and that such records are retained in accordance with published procedures and are readily accessible to all interested persons on a timely and reasonable basis;

"(8) That either a one-time written policy statement is maintained in the official procedures of the body or that standards literature published by the voluntary standards body specifically state that participation by Federal agency representatives in that body does not constitute Government endorsement of that body or the standards which it develops. A voluntary standard which includes a list of its developers and identifies Federal agency representation must include this disclaimer;

"(9) That voluntary standards bodies publish their official procedures and make them available to interested parties on a reasonable basis;

"(10) That voluntary standards are periodically reviewed and revised, as necessary, and that participation in the review process is granted to all interested persons;

"(11) That preference is given to the use of performance criteria in standards development when such criteria may reasonably be used in lieu of design, materials, or construction criteria." (*OMB Circular*).

The Federal Trade Commission once proposed a comprehensive regulation under its Trade Regulation Rule authority to hold voluntary standards organizations to specific substantive and procedural criteria. Congress then limited FTC's authority to develop a rule for standards-making. In late 1985, the Commission ultimately abandoned any general regulatory effort in the standards area, citing the *Hydrolevel* case in the Supreme Court as having called attention to the antitrust dangers of anticompetitive standards-making and noting that the FTC would continue to review standards programs on a case-by-case basis.

- Approaches by an association to government agencies to urge the adoption of standards beneficial to association members are generally protected from antitrust challenge by the First Amendment of the Constitution even when the resulting standards restrain trade in goods or services not covered. There may be exceptions to this protection, however, where the government agencies are purchasers of the goods or services on a commercial basis or the approaches by the association are mere shams designed to cover up what would otherwise be considered interference with competitors of members (see chapter on Approaches to Government).

- In addition to antitrust liability, associations should be aware that they could be held jointly liable with their members for injuries resulting from products made by members in conformity with association standards. The possibility is ordinarily remote; but one court had indicated that an association of explosives makers could be liable for injuries from use of blasting caps which had no danger warning labels on the individual caps where the association had considered and specifically rejected requiring warnings on individual blasting caps in the standard it developed for them (*Dupont*).

RESOURCES FOR CHAPTER 51

Books

Bradley, *The Role of Trade Associations and Professional Business Societies in America*, Penn. State Univ. Press, 1965, page 88.

Bucy, "Conducting Product Standards Programs Amid Changing Legal Ground Rules" in *Associations and the Law Book III*, U.S. Chamber, 1969, page 49.

Federal Trade Commission, "Preliminary Staff Study (Precis): Self-Regulation—Product Standardization, Certification and Seals of Approval," 1972.

Harter, "Antitrust Implications of Industry Standards Requiring Intermanufacturer Capability" in *Study of Strategies for Market Aggregation*, National Bureau of Standards, 1973.

Hemenway, *Industrywide Voluntary Product Standards*, Balinger, 1975.

Herold, "Antitrust, Trade Regulation, and Other Nontax Aspects of Association Activities" in *Managing Membership Societies*, Grief, Editor, ASAE, 1979, page 123.

Hoffman, "Antitrust Issues in Setting and Enforcing Product Standards" in *The Solar Market: Proceedings of the Symposium on Competition in the Solar Energy Industry*, Federal Trade Commission, 1978.

Howe & Badger, "Standards and Certification" in *Association Issues*, Jacobs, Editor, ASAE, 1983, page 47.

Lamb & Shields, *Trade Association Law and Practice*, Little, Brown, 1971, page 24.

MacArthur, *Associations and the Antitrust Laws*, U.S. Chamber, 1984, page 50.

National Commission on Product Safety, *Final Report*, 1970.

National Industrial Conference Board, *Industrial Standardization*, 1929.

Olverson, "Legal Problems in Conducting Product Standardization Programs" in *Associations and the Law Book III*, U.S. Chamber, 1969, page 1.

Rawie, *A Guide to Papers Citing Antitrust Cases Involving Standards or Certification*, National Bureau of Standards, 1979.

Shields, "Standards, Hazards, and Warnings" in *Associations and the Law Book VII*, U.S. Chamber, 1976, page 82.

Standards and Certification, Final Staff Report, Federal Trade Commission, April 1983.

Standards and Certification, Proposed Rule and Staff Report, Federal Trade Commission, December, 1978.

Webster, *The Law of Associations*, Matthew Bender, 1976, pages 12–25.

Webster & Herold, *Antitrust Guide for Association Executives*, ASAE, 1979, page 25.

Webster, Herold, & Dye, *Association Legal Checklist*, U.S. Chamber, 1983, pages 26–28.

Periodicals

"Antitrust Problems of a Trade Association Product Safety Standardization," *Iowa L. Rev.*, 1969, page 439.

Blecher, "Product Standards and Certification Programs," *Brooklyn L. Rev.*, Winter, 1980, page 181.

Braunstien & White, "Setting Technical Compatibility Standards," *Antitrust Bull.*, Summer, 1985, page 337.

Fellman, "Can Associations Develop Adequate Statistics and Participate in Standard Making Procedures on an Industry Basis Without Antitrust Liability?," *Antitrust Bull.*, 1974, page 723.

Garvin, "Deregulating and Self-Regulating," *Wharton Magazine*, Spring, 1981, page 57.

Hagan, "In Defense of Voluntary Standards System and the Law," *Standards Engineering*, June, 1975.

Hamilton, "The Role of Nongovernmental Standards in the Development of Mandatory Federal Standards Affecting Safety or Health," *Texas Law Review*, November, 1978, page 1329.

Herold, "Be Aware of Antitrust Risks in Statistical Reporting and Standard-Setting Programs," *Association Management*, September, 1978, page 85.

Hoffman, "Industry-Wide Codes, Advertising, Seals of Approval and Standards: As Participated in by the Trade Association," *Antitrust Bull.*, 1968, page 595.

Hummel, "Antitrust Problems of Industry Codes of Advertising,

Standardization, and Seals of Approval," *Antitrust Bull.*, 1968, page 607.

Jacobs, "FTC Proposes Rule on Standards and Certification," *Association & Society Manager*, August/September, 1979, page 65.

Jacobs, "Statistical Standardization and Research Activities," *ABA Antitrust Section*, 1955, page 80.

King, "Antitrust Laws and Standardization—What Role the Trade Association?," Federal Trade Commission, 1972.

Lane, "Trade and Professional Associations: Ethics and Standards," *ABA Antitrust L.J.*, 1977, page 653.

Lipstein, "Promoting Product-Quality Information: A Proposed Limited Antitrust Exemption for Producers," *Stanford Law Review*, February, 1978, page 563.

Rozel, "Progressive Trade Association Activity and the Antitrust Laws," *The Business Lawyer*, January, 1972, page 479.

Shields, "United States Voluntary Standards System and the Law," *Standards Engineering*, June, 1975.

Sivard, "Beware of Antitrust Pitfalls in Setting Metric Standards," *Association Management*, April, 1977, page 85.

Timberlake, "Standardization and Simplification Under the Antitrust Laws," *Cornell L.Q.*, 1949, page 301.

Verleger, "Trade Association Participation in Standardization and Simplification Programs," *ABA Antitrust Section*, 1965, page 129.

Wachtel, "Product Standards and Certification Programs," *Antitrust Bull.*, 1968, page 1.

Webster, "FTC Seeks to Regulate Voluntary Standards and Certification Activities," *Association Management*, September, 1978, page 85.

Webster, "Voluntary Standards: A Federal Retreat," *Association Management*, December, 1981, page 47.

Wolff & Peterson, "Association Standards: How to Avoid Charges of Negligence," *Association Management*, May, 1983, page 148.

Zeitbin, "How to Build Safeguards Into Your Standard-Setting Program," *Association Management*, January, 1983, page 79.

Cases

Maple Flooring Manufacturers Assn. v. United States, 268 U.S. 563 (1925). Commendation of standardization activity.

Tag Manufacturers Institute v. FTC, 174 F.2d 452 (1st Cir. 1949). Commendation of standardization activity.

National Macaroni Manufacturers Assn. v. FTC, 345 F.2d 421 (7th Cir. 1965). Association standard limiting amount of durum wheat in products was illegal.

United States v. Trenton Potteries Co., 273 U.S. 392 (1927). Association prohibition on the sale of "seconds" to avoid price competition.

Joseph Dixon Crucible Co., 29 F.T.C. 749 (1939). Order prohibiting not all pencil standardization activity if unrelated to price fixing.

C-O-Two Fire Equipment Co. v. United States, 197 F.2d 489 (9th Cir. 1952).

Roofire Alarm Co. v. Royal Indemnity Co., 202 F. Supp. 166 (E.D. Tenn. 1962), *aff'd.*, 313 F.2d 635 (6th Cir. 1963), *cert. denied*, 393 U.S. 1024 (1969). Failure of a plywood association to update its standard is not illegal.

United States v. Johns-Mansville Corp., (1967) Trade Reg. Rep. (CCH) para. 72,184 (E.D.Pa. 1967). Special requirements for foreign-made pipe not illegal.

Chance v. E.I. Dupont De Nemours and Co., Inc., 345 F.Supp. 353 (E.D.N.Y. 1972). Potential liability of developers of voluntary standard which inadequately provides for user safety from blasting caps.

Hydrolevel Corp. v. American Society for Mechanical Engineers, Inc., 456 U.S. 556 (1983). Apparent authority of association in misrepresentation of standard to restrain trade.

Other Resources

Shenefield, "Standards for Standards-Makers," Speech before American National Standards Institute, March 29, 1978.

Kirkpatrick, Speech before New York Bar Association, January 28, 1971.

Office of Management and Budget, Office of Federal Procurement Policy, *OMB Circular No. A-119*, issued at 45 Fed. Reg. 4326 (January 21, 1980); revised, with minimal procedural requirements withdrawn, at 47 Fed. Reg. 49496 (Nov. 1, 1982).

Federal Trade Commission, Notice of Proposed Rulemaking on Standards and Certification, 43 Fed. Reg. 57269 (Dec. 7, 1978); Staff Report, 48 Fed. Reg. 15484 (April 11, 1983); Pre-

siding Officer's Report, 48 Fed. Reg. 25218 (January 6, 1983);
Notice of Completed Action, 50 Fed. Reg. 44971 (October
29, 1985).
FTC Advisory Opinions 16 C.F.R. Sections 15.4 (1965); .407 (1970);
and .457 (1973).

Chapter 52

PRODUCT CERTIFICATION

Many associations that have developed and promulgated product standards have also instituted programs for certification of products that meet those standards. Products submitted by individual firms are tested or evaluated by the associations against the criteria of the associations' standards. If they comply with the standards, the products are permitted to be labeled or promoted as certified by the associations. Under variations of this typical approach, association certification programs may involve testing or evaluation of products by the individual firms themselves or these functions may be performed for the associations by independent testing laboratories. No matter who does the assessing, the essence of any association certification program is the objective measurement of products against reasonable standards requirements. To the extent that the standards are appropriate, and the measurement is done fairly, purchasers of association-certified products can be assured of their quality, safety, efficacy, accuracy, or whatever aspects have been the subject of certification.

It is clear that association certification programs are entirely legal if conducted according to guidelines derived from cases and opinions which deal with certification. Antitrust problems are raised by certification when it is arbitrarily denied to products for which certification is sought by firms, particularly when labeling or promotion of products as association-certified is essential or important to their success in the marketplace. Antitrust problems arise both when firms are improperly denied access to the association certification program or when products submitted for certification have certification improperly denied them.

In addition to the antitrust concerns raised by association certification of products, there may also be negligent misrepresentation or product liability implications inherent in certification. It is possible that false advertising claims could arise based on improprieties in association certification. In a few instances, certification programs have been involved in product liability suits by claimants who allege that they relied upon association certification as to the safety of certain products when they were purchased and that they were subsequently injured while using the products. The economic ramifications to associations from this potential liability must be examined realistically before beginning or continuing any certification programs.

This Summary outlines both the antitrust and product liability aspects of certification.

SUMMARY

- Association certification involves testing or evaluation by or for an association of products submitted to it in order to determine if the products meet the requirements of association standards.

- Products which are found to conform to association standards are allowed to carry certification labeling or seals of approval in packaging, advertising, and other promotion of the products. Some programs involve association endorsement of the products or enrollment on an association list of certification recipients.

- While association certification of products is basically legal, the programs have occasionally been attacked as anticompetitive by government antitrust enforcement authorities. In a leading case, a natural gas association created a standard for gas stoves which, if met, would allow stove manufacturers to use an association "seal of approval" but, if not met, would prohibit gas service to the stoves. The Supreme Court decided that the standard was not applied by the association objectively and that exclusion of a stove manufacturer from the market for failure to obtain the "seal of approval" was an unreasonable restraint of trade. (*Radiant Burners*).

- From a number of antitrust agency pronouncements on

association product certification come guidelines which suggest the most preferable methods of establishment and operation of certification programs to comply with the antitrust laws; note that some but not all of these are absolute rules or requirements; a few only reflect the government's view of optimum legal safeguards for association certification:

—Certification programs must not be used as devices for fixing prices or otherwise lessening competition.

—Certification programs must not have the effect of boycotting or excluding competitors.

—Certification programs must not have the effect of withholding or controlling production.

—No applicant for certification should be denied certification for any of the following reasons: (a) that he or she is a nonmember of any association or organization; (b) that he or she is a foreign competitor; or (c) that he or she is unable to pay the fee or cost charged for certification.

—Fees charged in connection with participation in a certification program must be reasonable as related to the direct and indirect costs involved.

—Nonmembers may be charged more than members are charged for association certification to the extent that the program is supported by general membership dues or assessments; nonmember fees must not be so large that they effectively compel joining the association.

—Membership in associations sponsoring, promulgating, or administering certification programs must be open to all competitors.

—Conditions or qualifications for nonmember access to association certification should be no more onerous than those for member access (except possibly with respect to fees).

—A uniform seal fo approval, certification mark, or registry on an endorsement list should be awarded to all whose products are certified.

—Due process must be accorded all parties interested or affected by a certification program, including suppliers, manufacturers, distributors, customers, and users; due process includes the conduct of timely hearings with prompt decisions on claims respecting the denial of certification.

—Certification programs, unless otherwise clearly required by considerations of safety, may not be used to reduce, restrict, or limit in any manner, the kinds, quantities, sizes, styles, or qualities of products.

—The function and responsibility of determining whether any product is to be certified should be performed by an appropriate organization such as the association, independent of those immediately affected by such program.

—Representations made with respect to testing procedures must be truthful.

—Certification programs should avoid the use of single "pass/fail" systems and, in lieu thereof, employ graded systems which preserve consumer and user options.

• In addition to antitrust concerns, associations should be aware that certification programs may be made the subject of negligent misrepresentation or product liability claims.

• It could be claimed that an association contributed to improperly promoting certified products when the products had not been adequately tested or, when tested, did not meet the applicable standards. A private claim against an association for negligent misrepresentation as to certified products may be unlikely for two reasons:

—Some state courts require that there be "privity," or contact along the chain of distribution between the claimant and the association, before the claimant can maintain a suit against the association.

—The complexity of technical issues, costs of litigation, and difficulty of proving actual negligence against an association would also discourage suits, at least where the association exercised even minimal care in evaluating the products that it certified.

• A suit against an association certifier for misrepresentation could also be brought by the federal government under the false advertising prohibitions of the Federal Trade Commission Act. In one such suit that resulted in settlement, FTC claimed that a plastics association, a standards and testing organization, and several

chemical firms misrepresented the burning character-
istics of insulation tested and certified as "non-burn-
ing" or "self-extinguishing."

- In an important Supreme Court case, a manufacturer
of loudspeakers sued a nonprofit testing and certification organization, which publishes *Consumer Reports*, arguing that its product was illegally disparaged
by a factual error in the article which described the
sound of instruments from the speakers as tending to
"wander about the room." Later the author of the article
admitted that, in fact, he thought the sound had really
wandered "along the wall" between the speakers. Although the lower court ruled against the testing and
certification organization, the appellate court reversed
and the Supreme Court agreed, holding that commercial disparagement of a product is subject to the famous
First Amendment constitutional rule from the *New York
Times v. Sullivan* case that the false statement must
be made with knowledge of the falsity and also with
actual malice for the disparagement to be illegal.

- Associations which use seals of approval or other certifying marks should consider seeking trademark protection against unauthorized use of the marks.

RESOURCES FOR CHAPTER 52

Books

American National Standards Institute, *Products Liability of
Standards Writing Committees*, 1975.
Howe & Badger, "Standards and Certification" in *Association
Issues*, Jacobs, Editor, ASAE, 1983, page 47.
Lamb & Shields, *Trade Association Law and Practice*, Little,
Brown, 1971, page 74.
MacArthur, *Associations and the Antitrust Laws*, U.S. Cham-
ber, 1984, page 56.
MacArthur, "Legal Implications of Association Certification
Programs" in *Associations and the Law Book V*, U.S. Cham-
ber 1973, page 50.
Webster & Herold, *Antitrust Guide for Association Executives*,
ASAE, 1979, page 25.

Periodicals

Blecher, "Product Standards and Certification Programs," *Brooklyn L. Rev.*, Winter, 1980, page 181.

Hoffman, "Industry-Wide Codes, Advertising, Seals of Approval and Standards: As Participated in by the Trade Association," *Antitrust Bull.*, 1968, page 595.

Howe & Badger, "The Antitrust Challenge to Non-Profit Certification Organizations: Conflicts of Interest and a Practical Rule of Reason Approach to Certification Programs as Industry-Wide Builders of Competition and Efficiency," *Washington University Law Quarterly*, May, 1982, page 357.

Hummel, "Antitrust Problems of Industry Codes of Advertising, Standardization, and Seals of Approval," *Antitrust Bull.*, 1968, page 607.

Jacobs, "FTC Proposes Rule on Standards and Certification," *Association & Society Manager*, August/September, 1979, page 65.

"Liability of Certifiers of Products for Personal Injuries to the User or Consumer," *Cornell L. Rev.*, 1976, page 132.

Cases

Radiant Burners, Inc. v. Peoples Gas Light & Coke Co., 364 U.S. 656 (1961). Illegality of stove certification program.

United States v. Johns-Manville Corp., (1967) Trade Reg. Rep. (CCH) para. 72,184 (E.D. Pa. 1967). Certification testing requirements held reasonable.

United States v. ASME, (1972) Trade Reg. Rep. (CCH) para. 74,028 (S.D.N.Y. 1972). Consent decree in which it is required that certification for foreign producers be established.

Bose Corp. v. Consumers Union of U.S., Inc., 104 S. Ct. 1949 (1984). Alleged commercial disparagement by a testing and certification organization subject to First Amendment requirement of "actual malice" to be illegal.

FTC Consent Order Docket No. C-2596, (1974) Trade Reg. Rep. (CCH) para, 20,669 (1974). Settlement of FTC complaint regarding misrepresentation in advertising of results of standards testing.

Albin v. Illinois Crop Improvements Assn., Inc., 174 N.E. 2d 697

(S.Ct. Ill. 1961). Privity required for action in tortious mis-representation. Overruled in *Rozny v. Marnul*, 250 N.E. 2d 656 (S. Ct. Ill. 1969). Privity not required in action against certifier.

Other Resources

FTC Advisory Opinions 16 C.F.R. Sections 15.96 (1966), .152 (1967), .350 (1969), and .457 (1973).

Chapter 53

HYDROLEVEL - THE "APPARENT AUTHORITY" DOCTRINE

In the *Hydrolevel* case, decided in May, 1982, the U.S. Supreme Court for the first time held a nonprofit association responsible for antitrust treble damages under the Sherman Act. The damages ultimately amounted to several million dollars. The Court concluded that the activities of the association's volunteer and lower staff members had caused competitive injury, even though the association leadership was unaware of those activities, had not approved them, and did not benefit from the activities. The *Hydrolevel* case has enormous implications for the antitrust liability of all trade and professional associations. This Summary reviews *Hydrolevel* and its implications in detail, because of the unique and lasting influence that the case is likely to have on association antitrust liability. The Summary also suggests policies and procedures that associations can employ to minimize the implications of *Hydrolevel*.

SUMMARY

- In *American Society of Mechanical Engineers, Inc. v. Hydrolevel Corp.*, the U.S. Supreme Court held that an association which issues and interprets product standards was liable under the antitrust laws for acts of its agents when the agents only appeared to be acting under the authority of the association, even though the association's volunteer and executive leadership neither authorized nor ratified the acts and even though the acts did not benefit the association.

- In applying the "apparent authority" theory to antitrust law for the first time, the Court stated that a rule that imposes liability on a nonprofit standards-setting organization is consistent with the intent of Congress that the Sherman Act be used to deter antitrust violations. The Court determined that an association is effectively strictly liable when it fails to prevent antitrust violations through the misuse of the association's reputation by its agents, including members who are only unpaid volunteers or lower level employees.

- The facts in *Hydrolevel* are unique but crucial to an appreciation of the importance of the case. The American Society of Mechanical Engineers (ASME) is a professional association that promulgates safety standards, including one for fuel cut-off valves that prevent boiler explosions. An ASME subcommittee had authority to respond to public inquiries about this standard. Hydrolevel Corporation entered the market with an innovative device. It was Hydrolevel's only product. The volunteer chairman of the ASME subcommittee contrived with its vice chairman, who worked for the major manufacturer of conventional fuel cut-off valves, to seek and issue an interpretation as to whether the innovative Hydrolevel device met ASME's standard. The interpretation went out on ASME letterhead over the signature of ASME's employed staff secretary to the subcommittee. It criticized Hydrolevel's product. The major manufacturer used the interpretation against Hydrolevel in the market. Hydrolevel went out of business.

- Hydrolevel filed suit against ASME. The trial judge issued jury instructions that ASME could only be held liable if it had ratified its volunteer and staff agents' actions or if the agents had acted in pursuit of ASME's interests; the jury returned a verdict for Hydrolevel.

- The appellate court affirmed and held that ASME was liable because its volunteer and staff agents had acted within the scope of their "apparent authority."

- The Supreme Court affirmed the appellate court, saying that it sought to "insure that standard-setting organizations will act with care when they permit their agents to speak for them." The Court repeatedly referred to the power that trade and professional associations have in affecting the entire economy of the country and noted that ASME is virtually "an extra-governmental agency, which prescribes rules for the regulation and restraint of interstate commerce." The majority decision pointed out that associations are "rife with opportunities" to violate the antitrust laws. The Court criticized ASME for failing to implement any meaningful safeguards that would prevent its reputation from being used to hinder competition in the marketplace. The Court noted that this antitrust violation could not have occurred without ASME's promulgation of product standards and the association's lax methods of administering them.

- Three dissenters argued that the Court's holding adopted an "unprecedented theory of antitrust liability . . . with undefined boundaries . . . ." They challenged the Court's apparent authority approach as a novel theory unsupported by law and unnecessary for resolution of the case against ASME, since the theory was not used in the lower court to produce a jury verdict against ASME. They particularly attacked the strict liability approach of assessing what are effectively punitive damages against a nonprofit organization for the fraudulent activities of volunteer members and lower staff that may not have been preventable by the exercise of any possible procedures by the association.

- The *Hydrolevel* case represents a mustering of several more or less established principles of legal liability joined together for the first time by the Supreme Court in an antitrust case involving an association:
  - —First is the principle that a voluntary product standard issued by a nonprofit association can be used to restrain competition by limiting entry of innovative products to the market and thereby effecting an antitrust boycott. *Hydrolevel* confirms and even expands this principle by declaring that interpretation of a product safety standard, as well as development and issuance of one, can be anticompetitive.
  - —Next is the ancient "apparent authority" doctrine which in common law declared that a principal, such as an employer, can be responsible for unauthorized wrongdoing of an agent, such as an employee, even

if the agent only appears to be authorized. Courts had ordinarily required, before invoking the doctrine, that the principal later somehow approve the wrongdoing or at least benefit from it. *Hydrolevel* ignores these later qualifications and utilizes the "apparent authority" doctrine in an antitrust case for the first time.

—Finally is the concept that the antitrust laws should be used to deter anticompetitive conduct. The Supreme Court declares in *Hydrolevel* that associations must take steps to avoid fraudulent conduct by their volunteers and other agents even though the very nature of fraudulent activity is that it eludes such steps. The majority holding is essentially one of strict liability.

- In view of the awesome theory and result in *Hydrolevel*—antitrust strict liability resulting in treble damages for an association when its representatives engage in unauthorized anticompetitive activities with no more than "apparent authority"—a trade or professional association must seek ways to reduce the chances of finding itself in a situation similar to that of ASME, the defendant association in the case.

- An antitrust compliance program has become essential for virtually all associations. Features of such a program are discussed in another chapter of this book. Some that pertain specifically to avoiding the results in *Hydrolevel* include:

  —A strong commitment by an association's volunteer and executive leadership to assure that an attitude of respect for the antitrust laws pervades the organization
  —A published statement of an association's position in favor of a continuing and undeviating policy to comply with all applicable antitrust laws and to require that all volunteers and staff do so
  —A simple and clear limitation on the prerogatives of volunteers and staff to communicate explicitly or implicitly in the association's name, such as in speeches and articles, as well as in private communications, such as letters and telephone conferences (limita-

tions on the use of an association's letterhead is an
obvious lesson from *Hydrolevel*)
—Review by counsel of any association-initiated communication that could raise some questions of anti-
competitiveness; and availability of counsel to answer
antitrust questions raised by volunteers and staff.

RESOURCES FOR CHAPTER 53

Periodicals

"Antitrust—Nonprofit Professional Association Liable for Antitrust Damages Under the Sherman Act for the Antitrust
Violations of Its Agents Acting Within the Scope of Their
Apparent Authority—*American Society of Mechanical En-
gineers v. Hydrolevel Corp.,*" *Santa Clara L. Rev.,* Spring,
1983, page 663.
"Antitrust Law—Nonprofit, Standard-Setting Corporation Sub-
ject to Treble Damage Liability for Antitrust Violations of
Its Agents Acting Under Apparent Authority," *Dick L. Rev.,*
1983, page 465.
"Apparent Authority Liability Theory Applicable in Antitrust
Suit Against Nonprofit, Tax-Exempt, Standard-Setting Or-
ganization," *Seton Hall L. Rev.,* 1983, page 334.
"Apparent Authority and Antitrust Liability: An Incompatible
Combination?, *American Society of Mechanical Engineers
v. Hydrolevel Corporation,*" *Nova L.J.,* Spring, 1983, page
641.
"Apparent Authority in Antitrust Law and Ruminations on a
New Antitrust Theory: The Implications of *American So-
ciety of Mechanical Engineers v. Hydrolevel Corp.,*" *Minn.
L.R.,* December, 1983, page 439.
"The Antitrust Threat to Technical Standards," *Business Week,*
June 7, 1982, page 31.
"Code-Setting Body Held Liable," *New York Times,* May 18,
1982.
Curran, "Volunteers . . . Not Profiteers: The *Hydrolevel* Myth,"
Catholic U. L. Rev., Fall, 1983, page 147.
Jacobs, "The Legacy of Hydrolevel," *Association Counsel,* CNA
Insurance, Fall, 1984.
Jacobs, "The Supreme Court's *Hydrolevel* Decision: Antitrust
Liability of Non-Profit Organizations," *Perspectives on the*

Professions, Center for the Study of Ethics in the Professions, Illinois Institute of Technology, September, 1983, page 2.

"Nonprofit Associations Are Subject to Antitrust Liability for the Acts of Their Agents With Apparent Authority: *American Society of Mechanical Engineers v. Hydrolevel Corp.*," *Wash. U.L.Q.*, Winter, 1983, page 1487.

Potter, "The *Hydrolevel* Decision: Increased Antitrust Vigilance Under Strict Liability Standard," *Chicago Bar Record*, May–June, 1983, page 356.

Webster, "Your Association Could Be Liable for Anticompetitive Acts of Members," *Association Management*, August, 1982, page 59.

Zeitland, "How to Build Safeguards Into Your Standards Program," *Association Management*, January, 1983, page 79.

Cases

American Society of Mechanical Engineers, Inc. v. Hydrolevel Corporation, 456 U.S. 556 (1982).

Other Resources

Favretto, "The *Hydrolevel* Case," Before the Bar Association of the District of Columbia's 18th Annual Symposium on Trade Association Law and Practice, February, 1982.

Chapter 54

JOINT RESEARCH

In this era of rapidly changing and increasingly expensive industrial technology affecting nearly every business enterprise large and small, means are often sought for firms to cooperate in developing and utilizing new basic and applied technological achievements. One obvious tactic which has proved successful is joint research conducted by competitors in an association setting. Associations promote, establish, and administer joint research projects in which many firms cooperate to share the costs and the benefits of research efforts. The research is sometimes conducted by an independent laboratory retained by the association and reporting to it; in other instances, the participating firms conduct research cooperatively at their own facilities and agree to share the results; occasionally, the association itself maintains research facilities in which it conducts research for the benefit of the entire industry or for firms which participate in funding special research projects.

The scientific areas appropriate for conducting association research projects are as broad or broader than the areas of individual firm research. They include investigations into new methods of manufacturing to increase productivity or improve products, new applications for an industry's primary products or waste materials, new uses of raw materials, machinery, testing equipment, or procedures, etc. Perhaps the major areas of association joint research have become those imposed or encouraged by government. New government controls over energy use, environmental discharges, workplace health and safety, toxic materials, and product safety, among others, have required industries to develop different and more sophisticated products and production procedures. Because the government requirements ordinarily apply to entire industries or segments of industries, association-sponsored joint research products are appropriate for these efforts to facilitate compliance with the requirements.

Association-sponsored industrial research has been praised

and approved in concept by courts and government officials. It is unquestioned that the basic idea of joint research is legally sound. But companies compete on the bases of research and development as well as on other bases. Competitive aspects of any association program can raise antitrust issues. Wherever association joint research projects include cross-licensing or patent-pooling arrangements, for example, the programs must be carefully scrutinized to assure compliance with the antitrust laws. Generally, the government will only condone licensing or patent exchanges in connection with joint research when they are "necessary and constructive." Some general guidelines to use in assessing research projects and making those kinds of determinations are available and are summarized here.

A specific modification of the antitrust laws provides for reduced antitrust exposure in some kinds of joint research and development endeavors. It is summarized in the next chapter.

SUMMARY

- Association-sponsored joint industrial research projects are often the most efficient and expeditious means for firms to develop necessary or desirable new technology.

- Joint research can cover nearly any area that individual firm research might cover, although antitrust concerns might dictate that areas of basic technology are more appropriate for cooperative research than areas of applied technology. Some areas where association research projects have been conducted include:
  —Manufacturing machinery or processes
  —Testing equipment or procedures
  —Raw material use
  —Waste disposal or recycling
  —Pollution control
  —Product safety
  —Occupational safety
  —Energy efficiency or conversion

—Alternative uses for products.

- The basic legality of association-sponsored research has been affirmed by courts and government officials; however, because firms compete for technology, joint research can raise legal issues if its purpose or effect is in any way anticompetitive.

- Some associations conduct research and make the results of the research freely available to the industry represented by the associations with no patent or licensing restrictions. Such research projects very likely could not be challenged on antitrust grounds because there are no competitive restrictions or inclusions involved in the use of the research.

- Cross-licensing and patent-pooling elements of joint research projects have sometimes rendered projects subject to antitrust challenge in cases where manufacturers agreed that (1) discoveries made in the research projects would be cross-licensed among all firms participating and (2) any new technology obtained outside of the projects by participating firms would be cross-licensed as well. Competition for technological development was said to be stifled by these agreements because any participating firm could do no research on its own and still benefit from that of all of its competitors (see auto manufacturers case in Resources).

- From decided and settled cases on joint research projects and from antitrust enforcement agency officials' pronouncements, general guidelines for association industrial research can be derived to help avoid antitrust scrutiny and challenge:
  —The greater the "necessity" for joint research, the more easily it can be defended. Factors to consider are the kind of problem being investigated, the state of the art, the resources available to individual firms, the anticipated costs, the need for fast action, etc.
  —The more "constructive" the joint research, the more easily it can be defended. Factors to be considered are the competitive impact of the project, whether its results will present problems to other industries, whether the research is needed to comply with socially desirable or government-mandated goals, etc.

—Exchanges of basic research information will be less likely to raise antitrust questions than attempts to develop new products or services.

—Research efforts conducted jointly by nondominant segments of an industry raise fewer questions than those by dominant firms or by all firms.

—Research ventures by firms in different and noncompeting industries have far less antitrust impact than those by direct competitors.

—The reasonableness of any joint venture can be assessed by relating the size of the proposed project to ventures which individual firms could successfully conduct on their own.

—Patent pools and cross-licensing are clearly illegal when they effect price-fixing, market allocation, or boycott arrangements.

—Patent-pooling which concerns only a limited number of existing patents, which settles competing interference claims, and which involves only a few companies is less likely to be scrutinized or condemned under the antitrust laws than patent-pooling which covers future patents, operates for a long period, or involves a whole industry.

—Results of association joint venture research efforts should be available on a nondiscriminatory basis to all competitors whether or not they are members, although nonmembers can be charged more for their participation to the extent members' dues and assessments help finance the efforts.

- The U.S. Department of Justice, Antitrust Division, has issued an extensive and erudite guide to antitrust and research joint ventures (listed in Resources). It should be carefully reviewed by anyone interested in pursuing the antitrust implications of association-sponsored joint research because it represents a rare display of the detailed positions on this subject that are held by a principle federal antitrust enforcement agency. The guide includes Justice Department analyses of sample joint research arrangements and provides references to decided antitrust cases to back up the Justice Department positions.

- A convenient summary of federal government guide-

lines on antitrust and joint research has been issued
by the Environmental Protection Agency in cooperation
with the Antitrust Division of the Department of Justice.
It is as follows:

—"Participants. Joint research ventures among firms
in noncompeting industries will create far less antitrust concern than ventures among direct competitors. Similarly, a venture whose participants are
smaller competitors will have fewer anticompetitive
effects than a joint project among the larger, dominant firms in an industry. Industry-wide joint ventures that effectively eliminate all competition in
research within their scope should be avoided.

—"Scope and Duration. The narrower the scope of, and
the shorter the time allotted for, the joint research,
the less anticompetitive effect will be created. More
specifically, a venture that is limited to basic research raises fewer antitrust problems than a joint
attempt to develop new commercial processes or
products.

—"Ability of Participants to Conduct Similar Research
Individually. If participants can show that the cost
and risks of the research are so great that they would
not have undertaken the project individually, then
the venture may have the effect of increasing rather
than decreasing competition. In this situation, there
is likely to be no antitrust objection to the formation
of the venture, especially if it is limited in scope and
duration and there is continuing competition in research and development from nonparticipants.

—"Access by Nonparticipants to Benefits of the Joint
Venture. The results of a joint research project may
give the participants a major advantage over non-
participating competitors. Where research and development efforts cannot be undertaken except
through a joint venture involving major competitors,
then, in order to avoid antitrust problems arising from
this competitive advantage, participation in a joint
venture should be open to all firms in an industry,
or the results of the project should be available to
competitors on reasonable and nondiscriminatory
terms.

—"Collateral Restraints. A joint venture that is otherwise legal may nevertheless violate the antitrust laws
if it imposes unreasonable collateral restrictions on
the participants. For example, restrictions on the
participants' right to use patents or information developed by the joint venture may raise antitrust problems. Similarly, an agreement by the participants
not to engage in independent research, or not to use
technology developed by others outside the venture
unless the technology is available to all participants,
tends to restrain competition in research and development and therefore raises serious antitrust concerns.

—"Exchanges of Information. Sharing of confidential
information about costs, productivity, prices, and
similar matters among participants to a joint venture
could lead to the reduction or elimination of competition among them. To minimize antitrust concerns, a joint venture should avoid such exchanges.
If such information is necessary for the research project, an independent entity could be used to collect
the data so that information exchange among competitors can be avoided.

—"Review of Proposals by Antitrust Agencies. The plans
for a proposed research and development joint venture may be submitted to the Antitrust Division of the
Department of Justice or to the Federal Trade Commission under their respective Business Review Procedures for a determination of this enforcement
intention under the antitrust laws with respect to the
proposed venture. These statements are, of course,
not binding on the agencies, but should provide you
with an indication of any antitrust problems raised
by your proposal. Naturally, before such a statement
is to be of any use, all pertinent information concerning the venture must have been submitted to the
reviewing agency and the actual operation of the
venture must comport with the plans originally submitted."

● Before initiating joint research that seems to raise antitrust issues, an association should consider seeking
antitrust review of the project in a Federal Trade Com-

mission advisory opinion or a Department of Justice business review letter. Either review may be time consuming and neither review will prevent private challenges to the projects or governmental challenges where the projects have been changed, but they do offer a measure of protection which may be valuable in avoiding antitrust problems.

- A recent law reduces antitrust exposure for some kinds of joint research and development endeavors. It is the subject of the next chapter.

RESOURCES FOR CHAPTER 54

Books

Bradley, *The Role of Trade Associations and Professional Business Societies in America*, Penn. State Univ. Press, 1965, page 98.

Herold, "Antitrust, Trade Regulation, and Other Nontax Aspects of Association Activities" in *Managing Membership Societies*, Grief, Editor, ASAE, 1979, page 123.

Lamb & Shields, *Trade Association Law and Practice*, Little, Brown, 1971, page 99.

MacArthur, *Associations and the Antitrust Laws*, U.S. Chamber, 1984, page 64.

Webster & Herold, *Antitrust Guide for Association Executives*, ASAE, 1979, page 94.

Webster, Herold, & Dye, *Association Legal Checklist*, U.S. Chamber, 1983, pages 33–34.

Periodicals

Anderson, "A Legal Guide to Association-Sponsored Joint Research Ventures," GWSAE *Executive Update*, September, 1985, page 43.

Holmes, "Research Joint Ventures and the Antitrust Laws— Recent Statutory and Administrative Changes," *Chicago Bar Rec.*, March/April, 1985, page 252.

"Joint Research Ventures Under the Antitrust Laws," *George Washington L. Rev.*, 1971, page 1112.

"National Institute on Joint Ventures," *ABA Antitrust L.J.*, 1986.

Pitofsky, "Joint Ventures Under the Antitrust Laws: Some Reflections on the Significance of *Penn-Olin*," *Harvard L. Rev.*, 1969, page 1007.

Turner, "Patents, Antitrust and Innovation," *U. Pitt. L. Rev.*, 1966, page 151.

Webster, "Avoid Antitrust Dangers When Conducting Association Research," *Association Management*, September, 1982, page 29.

Cases

United States v. Automobile Manufacturers Assn., (1969) Trade Reg. Rep. (CCH) para. 72,907 (C.D. Cal. 1969). Joint research with access to results limited to participants held illegal.

United States v. Penn-Olin Chemical Co., 378 U.S. 158 (1964). Joint venture by two competitors.

Other Resources

FTC Advisory Opinion 16 C.F.R. Section 15.478 (1973).

Baker, "Competition and Technical Innovation: The Continuing Search for That 'Better Mousetrap,' " Speech before the Federal Bar Association, September 4, 1974.

Ewing, "Legal Aspects of Cooperative Research, Innovation, Competition and Joint Activities: The Role of Antitrust Legal Analysis," Speech before Conference on Cooperative Research, February 19, 1980.

CHAPTER 55

COOPERATIVE RESEARCH ACT

In order to enhance the international competitiveness of United States firms, Congress passed the National Cooperative Research Act of 1984. The Act defines specific research conduct that may be undertaken by combined U.S. firms, including associations, and which benefits from the Act's substantial protections from antitrust challenges: (1) application of a "reasonableness" test to challenges against protected joint research endeavors, (2) limitation of antitrust liability for those ventures to actual damages rather than treble (triple) damages as elsewhere in antitrust challenges, and (3) availability of costs and attorney's fees to prevailing defendants in an antitrust challenge. To achieve these protections, a notification is filed with the Federal Trade Commission and the Department of Justice, who then publish a notice in the Federal Register, at which time the benefits become effective.

In addition to defining specific research conduct that qualifies for the antitrust protections under the Act, it also refers to several kinds of conduct that are excluded from eligibility for the protections. It is made clear that those excluded areas are not illegal; they are only not eligible for the special antitrust protection under the Act. Their legality must be determined by previous, conventional case law on joint research as outlined in the previous chapter of this book.

SUMMARY

- The legislative history of the National Cooperative Research Act provides a concise rationale for its need: "The international competitiveness of U.S. firms in both mature and emerging industries depends on their ability to remain at the frontiers of technological development. Equally important, the security of the United States vitally depends on the ability of U.S. firms to maintain their technological edge. Research and development is critical to the success of these efforts. In many industries, however, the research and development necessary to remain competitive has become increasingly costly and risky—indeed, often prohibitively so. In addition, limits on the available pool of skilled scientific and technical personnel may preclude any single company from gathering the talent needed to make an R&D project successful. In recent years, many of our trading partners have recognized the need for collaborative R&D efforts. Having seen the potential for tremendous economies that could be achieved through such efforts, firms in other countries have formed numerous joint R&D projects, often with government encouragement. Many U.S. firms have also recognized the potential value of joint R&D efforts. These firms recognize that joint R&D holds the promise of a more efficient use of both scarce R&D capital and human resources. In light of the increasing competitiveness of the world economy, joint R&D efforts also represent a necessary step to continued prominence of U.S. firms. Furthermore, stepped-up joint R&D activity, and the innovation that it will make possible, promises to increase productivity and employment, and to permit continued American leadership in important fields of research."

- The Act carefully defines a joint research and development venture, which is eligible for the antitrust protections that the Act provides, as activities that are engaged in for the purpose of:

  —Theoretical analysis, experimentation, or systematic study of phenomena or observable facts
  —The development or testing of basic engineering techniques
  —The extension of investigative findings or theory of a scientific or technical nature into practical application for experimental and demonstration purposes, including the experimental production and

testing of models, prototypes, equipment, materials, and processes
—The collection, exchange, and analysis of research information
—Any combination of these purposes.
The venture may include the establishment and operation of facilities for the conducting of research, the conducting of the venture on a protected and proprietary basis, and the prosecuting of applications for patents and the granting of licenses for the results of the venture.

- The Act also excludes some activities from eligibility for the antitrust protections it provides:
  —Exchanging information among competitors relating to costs, sales, profitability, prices, marketing, or distribution of any product, process, or service that is not reasonably required to conduct the research and development that is the purpose of the venture
  —Entering into any agreement or engaging in any other conduct restricting, requiring, or otherwise involving the production or marketing by any person who is a party to the venture of any product, process, or service, other than the production or marketing of proprietary information developed through the venture, such as patents and trade secrets
  —Entering into any agreement or engaging in any other conduct to restrict or require the sale, licensing, or sharing of inventions or developments not developed through the venture, or to restrict or require participation by a party in other research and development activities that is not reasonably required to prevent misappropriation of proprietary information contributed by a party to the venture or of the results of the venture.

- The Act declares that a covered joint research and development venture, if it should ever be challenged as illegal under the antitrust laws, is not to be considered illegal "per se," but instead must be judged by a reviewing court or agency under a "rule of reason" standard. Application of the "rule of reason" standard generally requires an analysis of all relevant factors affecting competition. Consideration of the effects of the research venture on competition in a properly defined relevant research and development market is to be an important focus of the analysis. If anticompetitive effects are identified, an assessment of procompetitive benefits must then also be made. Procompetitive benefits may include, for example, economic or research efficiencies resulting from a joint research and development venture. If the positive effects on competition outweigh the negative effects, the venture will survive antitrust scrutiny.

- The Act also provides for the limitation of antitrust liability, again in a challenge situation, to actual damages sustained, along with prejudgment interest and the costs of suit. Otherwise, the Clayton Act provides that in a suit for violations of the antitrust laws a defendant is customarily held liable for three times the actual damages sustained (known as "treble damages").

- Further, the Act provides that a "substantially prevailing defendant" can recover the costs of suit, including reasonable attorneys' fees, if the defendant can prove that "the claimant's conduct during the litigation of the claim, was frivolous, unreasonable, without foundation, or in bad faith."

- In order to obtain the antitrust protections of the Act, an association or other group proposing to engage in an eligible joint research and development venture must comply with the notification requirements of the Act. The requirements are these:

  —Written notification to the government must be made within 90 days after entering into an agreement to form an eligible venture; the notification is filed simultaneously with the Federal Trade Commission and the Department of Justice
  —The notification must disclose the identities of the parties to the venture, as well as the nature and objectives of the venture
  —One may file additional disclosure notifications using the same procedures in order to extend the antitrust protections.

- The nature and extent of the disclosure of the research

and development activities in the notification to the government is left to the discretion of the submitters; but the antitrust protections are based upon the contents of the notification.

- The Federal Trade Commission or the Department of Justice must, within 30 days after receiving notification of a proposed joint research and development venture, publish in the *Federal Register* a notice that identifies those participating in the venture and describes in general terms the area of planned activity of the venture. The submitting parties are given the opportunity for advance review of the notice to be published in the *Federal Register*. The submitters may withdraw their notification if the proposed *Federal Register* notice is unacceptable; but, of course, the antitrust protections are lost in the event of a withdrawal of notification by the submitters.

- Significantly, the antitrust protections become effective on the data of publication of notice in the *Federal Register*; or, if the notice is not published within the 30-day-time period imposed upon the government, after the expiration of 30 days beginning on the date the Federal Trade Commission or the Department of Justice receive the information required to be provided by the submitters.

- Except for information published in the *Federal Register*, all information and documentary material submitted as part of a notification under the Act, and all other information obtained by the government in the course of any investigation, administrative proceeding, or case with respect to a potential violation of the antitrust laws by the joint research and development venture for which notification was filed, is exempt from disclosure under the Freedom of Information Act.

- The government does not have the authority to release to the public information it obtains regarding a joint research and development venture, except for the information published in the *Federal Register* notice. The antitrust protections apply regardless of whether the information is exempt from disclosure under the Freedom of Information Act.

RESOURCES FOR CHAPTER 55

Periodicals

Anderson, "A Legal Guide to Association Sponsored Joint Research Ventures," GWSAE *Executive Update*, September, 1985, page 48.

Corrigan, "Antitrust Culture Shock Dazes Firms Freed to Join Hands in R&D Ventures," *National Journal*, November 17, 1984, page 2206.

Holmes, "Research Joint Ventures and the Antitrust Laws—Recent Statutory and Administrative Changes," *Chicago Bar Rec.*, March/April, 1985, page 252.

Katsh, "Act Sets New Standards for Research Ventures," *Legal Times of Washington*, November 26, 1984, page 11.

"National Institute on Joint Ventures," *ABA Antitrust L.J.*, 1986.

Webster, "Avoid Antitrust Violations When Conducting Association Research," *Association Management*, September, 1982, page 29.

Statutes

National Cooperative Research Act of 1984, 15 U.S.C. Sections 4301 and following.

Other Resources

Senate Report No. 98-427, 98th Congress, 2nd Session (1984).

Chapter 56

CREDIT REPORTING

Association members may find it helpful for their association to compile and distribute reports listing customers that have overdue accounts owed to the association members. Credit reporting activities are especially common among local associations and others whose members are apt to sell to the same customer groups. In a typical program, members periodically submit to their association reports naming customers whose accounts are past due for more than a stipulated period (for example, ninety days). The association makes a list of all the delinquent customers reported and sends the list to members. The information is useful to association members in evaluating potential credit risks.

The legality of association credit reporting in principle has been affirmed by the Supreme Court. Specific association credit programs have been forbidden by courts only when they were used by participants to make illegal agreements for activities such as boycotting overdue customers or fixing credit terms. In addition to these antitrust concerns, there are the possibilities that association credit reports might libel listed customers of members or might threaten tax-exempt status if they became too dominant as association activities (discussed in tax chapters).

SUMMARY

- An association exchange of information on the credit standings of customers of members has been declared an essential, legal joint activity by the Supreme Court. The Court's description and analysis of the program it condoned is useful as a guide in establishing and operating association credit-reporting programs:

"Members of the Association render monthly reports of all accounts of customers two months or more over due, giving the name and address of the delinquent debtor, the amount of the overdue account in ledger balance, accounts in hands of attorneys for collection, and any explanation, as for example when the account was treated by the debtors as offset of a balance due for (other products), or was otherwise disputed. There are also reports showing the general total of delinquent accounts in comparison with those for the last twelve months, and reports of payments of accounts placed in the hands of attorneys. There was a form, seldom used, for answering inquiries as to whether a particular name had appeared in the monthly report, and if so, where. There were never any comments concerning names appearing on the list of delinquent debtors. The Government neither charged nor proved that there was any agreement with respect to the use of this information, or with respect to the persons to whom or conditions under which credit should be extended. The evidence falls far short of establishing any understanding on the basis of which credit was to be extended to customers or that any co-operation resulted from the distribution of this information, or that there were any consequences from it other than such as would naturally ensue from the exercise of the individual judgment of manufacturers in determining, on the basis of available information, whether to extend credit or to require cash or security from any given customer." (*Cement* in Resources).

- From this and other decisions, several guidelines for assocation credit-reporting programs can be perceived:

    —An association credit-reporting program should have only one purpose—notifying participants of bad credit risks.

    —Information on overdue accounts should be given by participants on forms prepared by the association to minimize the likelihood that improper information is furnished by participants.

    —Information on overdue accounts may be given directly to the association or, preferably, may be given to some outside accounting or consulting firm on behalf of the association.

—Information on overdue accounts given to the association must be voluntarily provided.

—The information should be as accurate as possible.

—The credit information given to and reported by an association should include the name and address of the overdue account and how long the account is past due.

—The information may include the dollar amount due unless this would tend to identify to whom the account is owed. The identity of a creditor should not be reported.

—The information received and published should relate only to a customers' credit standings and should not include any comments other than standard accounting references like "given to attorney for collection," "notice of bankruptcy received," etc.

—The credit information published should indicate if a listed overdue account is disputed by the customer or withheld against some other claim; preferably, disputed accounts should not even be listed.

—If an association credit-reporting program includes information on past due accounts owed by consumers rather than businesses, the provisions of the Fair Credit-Reporting Act or other federal or state laws may apply and should be observed.

- Credit information supplied by participants on overdue customers should not be retained by the association after it is used to compile reports. Copies of reports by the association should not be retained beyond the time that they are current.

- Distribution of association credit reports should be made only to those with a legitimate interest in credit information. Distribution may be limited to those who participate by furnishing information to the association on overdue customers; participation may not be limited to association members only.

- An association might consider a short form agreement with each participant in its credit-reporting program in which the participant specifies the need for credit risk information and indemnifies the association against claims of libel or other legal claims based on information supplied.

- There must be no open or implied agreement or understanding among participants in an association credit-reporting program to boycott, "black list," avoid selling to, or otherwise deal uniformly with customers listed in the reports.

- There must be no open or implied agreement or understanding among the participants on what credit terms are offered to customers whether listed in the association credit reports or not.

- The association must not itself require, urge, or suggest a method of dealing with customers listed in its credit report.

- There should be no discussion of individual credit-report entries at association meetings.

RESOURCES FOR CHAPTER 56

Books

Lamb & Shields, *Trade Association Law and Practice*, Little, Brown, 1971, page 123.

MacArthur, *Associations and the Antitrust Laws*, U.S. Chamber, 1984, page 68.

MacArthur, "Credit Activities of Associations" in *Associations and the Law Book II*, U.S. Chamber, 1968, page 48.

Cases

Cement Manufacturers Protective Assn. v. United States, 268 U.S. 588 (1925). Extensive discussion of basic legality of association credit reporting program.

United States v. First National Pictures, Inc., 282 U.S. 44 (1930), *reversing* 34 F.2d 815 (S.D.N.Y. 1929). Ostensible credit reporting program struck down as anticompetitive.

Majestic Theatre Co., Inc. v. United Artists Corp., 43 F.2d 991
   (D. Conn. 1930). Illegal credit information exchange program.

Other Resources

FTC Advisory Opinion 16 C.F.R. Section 15.361 (1969).

Chapter 57

GROUP BUYING AND SELLING

Associations have often organized and operated group buying and selling programs, sometimes called cooperatives. Smaller firms band together to cumulate their purchases of supplies. In this way they take advantage of volume discounts, otherwise available only to their larger competitors, and minimize or avoid brokerage fees. They may also achieve savings by sharing purchasing, shipping, and warehousing costs. Similarly, smaller firms join with one another to engage in group selling. Savings from cooperative inventories, marketing, advertising, and distribution are sufficient to justify the efforts in many cases.

A specific law, the Capper-Volstead Act, applies to farm cooperatives. Group buying and selling of nonagricultural products are governed by the antitrust laws, particularly the Robinson-Patman Act which prohibits discriminatory pricing. A price may be discriminatory if it is higher than the price given to another buyer for the same product and the price to the other buyer cannot be justified because the other buyer purchased a larger quantity or was offered the same lower price elsewhere.

Associations involved in group buying and selling programs should be especially concerned about two rules. First, participation in the programs should not be restrictive. Second, prices received or given should not be discriminatory. If formed and run properly, association cooperative programs are effective in waging competition and do not raise the spectre of restricting competition.

SUMMARY

- Group buying and selling programs operated by associations can be effective business tools for members who choose to participate. Some rules governing participation include these:

—Participation in group buying and selling must be
available to all industry firms that are in competition
with one another.

—Participation must not be limited by the size, type,
or location of a firm.

—Participation must not be limited to members of the
association sponsoring the program.

- Group buying or selling must not be used to allocate
customers or territories; to raise, lower, or stabilize
prices; or to boycott suppliers or customers.

- Prices received by buying groups must be available to
other buyers of similar quantities; discounts can only
be based upon economies of scale.

- Buying groups should take precautions to assure that
the discounts they receive are cost-justified and not
induced or coerced from suppliers.

- Buying groups should be more than "shells" to channel
volume discounts to participants by cumulating in the
name of the groups transactions which are really made
individually. Buying groups should have administrative staffs; make transactions in the name of, and with
the credit of, the groups; and maintain warehouses if
possible.

- Selling groups can act as agents for participants but
must not establish participants' prices or terms of sale
and must not allocate orders or production among participants.

- Groups that want to cooperate in selling only to foreign
markets can form export associations under the Webb-
Pomerene Act to gain limited antitrust immunity. In
addition, the Export Trading Company Act provides for
reduced antitrust exposure in some circumstances for
entities organized to engage in trade abroad. These
are discussed in the next chapter.

- The potential antitrust ramifications of association-
sponsored group buying or selling programs can be
complex. Before proceeding with a program, consideration might be given to securing an opinion on the

program's details from one of the federal antitrust enforcement agencies. In any event, antitrust counsel should be involved in all aspects of the formulation and implementation of a group buying or selling program.

RESOURCES FOR CHAPTER 57

Books

Howe, "Cooperative Buying, Employment Contracts, Publications, Hotel and Exhibit Contracts: The Law of Associations" in *Trade and Professional Associations*, Hammond, Editor, Practising Law Institute, 1977, page 21.

Jacobs, "Shortages and Cooperative Buying" in *Associations and the Law Book VI*, U.S. Chamber, 1975, page 54.

Lamb & Shields, *Trade Association Law and Practice*, Little, Brown, 1971, page 138.

MacArthur, *Associations and the Antitrust Laws*, U.S. Chamber, 1984, page 71.

Waters, "Cooperative Buying as an Association Activity" in *Associations and the Law Book VIII*, U.S. Chamber, 1978, page 36.

Webster & Herold, *Antitrust Guide for Association Executives*, ASAE, 1979, page 53.

Webster, *The Law of Associations*, Matthew Bender, 1976, page 13.1.

Periodicals

Kintner, Romano, & Filippini, "Cooperative Buying and Antitrust Policy: The Search for Competitive Equality," *George Washington L. Rev.*, 1973, page 971.

Mezines, "Group Buying—When Is It Permitted Under the Robinson-Patman Act?" *N.Y.L. Rev.*, 1969, page 729.

Mezines, "Group Buying," *Antitrust Bull.*, 1967, page 539.

Selden, "Analysis of Cooperative Buying Associations—Including New Concerns for Franchise Systems," *Business Lawyer*, July, 1982, page 1569.

Steele, "Group Buying Under the Robinson-Patman Act," *Antitrust Bull.*, 1965, page 519.

Cases

Tri-Valley Packing Assn. v. FTC, 329 F.2d 694 (9th Cir. 1964).
Availability of participation in group cooperative programs.
Alhambra Motor Parts v. FTC, 309 F.2d 213 (9th Cir. 1962). F.T.C.
refusal to consider buying group as a separate entity.
Dayco Corp. v. FTC, 362 F.2d 180 (6th Cir. 1966). Participation
in group buying program.

Statutes

Robinson-Patman Price Discrimination Act, 15 U.S.C. Sections
13(a)–(f) (1970).

Other Resources

FTC Advisory Opinions 16 C.F.R. Sections 15.13 (1966), .23 (1966),
and .203 (1968).

Chapter 58

EXPORT ACTIVITIES

The United States balance of trade disadvantage in recent years has provided the impetus for many associations to consider planning and implementing major new efforts to assist members in marketing their goods and services in other countries. Joint export marketing assistance by associations is an attractive idea; but the perceived potential for antitrust law challenge against any kind of joint marketing by U.S. firms could have inhibited those efforts. So Congress passed legislation in 1982 to specifically protect associations and other U.S. entities engaged in joint export marketing activities from antitrust exposure. The 1982 legislation updates and expands, but does not replace, similiar legislation that has protected specific association export activity from antitrust challenges for nearly seventy years. Associations therefore now have a choice in seeking antitrust protection for their export assistance endeavors.

This Summary addresses both the Export Trading Company Act of 1982 and the Webb-Pomerene Act of 1918.

SUMMARY

- The Webb-Pomerene Act was passed in 1918 for the primary purpose of aiding and encouraging United States manufacturers and producers to extend foreign trade. Congress felt that American firms needed the power to form joint export associations to compete with foreign cartels. The Webb Act permits United States companies to combine into an association for the sole purpose of engaging in export trade; and, provided that it stays within the limits of the Webb Act, the associ-

ation's activity is exempt from the antitrust provisions
of the Sherman Act.

- Although Congress was willing to carve out this exemption from the antitrust laws, the exemption was
carefully limited to avoid substantial injury to domestic
firms. The Act contains a number of provisions obviously designed to protect domestic interests from the
associations that Congress authorized:

  —No act done by the export association can be "in
  restraint of trade within the United States."
  —The words "export trade" exclude, among other things,
  "selling for consumption . . . within the United States."
  —The association is forbidden to enter into any agreement "which artificially or intentionally enhances or
  depresses prices within the United States . . . or which
  substantially lessens competition within the United
  States or otherwise restrains trade therein."

- Judicial interpretations of the Webb Act have identified
prohibited and permissible activities under the Act:

  —The practices of allocating exclusive markets, fixing
  prices on an international scale, and selling through
  joint agents with foreign competitors were forbidden
  by one court because they do not constitute "agreements in the course of export trade."
  —Jointly-owned foreign factories were found to be
  without Webb Act immunity by another court because the Webb Act pertains only to joint exporting,
  not joint manufacturing.
  —The Supreme Court has held that the Webb Act does
  not cover joint overseas sales by an export association of commodities financed by the United States
  government under the foreign aid program.

- The FTC has also forbidden under the Webb Act any
practices that restrain the export of domestic producers, including agreements not to compete with nonmembers or arrangements in which the exports of
nonmembers are to be deducted from the export quota
of the association. In addition, the FTC prohibits practices that restrict the right of domestic producers to
compete within the United States as, for example, when
these producers control or attempt to control the terms

or conditions of sale within the United States. Accordingly, export associations cannot restrict imports into the United States or fix prices within the United States.

- A Webb Act export association is permitted, among other things, to:

  —Serve as an export agent for the members in all or some of their markets and for all or some of their products
  —Purchase products for resale from the members
  —Employ agents, direct members' agents, and promote conferences and agreements in export trade
  —Exploit members' products abroad, especially in new markets, and promote members' brands and patented goods
  —Agree with members upon prices for export
  —Adopt uniform contract forms.

- To qualify as an export association under the Webb Act, the association must register with the Federal Trade Commission. An association that fails to register faces a penalty of $100 per day, and loses the benefits of the Act. If the FTC has reason to believe that any act or agreement of the association is in restraint of the export trade of any domestic competitor or has done anything to artificially raise or depress domestic prices, the FTC may investigate and make recommendations to the Attorney General for whatever action he may deem proper. Although this sanction is much less stringent than an antitrust suit, as the United States Supreme Court has held, an antitrust suit may also be brought against an export association in addition to, or as a substitute for, an FTC investigation. In other words, the Webb Act does not preclude the possibility of a civil antitrust suit being filed against a Webb Act export association.

- Although the Webb Act permits export association activities, the Act's antitrust exemption has been narrowly construed. As a result, there is considerable apprehension in the business community concerning the use of the exemption. Only about 25 Webb Act associations are now qualified by the FTC; it is not known how many of them are active. To calm some of the apprehensions that have limited the utilization of the

Webb Act, in 1982 Congress passed the Export Trading
Company Act.

- The Export Trading Company Act was designed to add
  incentives for exports and to permit banks to invest in
  export trading companies.

- The Export Act permits an association or other entity
  to organize and operate principally for the purposes of
  exporting goods or services or facilitating the expor-
  tation of goods or services produced in the United States
  by unaffiliated persons by providing export trade services.

- Of special significance are sections of the Export Act
  which address the problem of uncertainty concerning
  the application of United States antitrust laws to export
  trade. These sections provide for a certification procedure under which an entity engaged in export trade
  can determine in advance whether its proposed export
  conduct qualifies for the specific antitrust protection
  provided under the Export Act. Any association or other
  entity involved in export activity can apply for this certificate. Two important definitions are these:

  —"Export trade" includes trade or commerce in goods,
    wares, merchandise, or services produced in the
    United States, which are exported, or are in the course
    of being exported, from the United States to any other
    country

  —"Services" has a broad meaning including, but not
    limited to, communication, financial, and profes-
    sional services.

- A certificate of review under the Export Act is issued
  by the Secretary of Commerce with the concurrence of
  the Department of Justice. It protects its holder and the
  members identified in the certificate from private treble
  damage actions and government criminal and civil suits
  under federal and state antitrust laws for the export
  conduct specified in the certificate.

- A certificate of review will be issued to an applicant
  which shows that its proposed export trade, export trade
  activities, and methods of operation will:

  —Result in neither a substantial lessening of compe-
    tition or restraint of trade within the United States

nor a substantial restraint of the export trade of any competitor of the applicant

—Not unreasonably enhance, stabilize, or depress prices within the United States of the goods, wares, merchandise, or services of the class exported by the applicant

—Not constitute unfair methods of competition against competitors engaged in the export of goods, merchandise, or services of the class exported by the applicant

—Not include any act that may reasonably be expected to result in the sale for consumption or resale within the United States of the goods, wares, merchandise, or services exported by the applicant.

- Although an association certificate holder is protected against private treble damage actions and government criminal and civil actions arising out of the certified conduct, any person who has been injured by the certified conduct may bring a suit for actual damages or for injunctive relief. Even here, however, the association certificate holder is protected in that these suits must be brought within two to four years depending on the circumstances, and must be brought only under the Export Act as opposed to the general antitrust laws. In addition, if a suit is brought there is a presumption of the association's compliance and, if the court finds that there is compliance, the court will award attorney's fees to the association. Besides a private suit for actual damages, the Attorney General may also sue to enjoin conduct threatening the national interest. Apart from those provisions, the association certificate holder, including members of the association engaged in the conduct specified, is shielded from all civil and criminal actions under the antitrust laws.

- To apply for a certificate, the interested association must complete an application detailing and including various information about the association, the goods or services, the export activity proposed to be certified, and other similar information. A nonconfidential summary of the application must also be prepared and submitted for publication in the *Federal Register*. Confidential business information may have to be dis-

closed during the application process; but the federal
government has taken several precautions to ensure
the confidentiality of this information. The average time
period in which a certificate may be obtained is 90 days
from the date the application is submitted.

- The Webb Act and the Export Act differ in several ways:
  - —The Webb Act covers the export of goods only, while
    the Export Act also covers services, including the
    licensing of technology.
  - —The Webb Act requires the entity registered with the
    FTC be an association, whereas the Export Act per-
    mits any person or entity to apply, including an as-
    sociation.
  - —Only those engaged solely in exporting are eligible
    to become a Webb export association; the Export Act
    does not limit the domestic or import activities of the
    certificate holder, although the certificate itself pro-
    tects only export conduct.
  - —Unlike the Export Act, the Webb Act does not provide
    an antitrust preclearance process for an exporter's
    proposed activities; the Webb Act serves only as a
    defense to an antitrust suit that has been brought, a
    function that the Export Act also performs.
  - —Unlike the Webb Act, the Export Act limits awards
    in private suits to single rather than treble damages,
    allows the payment of attorney's fees to a prevailing
    defendant, and limits the time to either four to two
    years in which a plaintiff may bring a suit.

- The primary disadvantages of the Export Act include:
  - —The somewhat cumbersome administrative proce-
    dure to apply for the certificate
  - —The publicity given to an applicant's export activities
    due to the publication of the application summary in
    the *Federal Register*, as opposed to the mere regis-
    tration with the FTC under the Webb Act
  - —The sometimes difficult requirement of specifying ex-
    port activities in detail for the certificate application.

Generally, however, despite these problems, the Export Act will give export associations greater antitrust
protection for their export conduct than they will receive under the Webb Act.

RESOURCES FOR CHAPTER 58

Books

Brochure for Exporters, Activities and Practices, Federal Trade Commission, 1982.

Periodicals

"The Export Trading Company Act of 1982: Theory and Practice," *Georgia Journal Int'l. & Corp. Law*, Fall, 1984, page 525.

Fugate, "The Export Trade Exemption to the Antitrust Laws: The Old Webb-Pomerene Act and the New Export Trading Company Act," *Vanderbilt Journal of Transnational Law*, 1982, page 673.

Golden & Kolb, "The Export Trading Company Act of 1982: An American Response to Foreign Competition," *Notre Dame L. Rev.*, April, 1983, page 743.

MacArthur & Jarrett, "Associations and the Export Trading Company Act of 1982," *Association Special Report*, U.S. Chamber, January, 1983.

Rosenthal & Yale-Loehr, "The Export Trading Company Act of 1982: Implications for International Antitrust Enforcement," *Private Investors Abroad*, 1983, page 73.

Ryan, "The Export Trading Company Act of 1982: Antitrust Panacea, Placebo, or Pitfall?," *Antitrust Bull.*, Fall, 1983, page 501.

Webster, "Associations Venture Into Foreign Trade," *Association Management*, July, 1982, page 29.

Zarin, "The Export Trading Company Act: Reducing Antitrust Uncertainty in Export Trade," *George Washington Journal Int'l. Law & Eco.*, 1983, page 297.

Cases

United States v. United States Alkali Export Assn., 86 F. Supp. 59 (S.D.N.Y. 1949). Limitations on Webb-Pomerene exemption.

United States v. Minnesota Mining & Mfr. Co., 92 F. Supp. 947 (D. Mass. 1950). Limitations on Webb-Pomerene exemption.

United States v. Concentrated Phosphate Export Assn., 393 U.S. 199 (1968). Limitations on Webb-Pomerene exemption.

Statutes

The Webb-Pomerene Act, 15 U.S.C. Section 61-65. The Export Trading Company Act of 1982, 15 U.S.C. Sections 4001 and following.

Chapter 59

PROFESSIONAL CREDENTIALING

A basic purpose of virtually every professional association—and many trade associations—is to improve the level of practice within the profession represented by the association. The goal of promoting professional competence is an extremely worthy one. Benefits from achievement of that goal are realized by members of the profession itself as well as by members of the public who deal with the profession.

There are many ways of promoting professional competence available to associations. They include presenting informative meetings and education programs, publishing literature of interest to professionals, sponsoring research in areas of concern to the profession, and promulgating and enforcing codes of acceptable conduct.

One further avenue for associations to improve their members' professionalism is credentialing. Credentialing by associations can encompass both certification of individuals who have been tested for proficiency and accreditation of educational institutions that have been approved for certain courses of study. A third kind of credentialing activity—occupational licensing—is also common, but is performed by state governments rather than by associations. State licensing of professionals generally exists as a legal condition for practicing an occupation rather than as a voluntary measure of competence.

Association professional credentialing—both certification and accrediation—has become a common activity in recent years. The number of associations involved in credentialing was put at 120 in 1965, but today the figure is most likely several times higher. Through association credentialing activities a profession is able to take responsibility itself for prescribing educational and ethical qualifications for candidates for certification, prescribing curriculum and faculty qualifications for potential accredited institutions, administering competitive examinations, and conducting assessment visits and awarding some sign of qualification to the successful. In addition, the profession retains jurisdiction to revoke creden-

tials from an individual or institution that ceases to meet qualifications.

For the credentialed individual or institution, the hallmark
provides prestige, recognition, and possibly increased earning
power for the individual or increased enrollment power for the
institution. Equally important, association credentialing enables the public (as well as government and private third party
payers for professional services) to distinguish between those
that have attained some qualifying level of competency from
those that have not.

In short, association professional credentialing programs
protect the public, by enabling anyone to identify competent
people or schools more readily, and simultaneously aid the
profession, by encouraging and recognizing professional and
institutional achievement.

Despite the ubiquitous benefits provided by association
professional credentialing, certain aspects of such programs
have at times come under legal attack. The Federal Trade
Commission and the Department of Justice have pursued alleged illegal practices by professions; some of the challenges
have involved credentialing. In addition, occasionally private
suits have arisen against association credentialing programs,
usually brought by those who have been excluded by the programs from qualification.

This Summary presents some legal background and guidance for professional credentialing programs based on the decision and opinions in governmental and private challenges
to the programs.

SUMMARY

- A Supreme Court case concerning a minimum fee
  schedule for professional legal services held that activities of the "learned professions" are subject to review under the antitrust laws as trade or commerce.
  However, the court did reserve some semblance of dis-
  tinction for professions by saying that it would be "un-
  realistic to view the practice of professions as inter-
  changeable with other business activities, and auto-

matically apply to the professions antitrust concepts which originated in other areas." (*Goldfarb*).

- The Supreme Court held that an engineer association's ban on competitive bidding was an antitrust violation, regardless of the ban's reasonableness. An important reference to professional credentialing appears in this decision in a concurring opinion stating that the court might be willing to grant some extra margin under the antitrust laws and analyze the reasonableness of, as an example, "a medical association's prescription of standards of minimum competence for licensing or certification." While not providing an antitrust exemption for association professional credentialing, it is possible that the court might view that activity with some additional leniency. (*National Society of Professional Engineers*).

- Little direction concerning association professional credentialing has been provided by the two federal antitrust enforcement agencies. The Department of Justice has never directly challenged credentialing programs, although it once charged an association of pathologsts with violations that involved accreditation of laboratories. In a settlement of the charges, the organization was specifically allowed to maintain "lawful, reasonable and non-discriminatory technical and performance standards for the operation or accreditation of laboratories." (*College of American Pathologists*).

- The Department of Justice has given its advice to an association on a proposed professional certification program. An audio-visual association proposed to confer the title of "Certified Media Specialist" upon qualifying individual professionals. In its advice to the association, indicating there would be no antitrust challenge, Justice relied on several aspects of the proposed program as important:

  —Initial certification would be granted without examinations on the basis of successful completion of certain association-sponsored courses or on the basis of a certain number of years of professional experience.

—Recertification would be granted after a certain number of years if additional courses were taken.

—Certification, recertification, and courses would be open to members and nonmembers alike (although fees for nonmembers could be higher to reflect members' support of the activities through payment of dues).

—Decertification would result only from failure to maintain certified status, not for ethical reasons.

—The association would not encourage anyone not to deal with uncertified individuals and would not overtly recommend certified individuals to customers or suppliers.

- FTC once refused to issue an advisory opinion approving a proposed plan by a moving consultants group to certify "professional moving consultants," who were described as estimators and salesmen for moving services. FTC claimed that:

  —The purposes of the program were too closely related to pricing of moving services.

  —Standards for refusing or revoking certification were too vague.

  —There were insufficient, less restrictive alternative methods for obtaining certification already available.

- More recently FTC has also refused to issue an advisory opinion approving a certification program for pedorthic professionals. While noting that "certification programs can be helpful to consumers by informing them that practitioners (and establishments) meet meaningful levels of occupational competency," the Commission cited what it considered several failings in the proposed plan:

  —The required qualifications for applicants were too indefinite.

  —There was no process for appealing adverse decisions to a body other than the credentialing group itself.

  —Certified professionals would be subject to "unreasonable" ethical restrictions such as a tacit ban on advertising.

- Legal precedent for the adequacy of policies and procedures of association professional credentialing programs can also be found in nongovernmental cases, usually brought against an association by some individual or institution denied or excluded from credentialing.

- One federal accreditation case held that an educational credentialing body was justified in denying accreditation to a women's junior college on the basis that the college was a proprietary rather than a nonprofit institution. The court found no antitrust violation as alleged by the college in its lawsuit. (*Marjorie Webster*).

- Two state cases are important because they extensively discuss issues of denial of individual certification to health care professionals. In one case the denial was upheld; in the other it was overturned.
  —In the case upholding denial, admission to a defendant psychological association (which was effectively a certification process) was not a prerequisite for employment as a professional psychologist because there already existed a separate state occupational licensing program.
  —In the case overturning a denial, admission to a defendant medical society (again effectively a certification process) was prerequisite for employment as a physician, because without admission a physician could not use local hospital facilities.
  The lesson is that courts will probably look more closely at, and overturn more readily, those certification decisions by professional associations where the certification is a prerequisite for employment as a professional.

- From the above background, it is possible to fashion a number of recommendations for credentialing programs conducted by associations. Recommendations are offered here separately for program criteria and for program procedures.

- The fundamental bases of any association credentialing program are requirements, conditions, prerequisites, standards, or qualifications that are established as criteria for certification or accreditation. In determining if the criteria are reasonable, the following guidelines should be considered:

—The criteria should be no more stringent than necessary to assure that minimum competency or quality levels have been attained by applicants for credentialing. This is particularly true when credentialing is of significant economic value, for example as a prerequisite for employment or third-party reimbursement.

—Any combination of reasonable education, experience, or examination requirements can be used as criteria for certification. However, it may be advisable to establish alternative criteria where the requirements for certification are difficult or expensive for many potential candidates.

—Criteria for credentialing must not have the purpose or effect of unreasonably restricting or boycotting competitors.

—Criteria for credentialing may include continuing requirements and periodic reassessment of those previously certified or accredited.

—Criteria should be established only after reasonable notice to all those who may be affected by credentialing requirements, including potential candidates and users of their services. Notice should include an opportunity to participate in the establishment of credentialing criteria.

• In addition to reasonable criteria, any association credentialing program should include policies and procedures assuring that the criteria are applied fairly to all candidates for certification or accreditation. The following guidelines should be considered:

—Participation in an association credentialing program must ordinarily be voluntary (except when agencies authorize associations to administer licensing or other mandatory programs).

—Participation in a credentialing program should not be denied because a candidate is not a member of the association. However, fees charged to nonmembers for credentialing may be higher than those charged to members to reflect any members' dues or assessments that contribute to funding the program.

—It is not clear whether it is legal to summarily "grandfather" current association members to a new credentialing program—i.e., provide automatic certification or accrediation without determining if the current association members meet reasonable requirements; the legality will depend upon the facts and circumstances in each case.

—Associations may promote their credentialing programs to potential participants or to the public as good measures for determining the qualifications of professionals or institutions. However, they should not promote credentialed individuals by name or disparage the noncredentialed.

—Denial of credentialing should not be used to "blackball" individuals or institutions, to limit the number of competitors, or to otherwise arbitrarily deny potential applicants access to credentialing or receipt of certification or accreditation.

—Denial of certification or accrediation should be made by written notice to the applicant giving the reasons for the denial—either in writing or at a hearing held for that purpose—with the ultimate decision made by a body other than the one making the original denial.

—Assessment of the qualifications of applicants for certification or accrediation may be best made by an objective body or organization not composed exclusively of those who have received their credentials.

—Any periodic reassessments of those who have been certified or accredited should be made on the same fair basis as the original assessments.

—All qualifying candidates should receive the same certification or accrediation title or denomination for which they qualify, with no discrimination between association members and nonmembers or any other differentiation.

—All policy-making functions of a credentialing group should be kept as independent as is feasible from influence or domination by a parent or related association whose functions include promoting the economic well-being of the profession. In short, the credentialing body should be autonomous with respect to policy-making. Indications are that federal antitrust enforcers would also prefer autonomy with respect to administration for professional voluntary credentialing organizations.

- Professional credentialing by voluntary associations is perhaps the best method of "self-regulation" to avoid excessive government regulation. To the extent that credentialing programs are conducted with fairness and impartiality, they are likely to withstand increased government scrutiny and controls. Therefore, associations involved in credentialing programs should take care to assure that they are aware of (or even ahead of) the rapid legal developments that could affect these activities.

RESOURCES FOR CHAPTER 59

Books

Bradley, *The Role of Trade Associations and Professional Business Societies in America*, Penn. State Univ. Press, 1965, page 95.

Horn, On *Professions, Professionals, and Professional Ethics*, Am. Inst. Prop. & Liab. Underwriters, 1978.

Jacobs, "Legal Aspects of Voluntary Professional Credentialing Programs," *The Study of Credentialing in Nursing: A New Approach*, American Nurses' Association, 1979, page 245.

Jacobs, "Professional Credentialing," in *Association Issues*, Jacobs, Editor, ASAE, 1983, page 61.

Jacobs, "Professional Credentialing by Associations—Some Cases and Guidelines" in *Associations and the Law Book IX*, U.S. Chamber, 1979, page 9.

Jacobs, "Vehicles for Self-Regulation: Codes of Ethics, Credentialing and Standards," in *Self-Regulation*, The Ethics Resource Center, 1982.

Langsley, Editor, *Legal Aspects of Certification and Accreditation*, American Board of Medical Specialties, 1983.

Reaves, *The Law of Professional Licensing and Certification*, Publications for Professionals, 1984, Supplement, 1985.

Periodicals

Gaumer, "Regulating Health Professionals: A Review of the Empirical Literature," National Center for Health Services

Research, U.S. Department of Health and Human Services, 1984, page 380.

Gilley, "Association Certification: Seeking the Common Pattern," *Association Management*, August, 1985, page 125.

Havighurst & King, "Private Credentialing of Health Care Personnel: An Antitrust Perspective," *American Journal of Law & Medicine*, 1983, page 131.

Jacobs, "Professional Codes of Ethics Have Antitrust Contents," *Association Letter*, U.S. Chamber, August, 1981, page 4.

Kaplin, "Accrediting Agencies' Legal Responsibilities: In Pursuit of the Public Interest," *Journal Law & Education*, January, 1983, page 87.

Oulahan, "Legal Implications of Evaluation and Accreditation," *Journal Law & Education*, June, 1978, page 193.

"Restrictive Practices in Accreditation of Medical Schools," *So. Cal. L. Rev.*, 1978, page 657.

Spahr, "Credentialing: A Consumer Necessity," GWSAE *Executive Update*, October, 1985, page 56.

Taylor & Hylden, "Judicial Review of Accrediting Agency Actions: *Marlboro Corporation d/b/a/ The Emory School v. The Association of Independent Colleges and Schools*," *Journal of College and University Law*, 1978, page 199.

"Voices of Experience," *Association Management*, August, 1985, page 129.

Webster, "Association Certification: Consider the Implications," *Association Management*, August, 1985, page 133.

Cases

Goldfarb v. Virginia State Bar, 421 U.S. 773 (1975). Illegality of attorney's minimum fee schedules.

National Society of Professional Engineers v. United States, 435 U.S. 679 (1978). Illegality of ban on competitive bidding.

United States v. College of American Pathologists, (1969) Trade Reg. Rep. (CCH) para. 72,825 (N.D. Ill. 1977). Accreditation of laboratories overly restrictive.

Marjorie Webster Junior College v. Middle States Assn. of Colleges & Secondary Schools, 432 F.2d 650 (D.C.Cir. 1969). Arbitrary exclusion of accreditation for proprietary school condoned.

Salter v. New York State Psychological Assn., 248 N.Y. 2d 867
   (Ct. App. N.Y. 1964). Denial of membership in society.
Falcone v. Middlesex County Medical Society, 170 A.2d 791 (S.
   Ct. N.J. 1961). Denial of membership in society.

Other Resources

FTC Advisory Opinions (uncodified) to Board for Certification
   in Pedorthics (1978); Georgia Assn. of Petroleum Retailers,
   Inc. (1977); and National Institute of Moving Consultants
   (1977).
U.S. Dept. of Justice Release of Oct. 31, 1978. Audio-visual
   specialist certification program.

Chapter 60

APPROACHES TO GOVERNMENT

Associations universally recognize that government is playing increasing roles in the business and professional endeavors of their members. The roles have not only grown quantitatively but have changed qualitatively. Until recent years most new federal legislation and regulation was concentrated in specific commercial areas, i.e., food and drugs, communications, transportation, etc. Even government agencies with broad statutory authority such as the Federal Trade Commission and the Securities & Exchange Commission generally attended to one industry or profession, or even one firm, at a time. The most recent federal laws and rules are more sweeping in scope. For example, they can apply uniformly to most any firm that has employees (Occupational Safety and Health Administration), that makes discharges into the air or water (Environmental Protection Agency), or that makes or sells products to consumers (Consumer Product Safety Commission). State and local government influence has likewise increased in size and scope.

As a result of this proliferation of government activity, it is a rare association that does not become actively involved in representing its members before legislatures or agencies—or even in court occasionally. Association approaches to government often seek laws, rules, or decisions favorable to association members. Alternatively, these approaches may be designed to change or avoid laws, rules, or decisions unfavorable to association members. These approaches effect the very purposes for which association government affairs activities are conducted. But occasionally, in advancing a position favorable to its members, an association directly or indirectly advances a position unfavorable to competitors of its members. The question is raised whether a particular united association government affairs effort, which because of its nature is necessarily harmful to competitors of members, is an unlawful "combination or conspiracy" in restraint of trade.

A series of Supreme Court cases have said "No." The First Amendment to the Constitution gives citizens—acting alone

341

or in groups—the right to petition their government. The Court
has said that legitimate approaches to government are ordinarily protected by the First Amendment even when they result
in competitive harm to others. Similarly, the resulting action
of a government entity itself may carry exemption from antitrust.

Some exceptions to this constitutional protection for association approaches to government have been carved out. To
avoid coming under the exceptions, and because it is sensible
for the establishment of long-term mutual respect between an
association and the government entities it deals with, care
should be taken to insure that association government activities
or presentations are legitimate, factual, reasoned, thoughtful,
and articulate.

Sample guidelines for association appearances at governmental hearings are included in the last section of this
book.

Quite apart from the antitrust implications of association
approaches to government, there are federal statutory provisions requiring that associations or others that collect or solicit
funds "for the principal purpose" of influencing passage or
defeat of federal legislation must register and file quarterly
reports. These federal lobbying provisions are covered in another chapter of this book.

This Summary describes the state of the law on association
antitrust protection for approaches to government as well as
the exceptions to that protection. It also outlines federal lobby
registration requirements.

SUMMARY

- Approaches by associations to legislative, administrative, or judicial arms of government are ordinarily protected from being considered antitrust violations even
  when they necessarily result in competitive disadvantage to those not represented by the associations such
  as competitors of members.

- The Supreme Court has held that the Constitution's
  First Amendment right to petition government ordinar-

ily supersedes the antitrust prohibitions against joint action that results in injury to competitors when that First Amendment right is legitimately utilized. Government action by states resulting from these petitions has also been given antitrust exemption in some circumstances.

● Protection from the antitrust laws for groups of competitors, such as in an association, making presentations to government was articulated in two Supreme Court cases where:

—A group of railroads successfully influenced a state legislature to impose laws and strengthen enforcement of them, restricting or impeding the activities of competing truckers which, the Court held, was protected from antitrust challenge because it was only solicitation of governmental action to pass and enforce laws and was political activity rather than business activity. (Noerr).

—A mine workers union and a group of large coal operators successfully convinced the federal government to set the minimum wage so high as to injure smaller coal operator competitors, which, the Court held, was joint effort to influence public officials which does not violate the antitrust laws even though intended to eliminate competition. (Pennington).

● The antitrust exemption for joint approaches to government, known as the Noerr-Pennington doctrine, is subject to several qualifications that have also been laid down in court decisions such as:

—That in which a group of truckers agreed to oppose every new trucking application filed with a state government regardless of the merits of the applications, in order to restrict additional competition. The Supreme Court held that this was an attempt to use governmental processes to directly restrain trade, and therefore was a "sham" and not protected by the First Amendment from antitrust challenge. (Trucking Unlimited).

—That in which a group of swimming pool builders and suppliers were successful in convincing government bodies to write procurement specifications favoring only them. A court found that this activity concerned the government's commercial role rather than its political role and was not protected from antitrust challenge. (*Paddock Pools*).

—That in which the approaches to government had to be considered attempts to influence the "policy-making" functions of the government rather than the administrative or regulatory functions (*Woods Exploration*).

- To assure constitutional protection from the antitrust laws for joint approaches to government the following guidelines should be followed:

    —"Sham" activities designed to directly restrain competition must be avoided.

    —Joint attempts to influence government commercial activities, such as procurement, rather than political or policy-making activities must be carefully considered.

    —Unethical or improper activities in influencing government must always be avoided. Particularly when such activities are made in areas other than the political arena, they may not have antitrust protection.

- Another exemption from the antitrust laws exists for actions of state governments which restrain trade or result in anticompetitive situations which, if undertaken by private firms or associations rather than by the state governments, would violate the antitrust laws. The existence of this exemption has led some associations to consider whether otherwise anticompetitive programs could be shielded from antitrust liability if state governments could be convinced to become involved in the programs.

- The "state action" exemption to the antitrust laws was most broadly set out by the Supreme Court in a 1943 case where a state government adopted and enforced an agricultural marketing program which resulting in restraint of trade but which, the Court held, did not violate the antitrust laws because it was state government action rather than action by individual firms or associations. (*Parker*). Since that decision, the Supreme Court has severely limited the applicability of the state action exemption to situations where the anticompetitive activities are directly compelled by a state government acting in its sovereign capacity (see cases in Resources). It is not clear exactly when state government involvement in an activity, such as one encouraged by association lobbying, will be sufficient to invoke the state action exemption to shield the activity from coverage of the antitrust laws.

- The exceptions to the antitrust laws for joint approaches to government and for state action are highly complicated and subtle legal areas where the observance of merely a few guidelines such as those given here may not be enough to avoid antitrust challenges. Associations should certainly be advised by experienced antitrust counsel in these areas to help avoid challenges.

- A subject raised by association approaches to government, and entirely different from the antitrust exemption ramifications of those approaches, is the federal law on registration of lobbying activities. The Federal Regulation of Lobbying Act of 1942 requires registration and reporting by those who engage in what the law and interpretive court decisions define very narrowly as federal "lobbying," whose elements are:
  —Collection or solicitation of funds
  —One of the main purposes of the collection or solicitation of funds having been to influence the passage or defeat of legislation by Congress, i.e., the U.S. House of Representatives or the U.S. Senate
  —The influence occurring in direct communications with members of Congress by those who solicited or collected the funds.

- Note that there are also implications of association lobbying activities in the area of tax exemption which are discussed in the tax section of this book.

RESOURCES FOR CHAPTER 60

Books

Herold, "Antitrust, Trade Regulation, and Other Nontax Aspects of Association Activities" in *Managing Membership Societies*, Grief, Editor, ASAE, 1979, page 123.

Jacobs, "Avoiding Antitrust Dangers from Lobbying" in *ASAE 2nd Annual Management Conference Proceedings*, 1984, page 300.

Jacobs, "The Law of Lobbying" in *ASAE 3rd Annual Management Conference Proceedings*, 1985, page 330.

Lamb & Shields, *Trade Association Law and Practice*, Little, Brown, 1971, page 162.

MacArthur, *Associations and the Antitrust Laws*, U.S. Chamber, 1984, page 73.

Shields, "Lobbying and the Antitrust Laws" in *Associations and the Law Book IV*, U.S. Chamber, 1981, page 8.

Webster, *The Law of Associations*, Matthew Bender, 1976, pages 17–30.

Webster & Herold, *Antitrust Guide for Association Executives*, ASAE, 1979, page 99.

Webster & Krebs, *Associations & Lobbying, A Guide for Non-Profit Organizations*, U.S. Chamber, 1957.

Webster & Krebs, *Associations & Lobbying Regulation*, U.S. Chamber, 1985.

Webster, Herold, & Dye, *Association Legal Checklist*, U.S. Chamber, 1983, page 32.

Periodicals

"Application of the Sherman Act to Attempts to Influence Government," *Harv. L. Rev.*, 1968, page 847.

Costilo, "Antitrusts' Newest Quagmire: The Noerr-Pennington Defense," *Mich. L. Rev.*, 1967, page 333.

Jacobs, "Association Appearances at Legislative and Regulatory Hearings," *Association & Society Manager*, June/July, 1979, page 29.

Kushner, "Challenging Federal-Agency Rulemaking: A Four-Tiered Approach," *Association & Society Manager*, December/January, 1980, page 17.

Richardson, "Lobbying and Public Relations—Sensitive, Suspect or Worse?," *Antitrust Bull.*, 1965, page 507.

Vandestar, "Presenting the Industry Viewpoint," *Antitrust Bull.*, 1967, page 565.

Cases

Eastern Railroad Presidents Conference v. Noerr Motor Freight, 365 U.S. 127 (1961). Exemption from antitrust laws for approaches to government.

United Mine Workers of America v. Pennington, 381 U.S. 657 (1965). Exemption from antitrust laws for approaches to government.

California Motor Transport Co. v. Trucking Unlimited, 404 U.S. 508 (1972). Sham exception to antitrust exemption for approaches to government.

George R. Whitten, Jr. v. Paddock Pool Builders, 424 F.2d 25 (1st Cir. 1970), *cert. denied*, 400 U.S. 840 (1970). Exemption from antitrust laws for approaches to government not applicable in pure commercial dealings with government.

Aluminum Co. of America v. Wood Exploration & Producing Co., 438 F.2d 1286 (5th Cir.), *cert. denied*, 404 U.S. 1047 (1972). *Noerr-Pennington* exemption applicable only to governments' political rather than administrative functions.

Parker v. Brown, 317 U.S. 341 (1943). State action exemption from antitrust laws.

Goldfarb v. Virginia State Bar, 421 U.S. 773 (1975). State action exemption not applicable in bar association minimum fee case.

Bates v. State Bar of Arizona, 433 U.S. 350 (1977). State action exemption applicable although ban on lawyer advertising overturned on constitutional grounds.

Cantor v. Detroit Edison, 428 U.S. 579 (1976). No state action exemption in state approval of tariff submitted by a utility.

City of LaFayette v. Louisiana Power & Light, 435 U.S. 389 (1978). State action exemption not applicable to political subdivisions of a state.

National Society of Professional Engineers v. United States, 435 U.S. 679 (1978). No state action exemption from alleged state government encouragement of professional society's ban on competitive bidding.

United States v. Harriss, 347 U.S. 612 (1954). Applicability of federal lobbying registration and reporting.

Statutes

Federal Regulation of Lobbying Act, 2 U.S.C. Sections 261-70.

Other Resources

D. Baker, "Exchange of Information for Presentation to Government Agencies: The Interplay of the Container and Noerr Doctrines," Speech before the American Bar Assn. National Institute, February 27, 1975.

Chapter 61

ANTITRUST COMPLIANCE PROGRAM

Because they are vehicles for bringing competitors together and conduits for moving information among competitors, associations are naturally closely scrutinized for violations of antitrust law. This unique exposure to antitrust scrutiny dictates that associations should take steps to minimize the danger of becoming involved in antitrust investigations or litigation.

The immense complexity of the various and often overlapping antitrust laws precludes the possibility of finding any association administrative policies or procedures which could absolutely guarantee immunity from antitrust scrutiny. The Supreme Court's *Hydrolevel* decision even suggests "strict liability" of associations for anticompetitive conduct of their representatives, real or "apparent." Nevertheless, the prospect of antitrust investigations or litigation is so unattractive that many associations take extraordinary measures to at least minimize their exposure.

Involvement in an antitrust investigation or lawsuit is singularly distasteful. Usually it is embarrassing. If a criminal antitrust case is lost, fines or jail terms are frequently imposed. On occasion, associations have been ordered to be disbanded. Even if an antitrust case is won, the demands upon the time of those involved can be enormous. The legal fees and costs can accumulate to six figures.

One way for an association to help avoid the possibility of antitrust investigations or litigation is to institute an antitrust compliance program. Major business corporations have for years used such programs to educate their employees in corporate policies and procedures designed to avoid antitrust problems. Associations whose potential exposure to antitrust scrutiny is at least as great as that of business corporations, can also use antitrust programs to educate their staffs, officers, directors, and members in the prevention of antitrust involvement.

349

This Summary outlines general features of association antitrust compliance programs. Naturally, the nature of the association and its members will dictate the policies or procedures to be emphasized for that association's compliance program.

Sample association antitrust compliance bylaw provisions and a sample association guidelines document on antitrust are included in the last section of this book.

SUMMARY

- An antitrust compliance program is one way for an association to provide some assurance that exposure to antitrust investigations or lawsuits will be minimized. Compliance programs can be adopted for use by associations of any size or kind.

- The central feature of an association antitrust compliance program is the establishment of a formal policy against antitrust violations. The policy should:
  —Be written in strong but clear language
  —Contain detailed prohibitions in areas where the association may have special concerns based upon past experience or upon the nature of the association or its members
  —Be approved by the association's governing body
  —Be circulated widely among staff, officers, directors, and members.

- An association's antitrust policy can be inserted in the bylaws or can be merely adopted by resolution of the membership or governing body.

- Association staff, officers, directors, and members should be provided with sufficient knowledge of the antitrust laws to be able to recognize antitrust problems when they arise. Association executives in particular should take a definite interest in antitrust compliance and make review of potential areas of antitrust problems a part of regular procedure.

- Legal counsel experienced in antitrust matters should

be readily available to an association to answer any inquiries about situations which may have antitrust consequences. The temptation to do without legal advice in this complicated field should be avoided. Familiarity between antitrust counsel and the association plus a flexible arrangement for legal fees can best encourage necessary communication in this area. Legal counsel should be asked to briefly review recent antitrust developments from time to time for the benefit of association staff, officers, directors, and members.

- Certain association activities require nearly continuous staff scrutiny and participation by legal counsel in planning, effectuation, and reporting. Examples include price activities, cost programs, standardization and simplification, professional credentialing, etc.

- Association records should be maintained in a way that insures that the records reflect factual, objective, and businesslike accounts of an association's activities without useless or outdated information. A record-retention program should be instituted to insure that only necessary materials are kept. Such things as noncurrent documents, penciled notes, document drafts, etc., may not have any lasting value and should be discarded.

- No association antitrust compliance program can be effective unless all those who deal with the association are kept acutely aware of potential antitrust dangers. Antitrust investigations or lawsuits can usually be avoided if those dealing with the association know the rules and are motivated to follow them.

- A sample association antitrust compliance program might include the following features:
  —The program should be summarized in the association bylaws and carefully detailed in some other document.
  —A strong and clear statement of the association's continuing and undeviating policy to comply strictly with the letter and spirit of all federal, state, and applicable international trade regulations and antitrust laws is the heart of the compliance program.
  —Procedures for conducting all association meetings

pursuant to agendas distributed in advance, limitation of meeting discussions to agenda items, and
prompt distribution of minutes to attendees should
be followed.

—Specific prohibitions should be included against activities or discussions which could be construed as
tending to: (a) raise, lower, or stabilize prices or fees;
(b) regulate production or the availability of services;
(c) allocate markets, customers, clients, or patients;
(d) encourage boycotts; (e) foster unfair practices; (f)
assist monopolization or in any way violate the antitrust laws and trade regulations.

—Provisions should be made for counsel to attend certain designated association meetings routinely and
to attend other association meetings when their subjects make it appropriate.

RESOURCES FOR CHAPTER 61

Books

Garrett, *Antitrust Compliance, A Legal and Business Guide*,
Practising Law Institute, 1978.

Jacobs, "The Ounce of Prevention: An Antitrust Compliance
Program for Associations" in *Associations and the Law
Book V*, U.S. Chamber, 1973, page 22.

MacArthur, *Associations and the Antitrust Laws*, U.S. Chamber, 1984, page 77.

Mezines & Fellman, *Antitrust Guide for Association Members*,
ASAE.

Webster, Herold, & Dye, *Association Legal Checklist*, U.S.
Chamber, 1983, page 19.

Periodicals

Anderson, "Antitrust Compliance in Action," *Antitrust Bull.*,
1975, page 731.

Anderson, "Effective Antitrust Compliance Programs and Procedures (An Outline)," *Bus. Law.*, 1963, page 739.

Barnett, "Problems of Compliance—Conflicts in State and Federal Antitrust Enforcement," *ABA Antitrust Section*, 1965,
page 285.

Beckstrom, "Destruction of Documents With Federal Antitrust Significance," *Nw. U.L. Rev.*, 1966, page 687.

Brinsley, "Antitrust Compliance Programs," *Los Angeles Bar J.*, 1976, pages 345–81.

Buchanan, "Avoiding Antitrust Troubles—Revisited," *Practical Law.*, 1964, page 45.

Fellman & Kelly, "Pricefixing, Collusion, Trade Restraint; Associations Need Compliance Programs to Avoid Antitrust Problems," *Association Trends*, May 3, 1985, page 4.

Freedman, "Antitrust: The Education of a Client," *Bus. Law.*, 1962, page 321.

"FTC's Model Antitrust Compliance Audit Program," *Legal Times of Washington*, August 27, 1979, page 18.

Galgay, "Corporate Plans and Policies for Voluntary Antitrust Compliance," *Bus. Law.*, 1964, page 637.

Grange & Oliver, "Head Off Trouble With a Legal Audit," *Association Management*, November, 1985, page 103.

Grange & Oliver, "The Legal Audit," *Association Management*, November, 1985, page 103.

Hale, "Practical Robinson-Patman Compliance," *Corporate Practice Commentator*, 1963, page 18.

Hale, "Preventive Law; Experience in the Antitrust Field," *So. Cal. L. Rev.*, 1965, page 391.

Herold, "Guidelines for Avoiding Antitrust Problems," *Association Management*, May, 1975, page 67.

Herold, "How Can an Association Avoid Antitrust Problems—A Private Practitioner's Perspective," *Antitrust Bull.*,1977, page 299.

Lipson, "How to Implement an Antitrust Compliance Program," *Practical Law.*, 1971, page 39.

McAllister, "Compliance With the Antitrust Laws," *Antitrust Bull.*, 1964, page 665.

Murphy, "How to Communicate Antitrust Philosophy to Corporate Personnel," *ABA Antitrust L.J.*, 1975, page 260.

"National Institute on Preventive Antitrust," *ABA Antitrust L. J.*, 1980, page 265.

Olson, "Trade Associations and Other Associations of Competitors," Chapter 7 of *Antitrust Advisor*, 2nd Edition, Hills, Editor, Shepherd's/McGraw-Hill, 1971, page 495.

Toll & Bauer, "Corporate Antitrust Audit—Establishing a Document Retention Program," *Practical Law.*, 1973, page 15.

Withrow, "Antitrust Compliance Programs," *Record of the New York City Bar*, 1964, page 151.

Chapter 62

ANTITRUST ENFORCEMENT

An association provides its members with a forum where antitrust law transgressions can occur, even if they do not occur intentionally. Associations by nature involve communications or activities among members who are business competitors. Extreme care must always be exercised by associations to avoid policies, programs, dialogs, or pursuits which could be seen as having an intention or result of restraint of trade. This is the very thing that the antitrust laws were designed years ago—and are used vigorously today—to prevent.

The antitrust laws are simple to read but difficult to understand. Decisions interpreting them are often lengthy and complicated; rulings and opinions based on one factual situation rarely apply perfectly to others. Nevertheless, those responsible for governing or administering associations must be able to recognize antitrust problems in order to avoid them.

The assistance of experienced antitrust legal counsel is important once the advice of counsel is sought. But before this can be done the potential for antitrust danger must be perceived by those working for the association or participating in it.

The following Summary sets out some aspects of the federal antitrust laws most pertinent to associations, and it describes the procedures used for enforcement of these laws. The Summary is not, however, an exhaustive or particularized treatment of antitrust laws and procedures. An adequate foundation in the proscriptions and prescriptions of the antitrust laws affecting associations is available from many sources, including some excellent books and articles on the subject, a few which are listed at the end of this chapter. Also informative seminars on antitrust laws and associations are offered by several organizations including the American Society of Association Executives and the Chamber of Commerce of the United States. Such a foundation should certainly be sought and obtained by anyone charged with the responsibility for recognizing potential association antitrust situations before they become major problems.

Note that sample association guidelines on antitrust, which explain antitrust enforcement, are included in the last section of this book.

SUMMARY

- The Sherman Act, the Clayton Act, and the Federal Trade Commission Act are the three principal antitrust laws which may affect associations. These laws, and especially the Sherman Act, were written many years ago in an effort to curtail abuses such as those of the large trusts, cartels, or monopolies which were perceived as threats to healthy competition and legitimate growth of other business.

- The Sherman Act was passed in 1890 and prohibits, among other things, "Every contract, combination . . . or conspiracy in restraint of trade or commerce" and any monopolization or "attempt to monopolize . . . trade or commerce."

- Although activities in violation of the Sherman Act and of the other antitrust laws must be in interstate commerce or must affect it, these qualifications have been narrowed by courts to the point that nearly any business activity is considered to meet the interstate commerce requirements. Even purely local activities may violate state antitrust laws in many states which have laws that are similar to the federal antitrust provisions.

- Early in the history of the Sherman Act, it was determined that not every contract, combination, or conspiring in restraint of trade violates the Act but only "unreasonable" ones. Certain restraints may be justifiable or tolerable. An exception exists for contracts, combinations, or conspiracies whose nature, effect, or purpose creates a presumption of illegality. These are called "per se" antitrust violations. One accused of a per se violation will be prohibited from explaining the reasonableness or other exculpatory aspects of their

purpose or effect. Per se Sherman Act violations include price fixing, boycotts, and market allocation.

- The Clayton Act was passed in 1915 and contains prohibitions concerning illegal situations arising from
mergers, price discrimination, brokerage, and exclusive dealing. Certain Clayton Act implications may exist for association price information activities or group
buying and selling programs.

- The Federal Trade Commission Act was also passed
in 1915. It prohibits "unfair methods of competition . . ."
and "unfair or deceptive acts or practices." No joint
action is required for violation of the FTC Act "unfair
methods of competition" prohibition; a single firm may
be attacked under the law. The test applied is generally
one of unfairness rather than of unreasonableness. The
"unfair or deceptive acts or practices" prohibition of
the FTC Act extends far beyond Sherman Act concerns
of competitive injury and covers injury to consumers as
well as competitors. Thus, association advertising and
promotion activities, among others, can come under
FTC attack for violation of this prohibition.

- Generally, the federal antitrust laws are enforced by
the Antitrust Division of the U.S. Justice Department
(for the Sherman Act), the Federal Trade Commission
(for the FTC Act), or private parties (for the Sherman
Act). There is some enforcement prerogative overlap
among those. Evidence of price fixing, for example,
which might be challenged by the Justice Department
under the Sherman Act, could also be challenged by
the Federal Trade Commission under the FTC Act. Similarly, corporate mergers could come under the antitrust enforcement areas of either agency.

- Government antitrust action ordinarily has its genesis
in a complaint by individuals or firms to the Justice
Department or the FTC, although either agency will
occasionally generate an action itself. Criteria for evaluating whether or not to act upon complaints exist in
both agencies and include consideration of the nature
of the violation alleged, the extent of the injury, the
implications for the public interest, and other factors.

- Notice of an antitrust investigation involving an association or its members can come from:

—A visit or call from a Justice Department attorney or
FBI agent, a civil investigative demand, informal letter requesting information, or grand jury subpoena
if it is a Justice Department investigation

—A visit or call from an FTC attorney, an investigative
subpoena, or an informal letter requesting information if it is an FTC investigation

—A summons and complaint, a subpoena, a list of in-
terrogatories, or a visit, call, or letter from an attorney if it is a private action involving the association.

- Whenever and however an association learns of an
antitrust action in which it may be involved, experienced antitrust counsel should be consulted immediately and before any informal or formal contact or
response of any kind is made concerning the action.
No agreement or understanding on any matter concerning the action should be made with government
officials or lawyers without the advice of association
antitrust counsel. No information of any kind should
be furnished by the association except on the advice
of counsel. Counsel will determine at least the general
nature of the action and prepare to invoke the fullest
measure of protection for the association in the proceeding.

- A Justice Department criminal antitrust action is ordinarily brought only for suspected per se violations. It
usually begins with an investigation by a federal antitrust grand jury which subpoenas documents and witnesses and determines whether to hand down an
indictment. Associations and individual or firm members, as well as association officers, directors, or staff
can be indicted. To avoid a trial, individuals may be
allowed to settle the action by pleading "no contest."
Under such a plea, or if guilt is determined at a regular
trial, the individual may be fined up to $100,000 and
imprisoned for up to three years. Corporate defendants, including associations that are incorporated, may
be fined up to $1,000,000 for criminal antitrust viola-
tions. In addition, an adverse judgment can be used
as evidence in suits brought by private parties.

- The Justice Department may bring a civil action instead
of, or in addition to, a criminal action for violation of

the antitrust laws. Sometimes only a civil action is brought when no per se violation is suspected. The purpose of the civil action is to obtain an order prohibiting the alleged antitrust violation in the future. Such orders have occasionally included forced dissolution of an association where flagrant violations, such as price fixing, have been admitted or proved. Civil actions may be settled without trial by entry of a consent decree approved by the court.

- A Federal Trade Commission action may be brought for any suspected violation of the FTC Act. It usually begins with an FTC staff investigation which may include informal letters of request for information and subpoenas for documents and witnesses. If the evidence warrants it, the FTC then issues a proposed complaint and frequently offers an opportunity to negotiate a consent order whereby one does not admit to a violation but agrees not to engage in an activity in the future. Once a consent order is issued and approved, actions for violations of it may be brought by the FTC to seek fines or other penalties. If no opportunity to negotiate a consent order is given, or if negotiations are unsuccessful, a hearing is held to determine if a cease and desist order should be issued to prohibit the conduct that the FTC considers illegal. The issuance of such an order can be appealed first to the FTC and then in court. Violations of cease and desist orders are punishable in the same way as are violations of consent orders.

- As an alternative to a separate FTC action seeking a cease and desist order against an association or business firm, the FTC has authority under the Magnuson-Moss Act to adopt trade regulation rules (TRRs). These declare, on an industrywide or professionwide basis, that certain practices are unfair or deceptive and are thus in violation of the FTC Act. Before it had this authority, the Commission concentrated on case-by-case actions against persons, companies, or associations that were thought to be in violation of the FTC Act. Armed with the TRR authority, the Commission is able to legislate for an entire industry or profession, even though many individual members of that industry or

profession may not have been in violation of the letter
or spirit of the law. A violation of a TRR constitutes a
violation of the FTC Act and is punishable by fines for
each day of continuing violation of the rule's requirements.

- Associations are singularly positioned to represent their
  industries or professions in FTC trade regulation rule
  proceedings:

  —TRR proceedings are lengthy and complicated and
  take years to complete. Enormous cost savings can
  be realized in cooperative industrywide or professionwide association participation in TRRs as against
  individual participation by association members.

  —When a TRR is first proposed, the Commission has
  not yet determined whether one should ultimately be
  issued: if an association can move quickly with the
  support of an entire industry or profession, the chances
  may be better to convince the FTC that no TRR at all
  is appropriate.

  —During TRR proceedings, the large number of participants usually requires that group representatives
  be designated to coordinate the presentation of certain positions; associations are best positioned to act
  as these group representatives.

  —The broad representation of associations makes them
  best able to marshal and present favorable evidence
  for their whole industry or profession.

  —Associations can take positions in TRR proceedings
  which individual members may prefer not to take
  publicly. Associations can thus forcefully advocate
  the positions and avoid any possible public relations
  response to members directly.

- Besides antitrust actions by the Justice Department or
  antitrust actions or rules by the Federal Trade Commission, certain antitrust violations may be made the
  bases for civil actions by private parties who attempt
  to show that they have been injured as a result of the
  violations. Such actions usually take an extensive period to resolve; they may involve a group of similar
  plaintiffs suing together in a "class action." If successful at trial in proving certain antitrust violations
  and the amount of damages to them, private parties

have their damages automatically multiplied by three—trebled—by law.

- One way for an association to help avoid antitrust enforcement actions involving itself or its members, apart from implementing an antitrust compliance program as described in the preceding chapter, is to seek government review of a proposed program that might have antitrust ramifications. In some circumstances the Federal Trade Commission issues Advisory Opinions, and the Antitrust Division of the Department of Justice issues Business Review Letters.

RESOURCES FOR CHAPTER 62

Books

Bierbower & Lazorus, *The Federal Dragnet, Associations and Government Investigations*, U.S. Chamber, 1978.

Fellman, "What to Do When the FTC Knocks," in *Associations and the Law Book IX*, U.S. Chamber, 1979, page 57.

Fellman & Jacobs, "New Antitrust Penalties & FTC Rules," in *Associations and the Law Book VI*, U.S. Chamber, 1975, page 32.

Handler, *Antitrust in Perspective, The Complementary Roles of Rule and Discretion*, Rothman, 1957.

Kanwit, *Federal Trade Commission*, Shepherd's/McGraw-Hill, 1979.

Kintner, *An Antitrust Primer*, McMillan, 1973, page 1.

Lamb & Shields, *Trade Association Law and Practice*, Little, Brown, 1971, page 20.

MacArthur, *Associations and the Antitrust Laws*, U.S. Chamber, 1984, page 1.

MacArthur, "Antitrust Improvement Act," in *Associations and the Law Book VIII*, U.S. Chamber, 1978, page 33.

Mezines & Fellman, *Antitrust Guide for Association Members*, ASAE.

Oleck, *Non-Profit Corporations, Organizations, and Associations*, Prentice-Hall, 1980, page 831.

Oppenheim & Weston, *Federal Antitrust Laws*, West Publ., 1968.

Van Cise, *Understanding the Antitrust Laws*, Practising Law Institute, 1970, page 1.

Waters, "Some Antitrust Basics in a Changing Climate" in *Associations and the Law Book IX*, U.S. Chamber, 1979, page 57.

Webster & Herold, *Antitrust Guide for Association Executives*, ASAE, 1979, page 1.

Webster, Herold, & Dye, *Association Legal Checklist*, U.S. Chamber, 1983, pages 17–18.

Periodicals

Barnes, "The Role of a Trade Association When the Government Looks Into Its Industry," *Antitrust Bull.*, 1968, page 585.

Brebbia, "The Role of Advisory Opinions and the Business Review Procedure," *Antitrust Bull.*, 1973, page 191.

Dolan, "How an Association Is Investigated and What Is the Government Looking For—A Federal Trade Commission Perspective," *Antiturst Bull.*, 1973, page 273.

Fellman & Pagano, "New Antitrust Law: More Power for Justice in Seeking Association Statistical Data," *Association Management*, December, 1976, page 69.

Herold, "Guidelines for Avoiding Antitrust Problems," *Association Management*, May, 1975, page 67.

Jacobs & Mann, "FTC Trade Regulation Rule Proceeding: Association Promotion of Members' Interests," *Association & Society Manager*, April/May, 1979, page 36.

Kanwit, "FTC Enforcement Efforts Involving Trade and Professional Associations," *ABA Antitrust L.J.*, 1977, page 640.

Offen, "How FTC Proposed Rules Affect Trade Associations and Their Members," *Antitrust Bull.*, 1977, page 317.

Olson, "Trade Associations and Other Associations of Competitors," Chapter 7 of *Antitrust Advisor*, 2nd Edition, Hills, Editor, Shephard's/McGraw-Hill, 1971, page 495.

Reeves, "How the Antitrust Division Can Use Its New Powers to Obtain Statistical Records and Testimony From Trade Associations and Trade Association Executives," *Antitrust Bull.*, 1977, page 355.

Reingold, "New Era of Antitrust Compliance: Can Associations Afford to Relax?," *Association Management*, November, 1981, page 83.

Thompson, "How Should an Association Under Investigation

React—A Former Federal Trade Commissioner's Perspective," *Antitrust Bull.*, 1977, page 287.

Walters, "The Federal Trade Commission Warns Associations: We're Not Going to Play Footsie, An Interview with James C. Miller, III," *Association Management*, January, 1984, page 53.

Waters, "How Legal Counsel for a Trade Association Participates in an FTC Rulemaking Proceeding and Protects His Members," *Antitrust Bull.*, 1977, page 341.

Webster, "Legal: FTC Investigation Seeks to Identify Antitrust Violations," *Association Management*, May, 1976, page 22.

Webster, "The Rule of Antitrust Law," *Association Management*, October, 1979, page 24.

Webster, "When the FTC Comes Knocking," *Association Management*, April, 1985, page 63.

Whiting, "The Role of a Trade Association When the Government Looks Into Its Industry: An Association and Industry View," *Antitrust Bull.*, 1968, page 567.

Statutes

The Sherman Anti-Trust Act, 15 U.S.C. 1-7 (1973).
The Clayton Act, 15 U.S.C. 12-27 (1973).
The Federal Trade Commission Act, 15 U.S.C. 41-58 (1973).

Other Resources

T. Kauper, "Antitrust Enforcement From the Inside," Speech before the American Bar Association, April 9, 1976.

K. Ewing, "Antitrust Enforcements: A Positive Force for Innovation," Speech before the Institute of Electrical and Electronics Engineers, Inc., September 20, 1978.

IV

ASSOCIATION TAXATION

Chapter 63

TAX-EXEMPT STATUS FOR ASSOCIATIONS

A trade or professional association is usually organized and operated as a "nonprofit" and "tax-exempt" entity. One would expect, therefore, that the association may not realize any excess receipts over expenditures and that it need not pay any taxes. Neither expectation is entirely warranted.

Even though it is "nonprofit," an association can ordinarily generate greater income than expenses at the end of its fiscal year and still remain a nonprofit entity. The result is more appropriately called "surplus" than "profit," but its financial effect is similar. The determination under state law of an organization's nonprofit corporate status focuses primarily on the reasons for which it is organized and operated rather than on its actual year-to-year financial situation. Likewise, even though it is tax exempt, an association may occasionally have to pay taxes. A determination by the Internal Revenue Service of an organization's tax-exempt status generally permits the organization to realize and accumulate income without the burden of federal income taxes. The association may, however, be subject to federal income taxes under circumstances when it has realized income from activities not related to the purpose for which tax exemption was originally granted. This is called "unrelated business income tax." An exempt association may also be required, depending upon the tax laws of the jurisdiction where it is located or organized, to pay local taxes on real estate or personal property, sales taxes on goods or services and certain other miscellaneous taxes.

Most trade and professional associations usually can qualify as nonprofit and tax exempt. However, exempt status is regarded by government as an exception to the norm. Associations are required to comply at all times with the guidelines for exemption to maintain their favored status under the tax laws.

Since the enactment of the first federal income tax laws in 1913, trade and professional associations have been able to qualify for exempt status under an Internal Revenue Code section granting that status to a "business league" which is "not organized for profit and no part of the net earnings of which inures to the benefit of any . . . individual." Some associations have been able to qualify for tax-exempt status as "scientific" or "educational" groups. However, most associations qualify for exemption as business leagues. Regulations promulgated by the Internal Revenue Service detail the requirements for obtaining and maintaining tax exemption as business leagues. Finally, numerous rulings by the IRS and decisions by the courts have interpreted the statutory and regulatory criteria and have given some specific, but not always consistent, guidance for organizations to follow in seeking and continuing their favorable federal income tax treatment.

Even though strict and specific requirements have long been established for many aspects of tax-exempt association formation and operation, the IRS and the courts have often allowed limited deviations from those rules without denying or revoking exempt status. When an association has activities that deviate from the established criteria but are minor and only incidental to the purpose of the association, the activities will not ordinarily jeopardize its tax-exempt status, although they may subject the association to unrelated business income tax on the net earnings from the activities. In most cases, only when these activities become "primary" or "principal" endeavors of the association will its exempt status be endangered. Federal income-tax-exempt status of an association can also be lost if it is determined that particular services being offered by the association to its members represent the principal activity of the association.

Generalizations are difficult in this area; but it is possible to appraise typical association activities—lobbying, trade shows, investments in real estate, etc.—under the requirements established since 1913 by Congress, by the IRS, and by the courts to illustrate their possible effects upon federal income tax exemption. As with the antitrust law area, however, the nuances and subtleties of association taxation are very extensive. Each situation ultimately turns upon its own unique facts. No generalizations such as those in this book can be relied upon to determine the outcome in a particular association's situation. Expert analysis and advice by experienced association legal or accounting advisors is necessary to avoid tax exemption problems and to assist in solving problems if they arise.

This Summary and the following ones cover organizational and operational criteria for association federal income-tax-exempt status, exemption requirements applicable to specific association programs or transactions, and procedures to be used for gaining and maintaining tax exemption.

SUMMARY

- Since 1913 when the first federal income tax laws were enacted in the United States, a trade or professional association has been eligible for tax-exempt status as a "business league" if it is one "not organized for profit and no part of the net earnings of which inures to the benefit of any private shareholder or individual." This provision now appears as Section 501(c)(6) of the Internal Revenue Code.

- Even though none of the specific denominations—"association," "trade association," "professional association," or "professional society"—appear in the Code provisions for tax exemption, it is clear from Internal Revenue Service pronouncements and court rulings that they are intended to be included within the purview of "business leagues" in Section 501(c)(6). Some trade or professional associations may alternatively qualify as "scientific," "educational," or similar tax-exempt organizations under Section 501(c)(3) of the Code. This Section confers tax-related and other benefits generally even more favorable than those available to "business leagues" under Section 501(c)(6).

- In addition to the statutory requirements for tax-exempt associations, IRS has by regulation promulgated under the Code detailed specific requirements for exemption. These regulations have been in effect without major changes for well over fifty years. Therefore, they have been sanctioned by Congress and the courts and generally have the effect of law. They state with respect to "business leagues," such as trade and professional associations:

"A business league is an association of persons
who have some common business interest, the purpose of which is to promote such common interest
and not to engage in a regular business of a kind
ordinarily carried on for profit. It is an organization
of the same general class as a chamber of commerce or board of trade. Thus, its activities should
be directed to the improvement of business conditions of one or more lines of business as distinguished from the performance of particular services
for individual persons. An organization whose purpose is to engage in a regular business of a kind
ordinarily carried on for profit, even though the
business is conducted on a cooperative basis or
produces only sufficient income to be self-sustain-
ing, is not a business league. An association engaged in furnishing information to prospective
investors, to enable them to make sound investments, is not a business league, since its activities
do not further any common business interest even
though all of its income is devoted to the purpose
stated. A stock or commodity exchange is not a
business league, a chamber of commerce, or a board
of trade within the meaning of section 501(c)(6) and
is not exempt from tax. Organizations otherwise
exempt from tax under this section are taxable upon
their unrelated business taxable income."

- The statutory and regulatory criteria for tax-exempt
  status of a trade and professional association qualifying as a "business league" have been listed by courts
  and commentators below. Among the criteria are the
  following:

  —That an association not be organized for profit
  —That no part of its net earnings inure to the benefit
  of any private shareholder or individual
  —That the organization be an association or persons
  having a common business interest
  —That its purpose be to promote that common business
  interest of members
  —That its activities be directed to the improvement of
  conditions in one or more lines of business

—That it not be engaged regularly in a business of a kind ordinarily carried on for profit

—That its activities not be confined to the performance of particular services for individual members

—That it be a "business league" and in the same general class as a chamber of commerce or board of trade.

- The criteria for association tax exemption are somewhat overlapping; neither the IRS nor the courts have consistently applied or emphasized all of them. Frequently, factual situations will be decided by relying on one or two of the criteria and disregarding the others. Although the task is often difficult, associations attempting to obtain or to maintain exempt status should review their organizations' governing documents, their activities, and their finances in light of the criteria developed by the courts and the IRS.

- There are two generic levels of scrutiny that could be used to determine if an association is entitled to tax-exempt status when exemption is applied for or challenged:

  —Initially, there is an *organizational* test which examines whether the association was formed according to Code Section 501(c)(6) and the regulations under the Code as a nonprofit organization or a "business league," whether any part of its earnings will inure to individuals, etc.

  —Next is an *operational* test in which is examined whether the association's activities are consistent with Section 501(c)(6) and the regulations so that it promotes common business interests, does not provide particular services, is primarily engaged in exempt activities, etc.

- The first of the combined statutory and regulatory criteria for a tax-exempt association is *that it not be organized for profit:*

  —This is a statutory requirement and is predominantly organizational rather than operational. It can usually be met by incorporation under a state nonprofit corporation law with clear language in the associ-

ation's governing documents that it is not organized
for profit.

—*Note:* The organization of an association as a nonprofit corporation under state law does not guarantee
federal income-tax-exempt status because several
other criteria must be met to qualify for and maintain
federal tax-exempt status.

—Governing documents of an association should be
carefully drafted to assure compliance with the organizational test. For example, if a statement is made
in the purpose clause that the association is not organized for profit but directly or indirectly contra-
dicted elsewhere (i.e., "the Board of Directors shall
endeavor to maximize surplus revenues for subsequent distribution to members"), the organizational
requirement may not be met.

- The second criterion for a tax-exempt association is
*that no part of its net earnings inure to the benefit of
any private shareholder or individual:*

—This is also a statutory requirement which precludes
distribution of an association's earnings or surplus
to individual members. The payment of cash dividends or the extension of services at less than their
cost elsewhere to individual association members
will ordinarily preclude exempt status. In the case
of cash payments, even an incidental amount of inurement to members may be enough to defeat tax
exemption when it is applied for or challenged by
the IRS. Generally, however, incidental particular
services to members (advice to a member from association staff, for example) will not be considered
inurement in violation of the statute.

—Although not specifically required to do so by the
law or by IRS, many associations provide against
any possible inurement of benefits to members upon
dissolution by stating in their governing documents
that funds remaining upon dissolution of the association shall be paid over to charitable organizations
or some other tax-exempt recipients not related to
members.

—Examples of inurement to the benefit of members
which have defeated the exempt status of associa-

tions include the routine furnishing of payments for legal fees of members, distribution to members of shares of income received from association-owned copyrights, elimination of dues of members made possible by profits from commercial activities of an association, and rebate of shares of net earnings of a trade show made by the sponsoring association to members who exhibited at the show.

- The third criterion for a tax-exempt association is *that the organization be an association of persons having a common business interest:*

  —Obviously, this provision is usually met if the association's members engage in the same trade or profession, such as the widget industry or the widgeters' profession, or even in the same functional level or geographic division within the trade or profession, such as widget wholesalers or Eastern widgeters.

  —The provision has been considered broad enough to include chambers of commerce or other general business or professional groups whose members are not engaged in the same line of commerce but otherwise have common business interests such as to promote general trade or professionalism in a subject or geographic area, to promote good industrial relations, etc.

  —In a specific instance, one federal appellate court some years ago upheld the tax exemption of an association of bottlers of a particular soft drink against the challenge that the members were not engaged in a line of commerce because they bottled only one soft drink brand. Another federal appellate court subsequently disallowed tax-exempt status for an association whose membership was limited to franchises of a particular automobile muffler company which the court did not consider to be a line of business. This decision was affirmed by the United States Supreme Court. The validity of the line of business requirement under the regulations, and the IRS position that an association of franchisees does not qualify for exemption, is now clearly settled. IRS strictly follows the reasoning of the Supreme Court muffler franchisees' association case. It has also extended that reasoning somewhat when it issued rulings denying exempt status to associations of dealers of a certain make of automobile and merchants in a particular shopping center. Note also that the American Automobile Association has been denied exempt status at least in part because its members are motorists who do not necessarily share a common business interest.

- The fourth criterion for a tax-exempt association is *that its purpose be to promote that common business interest of members:*
  —As a predominantly organizational rather than operational test, this one ought to be relatively simple to observe. An association should specify in its governing documents the common business interest of its members and indicate the purpose of the association to promote that interest.
  —Note that, in the operation of the association, the common business interest of members must be promoted. An association would violate this rule where its members had a common business interest but some other interest was the primary one actually promoted by the association (i.e., an association of widget manufacturers formed and run for social purposes).

- The fifth criterion for a tax-exempt association is *that its activities be directed to the improvement of conditions in one or more lines of business:*
  —The definition of an entire line of business—a trade, industry, or profession—can be an important factor in attempting to meet this requirement. In the Supreme Court muffler dealers' association case mentioned earlier, partly at issue was the question whether the purview of the association covered the required line of business or merely covered those marketing a particular brand or product line within a line of business.
  —Although there is no clear authority in the tax law for it, the exempt association requirement that it promote an entire line of business may mean that it must make its services available both to members and nonmembers alike. In one case, exempt status was

denied a research organization because its research was not available to both members and nonmembers. In this vein, and as an example of how the exempt association's statutory and regulatory criteria can be applied in ways that are inconsistent with each other and with unrelated legal principles such as antitrust policy, note that IRS has occasionally taken the position that charging nonmembers more for services than members are charged can result in prohibited "inurement." It is not likely that IRS will be sustained in that position.

- The sixth criterion for a tax-exempt association is *that it not be engaged regularly in a business of a kind ordinarily carried on for profit:*

  —This "similarity to business" requirement is rarely dispositive of the issue of tax-exempt status of an association, although it is frequently cited in rulings where exempt status is at is issue. Many activities of associations are similar to those conducted by profit-seeking companies but are designed to improve business conditions in a line of business and can be justified on that ground; so the practical result of this requirement is limited.

  —In an early Supreme Court case, the determination was made that it is the destination of income to an exempt organization, not its source in commercial activity, that is most important. Under this decision, some limited business-type activities of an exempt organization would be allowed so long as those activities were only "incidental" to the main purpose for which exemption was granted. The rule remains that limited commercial activities of associations will ordinarily not defeat tax exemption if they are considered only "incidental" to the associations' exempt purposes. Note, however, that any net gain from such activities may subject the associations to unrelated business income tax, as discussed in a succeeding chapter of this book.

  —An important recent decision denying tax exemption to an association of barbers and beauticians which conducted its own insurance program for members supports denial of exemption upon a finding that an

association is engaged in a business of a kind ordinarily carried on for profit after consideration of
the substantial time and financial resources devoted
to this type of activity.

- The seventh criterion for a tax-exempt association is
  *that its activities not be confined to the performance of
  particular services for individual members:*
  —The prohibited "particular services for individuals"
  has been defined by IRS to include any "activity that
  serves as a convenience or economy to members in
  the operation of their business rather than to promote
  or improve the industry represented by the association."
  —Again, courts have considered this apparent ban on
  particularized association services to members as a
  quantitative matter—exemption will not be denied
  where the particular services are minor or incidental.
  —Each association service must be viewed by itself to
  see if it could be considered a particular service for
  individual members and detrimental to exempt status. For example, specific associations have been
  denied exempt status when formed to give financial
  advice to members' customers, test products for hazards, publish a used car guide, etc. Denials of association exempt status were made in these instances
  on the basis that the primary purpose of each association was the performance of particular services.

- The eighth criterion for a tax-exempt association is *that
  it be a "business league" and in the same general class
  as a chamber of commerce or board of trade:*
  —Trade and professional associations can ordinarily
  meet this criterion with ease because, like "business
  leagues," chambers of commerce, and boards of trade,
  associations exist primarily to promote members'
  business and professional interests and, inevitably,
  those of the entire industrial or professional area of
  their memberships.
  —Since IRS has generally considered trade and professional associations as synonymous with "business
  leagues," this requirement is usually met simply by
  definition.

- There are a number of important reasons why an association would seek to obtain or retain tax-exempt status by meeting the statutory and regulatory mandates for exempt organizations. Among the advantages of exempt status (as offered by Statham & Buek) are the following:

—It enables the organization to receive dues and certain other income without paying taxes on that income.

—It generally allows the organization to accumulate income tax free.

—It is indicative of nonprofit status for many purposes, and may in some instances meet state or local requirements for exemption from property, sales, and other taxes.

—It can be a psychological advantage in working with the public, government officials, and members that may not be present if the organization were considered a for-profit corporation.

—It entitles the organization to the $1,000 specific deduction with regard to unrelated business income, which is not available to non-exempt organizations.

● It is rarely possible to make completely accurate predictions as to treatment by the IRS or by the courts of specific factual issues involving federal income tax exemption; nevertheless, an overriding rule of thumb is suggested by the statute, the regulations, the decisions, and the rulings: Was the association started, and is it run, not to make money but to promote generally the business interests of a trade or profession without furnishing a large number of individual services and without any members receiving financial return? If the answer is "yes," and if the specific criteria are met, exemption is almost always available.

RESOURCES FOR CHAPTER 63

Books

Greif, "Federal Income Tax Status" in *Managing Membership Societies*, Greif, Editor, ASAE, 1979, page 1.

Gross & Worshauer, *Financial and Accounting Guide for Non-profit Organizations*, Ronald Press, 1983.

Hopkins, *The Law of Tax-Exempt Associations*, Ronald Press, 1979, page 268.

Jordan, "Trends in Tax Exemption" in *Trends in Nonprofit Organizations Law*, American Law Institute, 1977, page 11.

Lamb & Shields, *Trade Association Law and Practice*, Little, Brown, 1971, page 240.

Lane, "Federal Income Tax Exemption" in *Legal Handbook for Nonprofit Organizations*, AMACOM, 1980, page 155.

Oleck, *Non-Profit Corporations, Organizations and Associations*, Prentice-Hall, 1980, page 601.

Statham & Buek, *Associations and the Tax Laws*, U.S. Chamber, 1978, page 5.

Touche Ross & Co., *Federal Income Tax Exemption for Trade and Professional Associations*, ASAE, 1985.

Webster, *Federal Tax Aspects of Association Activities*, U.S. Chamber, 1959.

Webster, *Associations and the IRS*, U.S. Chamber, 1966.

Webster, *The Law of Associations*, Matthew Bender, 1976, page 15.1.

Webster & Dye, "Trade Associations" in 331-2d *Tax Management*, The Bureau of National Affairs, Inc., 1976.

Webster, Herold, & Dye, *Association Legal Checklist*, U.S. Chamber, 1983, pages 41–42.

Periodicals

Anderson, "Sales and Use Taxes: How a Nonprofit Can Obtain an Exemption," GWSAE *Executive Update*, June, 1985, page 42.

Bittker & Rahdert, "The Exemption of Nonprofit Organizations From Federal Income Taxation," *Yale L.J.*, 1976, page 299.

"Business League Exemption Granted to Association of Bottlers of Non Name-Brand Product," *U. Kansas L. Rev.*, 1967, page 23.

Caytor, "What Activities Risk Trade Association Exemptions," *J. Taxation*, 1978, page 104.

Combs, "Should an Association Give Up Its Tax Exemption?," *Association Management*, September, 1974, page 22.

Duhl, "Tax-Exempt Organizations: The Attack on Unreasona-

ble Accumulations of Income," *Georgetown L.J.*, 1969, page
483.

Fischer, "Tax Status of Associations," *Life Association News*,
1969, page 135.

Fox & Jackson, "Trade Associations: Present and Future Problems," *Tax Law Rev.*, 1971, page 781.

Grief, "Making Money Through Strategic Tax Planning," *Association Management*, May, 1985, page 91.

Kinnamon, "How to Assure That Charitable, Civic, Business
League or Social Organizations Are Tax Exempt," *Taxation
for Accountants*, 1977, page 108.

LaRue & Lawler, "What You Should Know About Protecting
Your Tax Exemption," *Association Management*, November, 1981, page 71.

"Pepsi-Cola Bottlers' Association Case," *Fordham L. Rev.*, 1965,
page 738.

Reilly, "Lawyers Guide to Tax Exempt Organizations," *N.J. Bar
J.*, 1978, page 36.

Statham & Buek, "S. Ct's. Holding in National Muffler Precludes Exemption for Franchisee Associations," *J. Taxation*, 1979, page 80.

Teschner, "Tax Exemption v. Services to Members," *Taxes*, 1959,
page 669.

Webster, "Why Retain Federal Tax Exempt Status," *Association Management*, February, 1971, page 13.

Webster, "Why You Should Keep Your Federal Tax Exemption,"
Association Management, September, 1974, page 22.

Webster, "IRS Disputes Higher Charges for Services to Nonmembers," *Association Management*, April, 1978, page 18.

Webster, "Can a 501(c)(6) Qualify for a Nonprofit Mailing Permit?," *Association Management*, June, 1984, page 61.

Statutes and Regulations

Internal Revenue Code Section 501(c)(6)
Regulations Section 1.501(c)(6)-1.

Cases

Associated Industries of Cleveland, 7 T.C. 1449 (1946). Statement of requirements for "business league" exemption.
Trinidad v. Sagrada Orden de Predicadores, 263 U.S. 578 (1924).

The fact that an organization has earnings does not by itself defeat tax exempt status.

Waynesboro Manufacturers Assn., 1 B.T.A. 911 (1925). Issue of whether association is organized for profit.

National Chiropractic Assn. v. Birmingham, 96 F. Supp. 874 (N.D. Iowa 1951). Inurement of legal services.

Wholesale Grocers Exchange, Inc., 3 T.C.M. (CCH) 699 (1944). Inurement of copyright income.

Michigan Mobile Home & Recreational Vehicle Institute, 66 T.C. 770 (1976). Inurement of trade show income rebates.

Pepsi-Cola Bottlers' Assn., Inc., v. United States, 369 F.2d 250 (7th Cir. 1966). Common business interest of bottlers' association members.

National Muffler Dealers Assn., Inc., v. United States, 565 F.2d 845 (2nd Cir. 1977), *aff'd.*, 440 U.S. 442 (1979). No common business interest in muffler dealers' association.

American Automobile Assn., 19 T.C. 1146 (1953). Denial of exemption based on lack of common business interest.

Glass Container Industry Research Corp., 70-1 U.S.T.C. Section 9214 (W.D. Pa. 1970). Denial of exempt status for failure to make research available to nonmembers.

Associated Master Barbers & Beauticians of America, 69 T.C. 53 (1977). Denial of exempt status when association's self insurance activities more than incidental.

Chapter 64

SCIENTIFIC AND EDUCATIONAL ASSOCIATIONS

Although most trade and professional associations enjoy tax-exempt status as business leagues under Section 501(c)(6) of the Internal Revenue Code, a significant number of associations somewhat similar to trade and professional groups enjoy even more favorable tax-exempt status as "scientific" or "educational" organizations under Section 501(c)(3). This Section includes, in addition to scientific and educational groups, charitable, literary, public safety, anticruelty, amateur athletic, and other such organizations. Associations which are themselves exempt as business leagues have frequently formed controlled subsidiary organizations for specific purposes or to conduct specific activities which have qualified as exempt scientific or educational entities. The controlled Section 501(c)(3) organization is generally eligible for "charity" status with all of its corresponding benefits. Among other benefits, contributions to these entities are deductible to donors as charitable contributions.

A number of associations of professionals have long held Section 501(c)(3) status as scientific or educational organizations; but many of these are finding their more favorable exempt status under challenge in government attempts to downgrade them to Section 501(c)(6) associations.

This summary concerns requirements for tax exemption for scientific or educational organizations; it also describes some of the tax and other benefits available to these groups because of their special exempt status.

Once again, the laws, rules, and decisions on charitable organizations—which tax-exempt scientific and educational associations most closely resemble—are enormously intricate. Here, as elsewhere, each association situation is singular; so generalities are impossible to apply safely without closely examining the factual nuances of the situation. This Summary is intended to provide only the briefest overview. Those interested in learning more should turn to the books and articles

listed at the end of the chapter. Those with particular problems or potential problems should turn to professional advisors.

SUMMARY

- A number of associations, or entities related to associations, obtain federal income-tax-exempt status not as business leagues under Section 501(c)(6) of the Code but as scientific or educational organizations under Section 501(c)(3).

- The Internal Revenue Code provides exemption in Section 501(c)(3) for:

    "Corporations, and any community chest, fund or foundation, organized and operated exclusively for religious, charitable, scientific, testing for public safety, literary or educational purposes, or to foster national or international amateur sports competition (but only if no part of its activities involve the provision of athletic facilities or equipment), or for the prevention of cruelty to children or animals, no part of the net earnings of which inures to the benefit of any private shareholder or individual, no substantial part of the activities of which is carrying on propaganda, or otherwise attempting to influence legislation . . . and which does not participate in, or intervene in (including the publishing or distributing of statments) any political campaign on behalf of any candidate for public office."

- Scientific and educational organizations enjoy "most favored" tax-exempt status in the same category as churches, schools, and charities. In addition to freedom from payment of federal income taxes on revenue related to their exempt purposes, they may have other advantages. A few of them are listed here:

    —Contributions to these organizations can qualify for tax deductibility by donors as charitable contributions whereas dues to business leagues are deductible only as ordinary and necessary business expenses. In some circumstances, an association can more readily generate revenues if donations are deductible as charitable contributions. Private foundations, for example, often may only make grants to qualifying Section 501(c)(3) organizations.

—Scientific and educational groups often have more favorable postal categories and thus lower postal rates.

—Local sales and real estate taxes are often not applicable to scientific and educational organizations, whereas they are applicable to business leagues such as ordinary trade and professional associations.

—Special tax-shelter annuities are available to employees of scientific and educational organizations.

—It is usually perceived by an association as a public relations and membership relations advantage for the organization to be recognized by the government as a scientific or educational group rather than a business group.

- To obtain and retain tax-exempt status as a scientific or educational entity, an association must meet both organizational and operational requirements. It must be organized and operated "exclusively" for one or more exempt public, rather than private, purposes (the group can, for example, be scientific, educational, religious, and charitable at the same time). IRS defines "exclusively" as meaning "substantially." And, as with associations exempt from federal income tax under Section 501(c)(6) as business leagues, a scientific or educational association must be organized and operated so that "no part of (its) . . . net earnings . . . inures to the benefit of any private shareholder or individual."

- In addition to the requirements for exclusive exempt purposes and activities and for no private inurement, two other statutory criteria are specified for Section 501(c)(3) scientific, educational, and other exempt organizations which do not apply to Section 501(c)(6) business leagues. First, no "substantial part of the activities" of Section 501(c)(3) groups may constitute "carrying on propaganda, or otherwise attempting to influence legislation." Next, the group must "not participate in, or intervene in (including the publishing or distribution of statements), any political campaign on behalf of any candidate for public office." Thus, scientific and educational associations must limit lobbying activities and avoid political activities. However, certain qualifying Section 501(c)(3) organizations may elect, in lieu of the uncertain "substantial" test with respect to lobbying activities, to be governed by a limitation defined in terms of dollar expenditures. This procedure will enable these organizations to engage in lobbying activities with a reasonable degree of certainty concerning future tax-exempt status. Lobbying by Section 501(c)(3) organizations is discussed in detail in another chapter of this book.

- To meet the organizational requirements, the governing documents of the scientific or educational association:

   —Must state the exempt public purpose or purposes of the organization
   —Should limit the organization's activities to no more than an insubstantial amount of activities not in furtherance of its exempt purpose or purposes
   —Should indicate that no part of the net earnings of the organization may inure to the benefit of individual members and include a prohibition against distribution of assets to members upon dissolution
   —Should stipulate that no more than an insubstantial amount of the organization's activities will involve lobbying and that the organization is not authorized to intervene in political campaigns.

- To meet the operational requirements, the activities of the association:

   —Must be consistent with the requirement that the group is to be "operated exclusively for one or more exempt purposes" by assuring that no more than an "insubstantial" part of its activities are devoted to non-exempt purposes (thus, any more than an insubstantial amount of unrelated business income for the group jeopardizes its tax status). What constitutes an "insubstantial" part depends upon the facts although amounts of 5 percent and lower of a group's gross receipts have in specific situations been considered not insubstantial.

—Must be conducted so that no part of its net earnings inures to the financial benefit of individual members

—Must observe the proscription against devoting efforts toward political action

—Must avoid having a substantial part of its activities involved in lobbying or other attempts to influence legislation (the association may simply observe this rather vague test of having no more than an insubstantial part of activities in lobbying or, alternatively, may elect to limit lobbying activities to an amount prescribed by formula in the law for determining that they are not insubstantial).

- A number of scientific or educational groups that resemble professional associations are finding their favorable Section 501(c)(3) tax-exempt status under challenge in government attempts to downgrade them to Section 501(c)(6) associations. In some of these challenges, IRS has outlined activities of these groups which it considers more appropriate to business leagues than to scientific or educational exempt associations:

  —Continuing education programs that are oriented more to professional ends than purely educational ends

  —Placement services for professionals or assistants

  —Patient referral services

  —Publications that include advertising

  —Standard setting and codes of ethics

  —Public relations programs to enhance the image of the profession

  —Programs dealing with business aspects of professional practice

  —Sponsoring social events for professionals.

- Professional associations that have Section 501(c)(3) exempt status should carefully review their activities to determine whether the associations are in compliance with the above requirements.

- The law of tax-exempt scientific and educational associations is a trap for the unwary. Therefore, reference to legal treatises (Hopkins and Treusch and Sugarman listed at the end of this chapter are both excellent) and use of legal or accounting professionals who are experienced in dealing with this specialty of the tax laws should be explored to preclude loss of exempt status or other unexpected results.

RESOURCES FOR CHAPTER 64

Books

Bardsley, "Implications of IRS Reclassification Efforts" in *Associations and the Law Book VI*, U.S. Chamber, 1975, page 85.

Greif, "Federal Income Tax Status" in *Managing Membership Societies*, Greif, Editor, ASAE, 1979, page 1.

Hopkins, *The Law of Tax-Exempt Organizations*, Ronald Press, 1979, page 4.

Lane, "Federal Income Tax Exemption" in *Legal Handbook for Nonprofit Organizations*, AMACOM, 1980, page 155.

Oleck, *Non-Profit Corporations, Organizations, and Associations*, Prentice-Hall, 1980, page 601.

Reilly, "Trade Associations-Sponsored Public Service Foundations" in *Associations and the Law Book VI*, U.S. Chamber, 1975, page 85.

Statham & Buek, *Associations and the Tax Laws*, U.S. Chamber, 1978, page 104.

Treusch & Sugarman, *Tax-Exempt Charitable Organizations*, American Law Institute, 1979, page 49.

Webster, *The Law of Associations*, Matthew Bender, 1976, pages 15–58.

Webster, "Limitations of IRS Reclassification Efforts" in *Associations and the Law Book IX*, U.S. Chamber, 1975, page 85.

Periodicals

"Lobbying by Associations Exempt Under Section 501(c)(3) of the Code Under the Provisions of the Tax Reform Act of 1976," *Association Taxation*, August, 1977, page 1.

McGovern, "The New Declaratory Judgement Provision for Section 501(c)(3) Organizations: How It Works," *J. Taxation*, 1977, page 222.

Washburn, "New Tax Act Defines "Substantial" Lobbying—

But Charities Must Elect to Be Covered," *Taxes*, 1978, page 291.

Weaver, "Taxes & Lobbying—The Issues Resolved," *Geo. Washington L. Rev.*, 1963, page 938.

Webster, "IRS Inconsistent on Tax Exemptions for Professional Associations," *Association Management*, March 1978, page 22.

Webster, "Understanding the Tax Consequences of Association Foundations," *Association Management*, September 1981, page 33.

Weithorn, "Practitioners Planning Guide to the New Lobbying Rules for Public Charities," *J. Taxation*, 1977, page 294.

Statutes and Regulations

Internal Revenue Code Sections 501(c)(3), 509(a)(3).
Regulations Section 1. 501(c)(3)-1.

Cases

Seasongood v. Commissioner, 227 F.2d 907 (6th Cir. 1956). "Substantial" test for lobbying activities.

Harding Hospital, Inc., v. United States, 505 F.2d 1068 (6th Cir. 1974). Inurement of earnings to principal officers.

Lowry Hospital Assn. v. Commissioner, 66 T.C. 850 (1976). Inurement of earnings to principal officers.

Chapter 65

UNRELATED BUSINESS INCOME

Most associations are tax exempt as business leagues under Section 501(c)(6) of the Internal Revenue Code. Some have exempt status under scientific, educational, or other denominations of Section 501(c)(3). This means that the association is free from the obligation to pay federal taxes on exempt income. However, taxes may be due even from an exempt association if it receives certain kinds of business income from activities which are not related to the purposes for which the association was granted tax-exempt status.

Prior to 1950, if an exempt organization operated within the scope of its charter, there was really no threat of federal tax. So long as the ultimate recipient of the income was exempt, the income itself was considered tax free. The exempt organization was a special and sacrosanct entity. This long-standing rule permitted exempt organizations to operate businesses under the umbrella of their exemptions in direct competition with taxable entities.

The most cited abuse in this area was the acquisition by a tax-exempt university of a spaghetti company which permitted the company to operate as before except without federal income tax since it was a subsidiary of an exempt educational institution. The Revenue Act of 1950 represented an attempt to increase government revenues and to do away with the perceived unfair competition which tax-exempt corporations could exercise over taxable corporations. It introduced the concept of taxation on "unrelated business income." The concept was continued in the 1954 Internal Revenue Code and expanded in the Tax Reform Act of 1969.

After 1950, an exempt organization's insubstantial business activities would be permitted without taking away the exempt status by imposing a tax on that portion of its activities which are unrelated to its exempt purposes. In the event the unrelated activities are primary in relation to the organization's exempt activities, the tax-exempt status for the association may be forfeited completely.

This chapter summarizes the rules governing unrelated business income of tax-exempt associations. The legal and accounting aspects of association unrelated business income are, like most other aspects of federal income taxation, most complicated. Each rule seems to have its condition, qualification, corollary, exception, and modifer. Careful selection of association activities and careful allocation of expenses can generally minimize or eliminate the adverse consequences of unrelated business income for exempt associations. This Summary is intended only to touch upon the most basic features of unrelated business income taxation. It should certainly not be relied upon exclusively for direction in specific association circumstances.

SUMMARY

- Even though an association enjoys federal income-tax-exempt status, it may be required to pay taxes on the net gain received from activities which are considered unrelated to the purposes for which exempt status was granted the association.

- If the income of an association from activities unrelated to its exempt purposes becomes a primary portion of the association's total receipts from all sources, it could lose tax-exempt status altogether. Although there is no firm rule as to what is a "primary"portion. IRS has been successful in challenging association exempt status where the source of more than 50 percent of total revenues was from unrelated business activities. Individual circumstances of an association may justify a higher or lower percentage being designated a "primary" portion.

- Before an association will be subjected to unrelated business income tax or have its tax exemption jeopardized because unrelated business income constitutes too high a proportion of gross income, the IRS must establish that the association has conducted an "unrelated trade or business" under Section 513 of the Internal Revenue Code. Three requirements are given there to use in evaluating an association activity:

—The activity must be a trade or business.
—It must be regularly carried on.
—It must not be substantially related to an exempt purpose of the association.

- The first criterion for unrelated business activity is that it actually be a trade or business:

  —An activity conducted for the production of income through the sale of goods or the performance of services is considered a trade or business by IRS notwithstanding that it may be conducted within a larger aggregate of similar but exempt activities (e.g., paid advertising in a trade journal).
  —Whether or not an activity is actually profitable in some years, it can still be considered a trade or business if profits were intended or desired.
  —Where it can be shown that an association's profit-making activity is not in competition with that of any tax-paying business entity, this may help to mitigate the likelihood of a finding that the activity is a trade or business; but it may not be an absolute determinant.
  —If a commercial benefit is not derived or expected by beneficiaries of the activity, the IRS will not construe the activity as a trade or business (e.g., name only listing in a journal or membership directory sold to members only).

- The second criterion for unrelated business activity is that it be regularly carried on:

  —In general, an activity is regularly carried on if it is conducted frequently or continuously in a way comparable to that of commercial organizations which are required to pay taxes.
  —IRS regulations give examples of activities of tax-exempt organizations which are not considered to be regularly carried on—the operation of a sandwich stand for two weeks at a state fair or the publication of advertising in a program for a sports or cultural event are two IRS examples.
  —The regulations also give examples of activities which

are considered to be regularly carried on—the operation of a parking lot on Saturday every week during the year or the operation of a race track for several weeks each year during the normal season for race track operation are two IRS examples.

- The third criterion for unrelated business activitiy is that it must not be substantially related to an exempt purpose of the association:

  —To apply this criterion, one must evaluate the activity in question against the stated exempt purposes of the association; if the activity is substantially related to any exempt purpose, unrelated business income will not result.
  —To be "substantially related," an activity must contribute importantly to an exempt association's purposes and be aimed other than at an association's goal of generating income. The IRS has determined that sale of forms, operation of a mailing service, sale of mailing lists, and management of health and welfare plans are all unrelated; and therefore any income realized from such activities was subjected to the unrelated business income tax.

- In a few instances, Congress has determined that unrelated business income tax will not be applied where IRS might otherwise be inclined to do so. Some of those instances, as provided by statute, are:

  —Investment earnings, called by IRS "passive income," such as rents, royalties, interest, dividends, and gains from capital property, unless these earnings are received from property which the association acquired by borrowing funds (i.e., "debt-financed")
  —Income derived from research for federal, state, or local governments
  —Net gains on trade shows conducted in connection with meetings of associations exempt as business leagues under Section 501(c)(6)
  —A business activity conducted "primarily for the convenience" of members, students, patients, officers, or employees by a scientific, educational, or other association exempt under Code Section 501(c)(3)

—The selling of merchandise contributed to the association.

- A number of decisions or rulings give direction concerning unrelated business income tax in specific factual situations that may be encountered by associations:

    —An association formed to promote a professional sport was not subject to unrelated business income tax on tournaments it sponsored, media rights to competitions, or publications about rules of the sport.

    —The dental finance plan of a dental society was not subject to unrelated business income tax.

    —A ceramic society's business activities associated with conducting research in ceramics were not unrelated to the exempt purposes.

    —A labor organization was subject to unrelated business income tax on accounting and tax services it rendered to some members.

    —The management of an association of health and welfare plans as a service was subject to the tax.

    —Educational activities of a professional association conducted to help qualify individuals for the profession did not generate unrelated business income tax.

    —Consulting services performed by an organization exempt under Code Section 501(c)(3) for local businesses desiring to secure housing for their minority employees was not an unrelated business.

    —Furnishing of job inquiry histories of prospective employees was unrelated business activity.

    —A retail food store association's service of redeeming coupons was considered engaging in an unrelated business.

    —Use of an association's mailing equipment to provide services on a fee basis to other associations was an unrelated business activity whose net receipts were taxable.

    —Royalties received by an association from the publication by a commercial publisher of a book unrelated to the association's exempt purposes did not generate unrelated business income; but revenue from publication of such a book by the association itself was unrelated business activity.

    —Regular sales by a Section 501(c)(3) educational organization of its membership mailing list was an unrelated business activity.

- Some specific requirements for computation, payment, and reporting unrelated business income tax by exempt associations include:

  —Gains and losses from various unrelated business activities of an association can be lumped together to offset total gains with total losses.

  —A $1,000 special deduction is allowed against total taxable gains.

  —Regular business deductions are allowable against unrelated business income but only if they are directly connected with those unrelated business activities.

  —Taxation of unrelated business income is at corporate rates.

  —No periodic estimated tax payments are required.

  —A foreign tax credit is available to foreign associations.

  —A special tax return, IRS Form 990-T, is to be filed by associations with more than $1,000 in annual gross unrelated business income. Note that this requirement for filing a return is in addition to the requirement that an association file its informational report to IRS on Form 990 each year.

RESOURCES FOR CHAPTER 65

Books

Galloway, *The Unrelated Business Income Tax*, Ronald Press, 1982.

Greif, "Unrelated Business Income" in *Managing Membership Societies*, Greif, Editor, ASAE, 1979, page 23.

Hopkins, *The Law of Tax Exempt Organizations*, Ronald Press, 1979, page 560.

Kistner, "Unrelated Business Income From Advertising Revenue; How the Service's Unreasonable Allocations Can Cost You Tax Dollars" in *ASAE 1st Annual Management Conference Proceedings*, 1983, page 393.

Lane, "Unrelated Business Taxable Income" in *Legal Hand-*

book for Nonprofit Organizations, AMACOM, 1980, page 155.

Lehrfeld, "Federal Tax Treatment of Unrelated Business Income" in *Associations and the Law Book VIII*, U.S. Chamber, 1978, page 8.

Lehrfeld & Hezke, *Federal Tax Treatment of Unrelated Business Income*, U.S. Chamber, 1984.

Statham & Buek, *Associations and the Tax Laws*, U.S. Chamber, 1978, page 42.

Treusch & Sugarman, *Tax-Exempt Charitable Organizations*, American Law Institute, 1979, page 177.

Webster, *The Law of Associations*, Matthew Bender, 1976, pages 15–85.

Webster & Dye, "Trade Associations," 331-2nd *Tax Management*, The Bureau of National Affairs, Inc., 1976.

Webster, Herold, & Dye, *Association Legal Checklist*, U.S. Chamber, 1983, pages 60–63.

Periodicals

Ahern, "Unrelated Business Income Tax and the 1967 Regulations," *Missouri L. Rev.*, 1968, page 230.

Gottke, "Brush Up on Unrelated Business Income Requirements," *Association Management*, March, 1982, page 81.

"The Macaroni Monopoly: The Developing Concept of Unrelated Business Income of Exempt Organizations," *Harv. L. Rev.*, 1968, page 1280.

Middleditch & Webster, "The New Unrelated Business Income Tax Regulations," *J. Taxation*, 1968, page 174.

Meyers & Meyers, "How Art Oriented Exempt Organizations Can Skirt Unrelated Business Income Tax," *J. Taxation*, 1976, page 150.

Momberger, Simmons, & Squire, "Unrelated Trade on Business Income: A Panel," GWSAE *Executive Update*, October, 1985, page 28.

Pasvogel, "Unrelated Business Income of Tax-Exempt Organizations," *De Paul L. Rev.*, 1970, page 525.

Register, "Extensions and Expansions of UBIT," *Tax Advisor*, 1970, page 155.

Spevack, Whelan, & Reed, "Panel Discussion on Unrelated Business Income Tax," *Catholic Lawyer*, 1975, page 287.

Webster, "Unrelated Business Income," *Tax Lawyer*, 1970, page 471.

Webster, "Unrelated Business Income Tax," *Taxes*, 1970, page 844.

Webster, "Application of the Unrelated Business Income Tax to Exempt Organizations," *N.Y.U. 28th Annual Institute on Federal Taxation*, page 1317.

Statutes and Regulations

Internal Revenue Code Sections 511–513
Regulations Sections 1.513.1(a)–(d).

Chapter 66

ADVERTISING INCOME

Perhaps no area of association tax exemption has generated as much concern and controversy in recent years as that of unrelated business taxation on advertising income. Associations that receive substantial advertising income from publications may be subjected to payment of unrelated business income taxes on their net earnings from that advertising. Those managing or advising associations should be well aware of the impact of specific federal laws and regulations governing the matter and of increased Internal Revenue Service enforcement of those laws and regulations.

Although statutory provisions for the taxation of unrelated business income of tax-exempt organizations had existed since 1950, only in 1967 did the IRS decide to promulgate regulations treating the advertising portions of exempt organizations' publication activities as separate from the nonadvertising or editorial portions of publication activities so that revenue from advertising could be taxed by the government as unrelated business income. Those 1967 regulations were issued without specific statutory authority and some courts refused to apply them. So, in 1969, Congress enacted Section 513(c) of the Internal Revenue Code, which legitimatizes the separation of advertising portions of exempt organization publication activities for treatment as unrelated business whose income is taxable under Section 512 of the Code. A U.S. Supreme Court decision in 1986 confirmed the application of that treatment and held that advertising in a medical society's journal was primarily for the purpose of revenue production rather than education and thus unrelated to the society's exempt purposes. For taxable years after 1970, it is now quite clear that exempt organizations, including trade and professional associations, can be subject to unrelated business income tax on the sale of advertising in their publications under most circumstances.

Because of the complexity of this subject and the importance of the background and history of taxation of association advertising revenue, this Summary gives a somewhat detailed description of it. However, no summary can accurately convey all of the nuances of the statute, regulations, IRS pronouncements, and decisions involved in determining when and how association advertising income is taxable. Each association's factual situation is unique; and the general guidance given here cannot be applicable in every case. Once again, expert assistance is most essential.

SUMMARY

- Regulations on advertising income of exempt organizations were first issued by the IRS in 1967 but were successfully challenged in court cases. In 1969, Congress amended the tax laws to clarify that exempt organization programs can be segregated into portions related and portions unrelated to the organization's exempt functions for taxation purposes. The effect is that advertising in exempt association publications can be treated as unrelated business activity whose net revenues are subject to taxation as unrelated business income. In 1971, new proposed regulations on this subject were issued; they were finalized in 1975 and made applicable for tax years after December, 1976.

- As with other unrelated business activity of exempt associations, for a tax to be imposed upon advertising revenues from publications, the advertising activity must be regularly carried on. The law and regulations are not designed to impose taxation upon the advertising revenue from a unique, one-time publication issued by an association. Likewise, for the publications to be considered carried on to produce unrelated business income, an association must intend to realize income from advertising in its publications, from other income generated by the publications (such as subscriptions), or from both. Exempt organization publications that do not contain advertising are obviously not affected by these requirements.

- To determine if an association's publication is subject

to the tax on unrelated business income, a series of careful accounting procedures must be followed as dictated by IRS regulations. Most important of all is the allocation of income and costs for a publication between those related to advertising and those not related to advertising. Income and cost items for the publication which are related to both advertising and nonadvertising aspects must be fairly apportioned.

- Income generated by an association publication is considered ether:

  —*Circulation income,* which is that attributable to the production, distribution, or circulation of the publication (other than income from advertising) and includes subscription income, charges for reprints and, especially important, the portion of dues allocated as subscription income where the members of the association receive the publication as a benefit of membership (known as "allocable membership receipts"), or

  —*Gross advertising income,* which is that attributable to the advertising in the publication.

- Costs incurred by an association publication are considered either:

  —*Readership costs,* which are those attributable to the production and distribution of the readership or editorial content of the publication (writers' fees, editors' salaries and expenses, preparation and printing of the nonadvertising portions of the publication, etc.), or

  —*Direct advertising costs,* which are those attributable to the sale and publication of advertising (agency commissions, advertising salesperson salaries and expenses, preparation and printing of the advertising, etc.).

- The general rule for taxation of net advertising revenues from exempt association publications is that there is no unrelated business income tax imposed on a publication that does not net any overall revenues. No tax is due if total publication income (*circulation* and *gross advertising*) is no more than total publication costs (*readership* and *direct advertising*). In particular:

—*If gross advertising income* is equal to *direct advertising costs,* no tax is due (note that if the advertising income is less than its costs, the loss generated from advertising may be used to offset other association unrelated business activity income).

—Even if *gross advertising income* is greater than *direct advertising* costs, resulting in net revenues from the advertising, any excess readership costs over *circulation income* can be used to reduce those net revenues and their taxation as unrelated business income (note that if a publication loss is generated in this way, the loss cannot be used to offset other association unrelated business activity income).

—If *gross advertising income* is greater than *direct advertising costs* resulting in net revenues from the advertising, and no reduction is available from the publication's nonadvertising activities, the excess is subject to taxation as unrelated business income.

- These rules are best illustrated in several examples from the IRS regulations:

—First, an association publication carrying advertising generated, in one year, $40,000 in gross advertising income and $60,000 in circulation income (total publication income is thus $100,000). Readership costs were $40,000 and direct advertising costs were $50,000 (total periodical costs thus were $90,000). Since circulation income was in excess of readership costs (resulting in $20,000 in related income), the unrelated income rules look only to advertising income and costs, which in the example produce a $10,000 loss attributable to the advertising activity. Moreover, such a loss can be offset in computing taxable income from any other unrelated activity.

—Next, assume the same facts, except for $100,000 in circulation income, $40,000 is gross advertising income, $65,000 in readership costs and $25,000 in direct advertising costs. Since the circulation income again exceeds readership costs, the unrelated taxable advertising income is $15,000—the excess of the gross advertising income over direct advertising costs.

—Next, assume $60,000 in circulation income, $40,000 in gross advertising income, $70,000 in readership costs, and $20,000 in direct advertising costs. In this case, unrelated taxable income from the advertising is not $20,000 ($40,000 minus $20,000). Rather, since the readership costs are in excess of the circulation income, the unrelated business taxable income from advertising is the amount of total income attributable to the publication ($100,000), less the total costs of the publication ($90,000), or $10,000.

—Finally, assume $60,000 in circulation income, $40,000 in gross advertising income, $90,000 in readership costs and $30,000 in direct advertising costs. Because the readership costs exceed the circulation income, any unrelated business taxable income from advertising would be the net total income attributable to the publication (as in the previous example). Here, however, there is no unrelated taxable income because the total publication costs ($120,000) exceed total publication income ($100,000). Moreover, in computing unrelated business taxable income in general, only $70,000 of the readership costs are deductible, by reason of the above-noted rules that such costs may be deducted only to the extent they exceed circulation income and only to the extent they do not result in a loss from the advertising activity. Therefore, in this example, no amount is deductible on this account in computing taxable income from any other unrelated activity.

- The original 1967 IRS regulations provided for unrelated business income tax on net advertising income such as that from tax-exempt association publications. But the regulations did not prescribe the method of computation of *circulation income*. Most associations used the stated subscription price for the publication multiplied by the total number of subscriptions in computing this figure. Since the stated subscription price for association publications was typically nominal or nonexistent, *readership costs* generally exceeded *circulation income*. The net amount was used to reduce or eliminate any income from the sale of advertising. Thus, under the 1967 regulations, most associations escaped the tax consequences of treatment of advertising revenues as taxable.

- In 1975, the IRS finalized new regulations that had been proposed in 1971 based on congressional enactment of a statutory basis for taxation of advertising income. The 1975 regulations, of course, supersede those originally issued in 1967. They impose detailed requirements for determining if an exempt organization realizes net taxable income from the advertising revenues in its publications. The new regulations prescribe three mandatory rules which must be used by tax-exempt associations to allocate a portion of membership receipts to *circulation income* if a publication of the association is distributed as a condition of membership. The rules are:

  —(1) If 20 percent or more of the total circulation of a publication consists of sales to nonmembers, the subscription price charged to nonmembers determines the price of the publication for purposes of allocating membership receipts.

  —(2) If the first rule does not apply, and if membership dues from 20 percent or more of the members of an association are less than those received from other members because the former members do not receive the publication, the amount of the reduction in membership dues for a member not receiving the publication determines the price of the periodical for purposes of allocating membership receipts.

  —(3) If neither the first nor the second rule applies, as is the case in most associations, allocable membership receipts must be computed using a formula:

$$\text{Total Membership Receipts} \times \frac{\text{Total Costs of the Publication}}{\substack{\text{Total Publication Costs +} \\ \text{Other Exempt Activities Costs} \\ \text{to the Association}}}$$

- These three rules, including the formula in the third rule that is probably required for most associations, can be illustrated by three examples from the IRS regulations:

  —An exempt scientific organization has 10,000 members who pay annual dues of $15. Its monthly publication is distributed to all of its members, and it also distributes an addition 5,000 copies of the publication to nonmembers at an annual subscription cost of $10. Rule (1) is applicable because the nonmember circulation of the publication is 33 ⅓ percent of total circulation. Thus, the organization's allocable membership receipts are $100,000 ($10 times 10,000 members) and its total circulation income from the publication is $150,000 ($100,000 from members and $50,000 from nonmembers).

—Another example assumes the facts of the previous illustration, except that the organization sells only 500 copies of its publication to nonmembers at a price of $10 annually; and the organization's members may elect not to receive the publication, in which case their annual dues are reduced to $6. Three thousand members elect to receive the publication. The stated subscription price to members of $9 consistently results in an excess of total income attributable to the publication over its total costs. Since the 500 copies of the publication distributed to nonmembers represents only 14 percent of the 3,500 copies distributed, the $10 subscription price is not used to determine allocable membership receipts. Rather, rule (2) applies inasmuch as 70 percent of the members elect not to receive the publication and pay $9 less per year in dues; the $9 price is used to determine the subscription price charged to members. Thus, the organization's allocable membership receipts are $9 per member or $27,000 ($9 times 3,000 copies) and its total circulation income is $32,000 ($27,000 plus $5,000).

—Still another example concerns an exempt trade association having 800 members who pay annual dues of $50. The association's monthly journal is distributed to all of its members and no receipts are derived from nonmembers. The association's total receipts are $100,000 of which $40,000 ($50 times 800) are membership receipts and $60,000 is gross advertising income. Its total costs for the journal and other exempt activities are $100,000; its total publication costs are $76,000, of which $41,000 are direct advertising costs and $35,000 are readership costs. Rule (3) applies; based upon pro rata allocation of membership receipts ($40,000) by a fraction, the numerator of which is total publication costs ($76,000) and the denominator of which is the total costs of the journal and other exempt activities ($100,000), its circulation income is $30,500 ($40,000 times $76,000/$100,000).

- If an association has advertising in more than one publication, it is permissible to consolidate the publications for computing any unrelated business income taxation. However, this treatment has to be followed consistently and IRS approval must be obtained before changing the treatment.

- A case that has broad ramifications for the taxation of advertising revenue of association publications was decided by the U.S. Supreme Court in 1986; it is one of the very few cases ever in the Supreme Court on tax exemption issues affecting associations. The Court determined that revenue from advertising in the journal of the American College of Physicians is taxable because the advertising is not related to the organization's exempt purpose of professional medical education. The Court's decision is rare and important enough that those interested in the subject of taxation of association advertising revenue should have a detailed understanding of it.

  —The American College of Physicians is a Section 501(c)(3) tax-exempt organization that publishes *The Annals of Internal Medicine*, a journal containing articles on internal medicine as well as commercial and classified advertisements. The commercial ads are screened by the College for accuracy and relevance. The classified advertisements are primarily for employment opportunities.
  —The sale of advertising space in *Annals* generates revenue for the College. The Internal Revenue Service sought to tax this net income based on its longstanding position that Treasury regulations and legislative history establish a blanket or *per se* rule that the sale of advertising can never be substantially related to an exempt purpose and is always a taxable business. The College contended that each case must be decided on its own merits and stressed that the ads in *Annals* supplement the journal's editorial con-

tent and therefore are substantially related to the College's educational purpose.

—The U.S. Court of Claims decided in favor of the IRS. Although the court did not adopt the IRS' *per se* approach, it held that the educational function of the advertisements is only incidental to the College's primary purpose of raising revenue.

—The appellate court reversed on the ground that the lower court had improperly focused on the College's revenue raising purpose. The appellate court concluded that the content of the advertisements, rather than the existence of a profit motive, should be the focal point of inquiry. Since the content of the advertisements informs physician readers of new developments in their field, the appellate court found that the sale of advertising space furthers the College's exempt function to educate its members.

—The Supreme Court reversed the appellate court. It concentrated on two major issues: (a) whether the regulations and legislative history establish a blanket or *per se* rule whereby the sale of advertising space in a tax-exempt group's journal would always be subject to tax, or (b) if there were no blanket rule, whether, in this specific case, the advertisements are substantially related to the College's educational purpose.

—The Supreme Court rejected the IRS' blanket approach to the treatment of advertising income, noting that the IRS regulations require that the facts and circumstances of each case be examined to determine whether the sale of advertising space is an activity substantially related to an exempt organization's purpose. However, the Court also stated that the regulations and legislative history clearly do not support a blanket rule in *favor* of classifying income from the sale of advertising space in journals as tax-exempt income.

—The Court also stated that whether or not journal advertising is substantially related to an exempt purpose depends upon whether the advertising *contributes importantly* to the purpose for which the organization was granted tax-exempt status. In resolving this issue, the Supreme Court agreed with the IRS and the Court of Claims that the focal point of inquiry should be the exempt organization's conduct in selling advertising space rather than the educational quality of the advertisements themselves. Therefore, if an organization demonstrates an intention to publish advertisements primarily for their educational value rather than primarily for revenue, the advertising might be considered substantially related. In this case, the Court found that certain activities of the College indicate a lack of intent to sell advertising space in the journal primarily for the educational value of the advertisements: (a) the advertisements are laid out in the journal in a hit-or-miss manner, rather than in a comprehensive, systematic manner which would correlate with the journal's editorial content; (b) differences between advertisements reflect the marketers' advertising strategy rather than the probable importance of the advertisements to the reader; (c) only those companies willing to pay for advertising space receive it, while those companies not willing to pay do not receive advertising space; and (d) many of the advertisements are repeated from month-to-month, which undermines the College's argument that the advertising was designed principally to alert readers to recent developments. Based upon these facts, the Court concluded that the College sells advertising space in its journal in a commercial rather than an educational manner. As a result, the Court found that the educational function of the advertisements is only incidental to the College's primary intent to sell advertising space in order to raise revenue.

—Although the Supreme Court found that the College's primary intent in selling advertising space is not to further educational goals, it suggested that the College and presumably other exempt organizations could, under limited circumstances, demonstrate an educational purpose. For example, the Court noted that if the College had coordinated the content of the advertisements with the editorial content of the issue or published only advertisements reflecting current developments, its income might have been exempt from tax. The Court said that this would be indicative

of an intent to sell advertising space primarily for
its educational contribution to the journal.
—There is some comfort in the Supreme Court's clear
rejection of the IRS' long-standing blanket or *per se*
approach to the categorization of advertising income
earned by associations. Nevertheless, the opinion
would require a tax-exempt association to meet very
stringent standards in order to escape taxation of its
advertising revenue. The guidelines articulated by
the Supreme Court are extremely vague; it is difficult
to provide assurance that any method of structuring
advertising activities will result in exempt income.
—The opinion of the Supreme Court did not specifi-
cially address the issue of classified advertising. The
American College of Physicians includes such advertisements in *Annals*. In view of the Court's general holding, it would be difficult to establish that
classified advertisements promote an exempt purpose. In the context of trade or professional associations, classified ads may certainly promote the
interests of individual members. There remains a
question, however, as to whether they promote the
trade or professional as a whole and thus further an
exempt purpose.

- It is evident that requirements pertaining to taxation
of association advertising revenue are extremely involved. Judgments must be made often in the computations required. Any exempt association that has
advertising revenue from publications should seek expert legal or accounting advice to help assess whether
there is any exposure to unrelated business income tax
on the revenue or whether alternate planning approaches (such as the establishment of a taxable subsidiary) are available.

RESOURCES FOR CHAPTER 66

Books

Ellicott, "Taxing Association Publications Advertising Revenue" in *Associations and the Law Book I*, U.S Chamber,
1967, page 57.

Ellicott, "Publications Advertising Tax Adopted" in *Associations and the Law Book II*, U.S. Chamber, 1967, page 44.

Greif, "Unrelated Business Income" in *Managing Membership Societies*, Greif, Editor, ASAE, 1979, page 23.

Greif, "Unrelated Business Income Tax on Advertising Revenue of Associations" in *Association Issues*, Jacobs, Editor, ASAE, 1983, page 1.

Hopkins, *The Law of Tax Exempt Organizations*, Ronald Press, 1979, page 560.

Kistner, "Unrelated Business Income From Advertising Revenue; How the Service's Unreasonable Allocations Can Cost You Tax Dollars" in *ASAE 1st Annual Management Conference Proceedings*, 1983, page 393.

Lawler, "Controlling Taxes on Advertising Income" in *ASAE 2nd Annual Management Conference Proceedings*, 1984, page 245.

Lehrfeld, "Federal Tax Treatment of Unrelated Business Income" in *Associations and the Law Book VIII*, U.S. Chamber, 1978, page 8.

Statham & Buek, *Associations and the Tax Laws*, U.S. Chamber, 1978, page 42.

Treusch & Sugarman, *Tax-Exempt Charitable Organizations*, American Law Institute, 1979, page 177.

Webster, *The Law of Associations*, Matthew Bender, 1976, pages 15–85.

Periodicals

Barlow, "The New Treasury Tax on Exempt Organization Advertising: A Postscript and a Preview, Tax Problems of Non-Profit Organizations," *J. Taxation*, 1969, page 239.

De Filipps, "Advertising Can Generate Tax Liability as Well as Income for Tax Exempt Publication," *Taxation for Accountants*, 1972, page 368.

Ellicott, "Proposed Changes in the Taxation of Advertising Income of Exempt Organization Publications," *Tax Advisor*, 1971, page 710.

Harris, "How to Determine Your Unrelated Income From Advertising," *Association Management*, May, 1976, page 72.

Harris, "Tax Analysis: Impact of New Regulations on Association Publications," *Association Management*, February, 1976, page 30.

Lehrfeld, "Commercial Advertising Profits of Exempt Organizations," *Tax Lawyer*, 1970, page 223.

Liles & Weithorn, "Unrelated Business Income Tax; Changes Affecting Journal Advertising Revenues," *Taxes*, 1970, page 791.

Peck, "Advertising Income: How Much Is Taxable?," *Association Management*, July, 1984, page 66.

Peck, "Advertising Regulations: Special Considerations in Computing Unrelated Business Income," *Association Management*, April, 1978, page 61.

Simonetti, "Advertising Income of Exempt Organizations," *J. Accountancy*, 1972, page 79.

Spevack, "Taxation of Advertising Income of Exempt Organizations," *Catholic Lawyer*, 1975, page 268.

Sugarman & Vogt, "The New Advertising Regulations and Their Application to Exempt Organizations," *Taxes*, 1976, page 196.

"Taxing the Advertising Income of Trade Association Periodicals," *Association Taxation*, February, 1976, page 1.

Webster, "Your Association's Advertising Income May Now Be Tax Exempt," *Association Management*, December, 1984, page 47.

Webster, "Taxation of Association Advertising Revenue: The American College of Physicians Case," Jacobs, Editor, *Association Counsel*, CNA Insurance, Summer, 1985.

Statutes and Regulations

Internal Revenue Code Section 513(c).
Regulations Section 1.512(a).

Cases

Massachusetts Medical Society v. United States, 514 F.2d 153 (1st Cir. 1975). Invalidating early IRS regulations.

American College of Physicians v. United States, 530 F.2d 930 (Ct. Cl. 1976). Invalidating early IRS regulations.

American College of Physicians v. United States, 54 *US Law*

Week 4387 (April 22, 1986), No. 84-1737. Supreme Court determination that advertising in a professional medical journal is primarily for the production of revenue and thus unrelated to the exempt purposes of the organization which publishes the journal.

Chapter 67

GROUP INSURANCE PROGRAMS

Many associations, both trade and professional groups, are actively involved in group insurance programs for their members. Through group insurance programs, associations can make available to members various kinds of insurance policies such as general liability business policies; health, life or accident plans; workers' compensation coverage; malpractice or products liability indemnification and other types of protection. Association group policies can be tailored to the specific insurance needs and typical losses that have been experienced in the industry or profession represented by the association. The association membership communications channels may provide significant convenience and economy in marketing the insurance programs and in assisting members in keeping claims, and thus losses and premiums, to the minimum. As a result, association group insurance can sometimes be made available at premiums that are lower than those for comparable coverage available outside the association.

Associations vary greatly in the extent of their administrative activities connected with the group insurance programs and income derived from them. To some extent, state insurance laws may regulate association involvement. Some associations serve as actual insurers by underwriting coverage, drafting and marketing policies, and handling premiums and claims. A 1977 decision in the U.S. Tax Court makes this kind of extensive association self-insurance program very questionable for a tax-exempt association. More common is the association which leaves most of the administration of its group insurance plans to some outside commercial insurance carrier or insurance marketing firm; the association may only realize as "passive" income some percentage of the premiums paid by members to the plans. The exempt organization tax consequences of this activity are not entirely clear, although the IRS position is usually that the revenue from these endeavors is unrelated business income unless the association remains totally uninvolved in the administration, marketing, and all other aspects of offering the insurance. Further, some associations realize no income at all from group insurance programs to which the association name may be connected for promotional purposes. These associations consider it advantageous enough simply that a market for insurance coverage is available to members through the association. Obviously, this type of association involvement in insurance activity is the least questionable from the point of view of taxation because no income is flowing to the association, whether from an unrelated business activity or not. Finally, certain associations have established Section 501(c)(9) group insurance trusts as separate tax-exempt entities to operate the associations' insurance programs. This approach shields the association from unrelated business income tax exposure or loss of exemption.

The Internal Revenue Service is always interested in association income connected with group insurance programs for members. It behooves all associations that have insurance plans to assess carefully their impacts upon tax-exempt status and possible unrelated business income taxation.

This Summary presents some of the tax issues raised by association group insurance programs for members. Once again, the coverage here is only a summary of a complicated area of taxation. Affected associations should pursue further information and assistance.

SUMMARY

- Association involvement in group insurance programs for members is an area that raises significant issues for tax-exempt associations. The exact tax status of many kinds of association insurance situations is still evolving and should be watched closely by managers of associations and their advisors.

- Many types of insurance coverage are made available to members in association group programs; coverage can be tailored to the specific needs of a segment of an industry or profession and can be linked to an educational loss control effort to help keep claims, and ultimately to help keep premiums, as low as possible.

- There are many levels of association administrative involvement in insurance activities and of association income as a result of that involvement. It is becoming increasingly clear that IRS considers nearly any association income from insurance activities to be unrelated to association exempt purposes, thereby triggering unrelated business income tax or possibly even jeopardizing tax-exempt status if the activities are substantial. However, the levels of association involvement in group insurance programs have some bearing on the positions that IRS or the courts might take with respect to association revenues resulting from that involvement.

- Another factor besides tax considerations which may effect the type and level of association administrative involvement in group insurance programs is any applicable state insurance law or regulation which may dictate to what extent an association may administer and market its insurance program. Consideration should be given to "mass marketing" rules and statutes applicable to the various jurisdictions where the insurance will be offered.

- Some associations act as insurers themselves by underwriting insurance coverage; drafting and issuing policies; and handling premiums, investments, and claims. These activities may generate substantial amounts of revenues for the associations. A 1977 U.S. Tax Court case involving an association of barbers and beauticians found that the association's self-insurance program was sufficient to defeat exempt status because it:

  —Was a regular business of the kind ordinarily operated for profit
  —Was not devoted to the improvement of business conditions in one or more lines of commerce
  —Involved the performance of particular services for individual members.

  The court did not apply the test used in many earlier decisions and rulings as to whether the insurance activity of the association was a "primary" or "principal" one. It used a much more rigorous and, in view of precedents, inappropriate test of whether the activity was more than "insubstantial." Under this test, the activity failed; the result was revocation of the tax-exempt status of the association.

- Far more typical than self-insurance is the situation of an association which allows an outside commercial insurance underwriting or marketing firm to establish and promote group insurance programs for association members and other insureds. The association may lend its name and membership list to the insurance firm and may even perform some administrative functions connected with issuing or renewing policies. The association might receive income from the insurance firm in various ways—for example, as a percentage of premiums paid, as a lump sum, or in periodic fixed payments, as dividends assigned by members, and so forth. Some legal implications of this kind of program are:

  —The IRS ordinarily takes the position on audit that the income received in any way from an association group insurance program is unrelated to the exempt purpose of the association and is subject to unrelated business income tax (after allocable deductions and assuming no offsets from losses in other unrelated business activities of the association).

  —A 1969 federal district court case involving a state cattlemen's association (tax exempt as an agricultural association rather than as a business league) held that income the association received from an insurance company in the form of a 5-percent rebate on premiums paid to an association-sponsored group insurance program *was* related to the exempt purposes of the association and not subject to unrelated business income tax. IRS disagrees with this decision.

  —In another case, the Court of Claims held that a state hardware association was not entitled to tax exemption because a large percentage of association income and substantial staff involvement related to what the court considered particular services for

members. Among those services was active association involvement in group health, accident, and life
insurance offered through the association.

—One argument against the IRS position is that if an
association has no active participation in administering, marketing, or otherwise offering a group insurance plan run by an outside firm, any association
income from the plan is passive in nature and is not
realized from a trade or business. In at least one non-
precedent-setting IRS proclamation, a private letter
ruling in 1980, this IRS position was substantiated.
It can be argued that the statutory exemption from
unrelated business income taxation for "passive income" such as interest, rents, and royalties should
apply in these situations of insurance company premium rebates. Proper planning in characterizing rebates as royalties pursuant to a written agreement
is essential to support this argument.

—It may be important that in some instances an association group insurance plan is the only practicable source of some specialized types of insurance,
i.e., professional malpractice coverage, products liability coverage, etc. Under these circumstances,
promotion of the particular line of business or industry is achieved by the insurance activity; and,
therefore, it should not be considered "unrelated" to
the association's exempt purpose. One federal district court case generally supports this proposition.

• Some associations may sponsor or promote group insurance plans for members but receive no income from
them. The associations may perceive some value in
merely having a source of insurance coverage available to members. Members sometimes receive discounts from the insurance companies when they
participate in the plans. If the associations receive no
income from the plans, there are very likely no tax
implications.

• Note that if participation in association group insurance programs is restricted to association members, or
significant discounts are available only to association
members without justification in terms of members' dues

income supporting the administration of the plans, antitrust issues may be raised. If there is any significant competitive or economic value inherent in subscribing to the association group insurance program, it is best to make participation available to both members and nonmembers.

● Historically, some associations have attempted to avoid unfavorable tax consequences of income from employee benefit group insurance programs offered to members' employees by operating the programs through insurance trusts exempt under Section 501(c)(9). However, IRS issued regulations in early 1981 which severely limit the ability of associations to avoid taxable insurance program income through Section 501(c)(9) trusts. Under those regulations, participants in such a trust must share a common employment and geographic bond. For national associations, it is unlikely that the Internal Revenue Service will agree that the association members' employees participating in the employee benefit insurance programs are all participants with an "employment-related common bond" such as "employers engaged in the same line of business in the same geographic locale." Associations that have had a Section 501(c)(9) insurance trust, or are contemplating one, should carefully consider the regulations.

● In conclusion, perhaps the clearest statement of the attitude of the Internal Revenue Service regarding association-sponsored group insurance programs was made by the IRS Commissioner in a speech in 1973. He said:

> "We are studying the ramification of (c)(6) organizations carrying on insurance activities. As you may know, a number of associations provide their members low cost insurance—usually term life insurance—on a voluntary basis. Usually a profit factor is involved. The association normally retains dividends paid. In some instances, it makes money by collecting the premiums and then remitting a lesser agreed-upon amount to the insurer who saves administrative costs. In any event, the association usually does more than meet ex-

penses. We are inclined to feel that anything in excess of expenses represents unrelated business income and, therefore, is subject to tax."

RESOURCES FOR CHAPTER 67

Books

Combs, "Unrelated Business Income: Insurance" in *Associations and the Law Book VI*, U.S. Chamber, 1975, page 8.

Dye, "Unrelated Business Income Tax on Insurance Revenue of Associations," page 15, "Availability of Tax-Exempt Status for IRC Section 501(c)(9) Insurance Entities," page 25, in *Association Issues*, Jacobs, Editor, ASAE, 1983.

Greif, "Unrelated Business Income" in *Managing Membership Societies*, Greif, Editor, ASAE, 1979, page 23.

Statham & Buek, *Associations and the Tax Laws*, U.S. Chamber, 1978, page 87.

Webster, *The Law of Associations*, Matthew Bender, 1976, pages 15–120.

Webster & Dye, "Trade Associations," 331-2d *Tax Management*, The Bureau of National Affairs, Inc., 1976.

Periodicals

Dye, "Tax Court Revokes Exemption Based on Association Self-Insurance Program," *Association Management*, December, 1977, page 16.

Hart, "Association Insurance Programs," *Association Special Report*, U.S. Chamber, 1980.

Stuchiner, "Using a 501(c)(9) Trust to Fund Employee Benefits," *Trusts & Estates*, 1973, page 242.

Webster, "How the IRS Views Association Insurance Programs," *Association Management*, June, 1976, page 20.

Webster, "State, National Associations Fail New Criteria for 501(c)(9) Insurance Trusts," *Association Management*, March, 1982, page 33.

Webster, "What Are the Ins and Outs of Forming a 501(c)(9) Insurance Trust?," *Association Management*, May, 1984, page 57.

Cases

Oklahoma Cattlemen's Assn., Inc., v. United States, 310 F. Supp. 320 (W.D. Okla. 1969). Rebates to agricultural association from group insurance program for members held not unrelated business income.

Associated Master Barbers & Beauticians of America, Inc., 69 T.C. 53 (1977). Association self-insurance program income held substantial and sufficient to defeat tax-exempt status.

New York State Assn. of Real Estate Boards Group Insurance Fund, 54 T.C. 1325 (1970). Association insurance income held to be not taxable, except as to interest, as a trust.

Indiana Retail Hardware Assn. v. United States, 366 F.2d 998 (Ct. Cl. 1966). Group insurance one of several association unrelated business activities defeating exempt status.

Independent Insurance Agents of Northern Nevada v. United States, 79-2 U.S.T.C. Section 9601 (D. Nev. 1979).

Other Resources

D. Alexander, Speech before the American Society of Association Executives, August 29, 1973.

Chapter 68

REAL ESTATE

Whether an association should invest its funds in real estate is initially a question for determination by association management, board of directors, and membership based upon a variety of investment factors.

Tax-exempt trade and professional associations exist to advance the interests of their respective trades or professions. The acquiring, occupying, leasing, or disposition of real estate is rarely one of their essential functions. But as they expand their memberships, budgets, services and staffs, associations sometimes find it convenient or necessary to engage in real estate ventures.

A typical venture for an association is the acquisition of a building to serve as its headquarters. So long as use of the property is confined primarily to association functions, there are no more legal problems for the association in this type of real estate venture than those which any corporation would experience. Indeed, as an exempt organization, the association's eventual disposition of real estate which was used for its exempt purpose may be even simpler than for the business corporation, since the association will not ordinarily have liability for taxes on the gain received.

A more difficult situation exists when an exempt association acquires real estate it does not intend to use mainly for exempt purposes but as investment property. If the real estate is acquired in circumstances where the association directly or indirectly incurs debt to make the acquisition, a portion of the rental income and net gain at the time of sale may be taxable as unrelated business income to the association.

Before a tax-exempt association becomes involved in any real-estate venture, careful consideration must be given to the legal and accounting implications of the Internal Revenue Code. The advice of an experienced association tax advisor is essential in this area.

Federal income tax law provisions for "unrelated debt-financed income" of exempt organizations such as associations were adopted in 1969 to curb abuses by some exempt groups which were trading upon their exempt status in various ventures such as "bootstrap sale and leaseback transactions" involving taxable entities. The provisions apply not only to real estate but to any exempt association property whose acquisition is not related to the association's exempt purposes and is debt-financed. The unrelated debt-financed income provisions are considered in this Summary, however, in the context of association real-estate transactions because it is in these transactions that the impact of the provisions most frequently arise for trade and professional associations.

The statutes, regulations, and decisions which govern the tax aspects of debt-financed association real-estate holdings are enormously complicated. The following treatment is necessarily no more than a summary of these intricate rules. One must not assume that the content of this Summary is completely comprehensive or universally applicable to the tax consequences of all association real-estate transactions.

SUMMARY

- Although usually not required to pay federal income taxes, exempt associations may have taxes due on net income from activities unrelated to the purposes for which the favorable tax status was originally granted. Unrelated business income taxes can apply in some circumstances to association income from real-estate investments or transactions when they are debt-financed.

- Two primary types of unrelated business income which might result from association real-estate holdings in certain cases are rental fees when the property is occupied by those outside the association and gains realized when the association sells the property. Note also that some states may levy property or income taxes against association real estate and real estate income completely apart from federal taxes. State laws on income and property taxation vary considerably and should also be carefully checked before an association enters into any real estate transaction.

- A general rule is that real estate property which a tax-exempt association holds for the production of income, which *(1) is not substantially related to the functions for which the association has its exemption and which (2) was purchased in connection with the borrowing of any funds,* may have its rental income or investment gain subject to tax as unrelated business income to the extent of the borrowings which the association incurred in making the purchase. The rule has numerous qualifications and exceptions, but its effects mainly relate to three circumstances.

—First, the income on any real estate or other property which an exempt association purchases, holds or sells is not subject to any federal tax so long as the property is substantially used by the association in pursuit of its exempt purposes and functions. For example, if an association sells at a substantial profit a building which it has used exclusively for its headquarters, whether or not the acquisition was debt-financed, there is no federal income tax on the gain realized.

—Second, if an exempt association purchases real estate by using only surplus funds, there is likely to be no federal income tax on any rental income or investment gain on the property regardless of the purpose for which it is used. Usually, there is no federal income tax on income from property purchased by an exempt association without having to go into debt to make the purchase. This is because the definition of "unrelated business income" specifically excludes real-estate rents, rents on incidental amounts (less than 10 percent) of personal property leased together with real estate, and gains from the sale or disposition of such property as real estate. Note that if personal property rented with real estate is more than 10 percent, the rent on the former is taxable; and if the personal property rent exceeds 50 percent, both it and the real estate rent may be taxed. To repeat, if no borrowed funds were used to acquire association real estate, there is generally no federal tax due on its income.

—Third, there are the unrelated debt-financed income provisions. As their name indicates, these provisions apply to the real-estate income of an exempt association only if that income is both unrelated to the exempt functions of the association and if it is debt-financed. The effect of the provisions is to render unrelated debt-financed income taxable at ordinary corporate income tax rates. For example, assume that an exempt association acquires a business or investment property subject to mortgage and that the functions for which it is used are not related to those for which the association was granted tax-exempt status. Assuming that no special exceptions are applicable, a proportionate percentage of the income and the deductions are taken into account for tax purposes. As the mortgage is paid off, the percentage taken into account diminishes. Capital gains on the sale of such debt-financed property will also be taxed in the same proportions. A complicated averaging formula is set out in Internal Revenue Service regulations to determine the applicable percentage to which income and deductions for this kind of property must be taken into account for unrelated business income tax purposes. The usual deductions are allowable. These would include depreciation (which can only be computed by the straight-line method), salaries, overhead, and other expenses.

- Two minor points in the tax statute and regulations have important implications for an association planning to dispose of "unrelated debt-financed" real estate. First, for the property to be considered "debt-financed," there need not be debt encumbering the property itself. If real estate is purchased with funds that would otherwise be used for the operating budget, for example, and a loan is used to operate the association, IRS will consider the real estate debt-financed. Second, for property that is sold or disposed of, it is enough that an indebtedness existed on the property at any time during the 12-month period ending with its sale or disposition. That property will be considered "debt-financed" at the time of the sale. For an association to have a tax-free sale on unrelated, encumbered real estate, the encumbrance must have been paid off for a full year before the real estate is sold by the association.

- The federal tax statute and the IRS regulations resolve the practical question of whether an association can transact a tax-free sale of only a portion of a tract of "unrelated debt-financed" real estate. It seems clear that by paying off the debt only on the severed part of the whole tract, waiting a year (for the reason given above), and then selling that severed part, a tax-free transaction could be accomplished. In such a situation, the rules require *pro rata* apportionments between the main tract and the severed part for indebtedness, deductions, and the rest.

- There are several major exceptions to the rules regarding unrelated debt-financed income. If any of the exceptions are applicable, it may well be that income from association real estate is not taxable even if that income is realized from debt-financed property.

- One exception is that real estate or any property will not be considered debt-financed if "substantially all" of its use is "substantially related" to the exercise or performance of the functions for which the association was granted exempt status. Generally, the test is met when 85 percent or more of the property use is devoted to the association's exempt purposes. This exception allows the exempt association a degree of flexibility. Its effect is to exclude the entire property if substantially all of it meets the "related" test, but, in any event, to exclude that portion less than "substantially all" of which meets such test.

- Another exception exists for property used by a related exempt organization. If an exempt association leases debt-financed real estate to a related exempt association, the income won't be treated as taxable unrelated debt-financed income so long as the real estate is used in the exempt functions of either of the associations. The regulations define "related" associations in a variety of ways, including those with 50 percent or more common membership, local affiliates of a national organization, etc.

- The "neighborhood land rule" is one more major exception to the unrelated debt-financed income provisions. The requirements specify that where an exempt organization acquires real estate for the "principal purpose" of using it in the exercise or performance of its exempt function and, if at the time of acquisition, the real estate is in the neighborhood of other organization-owned property which is used for that exempt function, then the newly acquired real estate is considered to be for future use. As such, it will not be subject to the unrelated debt-financed income provisions. Its income will be tax-free. This rule applies only for as long as there is an intention to use the real estate for the exempt purpose within ten years from its acquisition. Moreover, after the first five years, the organization must affirmatively establish that it is reasonably certain to use the land for its exempt purposes before the 10-year period expires. This may be done by showing construction or renovation building plans, contracts, etc.

- There are some limitations to the "neighborhood land rule" exception:
  —If the income from the property is to be tax-free, then it must not come from "business leases," i.e., leases more than five years in duration.
  —The concept of "neighborhood land" is arbitrarily defined as land which is either contiguous to the association's present land, just across the street from it, or in some circumstances, a maximum of a mile away.

RESOURCES FOR CHAPTER 68

Books

Beller, "Unrelated Debt-Financed Income," *338 Tax Management*, The Bureau of National Affairs, Inc.
Galloway, "The Unrelated Debt-Financed Income Tax" in *The Unrelated Business Income Tax*, Ronald Press, 1982, page 113.

Greif, "Unrelated Business Income" in *Managing Membership Societies*, Greif, Editor, ASAE, 1979, page 23.

Hopkins, *The Law of Tax-Exempt Organizations*, Ronald Press, 1979, page 43.

Jacobs, "Taxation of Association Real Estate Holdings" in *Associations and the Law Book V*, U.S. Chamber, 1973, page 27.

Lamb & Shields, *Trade Association Law and Practice*, Little, Brown, 1971, page 252.

Statham & Buek, *Associations and the Tax Laws*, U.S. Chamber, 1978, page 82.

Treusch & Sugarman, *Tax-Exempt Charitable Organizations*, American Law Institute, 1979, page 198.

Webster, Herold, & Dye, *Association Legal Checklist*, U.S. Chamber, 1983, pages 69–70.

Periodicals

Beller, "Exempt Organizations: Taxation of Debt-Financed Income," *Tax Lawyer*, 1971, page 489.

Canter, "Owning a Building: Tax on Unrelated, Debt-Financed Income," *Association Letter*, September, 1981, page 4.

Greif, "Tax Implication of an Exempt Organization Constructing and Operating a Building," *Tax Advisor*, 1975, page 354.

"The Macaroni Monopoly: The Developing Concept of Unrelated Business Income of Exempt Organizations," *Harvard L. Rev.*, 1968, page 1280.

Reed, "Exemptions From Unrelated Business Tax—Rental Income," *Catholic Lawyer*, 1975, page 282.

Statutes and Regulations

Internal Revenue Code Sections 514 and 1011.
Regulations Section 1.514.

Chapter 69

MISCELLANEOUS ASSOCIATION ACTIVITIES

In addition to association activities connected with advertising, insurance, and real estate, whose tax implications are summarized in separate chapters, there are other typical association activities which may have important tax consequences for exempt associations. They are the subjects of the Summary contained in this chapter.

Two typical association activities, trade shows and lobbying, were once highly controversial because there existed conflicting or confusing decisions and rulings about them. Recent statutory changes have made the tax consequences of those two kinds of association activities somewhat more predictable.

Other activities, while perhaps not controversial, are at least unclear in their tax implications. For these activities, one can only review whatever authority does exist and attempt to predict the positions that IRS or the courts would take were the activities under review from a taxation viewpoint. Before an analysis of the tax consequences of any particular association endeavor can be intelligently assessed, all of the facts of the endeavor must be analyzed and weighed against statutory and regulatory provisions as well as against rulings and decisions that may be applicable.

This Summary can only outline some issues raised in authorities or precedents concerning typical association activities; it should not be used to form legal conclusions about the particular facts of specific association activities but only to alert readers to questions about them.

SUMMARY

- *Trade shows* conducted by associations exempt from federal taxation as business leagues under Section

423

501(c)(6) of the Internal Revenue Code once had unclear tax consequences because the IRS had ruled that the net income derived from trade shows was unrelated business income if selling of goods or services occurred on the floor of the trade show. The Tax Reform Act of 1976 changed this as follows:

—A new provision of the Code, Section 513(d), applies to associations exempt as business leagues which regularly conduct trade shows to stimulate interest in an industry's products.

—Under Section 513(d), net income from a trade show is not subject to unrelated business income taxation whether or not selling occurs if these conditions are met:

    (1) The trade show must be conducted in connection with an international, national, state, regional, or local convention.

    (2) One of the purposes of the organization sponsoring the trade show must be to stimulate interest in an industry's products or services.

    (3) The trade show must promote that interest through the character and the extent of the displays.

—The provision does not apply to associations exempt in scientific, educational, or similar categories of Section 501(c)(3).

- *Credit programs* have been the subject of a number of court decisions where the exempt status of associations was challenged. In cases where the associations were engaged in substantial credit activities such as furnishing credit reports or information to members or conducting collection services, tax-exempt status has generally been denied the associations. The rationale for denial of exemption has generally been that these kinds of activities are ordinarily carried on for profit by commercial firms or that the activities involve the rendering of particular services to members. IRS has ruled that an association whose primary activity is to provide credit and collection services is not entitled to exempt status. Associations which have only an "incidental" or small amount of activity in this area may not be jeopardizing exempt status but, in certain cases, may still be required to pay unrelated business income tax on any net gains from income received in connection with the activity.

- *Lobbying* is clearly an appropriate and permissible activity of associations exempt as business leagues under Section 501(c)(6). An IRS ruling has held that the exempt status is appropriate even for an association whose sole or principal activity is lobbying. Prior to 1963, there existed the possibility that a portion of a member's dues to an association might not be deductible to the member if lobbying were carried on by the association; but statutory amendments have clarified that dues paid to associations engaged in lobbying efforts germane to the business interests of members are deductible under most circumstances as business expenses. Note that as a result of congressional inquiry, the IRS has taken the position that a trade or professional association which engages in a substantial amount of lobbying on issues not of direct benefit to its members or which engages in "grassroots" lobbying to influence the public on legislative issues still risks having an apportionate share of members' dues declared nondeductible. This is discussed in another chapter. Associations which are tax exempt under Section 501(c)(3) of the Code are clearly prohibited by statute from engaging in more than an "insubstantial" amount of lobbying activity or grass roots public opinion expenditures. Legislative provisions enacted in 1976 allow those associations to elect to follow a formula to determine precisely how much of such activity will be considered insubstantial with the excess subject to taxation. This is also discussed in another chapter.

- *Cooperative buying and selling* efforts of associations have been the subject of numerous decisions and rulings. It has generally been held that tax-exempt status is to be denied an association whose primary activities are in the area of cooperative buying and selling. On the other hand, where an association engages in such minor cooperative activities as purchasing of business forms for members to use in reporting statistics to the association as well as to use in their own businesses, an IRS ruling found that the activity benefited the association and use by members of the forms was inci-

dental. The association's tax-exempt status was not
jeopardized and no unrelated business income tax was
levied. In general, if cooperative buying or selling activities of an association are kept at levels which could
be defended as insubstantial or incidental, they will
not endanger exempt status; but they may, depending
upon the facts, incur unrelated business income tax on
any net receipts (after deductions and assuming no
offsetting losses from other unrelated business activities).

- *Research activities* conducted by associations where
  the results benefit an entire industry or profession may
  have no disadvantageous tax consequences for the exempt association unless the results are restricted only
  to association members. In an IRS ruling and a court
  decision upholding it, an association which conducted
  research for an industry but restricted the results to
  association members was held not entitled to a tax
  exemption.

- *Testing and certification activities* of associations have
  tax consequences similar to research activities. If the
  testing and certification activities are offered on a nondiscriminatory basis to association members and nonmembers, they will probably not disqualify the association for the tax-exempt status. It may also be important
  to be able to show that the testing and certification
  activities were incidental to other primary association
  exempt purposes, according to IRS rulings in individual cases where exemption was allowed to stand despite some testing and certification activities of the
  associations involved.

- *Labor negotiations* by an association formed to conduct
  them for members can be a significant benefit to an
  entire line of commerce and entitle an association to
  tax-exempt status even when joint employer bargaining and interpretation of labor agreements are the only
  functions served. Rulings have held that associations
  can engage in these activities in most instances without fear of threatening exempt status or incurring unrelated business income tax. However, association
  representation of employers in arbitration and griev-
  ance hearings may result in a claim by the IRS that

the association is performing particular services for members. This claim, however, may be disputed where the subject of a hearing—for example, an issue arising under an industry collective bargaining agreement—has an impact upon all the association members.

- *Advertising* activities of associations performed to promote the products or services of an entire industry or merely of some industry members can raise tax exemption questions in some circumstances. If joint industry advertising is other than "institutional advertising" contrasted with promotion of named association members, tax-exempt status may be challenged by the IRS. The principal issue has been whether the advertising activities were particular services for members. Also, the advertising activity may be deemed unrelated to the exempt purposes of the organization and thus subject to tax.

- The above summaries of miscellaneous association activities should alert readers who are responsible for managing or advising associations to the kinds of issues IRS can be expected to raise on audit. These summaries are obviously not exhaustive, however, and interested readers are urged to probe further into the literature on exempt association activities listed below.

RESOURCES FOR CHAPTER 69

Books

Greif, "Unrelated Business Income" in *Managing Membership Societies*, Greif, Editor, ASAE, 1979, page 23.

Hopkins, *The Law of Tax-Exempt Organizations*, Ronald Press, 1979, page 260.

Hopkins, "Unrelated Business Income Tax on Trade Show Revenue of Associations" in *Association Issues*, Jacobs, Editor, ASAE, 1983, page 11.

Lamb & Shields, *Trade Association Law and Practice*, Little, Brown, 1971, page 240.

Statham & Buek, *Associations and the Tax Laws*, U.S. Chamber, 1978, pages 42, 81.

Webster, *The Law of Associations*, Matthew Bender, 1976, page 5.1.

Webster & Dye, "Trade Associations," 331-2d *Tax Management*, The Bureau of National Affairs, Inc., 1976.

Webster, Herold, & Dye, *Association Legal Checklist*, U.S. Chamber, 1983, pages 64–65.

Webster & Krebs, *Association & Lobbying, A Guide for Non-Profit Organizations*, U.S. Chamber, 1979, page 14.

Periodicals

Caytor, "What Activities Risk Trade Association Exemptions," *J. Taxation*, 1978, page 104.

Fones, "Taxation of Trade Shows and Public Entertainment Activities," *A.B.A.J.*, 1978, page 913.

Kannry, "Analysis of IRS Trade Show Rulings," *Association Management*, April, 1976, page 69.

Kannry, "Trade Shows Must Bar All Selling to Avoid Unrelated Business Income Tax," *J. Taxation*, 1976, page 300.

McKinney, "The Application of Section 277 to Business Leagues and Income Derived From Trade Shows," *Taxes*, 1970, page 266.

"Trade Shows—Changes in the Tax Reform Act of 1976," *Association Taxation*, November, 1976, page 2.

Webster, "Tax Status of Business Conventions and Trade Shows," *Association Management*, August, 1972, page 70.

Webster, "What Is the Bottom Line on Taxation of Trade Shows?," *Association Management*, November, 1983, page 41.

Webster & Lehrfeld, "The Current Tax Treatment of Trade Shows; Attacks Now Being Made by the IRS," *J. Taxation*, 1966, page 10.

Weinberg, "Current Taxation of Trade Show Revenues: When Are They Unrelated Business Income?," *J. Taxation*, 1977, page 294.

Statutes

Internal Revenue Code Sections 513(d), 162(e).

Cases

Retail Credit Assn. of Minneapolis v. United States, 30 F. Supp. 855 (D. Minn. 1938). Credit activities by tax-exempt association.

Indiana Retail Hardware Assn. v. United States, 366 F.2d 998 (Ct. Cl. 1966). Cooperative buying one of several association unrelated business activities defeating exempt status.

Glass Container Research Corp. v. United States, 70-1 U.S.T.C. 9214 (W.D. Pa. 1970). Failure to make research results available to nonparticipants held inconsistent with exempt status.

American Plywood Assn. v. United States, 267 F. Supp. 830 (W.D. Wash. 1967). Testing program of association held incidental to total activities of association and thus not particular services.

Washington State Apples, Inc., 46 B.T.A. 64 (1942). Advertising program designed to benefit one entire industry without monitoring specific firms held not particular services jeopardizing exempt status.

Chapter 70

ASSOCIATION SUBSIDIARIES

Until recently, trade and professional associations had become identified with a handful of conventional programs intended to enhance and advance the industries or professions they represented: conventions, trade shows, seminars, and other educational meetings; journals, newsletters, manuals, and all sorts of educational publications; public affairs projects to influence the government and the populace; product and professional standards and certification; joint statistical gathering, labor negotiations, research, marketing, and advertising.

Associations still do all of those things, and they do them bigger and better than ever. But association endeavors are no longer limited to the conventional. Associations are expanding beyond their conventional roles and traditional activities to further the common business and professional interests of members. The accent is on servicing the members using whatever creative and innovative policies and programs, within the law, work best. A secondary but important consideration is generating non-dues income, since many associations have already "tapped" dues revenue to its maximum and since often the new endeavors do not benefit all members equally; funding them with dues paid by all the members might seem unfair.

Inevitably, associations are turning more and more to the establishment of subsidiaries as the organizational entities from which to operate these creative or innovative programs to service members. There are two major reasons for using subsidiaries. First, as new programs approach the fringes of what has been determined as the appropriate scope of endeavor for federal income-tax-exempt associations, or even move beyond those fringes, the establishment of a separate subsidiary is necessary to protect and preserve the exempt status of the main association. Second, some of the new endeavors may raise additional or different issues of legal liability exposure than that which the main association has long experienced; it is therefore often best to limit that exposure if possible to the assets of a separately incorporated subsidiary. This Summary considers both tax exemption and liability aspects of association subsidiaries.

SUMMARY

- Easily the most common use of an association subsidiary is to avoid tainting the federal income-tax-exempt status of the main association. Subsidiaries established for this purpose are usually for-profit (not tax exempt) corporations equivalent to any tax-paying business and owned by the parent associations.

- For-profit subsidiaries are ordinarily essential for the conducting of "business" activities which are clearly and obviously unrelated to the purposes for which an association holds tax-exempt status and are likely to generate substantial net revenues.

- In general, a for-profit subsidiary should be used whenever an unrelated business activity of a trade or professional association is likely to threaten the tax-exempt status of the main association. The generation of substantial *net revenues* from the unrelated activity is one of the danger signals that should certainly trigger consideration of a for-profit subsidiary. But there are some other fact patterns in which a for-profit subsidiary may be desirable:

  —A high percentage of association *staff time* devoted to an unrelated business activity is also a danger signal. The Internal Revenue Service routinely looks to the percentage of the time devoted to the unrelated business activity by paid employees to determine whether the activity is "substantial." This percentage is often readily ascertainable, because the association usually allocates a percentage of its salaries to its unrelated activity as an offset to income from the unrelated activity. The IRS thus needs only to compare the deduction on an association's Form 990-T, the tax return for unrelated business income ac-

tivities, to the total salaries shown on Form 990, the
information return for tax exempt activities, in order
to determine what percentage of staff time is allocable to the unrelated activity. An association might
make the mistake of allocating a high percentage of
staff time to unrelated activities to generate substantial expenses which will offset income from the
unrelated activities. It is thus creating what amounts
to an admission that the unrelated activities are
"substantial" in relation to the exempt activities of
the association.

—Another danger signal is a high percentage of *gross
income and gross expenses* generated by the unrelated business activity. The Internal Revenue Service
has been known to look not only to net revenues, but
to gross income and gross expenses, to determine
whether an unrelated activity is substantial in relation to exempt activities. This is often the case;
unrelated activities can involve hundreds of thou-
sands or millions of dollars of gross income and gross
expenses for associations while membership dues
are substantially less. The law and regulations suggest that IRS should look only at net revenue, not
gross income or expenses, in reviewing the tax-exempt status of an association. But there is not much
firm legal authority on this point. It is not clear which
way courts would rule on it.

—Generation of *loss* by the unrelated activity is a third
danger signal. If the unrelated activity is consistently generating a substantial loss, this means to
the IRS that the excess of expenses over income is
being covered by the exempt income of the association. If the loss is substantial, the IRS could consider
this to be an abuse of the nonprofit, tax-exempt status of the association. It may be advisable to create
a for-profit subsidiary to avoid this situation.

• Associations often sponsor activities which are related
in part and unrelated in part to their exempt purposes.
In such cases, only the income generated by the unrelated activity is subject to tax, and the association
may deduct only those expenses specifically allocable
to the unrelated portion of the business activity. It is

quite common to have a net revenue from the unrelated portion of the activity but to have a net loss when the activity is considered as a whole. In such cases, it may be advisable to create a for-profit subsidiary so that the entire income from the activity, and all of the expenses attributable to it, will be counted in determining income.

- It is not likely that the Internal Revenue Service would require separate boards of directors or separate headquarters for associations and for their for-profit subsidiaries. What the IRS does require is strict *financial separation*. There must be a very precise allocation of all of the expenses of the main association and the subsidiary which are in any way related. Furthermore, it is important to be able to substantiate the allocation on audit. For example, staff time should be allocated by having employees keep an accurate daily log of the number of hours devoted to the matters of the for-profit subsidiary. Legal and accounting fees should be allocated by the service provider. A separate log can be kept for telephone and mail expenses.

- Another way to achieve the necessary financial separation is to have the for-profit subsidiary retain the main association to manage it and to pay a flat management fee. Care must be taken to have the management fee approximate the fair market value of the services. It may be advisable to ask for quotes from association management companies for the same services; these quotes can be shown to the Internal Revenue Service as substantiation for the fair market value of the service fee paid by the subsidiary to the main association.

- Separate from considerations of tax exemption, another major reason for conducting a new association program through a subsidiary, rather than through the main association, is the desire to isolate the association from liability for the program if possible.

- As trade and professional associations become more innovative, more aggressive, and more visible in their policies or activities, they inevitably also become almost lightning rods for legal claims. In the monumental

1982 *Hydrolevel* case, the Supreme Court first held an association responsible for antitrust treble damages because of an anticompetitive interpretation of product standards that the association had issued. In doing so, the Court declared that in some circumstances an association can become virtually "an extra-governmental agency, which prescribes rules for the regulation of interstate commerce," and that associations are "rife with opportunities" to violate the antitrust laws.

- Apart from antitrust, associations are increasingly named as defendants in personal injury or property damage cases because of communications, standards, or policies issued by associations that are claimed to have caused damages.

- As associations expand into new services for members which sometimes more closely resemble those offered by commercial enterprises, they are becoming entangled in the myriad of disputes which seems symptomatic of American business operations—claims for contract violation, copyright or trademark infringement, etc.

- One strategy that may sometimes help to protect the assets and reputation of an association against antitrust, damage, and other kinds of claims for liability from a new association service is to offer the service through an independently incorporated subsidiary of the association.

- The extent to which an association can successfully isolate itself from liability arising through a separate subsidiary corporation will always depend upon the specific situation of the association and its subsidiary. Predictions on this subject are unreliable because there is as yet almost no precedent on liability of a nonprofit parent for the claimed misdeeds of its subsidiary. Generally, however, one can look for guidance to the body of law that has grown up on the subject of commercial corporation liability for the illegal or harmful acts or omissions of its incorporated subsidiaries. Here one finds that courts typically focus upon two fundamental elements:

  —The extent of control exercised by the parent over the subsidiary

—The extent to which the parent actually participated in the challenged policy or activity.

- The cases on corporate parent liability for incorporated subsidiaries typically discuss the extent of control a parent can exercise over its subsidiary before the subsidiary loses its separate legal existence and must be considered a "mere instrumentality" of the parent. In these cases, courts will "pierce the corporate veil" of the subsidiary and hold the parent liable.

- Likewise, if it can be shown that the parent participated in the claimed wrongdoing of the subsidiary, the "mere instrumentality" rule is unnecessary; the parent will be held responsible for its own participation and the consequences of the wrongdoing.

- Associations may have as one purpose the isolation of themselves from potential liability for new services when they consider offering the new services through separately incorporated subsidiaries. If that is a purpose, it is very important to plan for the issues of control and participation to maximize the likelihood of legal isolation between the main association and the subsidiary.

- It is clear that associations are expanding the nature and scope of their endeavors. Neither tax exemption nor legal liability restrains the offering of creative and innovative services to members. For many associations, subsidiaries provide the appropriate legal vehicle to use in providing the new services.

RESOURCES FOR CHAPTER 70

Books

Galloway, "The Organization's Legal Form and Subsidiaries" in *The Unrelated Business Income Tax*, Ronald Press, 1982, page 163.

The Role of Association Foundations Today, ASAE Foundation, 1981.

Webster, Herold, & Dye, *Association Legal Checklist*, U.S. Chamber, 1983, pages 66–68.

Periodicals

Bistline, "Service Corporations: The Profits Side of Nonprofits,"
    Association Management, August, 1982, page 74.
Gratz, "Examining Subsidiaries: Formation, Policy Consider-
    ations," *Association Letter*, July, 1981, page 3.
Jacobs, "Association Subsidiaries and the Law," *Association
    Digest*, January/February and March/April, 1986, page 27.
Statham, "Should Your Association Form a Subsidiary?," *As-
    sociation & Society Manager*, October/November, 1981, page
    17.
Webster, "How to Work With For-Profit Partners," *Association
    Management*, September, 1983, page 65.
Webster, "Subsidiary Corporation Can Limit Your Tax Liabil-
    ity," *Association Management*, June, 1981, page 35.
Webster, "Understanding the Tax Consequences of Associa-
    tion Foundations," *Association Management*, September,
    1981, page 33.

Chapter 71

DEDUCTIBILITY OF MEETING EXPENSES

Expenses incurred by members in attending trade or professional association conventions, seminars, and other meetings generally are tax deductible as ordinary and necessary business expenses if the attendance is primarily for business or professional reasons rather than for pleasure or personal reasons. Items that typically are deductible under these circumstances include meeting registration fees, travel to and from the meetings, transportation at the meetings, lodging, meals, and other incidental expenses. If an individual's firm pays for the expenses of attending the association meeting, the expenses would be deductible on the firm's tax return. If an individual pays for the expenses and is not reimbursed by the firm, the expenses would be deductible on the individual's tax return.

Problems for members may arise in the area of tax deductibility of expenses incurred in attending association meetings where individuals combine trips to the meetings with pleasure trips, where individuals bring their spouses to the meetings, or where the meetings are held in locations outside North America. Tax deductibility of expenses of attending of meetings outside North America is subject to special statutory rules, which are included in the next chapter of this book.

SUMMARY

- Expenses incurred by U.S. citizens in attending association conventions, seminars, and other meetings generally are tax deductible by whomever pays for the expenses as ordinary and necessary business expenses where the attendance is primarily for business or professional reasons rather than for pleasure or personal reasons.

- If a firm or employer pays the expenses of an individual to attend the association meeting, the expenses would be deductible by the firm as ordinary and necessary business expenses.

- If an individual pays the expenses and is not reimbursed by the firm or employer, the meeting expenses would be deductible by the individual as nonreimbursed business expenses.

- Deductible expenses for attendance at association conventions, seminars or other meetings may include:
    —Registration fees or other charges made by the association
    —Travel to and from the place where the meeting is held
    —Local transportation at the meeting location
    —Hotel, motel, or other lodging charges
    —Meals
    —Business entertainment expenses directly related and necessary to attendance at the meeting
    —Tips
    —Service charges
    —Telephone charges
    —Laundry and cleaning
    —Other incidental expenses.

- The expenses of attending an association meeting are deductible only if the primary purpose for attending is to derive a business or professional benefit, according the the IRS regulations. This is a determination which has to be made in each case.

- In determining whether the primary purpose of attending an association meeting is to enhance one's business or profession, the government will look mainly at the amount of time devoted to business or professional activities at the meeting when compared to the amount of time devoted to recreational or social activities. But other factors may also be considered. In one case, for example, a reviewing court considered these factors in deciding upon the deductibility of an insurance company's employee expenses for attending a convention:

—the amount of time on the trip, for which the expenses were claimed as deductible, that the individual spent on directly business-related activities versus personal activities

—The fact that the meeting at issue was sponsored by the individual's employer and the only attendees were fellow employees

—The fact that the meeting was held at a vacation site

—The sponsor's general attitude toward the meeting.

In this case, the reviewing court decided against deductibility.

- The fact that an association meeting is held at a resort site will not, by itself, disqualify the tax deductibility of expenses of those who attend as long as there is primarily a business or professional purpose involved. Note, however, that there is a statutory prohibition against deductibility of expenses of attending meetings held aboard cruise ships (except certain U.S. flag vessels).

- When a trip to attend an association meeting is combined with activities such as social entertaining or sightseeing, the expenses related to the personal activities are not deductible.

- The IRS may be expected to look more closely at business expense deductions for association meeting attendance where the individuals attending have their expenses reimbursed by small, closely-held or family corporations since the government will want to insure that these firms are not, in effect, paying dividends to their principals in the form of reimbursement for pleasure trips. If that were the case, the expenses would be considered nondeductible to the firms and the reimbursements would be considered taxable to the individuals.

- Beyond the general rules on deductibility of members' expenses for attendance at association meetings, questions sometimes arise as to deductibility of members' spouses' expenses when the spouses attend also.

- The deductibility of spouses' expenses depends first of all upon the deductibility of the members' expenses. Initially it must be established that the trip to an association meeting is an "ordinary and necessary business expense" for the member. Beyond that, the Internal Revenue Service regulations provide that "where a taxpayer's wife accompanies him on a business trip, expenses attributable to her travel are not deductible unless it can be adequately shown that the wife's presence on the trip has a bona fide business purpose."

- In short, the spouse's attendance at the association meeting must, in the view of IRS, have as its dominant purpose the advancement of the member's business or professional interest in attending rather than some other interests such as vacationing, shopping, sightseeing, or visiting friends or relatives.

- Incidental business or professional purposes for attendance at meetings by spouses such as to assist in entertaining, to attend general interest programs, to take notes, etc., may be helpful to the members' businesses or professions but may be insufficient by themselves to justify deductions for the expenses of the spouses. Each situation turns upon its own facts.

- If there is no dominant business or professional purpose for attendance by a spouse or another family member at an association convention, seminar, or meeting, the portion of the total expenses attributable other than to the association member's attendance cannot be deducted (i.e., total automobile expenses could be deducted but only one airfare; single room rates could be deducted but not double room rates, etc.) If in these circumstances the member's employer reimburses for the spouse's expenses, taxable income results for the member.

- Courts that have reviewed IRS disqualifications of spouses' expenses for attending association meetings have often been more lenient than the government's regulations and other pronouncements on the subject. For example, an important 1977 case demonstrates a factual situation in which a court overruled the Internal Revenue Service determination of nondeductibility of spouses' expenses for attendance at conventions. A bank was challenged on the tax deductions it claimed for expense reimbursements to employees for attendance of their spouses at banking conventions. The bank satisfied the reviewing court that its banking business benefited from close relationships between its employees and personnel of other banks and that those relationships were developed at banking conventions and furthered by spouses' attendance. The court recognized a number of features of the spouses' attendance at the banking conventions which it considered to be helpful to the business of the bank. In the view of the court, the spouses:

—*Participated* in the educational aspects of the convention by broadening their understanding of banking
—*Attended* general and business sessions of the convention including programs specifically designed for wives of bankers
—*Organized, planned,* and *effectuated* numerous convention activities as official duties of officer's wives
—*Arranged* various functions, including dinners, and helped run the convention registration booth
—*Coordinated* and were instrumental to the success of the social activities such as the convention's golf and tennis tournaments
—*Entertained* and *socialized* with other bankers and their wives with whom the taxpayer's officers transacted business and from whom they sought advice
—*Aided* the officers in the activities in making new contacts, renewing old contacts, becoming better acquainted with other bankers, and in developing business relationships with other bankers
—*Enhanced* the image and public relations of the taxpayer and its officers by their presence and demeanor at the convention
—*Acted* as hostesses for the taxpayer's hospitality rooms, convention dinners, and receptions
—*Performed* such services as taking notes, carrying messages, and typing for the officers.

• From the relevant Internal Revenue Code provisions, from IRS regulations and other pronouncements, and from numerous court decisions can be gleaned some arbitrary guidelines for associations to consider in planning conventions, seminars, and other meetings to maximize the likelihood of tax-deductible treatment for expenses of members and spouses. Note, however, that each case turns upon its own facts and no guidelines in this area can be universal or unequivocal. Here are the guidelines:

—The program of any meeting should be planned to reflect the business or professional interests of members.

—Announcements, brochures, agendas, printed programs, and all other documentation of a meeting's subject matter should emphasize its business and professional aspects and de-emphasize any incidental social or pleasure aspects.

—No hard and fast rule requires that some minimum number of program hours be dedicated to business or professional activities. However, good sense dictates that the major portion of a program should be business-related or profession-related.

—Likewise, no rule disqualifies expense deductibility for meetings simply because they are held at resort sites (other than on cruise ships); but, again, there are requirements that the emphasis of a meeting be on business rather than pleasure wherever it is held.

—Associations should maintain records of meeting programs and attendance for at least several years in case some member might need these records to help support a case for deductibility of expenses.

—Promotion of an association convention, seminar or other meeting as "tax deductible" runs certain risks since the association cannot control all factors that are used to determine for a specific individual if expenses for attending are indeed deductible.

—Spouses' programs at associations should be planned carefully to maximize the business-related or profession-related content of the programs.

—Spouses may be encouraged to attend some or all of the regular meeting sessions held for members.

—Even at social or other noneducational events scheduled during association meetings, spouses should be given active participatory roles.

—Special separate rules apply for association conventions, seminars, or other meetings held outside North America (see next chapter).

—Tax deductibility of expenses of association meeting attendance raises difficult questions that should be referred to experienced tax consultants.

RESOURCES FOR CHAPTER 71

Books

Goldberg, "Planning Convention Programs to Allow Tax Deductions for Spouses' Expenses" in *Associations and the Law Book IX*, U.S. Chamber, 1979, page 54.

Lamb & Shields, *Trade Association Law and Practice*, Little, Brown, 1971, page 258.

Statham & Buek, *Associations and the Tax Laws*, U.S. Chamber, 1978, page 114.

Webster, "Conventions, Meetings and Wives: Taxes" in *Associations and the Law Book II*, U.S. Chamber, 1968, page 32.

Periodicals

"Deductibility of Spouse's Attendance at Conventions and Other Meetings," *Association Taxation*, December, 1977, page 1.

Feinschreiber, "New Limits on Foreign Convention Deductions," *Taxes*, 1977, page 358.

Heffernan & Terr, "Tax Planning for Foreign Conventions After the Tax Reform Act of 1976," *Tax Law Rev.*, 1977, page 273.

"Is Attendance at Your Convention or Meeting Tax Deductible?," *Association Taxation*, May, 1974, page 2.

Osborn, "How to Protect a Deduction for Going to a Foreign Convention Under Current Law," *J. Taxation*, 1977, page 336.

Postlewaite, "Deductibility of Expenses for Conventions and Educational Seminars," *Minnesota L. Rev.*, 1977, page 61.

Sheehan & Sullivan, "Convention Expenses; How to Prove Business Connection to the IRS's Satisfaction," *Taxation for Accountants*, 1971, page 146.

Webster, "Deducting Your Spouse's Convention Expenses," *Association Management*, December, 1982, page 43.

Webster, "Guidelines for Deducting Spouse Convention Expenses," *Association Management*, October, 1977, page 24.
Webster, "Wives Expenses at Conventions," *Association Management*, March, 1970, page 16.

Statutes and Regulations

Internal Revenue Code Sections 162 and 274(h) 1–7.
Regulations Section 1.162.

Cases

Patterson v. Thomas, 189 F. Supp. 230 (N.D. Ala. 1959), *rev'd.*,
289 F.2d 108 (5th Cir. 1961), *cert. denied*, 368 U.S. 837 (1962).
Insurance company employee attendance at convention.
United States v. Disney, 413 F.2d 783 (9th Cir. 1969). Spouse
expenses for business travel.
Bank of Stockton v. Commissioner, 36 T.C.M. (CCH) 114 (1977).
Deductibility by bank of expenses for employees' spouses'
attendance at conventions.

Chapter 72

DEDUCTIBILITY OF FOREIGN CONVENTION EXPENSES

Expenses incurred by members in attending association conventions, seminars, and similar meetings held at locations outside the United States, Canada, Mexico, and certain Caribbean sites are eligible for tax-deductible treatment for those members only in accordance with special rules imposed by tax legislation enacted in 1980.

Foreign convention expenses must first be of the type that would be deductible if the meeting were not held abroad. The general requirements for deductibility of expenses of attending meetings are included in the previous chapter of this book. In addition to the general requirements, when a convention is held outside North America, special provisions for tax deductibility also apply.

No deduction is allowed for the expenses of attending a convention, a seminar, or a similar meeting held outside North America unless it can be demonstrated that it is "as reasonable" to hold the meeting there as it would be to hold the meeting within North America. Criteria are given for determining when a foreign location is "as reasonable" as a domestic one. A flat prohibition exists for deductibility of expenses incurred in attending meetings held aboard cruise ships (except certain U.S. flag vessels).

This Summary outlines the foreign convention provisions passed in 1980.

SUMMARY

- Special rules apply for federal income tax deductibility of expenses incurred by members in attending foreign conventions, seminars, and similar meetings such as those sponsored by associations.

- Essentially, U.S. citizens who attend conventions or seminars held abroad cannot deduct for federal income tax purposes their expenses of attendance unless they can show that it was "as reasonable" for the sponsoring association to hold the convention or seminar abroad as it would have been to hold it in North America.

- The special provisions for deductibility of U.S. taxpayers' expenses at conventions or seminars held abroad do not affect ordinary business meetings, incentive travel, or trade exposition attendance, apparently. The provisions apply to "conventions, seminars, and other similar meetings" held outside the "North American territory," such as those sponsored by trade and professional associations (whether U.S. associations or not). The North American territory includes the United States (including Puerto Rico and the Virgin Islands), Canada, Mexico, and certain Caribbean nations. Additional Caribbean nations are expected to be added under the provisions of the Caribbean Basin Economic Recovery Act.

- As of early 1986, only Barbados had qualified to be considered as within the "North American territory," for purposes of the deductibility of expenses of attendance at conventions and seminars by U.S. citizens, under the Caribbean Basin Economic Recovery Act. Jamaica was added as a "North American" country under a separate treaty. Other Caribbean nations that might in the future qualify as Barbados has done include Anguilla, Antigua and Barbuda, the Bahamas, Belize, Bermuda, Costa Rica, Dominica, the Dominican Republic, El Salvador, Grenada, Guatemala, Guyana, Haiti, Honduras, Nicaragua, Panama, Saint Lucia, Saint Vincent and the Grenadines, Surinam, Trinidad and Tobago, the Cayman Islands, Montserrat, the Netherland Antilles, Saint Christopher-Nevis, Turks and Caicos Islands, and the British Virgin Islands. To qualify, these nations must sign a treaty with the U.S. on exchange of income information for tax enforcement and must not themselves discriminate on tax deductibility of their citizens' expenses for attendance at meetings in North America.

- Factors which, according to U.S. tax law, will lead to a determination that it was "as reasonable" for the sponsoring organization to hold the meeting outside North America as it would have been to hold it within North America are these:

  —Whether there are appropriate business or professional reasons for holding the convention or seminar abroad

  —Whether the sponsoring association has among its purposes some which can be related to the international site of the convention or seminar

  —Whether the sponsoring association includes regular and active members from other countries

  —Whether the sponsoring association has held or is planning other conventions or seminars abroad.

- Additional related factors which might logically also be considered in this "as reasonableness" test determination are these:

  —Whether the convention or seminar is scheduled to coincide with other business or professional events abroad (such as an international exhibition or a convention or seminar of a related organization abroad)

  —Whether non-U.S. citizens will attend

  —Whether business or professional programming is extensive and international in content

  —Whether promotional materials emphasize the business and professional aspects of the convention or seminar, rather than the travel and tourism aspects (post-convention trips with minimal business or professional connections should be promoted and priced separately).

- The presence or absence or any of these factors will not in itself determine whether it is "as reasonable" to hold a convention or seminar abroad. Instead, all factors will be considered upon review by the IRS.

- These special tax deductibility provisions apparently dictate apportionment of expenses when a U.S. citizen combines attendance at a convention or seminar outside North America with other business or tourism purposes. They apparently do not apply to "associate" or "supplier" participants attending conventions or seminars abroad for the purpose of promoting goods or services to other attendees rather than for educational purposes. They also do not apply, of course, to the sponsoring U.S. association's own executives and staff, assuming the association is tax-exempt and thus does not need to consider tax deductibility of expenses, at least for endeavors such as meetings which are related to the exempt purposes of the association.

- The reasonableness test for the deductibility of foreign meeting expenses applies to conventions, seminars, or similar meetings held after the end of 1980.

- The result of the reasonableness test is to eliminate all record-keeping requirements, all logging-in of delegates, and all per diem or other limitations on deductions that previously existed for deductibility of foreign meeting expenses as a result of the Tax Reform Act of 1976. In addition, the 1980 provisions eliminate all previous special requirements on meetings held in Canada and Mexico.

- Conventions, seminars, and similar meetings that are held aboard certain non-U.S. flag cruise ships traveling inside or outside of North America are flatly denied deductibility for expenses.

- Before planning any meeting in a location outside of the defined "North American territory," i.e., the United States, Canada, Mexico, and certain Caribbean sites, an association should review closely the potential tax implications for members of deductibility of expenses. The assistance of a tax expert is essential in this review.

RESOURCES FOR CHAPTER 72

Books

Statham & Buek, *Associations and the Tax Laws*, U.S. Chamber, 1978, page 120.
Vickerman, "Tax Treatment of Overseas Meetings" in *Association Issues*, Jacobs, Editor, ASAE, 1983, page 29.

Webster, *Foreign Convention Tax Guidelines*, ASAE, 1976.

Periodicals

Anderson, "IRS Rules Regarding Foreign Convention Travel," GWSAE *Executive Update*, June, 1984, page 12.

Bostwick & Terr, "An Analysis of the Changes Made to the Foreign Convention Rules by the 1978 Act," *J. Taxation*, 1979, page 206.

"Foreign Conventions, Educational Seminars, and Similar Meetings," *Association Taxation*, October, 1976, page 2.

"How Associations Are Complying With Foreign Convention Tax Law," *Association Management*, April, 1977, page 53.

"Impact of Tax Reform Act on Foreign Conventions," *Association Management*, December, 1976, page 37.

Owen, "Congress Acts on Foreign Convention Provision," *Association Letter*, January, 1981, page 7.

Postlewaite, "Deductibility of Expenses for Conventions and Educational Seminars," *Minnesota L. Rev.*, 1977, page 253.

Savitt, "Update: Caribbean Basin Initiative," *Association & Society Manager*, February/March, 1984, page 44.

Statham, "Revised Foreign Convention Rules," *Association & Society Manager*, April/May, 1981, page 39.

Sullivan, "Planning a Conference Cruise That Complies With New Tax Law," *Association Management*, April, 1977, page 68.

Vickerman, "Viewpoint: What Does the New Law on Foreign Conventions Mean to Associations?," *Association Management*, April, 1981, page 81.

Webster, "Tax Aspects of Foreign Convention Travel," *Association Management*, January, 1972, page 17.

Statutes

Internal Revenue Code Sections 274(h) 1–3.

Other Resources

S. Rep. No. 1031, 96th Cong., 2nd Sess. (1980).

Floor debate at Cong. Rec. S16508-10, H12488-90, December 13, 1980.

H.R. Rep. No. 658, 94th Cong., 1st Sess. (1975).

H.R. Rep. No. 1515, 94th Cong., 2nd Sess. (1975).

Chapter 73

DEDUCTIBILITY OF GRASS-ROOTS LOBBYING EXPENSES

One tax issue that does not affect associations directly, but affects association members based upon the activities of their associations, is "grass-roots lobbying" expense deductibility. When associations incur substantial expenses in attempting to influence the public on legislative issues, there is some risk that a portion of the association members' dues, which would otherwise be tax deductible to the members, may not be fully deductible.

This Summary concerns association members' federal income tax deductibility of association dues when those dues are used in part to pay for associations' grass-roots lobbying expenses.

SUMMARY

- Generally, direct lobbying expenses of a company are deductible for federal income tax purposes as "ordinary and necessary" business expenses if the lobbying has a sufficient connection with the company's business.

- However, expenses of "grass-roots lobbying"—attempts to influence the general public or segments of the public—are specifically prohibited as tax deductible.

- Associations which engage in "substantial" grass-roots lobbying risk having a portion of members' dues held nondeductible to the members in proportion to the extent of grass-roots lobbying costs compared with other association costs. What constitutes "substantial" grass-roots lobbying has never been defined adequately.

- Tax advisers once felt that if less than 5 percent of an association's budget was used for grass-roots lobbying, that would be less than a "substantial" amount and would avoid jeopardizing members' dues deductibility. More recently, IRS agents were informally suggesting 15 percent as the threshold of substantiality. However, in 1978, IRS notified its agents that there was no 15 percent test and anything more than a de minimus amount of grass-roots lobbying by an association will affect members' dues deductions.

- It is clear that communications regarding legislation at any level of government—federal, state, or local—could be considered grass-roots lobbying.

- Congressional investigations and hearings held in 1976–1978 under the late Rep. Benjamin Rosenthal explored and publicized the issue of tax deductibility of expenses of grass-roots lobbying. Partly as a result, IRS required associations to state in the annual Form 990 information return if they engage in grass-roots lobbying. Also in 1978, the IRS issued four revenue rulings on this subject. Among the points made in the rulings are these:
  —A communication need not specifically exhort action regarding legislation to be considered grass-roots lobbying.
  —Mere distribution of testimony presented to a legislature can be grass-roots lobbying.
  —Association communications to association members are generally not considered as made to the public; but if the communications are intended to go beyond members and to reach their employees or customers, this is grass-roots lobbying.
  —Prospective members of an association are members of the public.

- In 1980, the Internal Revenue Service issued proposed regulations that take a much stricter view of what is deductible and broaden the definition of grass-roots lobbying:
  —The proposal eliminates the "substantiality" test and

requires associations to advise members of any grass-roots lobbying, thereby disallowing a portion of the members' dues deductions.

- The proposal treats a communication as grass-roots lobbying if it:
  —Pertains to action by a legislative body
  —Reflects a view on that action
  —Is distributed to reach individuals as voters or constituents.

- Associations engaged in any communications that might be considered grass-roots lobbying by the Internal Revenue Service should be familiar with the dues deductibility ramifications for members and should follow the progress of possible IRS final regulations in this area.

RESOURCES FOR CHAPTER 73

Books

Krebs, "Deductibility of Business Expenses for Grassroots Lobbying" in *Association Issues*, Jacobs, Editor, ASAE, 1983, page 31.
Jacobs, "The Law of Lobbying" in *ASAE 3rd Annual Management Conference Proceedings*, 1985, page 330.

Periodicals

Cooper, "Tax Treatment of Business Grassroots Lobbying: Defining and Obtaining the Public Policy Objectives," *Col. L. Rev.*, 1968, page 801.
Krebs, "Grassroots Lobbying Defined: The Scope of I.R.C. Sec. 162(e)(2)(B)," *Taxes*, 1978, page 516.

"Summary of I.R.S. 'Grassroots' Lobbying Rulings," *Association Taxation*, March, 1978, page 2.

Regulations

Internal Revenue Code Section 162(e).

Other Resources

Revenue Rulings 1978 - 11, 12, 13, 14.

Chapter 74

LOBBYING BY SECTION 501(c)(3) ASSOCIATIONS

Associations that have been determined by the Internal Revenue Service to be exempt from federal income tax under Section 501(c)(3) of the Internal Revenue Code are subject to limitations on their permissible lobbying activities. These "charitable, scientific or educational organizations," which in the association community are typically recognizable or primarily scientific or educational associations, may continue to hold their special federal tax exempt status if "no substantial part" of their activities involve lobbying. By comparison, trade and professional associations—classified as tax-exempt "business leagues" under Section 501(c)(6) of the Code—have essentially no tax-exemption-related limits on lobbying.

For scientific and educational associations, "(c)(3)s," the limit on "substantial" lobbying was for a long time a very vague limit. It often led these associations to avoid all lobbying in order to ensure that they thereby avoided "substantial" lobbying. Even under this vague proscription, however, many Section 501(c)(3) associations have become comfortable with limited lobbying activities based upon a comparison of those activities with all of the associations' endeavors.

Moreover, in 1976 an elective alternative provision was added to the law to permit Section 501(c)(3) scientific and educational associations to be guided by an absolute numerical percentage test for determining what is permissible insubstantial lobbying activity and to be subjected to penalties when the test is violated.

This Summary discusses limits on lobbying by Section 501(c)(3) scientific and educational associations.

SUMMARY

- The federal income tax exemption laws and regulations have long provided for different treatment of different kinds of exempt organizations. Those exempt as "charitable, scientific or educational" groups under Section 501(c)(3) of the Internal Revenue Code may offer contributors guaranteed tax deductibility for contributions but may not engage in "substantial" lobbying. Likewise veterans' organizations exempt under Code Section 501(c)(19) are limited in their lobbying activities. The Supreme Court considered several years ago whether the disparate treatment with respect to lobbying by tax exempt organizations is unconstitutional; the Court decided that it is not unconstitutional.

- Trade and professional associations exempt from federal income tax as "business leagues" under Code Section 501(c)(6) are not limited in their lobbying activity at all—IRS has provided tax exemption determinations to these groups even when one hundred percent of their activities involve lobbying.

- Section 501(c)(3), on the other hand, provides federal income tax exempt status for scientific and educational associations if "no substantial part" of their activities entail "propaganda, or otherwise attempting to influence legislation . . . ."

- The law bans completely any participation by a Section 501(c)(3) association, directly or indirectly, in a political campaign for or against a federal, state or local candidate—this likely precludes such an association from administering a related political action committee even if PAC finances are kept segregated from those of the association.

- The problem for Section 501(c)(3) scientific and educational associations is that the limit on lobbying is determined by a vague, uncertain standard, i.e., no "substantial" lobbying is permitted:
  - One court case has held that the meaning of "substantial" varies between different types of tax-exempt organizations.
  - The chilling effect of this uncertainty historically has

caused many Section 501(c)(3) associations to avoid most or all lobbying in order to preserve their federal income-tax-exempt status.

- A "rule of thumb" once prevailed informally that up to five percent of the total activities of a 501(c)(3) association could be in lobbying and not considered "substantial"; but the IRS never accepted any fixed percentage of activities or expenditures as the limit for what would be considered insubstantial.

- The 1976 Tax Reform Act added Section 501(h) to the Internal Revenue Code; it gives Section 501(c)(3) exempt associations the option of complying with specific monetary limits on lobbying expenses rather than having to cope with the vague substantiality test.

- There are six eligible categories of 501(c)(3) organizations that may use this alternative specific test:
  —Educational institutions
  —Hospital and medical research organizations
  —Organizations supporting government schools
  —Organizations publicly supported by charitable contributions
  —Organizations publicly supported by admissions, sales, performance of services, or furnishing facilities
  —Organizations supporting qualified public charities

- There are also several kinds of unqualified organizations:
  —Private foundations (these are subject to separate lobbying rules)
  —Labor unions
  —Trade associations
  —Civic organizations.

- What is considered "lobbying"? These definitions appear in the Code or the IRS regulations:
  —*Lobbying expenditures*—money spent to influence legislation.
  —*Influencing legislation*—contact with legislature or grass-roots lobbying.
  —*Legislation*—any local, state, or national bill, resolution, referendum, or initiative.
  —*Legislative action*—introduction, amendment, re-

peal, enactment or defeat of legislation; *not* general
investigations or oversight.
—*Grass-roots lobbying*—trying to influence opinions of
the general public or any segment of it to affect legislation.

- "Contact with a legislature" includes legislative staff
  contacts; it includes contact with nonlegislative government officials only if the principal purpose of the
  contact is to influence legislation.

- "Grass-roots lobbying" includes communications that
  do not urge contact with a legislature, *e.g.*, newspaper
  ads that include an association's objections to legislation; it also includes contacts with prospective association members, but *not* contacts with present
  association members on matters of their direct interest.

- What is *not* considered lobbying?
  —Making available results of non-partisan analyses
  —Providing technical advice or assistance in response
  to a governmental body's request
  —"Self-defense" lobbying contacts with a legislature
  (not with the public) regarding legislation that might
  affect an association's existence, powers and duties,
  exempt status, or deductibility of contributions to it
  —Communications with bona fide members of an association regarding legislation that is related to the
  exempt purposes of the association, unless it directly
  urges members to influence legislation or engage in
  grass-roots lobbying
  —Communications with a nonlegislative government
  employee if the principal purpose is not to influence
  legislation.

- The expenditure limits under the alternative test are
  according to a formula. These definitions apply:
  —"Exempt Purpose Expenditures" ("EPE")—Total paid
  or incurred for exempt purposes; it includes administrative costs and all lobbying costs; it does not include amounts paid or incurred to a separate fund
  or unit of the organization or another organization.
  —"Lobby Nontaxable Amount" ("LNA")—Expenditure
  limit to avoid penalty tax.

- The formula is this:

Exempt Purpose Expenditures (EPE)	*Lobby Nontaxable Amount (LNA)*
Not over $500,000	20% of EPE
Over $500,000 but not over $1,000,000	$100,000 plus 15% of excess of EPE over $500,000
Over $1,000,000 but not over $1,500,000	$225,000 plus 5% of excess of EPE over $1,500,000

- There is an absolute limit of $1,000,000 on LNA which only affects organizations with over $17,000,000 in EPE.

- The grass-roots nontaxable amount equals 25 percent of LNA.

- Excess lobbying expenditures are the greater of:
  —Lobbying expenditures in excess of the LNA; or
  —Grass-roots expenditures in excess of the grass-roots nontaxable amount.

- A 25 percent penalty tax is imposed on excess lobbying expenditures.

- The lobbying ceiling amount equals 150 percent of the LNA.

- The grass-roots ceiling amount equals 150 percent of the grass-roots nontaxable amount.

- Loss of tax exemption occurs if either ceiling amount is "normally exceeded" (exceeds the ceiling average over a four-year period).

- Affiliated associations are treated as one for purposes of calculating nontaxable and ceiling amounts under these rules:
  —If the group has excess lobbying expenditures, each affiliate is credited with a proportionate amount of those excess expenditures
  —If a ceiling violation results in loss of tax exemption, that loss extends to each affiliate
  —The definition of "affiliation" includes circumstances in which the governing instrument of one association

requires it to be bound by decisions of another on legislation; or the governing board of one is dominated by representatives of another that can cause or veto legislative action.

- Election of the dollar ceilings option can be made any time before the end of the tax year for that year. It extends to future years until it is revoked. It is better to make the election early to insure adequate recordkeeping. Revocation can only be prospective. An association cannot avoid sanctions by revoking the election retroactively.

- Despite the enactment of this quantifiable ceiling option, many Section 501(c)(3) associations still do not engage in lobbying for fear of tax consequences. This fear is unwarranted. With careful planning and recordkeeping, there is no reason to worry because the maximum lobbying expenditures to avoid penalty tax and loss of exemption are clear, easily calculable, and high enough to permit lobbying activities that the vast majority of 501(c)(3) associations might reasonably wish to engage in.

RESOURCES FOR CHAPTER 74

Books

Jacobs, "The Law of Lobbying" in *ASAE 3rd Annual Management Conference Proceedings*, 1985, page 330.

Webster & Krebs, *Associations & Lobbying Regulation*, U.S. Chamber, 1985.

Periodicals

Webster, "Aspects of Association Lobbying," *Association Management*, November, 1985, page 53.

Webster, "What Are the Lobbying Limits on 501(c)(6) and 501(c)(3) Groups?," *Association Management*, February, 1983, page 39.

Statutes

Code Sections 501(c)(3), 501(c)(6), and 501h.

Cases

Taxation With Representation of Washington v. Reagan, 103 S. Ct. 1997 (1983). No constitutional violation in limiting lobbying activities of certain tax exempt organizations.

Korhn v. United States, 246 F. Supp. 341 (D. Colo. 1965). What constitutes "substantial" lobbying differs depending upon the organization involved.

Seasongood v. Commissioner, 227 F.2d 907 (6th Cir. 1955). Permissible lobbying activities to avoid "substantial" test.

Chapter 75

IRS FORMS AND PROCEDURES

As one might expect, the Internal Revenue Service has promulgated detailed forms and procedures for associations to use in applying for federal income-tax-exempt status, appealing adverse determinations on exempt status, filing annual informational returns, and filing annual tax returns for any unrelated business income.

This Chapter contains a summary of those forms and procedures.

SUMMARY

- There are initial and continuing procedural requirements promulgated by the Internal Revenue Service for associations to follow in seeking to obtain and working to maintain federal income-tax-exempt status.

- There is no clear requirement that associations seeking tax-exempt status as business leagues under Section 501(c)(6) of the Internal Revenue Code must actively seek a written determination of that status from the IRS; but it is advisable to do so. Once a determination of exempt status is received from the IRS, the association is in a better position to budget and plan its financial affairs. In addition, the IRS, absent unusual facts, will be precluded from retroactively revoking the association's exempt status. For associations seeking exempt status as scientific, educational, or other types of organizations listed under Section 501(c)(3) of the Code, it is clear that the notice of formation, which may be in the form of a request for written determination of exempt status, must be made within 15 months after the end of the month in which they are created in order

461

for an eventual determination to be retroactive to the date of creation.

- Associations seeking exemption under Section 501(c)(6) use IRS Form 1024 to request the determination. Associations seeking exemption under Section 501(c)(3) use Form 1023. In either case the form is filed with the IRS Key District Office having jurisdiction over the state in which the association will have its main office; there are 17 such offices with authority to process and decide exemption requests.

- If an association receives an adverse determination of exempt status, it may file a protest and seek a conference with the Regional Appeals Office having jurisdiction over the Key District Office which issued the adverse determination. The protest must be filed within 30 days from the date of the determination letter and must be filed with the Key District Office. The association may obtain review by IRS at the National Office level either upon request by the association or the Key District Office by means of a Technical Advice procedure. Once the administrative levels of review are exhausted by the association, it may sue the IRS in a federal district court in the form of a tax refund suit alleging that the adverse determination was incorrect. It may refuse to pay any tax assessed and file a petition in the U.S. Tax Court claiming tax-exempt status; and, in the case of an association seeking exempt status under Section 501(c)(3), it may sue for a declaratory judgment in the U.S. Tax Court.

- Revocation of federal income-tax-exempt status from an association is processed by the IRS under procedures similar to those used upon the issuance of an adverse determination of exempt status. Revocation is generally announced by the Key District Office; appeals may be available at the Regional Appeals Office and National Office under certain circumstances. The same judicial remedies described above are also applicable.

- Associations exempt from taxation under either Section 501(c)(6) or 501(c)(3) are required to file annual informational returns unless they do not normally have gross receipts of more than $10,000 in each taxable year. Associations exempt under either section use IRS Form 990, which was revised in 1979, as their informational return. The data required of Section 501(c)(3) associations on Form 990 is more detailed than that required of Section 501(c)(6) associations. These forms will be made available by IRS for public inspection.

- An organization that is seeking a tax-exempt status determination from IRS, but has not yet received it, may nevertheless file its informational return as an exempt organization but should indicate on the form that its request is pending. This procedure will release the organization from possible penalties and interest and will likewise commence the applicable statute of limitations.

- Exempt associations that have unrelated business income over $1,000 in a taxable year must report that income on IRS Form 990-T.

- An exempt association which has undergone a dissolution, termination, or other major disposition of assets must file an informational return on IRS Form 966-E, which is due within 30 days after a resolution is adopted for the dissolution or termination.

- Associations which fail to file required returns or reports to IRS may be subject to penalties of $10 per day of delinquency with a maximum penalty of $5,000.

- Associations which are federations of national and local organizations or are otherwise affiliated in a group may obtain a determination from IRS that all affiliated associations are tax exempt and subject to reporting by only a central entity. The following qualifications apply to group exemption applications and returns:
  —The central association applying for group exemption must itself be tax exempt under code provisions, for example, Sections 501(c)(6) or 501(c)(3).
  —The affiliated associations must be related to the central one and subject to its control.
  —The affiliated associations must have some governing document.
  —The affiliated associations must all be exempt under

the same section of the Code, although the section
may be different from that of central association.
—An officer of each affiliated association must authorize the central association to seek group exemption.
—Only affiliated associations created with 15 months
of the application for group exemption may be included if the status is sought under Section 501(c)(3)
of the Code.
—The central association files an annual informational
return on IRS Form 990 for all of the affiliates under
the group exemption; affiliates then do not have to
file their own returns.

• The correct use of IRS forms and procedures for tax-
exempt associations can result in important advantages just as incorrect use can defeat, delay, or jeopardize association aims. The laws affecting tax-exempt
associations are often strikingly different from those
affecting business corporations. Tax-exempt organization legal and accounting practice is a specialty not
maintained by most lawyers or accountants. Associations should seek out specialists in exempt-organiza-
tion law when assistance is needed.

RESOURCES FOR CHAPTER 75

Books

Gilchrist, "What to Do When the IRS Knocks" in *Associations
and the Law Book IV*, U.S. Chamber, 1971, page 41.
Greif, "Federal Income Tax-Exempt Status" in *Managing Mem-
bership Societies*, Greif, Editor, ASAE, 1979, page 1.
Gross & Warshauer, "Tax and Compliance Reporting Requirements" in *Financial and Accounting Guide for Nonprofit
Organizations*, Ronald Press, 1983, page 393.
Internal Revenue Manual, "Exempt Organizations Hand-
books," IRS.
Lamb & Shields, *Trade Association Law Practice*, Little, Brown,
1971, page 255.
Statham & Buek, *Associations and the Tax Laws*, U.S. Cham-
ber, 1978, pages 30, 149.
Webster, *The Law of Associations*, Matthew Bender, 1976, pages
15–129.

Webster, Herold, & Dye, *Association Legal Checklist*, U.S. Chamber, 1983, pages 55–59.

Periodicals

Arnold, "The IRS's Exempt Organization Program: How It's Working," *Practical Accountant*, 1976, page 46.

Bacon, "The New Exempt Organizations Program in Audit," *Tax Advisor*, 1970, page 69.

Greif, "Federal Income Tax Recordkeeping—1985 Changes," GWSAE *Executive Update*, August, 1985, page 49.

"I.R.S. Tax Audit Guidelines for Exempt Organizations," *Association Taxation*, July, 1974, page 3.

Kennedy & O'Reilly, "What to Do When the Tax Man Cometh," *Association Management*, January, 1978, page 69.

Lehrfeld & Webster, "Administration by the IRS of Non-Profit Organization Tax Matters," *Tax Lawyer*, 1968, page 591.

Leonard, "Case Report: What To Do When IRS Strikes," *Association Management*, April, 1973, page 54.

Statham, "Law," *Association & Society Manager*, August/September, 1982, page 53.

Stratton, "A Guide to Dealing With the IRS," *Association Management*, August, 1979, page 45.

Thrower, "The IRS's New Enforcement Program for Exempt Organizations," *Practical Accountant*, 1970, page 34.

Webster, "Changes Possible in Way IRS Reviews Tax-Exempt Determination Cases," *Association Management*, July, 1978, page 16.

Webster, "How an Association Can Lose Its Tax Exemption," *Association Management*, January 1986, page 60.

Webster, "IRS Review: Tax Exempt and Reporting Requirements for Associations," *Association Management*, January, 1978, page 16.

Webster, "Pointers for Maintaining Association Tax Records," *Association Management*, February, 1978, page 18.

Webster, "Tax Forms: How and What to File," *Association Management*, July, 1984, page 39.

Webster, "What to Do When the IRS Audits Your Association," *Association Management*, September, 1972, page 22.

Regulations

Regulations Sections 601.201 (N)(5) and (6).

Other Resources

Reilly, "How to Survive an IRS Audit," 1980 National Conference on Tax, Legal & Other Problems of Trade and Professional Organizations, Washington Seminar Center, January, 1980.

Rev. Pro. 80-25, I.R.B. 1980-26, 39. Procedures for applying for exempt status and appealing adverse determinations.

Rev. Pro. 80-27, I.R.B. 1980-26, 49. Procedures for group exemptions.

Rev. Pro. 80–26, I.R.B. 1980–26, 43. Procedures for obtaining Technical Advice from National Office.

V

Appendices

SAMPLE ASSOCIATION DOCUMENTS

Notes on Appendices

The following appendices contain sample association documents which were drafted specifically for inclusion in this book and are offered for use in forming or operating trade or professional associations.

First are unique "plain English" articles of incorporation for an association. An attempt has been made in drafting these articles to include all legally required statements and information while also presenting the articles in the most basic and understandable language. These articles fully comply with the legal requirements for articles of incorporation for a nonprofit association incorporated in the District of Columbia. They have been accepted for filing by several national trade and professional associations in that jurisdiction. State corporation law requirements for articles of incorporation vary considerably from one state to another, however; and these sample articles likely cannot be used in other jurisdictions without modifications based upon the legal requirements of those other jurisdictions.

Second are sample association bylaws. These too are drafted in plain English and are being used successfully by several national trade or professional associations. The sample bylaws cover most substantive and procedural areas that are important to typical associations. They recognize and include language relating to federal income-tax-exempt status and to antitrust compliance. Although these bylaws seem unusually short and simple, they may well be adequate with only minor changes for the majority of trade or professional associations.

Third are more extensive bylaw provisions regarding antitrust compliance. Associations with special interests or concerns in this area might consider adoption of bylaw provisions such as these as part of their overall antitrust compliance programs, as discussed in Chapter 61.

Fourth are sample bylaws for association political action committees which follow the recommendations made in Chapter 32. The possibilities for structure and administration of PACs are somewhat broader than they are for incorporated tax-exempt associations because very few legal mandates exist for PAC structure and administration. These sample PAC bylaws present one set of alternatives, while taking into account those requirements which do exist in the federal election and federal tax laws and regulations.

Fifth are sample guidelines on antitrust. This document explains and expands upon the requirements of federal antitrust laws and trade regulations; it is intended for distribution to association members. The guidelines are based upon similar documents that have been published by several national trade or professional associations and by several major business corporations. They conclude with a series of clearly-stated "Do's and Don'ts."

Sixth are sample guidelines on association statistical programs which follow the recommendations made in Chapter 48. These or other similar guidelines might appropriately be adopted by an association and distributed to those who participate in a statistical program and to those who administer it.

Seventh are guidelines for appearances by association representatives at governmental hearings. The guidelines provide common sense direction both in preparing for appearances and in making presentations. They are designed to be furnished to association representatives in advance of their appearances at governmental hearings.

All of the sample association documents in the appendices are offered for duplication and use by trade or professional associations. In many cases, some modifications will be necessary to adapt the sample documents to the needs and circumstances of particular associations. Professional assistance will likely be required in making those adaptations. Although this book bears a copyright notice, the publisher specifically waives its copyright protection as to the sample association documents contained in the following appendices.

Appendix 1

ARTICLES OF INCORPORATION OF THE ELIXIR MANUFACTURERS ASSOCIATION
A Nonprofit Corporation

We have signed these articles as incorporators of a nonprofit corporation formed under the District of Columbia Nonprofit Corporation Act; we are over the age of twenty-one; and we state:

1. *Name.* The name of the corporation is the *Elixir Manufacturers Association.*

2. *Duration.* The duration of the corporation is perpetual.

3. *Purposes.* The purposes of the corporation are (a) to provide members and others with opportunities for dialogue, education, advancement, and improvement of all aspects of the elixir manufacturing industry through meetings, seminars, communications, publications, and other programs and activities; (b) to articulate and advocate the needs and interests of the elixir manufacturing industry before legislative, administrative, and judicial branches of local, state and national governments; (c) to cooperate on behalf of the elixir manufacturing industry with suppliers, distributors, dealers, insurers, and customers directly and through their associations in matters involving the business and governmental affairs of the industry; and (d) to promulgate policies and conduct activities for the betterment of all those individuals or firms involved in some aspect of the elixir manufacturing industry; provided that all policies and activities of the corporation be consistent with applicable federal, state, and local antitrust, trade regulation, or other legal requirements and with the tax exemption requirements that the corporation not be organized for profit and that no part of its net earnings inure to the benefit of any private individual.

4. *Membership.* Membership in the corporation is available and gives voting privileges to one or more classes of individuals or firms involved in some aspect of the elixir manufacturing industry as stated in the bylaws of the corporation.

5. *Directors.* The matter of election of directors is as stated in the bylaws of the corporation.

6.   *Initial Directors.* Three directors serve as the initial Board of Directors of the corporation until successors are elected; their names and addresses are:

David D. Doe	100 New York Ave. New York, NY 12345
James J. Jones	200 Illinois St. Chicago, IL 23456
Stephen S. Smith	300 California Blvd. Los Angeles, CA 34567

7.   *Incorporators.* The names and addresses of the incorporators of the corporation are:

David D. Doe	100 New York Ave. New York, NY 12345
James J. Jones	200 Illinois St. Chicago, IL 23456
Stephen S. Smith	300 California Blvd. Los Angeles, CA 34567

8.   *Registered Office and Agent.* The initial registered office of the corporation is 400 District of Columbia Dr., Washington, DC 45678. The initial registered agent of the corporation at that address is Anthony A. Attorney, who is a resident of the District of Columbia.

9.   *Dissolution.* If the corporation should be dissolved, no member will receive any portion of its remaining assets or property; upon dissolution, the balance of any assets or property of the corporation which remains after all debits or obligations are paid will be distributed to any other nonprofit corporation which has been determined by the Internal Revenue Service to be exempt from federal income taxes.

As witnesses to our statements, we have signed these articles on July 7, 1986.

_____

David D. Doe

_____

James J. Jones

_____

Stephen S. Smith

CITY OF WASHINGTON
DISTRICT OF COLUMBIA

Signed and sworn to in my presence on July 7, 1986.

_____

Notary Public

My Commission expires on August 8, 1991.

BYLAWS OF THE ELIXIR MANUFACTURERS ASSOCIATION
A Nonprofit Corporation

Article I

1. *Name.* The name of the association is the *Elixir Manufacturers Association,* a nonprofit corporation incorporated in the District of Columbia.

2. *Location.* The principal office of the Association is located in the District of Columbia.

3. *Purposes.* The purposes of the Association incude:

   a) providing opportunities for dialogue, education, advancement, and improvement of all aspects of the elixir manufacturing industry through meetings, seminars, communications, publications, and other programs and activities;

   b) articulating and advocating the needs and interests of the elixir manufacturing industry before legislative, administrative, and judicial branches of local, state, and national governments;

   c) cooperating on behalf of the elixir manufacturing industry with suppliers, distributors, dealers, insurers, and customers directly and through their associations in matters involving the business and governmental affairs of the industry; and

   d) promulgating policies and conducting activities for the betterment of all those individuals or firms involved in some aspect of the elixir manufacturing industry.

4. *Restrictions.* All policies and activities of the Association shall be consistent with:

   a. applicable federal, state, and local antitrust, trade regulation, or other legal requirements; and

   b. applicable tax exemption reqirements including the requirements that the Association not be organized for profit and that no part of its net earnings inure to the benefit of any private individual.

Article II

1. *Membership Qualifications.* Membership in the Association

is available to persons or firms involved in, or associated with, the manufacturing of elixirs.

2.   *Regular Membership.* Regular voting membership in the Association is limited to persons or firms engaged in the manufacturing of elixirs for sale and who pay regular dues. Regular members may serve as directors and hold office.

3.   *Non-Voting Memberships.* The following membership classes have no vote nor are they eligible to serve as directors or hold office in the Association:

   a)   *Supplier Membership.* Supplier membership is available to persons or firms furnishing goods or services to the the elixir manufacturing industry. Dues and other terms of supplier membership are specified by the Board of Directors.

   b)   *Affiliate Membership.* Affiliate membership is available to educators and government officials having a special interest in the elixir manufacturing industry. Dues and other terms of affiliate membership are specified by the Board of Directors.

   c)   *Life and Honorary Membership.* Life and honorary membership is conferred upon individuals or firms according to terms specified by the Board of Directors. No dues are paid by the life or honorary members.

4.   *Applications for Membership.* All applicants for membership must complete and sign the application form provided by the Association and submit the application to the principal office of the Association, located in the District of Columbia.

5.   *Admission of Members.* Admission to membership is by majority vote of the Board of Directors.

6.   *Resignation.* Any member may resign by filing a written resignation with the Board of Directors; however, resignation does not relieve a member from liability for dues accrued and unpaid as of the date of resignation.

7.   *Expulsion.* Any member may be expelled for adequate reason by a two-thirds vote of the Board of Directors. Failure to pay dues or to meet the criteria for membership is presumed to be adequate reason for expulsion and does not require advance notice to the member and deliberation by the Board. Any member proposed for expulsion for another reason is given advance written notice including the reason for the proposed expulsion, opportunity to contest the proposed expulsion in writing or in person before the Board of Directors, and final written notice of the Board's decision.

Article III

1.   *Dues.* Dues are established by the Board of Directors.

2.   *Delinquency.* Any member of the Association who is delinquent in dues for a period of ninety (90) days is notified of the delin-

quency and suspended from membership. If dues are not paid within the succeeding thirty (30) days, the delinquent member forfeits all rights and privileges of membership and is expelled.

3. *Refunds.* No dues will be refunded.

Article IV

1. *Directors.* The governing body of the Association is the Board of Directors, which has authority and is responsible for the supervision, control, and direction of the Association.

2. *Composition of the Board.* The Board of Directors consists of nine persons elected by and from the regular membership.

3. *Election and Term of Office.* At each annual meeting of the Association an election is held to choose three new members of the Board of Directors. Directors serve staggered terms of three years. No director may serve succeeding terms; however, a person who has previously served as a director may again be elected one year after having held the position.

4. *Vacancies.* If a vacancy occurs on the Board for any reason, the position is filled for the unexpired portion of the term by the Board.

5. *Meetings.* The Board of Directors meets at least annually at whatever time and place it selects. The presence of any four directors constitutes a quorum. A majority of directors where a quorum is present is necessary to make a decision except where some other number is required by law or by these Bylaws. Proxy voting is not permitted. Mail voting is permitted.

6. *Removal.* A director may be removed for adequate reason by a two-thirds vote of the regular membership.

7. *Compensation.* Directors do not receive compensation for their services.

Article V

1. *Officers.* The officers of the Association are a President, a Vice President, a Treasurer, and an Executive Director.

2. *Qualifications.* Officers, except for the Executive Director, must be regular members of the Association who have been elected directors. No person may hold more than one office at the same time. Oficers may serve consecutive terms.

3. *Election and Term of Office.* Officers, except for the Executive Director, are elected by written ballot of the Board of Directors each year before the annual meeting of the Association's regular membership. Officers, except for the Executive Director, serve for one year.

4. *Duties.* The officers perform those duties that are usual to

their positions and that are assigned to them by the Board of Directors. In addition, the President of the Association acts as Chairman of the Board of Directors, the Vice President acts in place of the President when the President is not available, the Treasurer is the financial officer of the Association, and the Executive Director, appointed or terminated by the Executive Committee, is the Association's chief employed administrative officer.

    5.   *Vacancies.* If a vacancy occurs among the officers, other than the Executive Director, for any reason, the position is filled for the unexpired portion of the term by the Board.

    6.   *Removal.* An officer may be removed for adequate reason by a two-thirds vote of the Board of Directors.

    7.   *Compensation.* Officers do not receive compensation for ther services.

Article VI

    1.   *Annual Membership Meeting.* The Association holds an annual meeting of the regular membership at the place and on the date that the Board of Directors determines.

    2.   *Special Meetings.* Special meetings of the Association regular membership may be called by the Board of Directors at any time.

    3.   *Notice.* The Board of Directors must give Association members reasonable notice of all annual and special meetings. The notice must include a description of the business to be discussed.

    4.   *Voting.* The presence of twenty percent of the regular membership constitutes a quorum. A majority of members where a quorum is present is necessary to make a decision except where some other number is required by law or by these Bylaws. Proxy voting is not permitted. Mail voting is permitted.

Article VII

    1.   *Committees.* An Executive Committee consists of the officers of the Association and may act in the place of the Board of Directors when authority is designated by the Board or in emergency matters where Executive Committee action is temporary and subject to subsequent approval by the Board at its next meeting. The President appoints whatever other committees are necessary.

    2.   *General Counsel.* A General Counsel is appointed or terminated by the Executive Committee.

    3.   *Auditors.* Auditors are appointed or terminated by the Executive Committee.

    4.   *Rules.* The Board of Directors may establish rules that are

consistent with these Bylaws for the policies, procedures, and programs of the Association.

5. *Amendment.* Amendments to these Bylaws may be made without prior notice at an annual meeting of the Association by a two-thirds vote. Emergency amendments may be made at any time by a two-thirds vote of the Board of Directors, but emergency amendments are temporary and subject to subsequent approval by a two-thirds vote at the next meeting of the Association's regular membership.

ASSOCIATION BYLAW PROVISIONS FOR ANTITRUST COMPLIANCE

Section 1. POLICY

It is the undeviating policy of the Association to comply strictly with the letter and spirit of all federal, state, and applicable international trade regulations and antitrust laws. Any activities of the Association or Association-related actions of its staff, officers, directors, or members which violate these regulations and laws are detrimental to the interests of the Association and are unequivocally contrary to Association policy.

Section 2. IMPLEMENTATION

Implementation of the antitrust compliance policy of the Association shall include, but shall not be limited to, the following:

A. Association Membership, Board of Directors, Executive Committee, and other Committee meetings shall be conducted pursuant to agendas distributed in advance to attendees; discussions shall be limited to agenda items; there shall be no substantive discussions of Association matters other than at official meetings; minutes shall be distributed to attendees promptly.

B. All association activities or discussions shall be avoided which might be construed as tending to: (1) raise, lower, or stabilize prices; (2) regulate production; (3) allocate markets; (4) encourage boycotts; (5) foster unfair trade practices; (6) assist in monopolization; or in any way violate federal, state or applicable international trade regulations and antitrust laws.

C. No officer, director, or member of the Association shall make any representation in public or in private, orally or in writing, which states, or appears to state, an official policy or position of the Association without specific authorization to do so.

D. General Counsel shall attend all Association Executive Committee, Board of Directors, and Membership meetings. Attendance of counsel at other meetings shall be at the discretion of the President or Executive Director.

E.   Associate members, officers, directors, or employees who participate in conduct which the Board of Directors, by a two-thirds majority vote, determines to be contrary to the Association antitrust compliance policy shall be subject to disciplinary measures up to, and including, termination.

Appendix 4

BYLAWS OF THE ELIXIR MANUFACTURERS ASSOCIATION POLITICAL ACTION COMMITTEE

1. *Name.* The name of this organization is the *Elixir Manufacturers Association Political Action Committee* (the "Committee"). The name of the Committee may be abbreviated as *EMAPAC* when permitted by Federal law.

2. *Address.* The Committee's address is in the District of Columbia.

3. *Nature.* The Committee is a "political committee" which intends to qualify as a "multicandidate committee" under Federal election law. It is a "political organization" under federal tax exemption law. The Committee is an unincorporated nonprofit association under the law of the District of Columbia.

4. *Affiliation.* The Committee is affiliated with the Elixir Manufacturers Association. Neither the Committee nor that Association has other affiliates.

5. *Books and Records.* Books and Records of the Committee are maintained by the Treasurer of the Committee at the principal office of the Elixir Manufacturers Association in the District of Columbia. The Treasurer is assisted in this responsibility by one or more staff members of the Association.

6. *Officers.* The Committee has a Chairman and a Treasurer. Both officers are appointed annually by the Board of Directors of the Elixir Manufacturers Association from its regular membership. The officers may serve succeeding terms. Vacancies that occur in either office are filled in the same manner as the original appointment and as soon as possible. The Chairman automatically occupies the office of Treasurer if it is temporarily or permanently vacant until the Treasurer re-assumes the office or is replaced. The Committee does not accept contributions or make expenditures if there is a vacancy in the office of Treasurer that has not been filled by the Chairman. No expenditure is made on behalf of the Committee without the written or oral authorization of the Treasurer. The Chairman of the Committee is the chief operating officer of the Committee. The Chairman is responsible for the overall direction and implementation of the Committee's policies and activities. The Chairman presides at meetings of the Board of Advisors of the Committee. The Treasurer is responsible for its registration, record-keeping, and reporting as re-

quired by federal election law. Both officers may be assisted in their responsibilities by one or more staff members of the Elixir Manufacturers Association.

7. *Depository.* The designated depository used by the Committee is the Upright National Bank of Washington, D.C. where the Committee maintains a checking account and other accounts if necessary. A different depository or additional ones may be designated by the Treasurer, if they meet the requirements of federal election law.

8. *Purposes.* The purposes of the Committee are:

   a.   to solicit and receive contributions to be used to make political campaign expenditures to those candidates for federal elective office who have demonstrated understanding and interest in the views and goals of the Committee or of the Elixir Manufacturers Association;

   b.   to exist and operate as a "political committee" and a "separate segregated fund" which receives "contributions" and makes "expenditures" to any "candidate" for "federal office" as those and related terms are defined and construed under federal election law;

   c.   to exist and operate as a "political organization" and a "separate segregated fund" primarily for the purpose of directly or indirectly accepting contributions or "making expenditures," or both, for its "exempt function," e.g., influencing or attempting to influence the selection, nomination, election, or appointment of any individual to any federal office, as those and related terms are defined and construed under federal tax exemption law; and

   d.   to comply fully with all other applicable federal election or tax exemption laws and with other applicable laws in carrying out those purposes.

9. *Members.* Each individual, noncorporate contributor becomes a Committee member upon acceptance by the Committee of a contribution from the individual. The contributor remains a member of the Committee for one year following acceptance of that contribution or, if advance approval for solicitation of the contribution from the individual was required under federal election law, the individual remains a member for the period following acceptance of that contribution during which the advance approval for the solicitation is valid. Members of the Committee have no rights or responsibilities other than those specifically designated by the Committee's Chairman which are consistent with applicable federal election and tax exemption laws and with other applicable laws.

10. *Board of Advisors.* The Committee has a Board of Advisors consisting of three, five, or seven individuals in addition to the Chair-

man and Treasurer of the Committee. The Chairman appoints individuals to the Board of Advisors for one-year terms, has discretion to accept resignations or terminate individuals from the Board for cause, and fills vacancies on the Board if they occur. The Chairman makes the determination whether to maintain three, five, or seven individuals on the Board of Advisors in addition to the Chairman and Treasurer. The function of the Board is to advise the Chairman in all aspects of the organization and operation of the Committee. In particular, the Board of Advisors recommends criteria for candidates for federal elective office to which the Committee makes expenditures; and the Board assists the Chairman in determining whether specific candidates meet those criteria. The Board of Advisors conducts its functions by telephone, in correspondence, or at meetings, in the discretion of the Chairman.

11. *General Counsel.* The Committee maintains a continuing relationship with General Counsel familiar with federal election, federal tax exemption, and other laws that may be applicable to the Committee.

12. *Amendments.* These Bylaws are amended by the Chairman of the Committee in consultation with the Board of Advisors and with the specific ratification of the Board of Directors of the Elixir Manufacturers Association.

Appendix 5

GUIDELINES ON ANTITRUST FOR ELIXIR MANUFACTURERS ASSOCIATION MEMBERS

Antitrust and the Elixir Manufacturers Association

The purpose of the antitrust laws is the preservation of competition within lines of commerce. Both the Federal Trade Commission and the Department of Justice have regarded exchanges of certain types of information as tending to threaten or eliminate competition. Because they are vehicles for bringing competitors together and conduits for moving information among competitors, associations have naturally been viewed with the closest scrutiny under the antitrust laws. The unique exposure of associations to antitrust scrutiny dictates that measures should be taken to minimize the risks of their involvement in antitrust investigations or litigation.

The immense complexity of the various and often overlapping antitrust laws precludes the possibility of finding any association administrative policies or procedures which could absolutely guarantee immunity from antitrust scrutiny. Nevertheless, the prospect of antitrust investigations or litigation is so unattractive that many associations take extraordinary measures to at least minimize their exposure.

Involvement in an antitrust investigation or lawsuit is singularly distasteful. Usually it is embarassing. If a criminal antitrust case is lost, fines or jail terms are frequently imposed. On occasion, associations have been ordered to be disbanded. Even if an antitrust case is won, the demands upon the time of those involved can be immense; the legal fees and costs can be astronomical.

One way for an association like the Elixir Manufacturers Association to help avoid the possibility of antitrust investigations or litigation is to institute an antitrust compliance program. Major business corporations have for years used such programs to educate their employees in corporate policies designed to avoid antitrust problems. The Association, whose exposure to antitrust scrutiny is theoretically as great as that of a business corporation, can also benefit from an antitrust informational program to educate its staff, officers, directors, and members in the prevention of antitrust involvement.

From the date of its formation, the Elixir Manufacturers Association has required that all of its activities be conducted strictly in accordance with federal and state antitrust laws. To help remain consistent with that policy, this guide outlines those areas of the antitrust laws which should be of particular concern to the Association and its members, the obvious dangers which they should avoid in order to minimize the risk of antitrust liability, and the policies and procedures which they should follow in order to comply with the law. This guide does not pretend to be an all-encompassing delineation of potential antitrust problems and the means to avoid them. In instances of doubt, Association members should always seek the assistance of legal counsel experienced in antitrust.

Antitrust Laws in General

The basic federal antitrust statutes are the Sherman Act, the Clayton Act, the Federal Trade Commission Act, and the Robinson-Patman Act.

The Sherman Act prohibits contracts, combinations, and conspiracies in restraint of trade. It also condemns monopolization and attempts and conspiracies to monopolize.

The Clayton Act prohibits various kinds of business behavior which tend to lessen competition or monopolize trade. Among the activities prohibited by the Act are exclusive dealing arrangements, acquisitions, and mergers which tend to lessen competition and interlocking directorates.

The Federal Trade Commission Act, in addition to prohibiting the anticompetitive activities made illegal by the Sherman and Clayton Acts, bans unfair methods of competition and unfair or deceptive acts and practices.

The Robinson-Patman Act prohibits price discrimination where the effect is to lessen competition.

In addition to the federal laws, most states have enacted statutes similar to the Sherman and Federal Trade Commission Acts.

Antitrust Laws Applicable to Activities of Associations

Of principal concern to individuals and firms that take part in association activities are Section 1 of the Sherman Act and Section 5 of the FTC Act. These laws make illegal contracts, combinations, and conspiracies in restraint of trade.

The Supreme Court has interpreted these statutes as prohibiting only those contracts and combinations which have the effect of *unreasonably* restraining trade. A court will, therefore, examine all the facts and circumstances surrounding the conduct in question in order to ascertain whether the contract or combination is in violation of the law by restraining trade unreasonably.

Certain activities have, however, been regarded as unreasonable by their very nature and are, therefore, considered illegal "per se." Individuals and firms are conclusively presumed to engage in such conduct for no other purpose than to restrain trade. Practices within the "per se" category include agreements to fix prices, agreements to boycott competitors, suppliers, or customers, agreements to allocate markets or limit production, and certain tie-in sales. A tie-in sale is one in which the customer is required to purchase an unwanted item in order to purchase the product or service desired.

Antitrust Enforcement

The Sherman Act is enforced by the Antitrust Division of the Department of Justice and the Bureau of Competition of the Federal Trade Commission, as well as by private suits for treble damages instituted by persons or firms injured by antitrust violations. Government suits may be either civil or criminal in nature. The remedy on the civil side in an action brought by the government is an injunction prohibiting the offender from future violations. On the criminal side, the penalty can be a fine, imprisonment, or both.

The Federal Trade Commission enforces the FTC Act by issuing cease and desist orders for practices found to violate the law. The violation of an FTC order may result in a penalty of as much as $10,000 per day. In addition, any association adjudged to be in violation of the antitrust laws can be dissolved by court order.

Recent years have seen a marked increase in antitrust proceedings undertaken by federal and state governments and by private parties. Another significant change is the increased severity of punishment available for criminal violations of the Sherman Act. A violation, formerly a misdemeanor punishable by no more than one year, is now a felony, punishable by imprisonment of up to three years. In addition, the fine for Sherman Act violations—previously limited to $50,000 for corporations and individuals—has been increased to a maximum of $1 million for corporations and $100,000 for individuals. To note but one more ground for cautious behavior when dealing with the antitrust laws, the Antitrust Improvements Act of 1976 gave new authority to state attorneys general to file treble damage suits on behalf of citizens who have allegedly been injured by antitrust violations.

Special Antitrust Problems for Associations

The legality of activities under the antitrust laws is determined by the application of the standards no different from those used to determine the legality of the activities of other groups of persons or firms. Special problems do arise, however, from the fact that an association is, by definition, a *combination* of competitors, and the act of bringing these competitors together creates the means by which collusive action can be taken in violation of the antitrust laws. A second antitrust problem arising from the nature of associations is that many of their most valuable programs directly impinge upon areas of particular antitrust concern. Among these are credit and statistical reporting, product standards, credentialing, certification, and customer relations.

Conspiracy in Restraint of Trade

As noted above, Section 1 of the Sherman Act prohibits any arrangement or agreement in restraint of trade. The prohibition extends to any such agreement, whether oral or written, formal or informal, expressed or implied. For example, a "gentleman's agreement" to hold the line on prices is sufficient evidence of an unlawful conspiracy to fix prices.

Antitrust liability is frequently a result of circumstantial evidence of a course of business conduct from which a jury infers the existence of an illegal conspiracy. A set of circumstances may be entirely innocent and lawful when viewed separately. But the same set of circumstances, when viewed in the aggregate, may be held to constitute a conspiracy. For example, a jury might infer the existence of a conspiracy from the fact of price instability in an industry, a meeting of competitors at which prices are discussed, followed by increased prices by those participating in the discussion. The fact that without the price discussion it would be impossible to prove a conspiracy is an indication of why it is crucial to avoid price discussions at Association meetings. Mere attendance at a meeting where businessmen engage in a discussion concerning price-fixing may imply acquiescence and make a nonparticipant criminally responsible and subject to as great a penalty as the active participants in the discussion.

Basic Antitrust Rule for Association Members

The essential principle which should guide the policies and activities of the Elixir Manufacturers Association in order to avoid antitrust violations is that no illegal agreements should be either reached or carried out through the Association. Conduct which might give the appearance of an illegal agreement must also be avoided.

Staff, officers, directors, and members of the Association should be particularly on guard as to conduct or agreements affecting areas of particular antitrust concern, especially pricing, association membership, standardization, certification, and statistical programs.

Pricing—Price-fixing is the most common antitrust violation. To avoid the risk of liability, Association members should *never* discuss prices, pricing systems, or discounts, nor should the Association ever be involved in members' pricing practices.

Statistical programs involving members' past prices are permissible but should be established and conducted under the careful supervision of legal counsel. Present and future prices may never be the subject of such programs.

Membership—Membership qualifications should be reasonably drawn and interpreted in order to allow the inclusion of all companies that share the common concerns of the industry. Qualifications should be objective. Companies meeting the qualifications should be automatically admitted.

Association services of potential competitive benefit must be made available to nonmembers. The Association may charge nonmembers higher fees for these services than are charged Association members if dues income helps to support the services.

Normally, no member may be expelled unless the member is no longer in the industry or has not paid its association dues. Counsel should be consulted before consideration is given to expelling a member for any other reason.

Industry Self-Regulation—Industry rules proposed or established by the Association should be reviewed by counsel to ensure that they do not unreasonably restrict competition. Especially to be avoided is any rule or conduct which might be construed as an agreement not to deal with competitors, suppliers, or customers in the industry.

Standardization, Certification, and Statistical Programs—These programs are proper so long as they are not used to restrict competition. Self-regulation criteria must be reasonable and procedures must be fair. Interpretation of criteria must be nonrestrictive. Counsel is the best source of advice as to the manner in which these programs may be conducted.

Do's and Don'ts

Members can participate fully in Elixir Manufacturers Association programs and activities with minimal possibility of antitrust problems by following a few simple "do's" and "don'ts":

1. *DO* schedule and attend meetings only when there are proper items of substance to be discussed that justify your attendance.

2. *DO* review the meeting notice or agenda in advance of every meeting. It should be specific, without broad topics such as "marketing practices," which might look suspicious from an antitrust standpoint.

3. *DO* adhere strictly to the stated agenda. In general, subjects not included on the agenda should not be considered at the meeting.

4. *DO* assure that no matter of doubtful legality is brought up for discussion. This, of course, is counsel's responsibility; but in his absence, the Association staff representative or any member present who becomes aware of legal implications of a discussion should attempt to halt the discussion. Should the discussion continue despite protest, it may be wise to leave the meeting.

5. *DO* make sure that minutes of all meetings are kept (usually by Association staff); they must accurately report what actions were taken.

6. *DO* use the Association as a vehicle for promoting the industry as a whole.

7. *DO* assure that Association counsel is in attendance at all meetings of the Association where legally sensitive subjects might be discussed.

8. *DO* check with Association staff, who will likely contact counsel, if there is doubt about the legality of any Association policy or program.

9. *DO* cooperate with Association counsel in all matters, particularly when counsel has ruled adversely about a particular activity.

10. *DON'T* allow or participate in secret or "rump" meetings. These meetings may have no purpose other than to discuss illegal activities. They could seriously jeopardize legitimate Association activities and create a risk that those activities will be investigated.

11. *DON'T* allow recommendations with respect to sensitive antitrust subjects to be made during meetings, especially those relating to price, production, markets, and the selection of suppliers or customers. Prices should not be discussed at all. In the less sensitive areas, such as standardization activities, recommendations may be permissible.

12. *DON'T* be coerced into taking part in Association activities. There must be no policing of the industry to see how individual members are conducting their business.

13. *DON'T* establish programs or guidelines which are for the primary purpose, explicit or implicit, of excluding some members of the industry.

14. *DON'T*, without specific authorization, make public or private communications about policies or positions of the Association.

Appendix 6

GUIDELINES FOR ASSOCIATION STATISTICAL PROGRAMS

It is the policy of this Association to adhere to these guidelines in preparing, conducting, and promulgating statistical programs:

- Programs are undertaken in strict compliance with the letter and spirit of any applicable federal antitrust laws and trade regulation rules. Publication of results of programs is also in strict compliance with any applicable federal securities laws.

- Programs are not undertaken if publication of the results would tend to:
  —raise, lower, or stabilize prices;
  —affect production;
  —allocate customers or markets; or
  —encourage boycotts.

- Participation in programs is completely voluntary; no company or individual is forced, coerced, or required to participate.

- Participation in programs and/or receipt of results of programs is available to all companies or individuals engaged in the area of endeavor represented by this Association under the conditions described here. *Participation and/or results:*
  —may be made available to other companies or individuals at the discretion of the Association and upon notice to all program participants;
  —are not denied any company or individual because the company or person is not a member of the Association;
  —for a company or individual that is not an Association member will be subject to a reasonable supplemental fee when a program is wholly or partially supported by Association members' dues;
  —are not solicited from companies or individuals that are not Association members; and
  —may be denied any company or individual which does not agree in advance of participation to keep the results confidential.

- All reasonable measures are to be taken to *maintain the confidentiality of data or information* submitted by participants in Association statistical programs. Whenever proprietary or sensitive statistics are surveyed:
    —an independent firm of accountants or consultants is retained to receive, analyze, and tabulate the statistics;
    —no individual participant's name or statistics submitted are disclosed by the Association or by the independent firm;
    —a coding system is employed in which the Association alone possesses the names of program participants and the independent firm alone receives the statistics submitted by participants;
    —names of particpants are not revealed to the independent firm and individual participants' statistics are not revealed to the Association; and
    —after analysis and tabulation of statistics by the independent firm, individual submissions of participants are destroyed and any computer memories are purged of all individual participants' statistics.
- Publication of the results of Association statistical programs:
    —does not include statistics based upon submissions by three or fewer participants or upon submissions where one participant accounts for fifty percent or more of the observed variable;
    —does not include any statistics on past, present, or future prices or fees of participants; and
    —is not accompanied by recommendations or encouragement of any action by participants or others based upon the statistics.

Any questions or comments or any aspects of these guidelines for Association statistical programs should be addressed to the Association headquarters.

GUIDELINES FOR ASSOCIATION APPEARANCES AT HEARINGS

Association executives or other association representatives are often called upon to make appearances at hearings before public bodies such as legislative or administrative committees. The procedural aspects of presentations should be carefully attended to and prepared for diligently. Too often a deliberative body misses a substantive message because of an annoying and inept presentation.

There is simply no substitute for rehearsal. Whether the association presenter has written the intended remarks or they have been written by others (such as an association executive, attorney, or other advisor), the remarks should be rehearsed as many times as is feasible to assure a smooth and polished delivery. If an association committee has been responsible for a project that includes making a presentation at a hearing, such as an association government-relations committee, it would be ideal for the presenter to rehearse the remarks before the committee to gauge their accuracy and effect. Otherwise, rehearsal of the presentation with a tape recorder or with videotape equipment are good ways for presenters to judge for themselves the quality of their intended speeches. In short, do not underestimate the importance of making an articulate, professional presentation when an association has the opportunity to address a public body to advance the views of its industry or profession.

Beyond the preliminaries of style, the quality of the substance of an association's publicly articulated views is the most essential aspect of its appearance before a public body. No amount of oratorical skill can conceal an inane position or statement from any reasonably intelligent legislators or administrators at a hearing.

A 1977 publication of the Association Division of the Chamber of Commerce of the United States entitled *Legislators and Regulators Appraise Associations* gives useful advice on improving the substantive quality of association presentations at hearings based on a survey of members of legislative and administrative bodies. Some specific suggestions edited from the Chamber's publication that relate to presentations before government bodies include the following:

- Begin presentations with an honest, well-written summary and conclusion.
- Concentrate on the facts, develop a clear statement of your

position and the opposition's, offer an alternative, and list
key resources.

- Unsupported statements and summaries are suspect of bias.
  They should be accompanied by the reports upon which they
  are based, even if you suspect that the recipient does not
  have time to read them. He or she will be able to transmit
  the report to the staffer who is responsible for examining
  the problem and the reasoning that led to the association's
  conclusion.

- Staffers of legislative bodies are interested in detailed reports, research, and case studies. Some say that they read
  everything that associations submit in order to understand
  different points of view.

- Staffers in government departments and agencies also want
  to see the basic materials on which associations base their
  conclusions, not just general summaries. They want to take
  note of all the cautionary observations that professional research projects usually include.

- Recognize that opinions and relationships are colored by the
  political, social, moral, legal, and philosophical views of
  legislators, regulators, and their staffers.

- Agency and department administrators often see themselves
  as being devoted to the public interest. An association,
  therefore, should be prepared to demonstrate how its position would benefit consumers, small businessmen, farmers,
  minority groups, and others perceived as "the public."

Association presentations at government hearings depend for
their success upon both an effective presentation and accurate substance. To assist in preparing association witnesses for appearances
at legislative or administrative hearings, here is a checklist of do's
and don'ts:

1. An association witness may be appearing at the hearing of
a legislative or regulatory body for any of several reasons, e.g., to
convince the body to adopt the position advocated by the association,
to give views on the subjects about which the witness or the association has some special knowledge or experience, to support or
enforce the positions or views of others, etc. Whatever the reason
for an appearance, it is essential that information provided at the
hearing be accurate and that it be presented professionally. The
ultimate aim is *credibility*.

Do provide only accurate information.

Do present it professionally.

2. Before appearing, the association presenter should carefully
outline all the points that will be stressed in the appearance and
any points that ought to be bypassed. Ideally, the presentation should

be written out in full and edited; it should be rehearsed several times orally by following the outline or the full script, depending upon the formality or informality of the hearing.

Do outline your presentation and rehearse it.

Don't plan to ad lib.

3.   Both in preparing and delivering the presentation, an association presenter should confine its coverage to matters over which the legislative or regulatory body has authority to effect some action.

Do keep the remarks relevant.

4.   It may be helpful to learn something about the official positions, backgrounds, and views of those who are presiding at the hearings in order to tailor the witness' presentation to them and to anticipate any questions or comments.

Do learn as much as possible about those presiding at the hearing.

5.   It is often helpful, and sometimes essential, to have copies of the outline or full text of the witness' statement available on request for those who are presiding at the hearing, for representatives of the press, or for others in attendance.

Do have extra copies of the remarks.

6.   At the outset of the appearance, an association spokesman should clearly orient those presiding at the hearing as to the exact name and title of the individual, the reason for the appearance, and the association on whose behalf the appearance is made.

Do carefully identify the witness.

Do indicate exactly whose position or views are being represented.

7.   Avoid microphone tapping, coughing into a mike, stammering, and any signs of nervousness as much as possible.

Do be relaxed and professional.

8.   An association presenter should ordinarily not object to being interrupted briefly during the presentation to respond to an inquiry from someone who is presiding at the hearing; but the witness should not allow the interruption to upset any devised order or progression for the presentation, to distract him from the important elements of the presentation, or to dim the emphasis of a point being made before being interrupted.

Do allow brief interruptions.

Don't be confused by them.

9.   In any debate that occurs with someone who is presiding at the hearing or questioning the spokesman, excessive zeal in argumentativeness should be avoided.

Don't argue excessively.

10. If questions or comments arise for which the association representative has no immediate and accurate response, an offer can be made to find an answer and to submit it later.

Don't guess at answers to inquiries.

Do offer to research and respond later.

11. If suppositions or predictions are requested, the witness should be careful to avoid both understatement and overstatement. For example, both reticence and exaggeration are dangerous when discussing economic consequences.

Don't understate or overstate an opinion.

12. When facts or opinions are questioned, the speaker may offer to provide references to authoritative writings or to association survey responses, or to offer additional sources to corroborate positions and views. References should only be given when their accuracy and import are clearly known.

Do cite other authorities accurately.

GENERAL RESOURCES

Books

Antitrust Guide for Association Executives, by George D. Webster and Arthur Herold (Washington, DC: American Society of Association Executives, Second Edition, 1979) 204 pages.

Associations and the Antitrust Laws, by Malcolm D. MacArthur (Washington, DC: Chamber of Commerce of the United States, 1976) 81 pages.

Associations and the Law, Books I-IX (Washington, DC: Chamber of Commerce of the United States, 1967-1979).

Associations and the Tax Laws, by Robert R. Statham and Richard W. Buek (Washington, DC: Chamber of Commerce of the United States, 1978) 157 pages.

The Law of Associations, by George D. Webster (New York, NY: Matthew Bender Co., Revised Edition, 1976).

The Law of Tax-Exempt Organizations, by Bruce R. Hopkins (New York, NY: Ronald Press, John Wiley & Sons, Third Edition, 1979) 653 pages.

Managing Membership Societies; A Tax, Legal and Financial Handbook for Officers and Executives, Joseph Grief, Editor (Washington, DC: Foundation of the American Society of Association Executives, 1979) 159 pages.

Non-Profit Corporations, Organizations, and Associations, by Howard L. Oleck (Englewood Cliffs, NJ: Prentice-Hall, Third Edition, 1974) 1,000 pages.

Principles of Association Management (Washington, DC: American Society of Association Executives and Chamber of Commerce of the United States, 1975) 437 pages.

The Role of Trade Associations and Professional Business Societies in America, by Joseph F. Bradley (University Park, PA: The Pennsylvania State University Press, 1965) 166 pages.

Trade and Professional Associations, Course Handbook, Alexander Hammond, Chairman (New York, NY: Practising Law Institute, 1977) 280 pages.

Trade Association Law and Practice, by George P. Lamb and Carrington Shields (Boston, MA: Little, Brown and Co., Revised Edition, 1971) 287 pages.

Periodicals

Association & Society Manager, Magazine (Los Angeles, CA: Barrington Publications Inc., published bi-monthly).

Association Letter, Newsletter (Washington, DC: Chamber of Commerce of the United States, Published monthly until 1982. Law article accumulated and published as *Associations and the Law*).

Association Management, Magazine (Washington, DC: American Society of Association Executives, published monthly).

Association Taxation, Newsletter (Washington, DC: Chamber of Commerce of the United States, published at irregular intervals).

Leadership, Magazine (Washington, DC: American Society of Association Executives, published quarterly).

INDEX

502 ASSOCIATION LAW HANDBOOK

I

Income and taxes (see Taxation)
Incorporation
    advantages 16–19
    articles of 21, 23–26, 83
        sample document 471–473
    disadvantages 18–19
    political action committees 167
    procedures 20–22
    record retention 72
    risk retention groups 144–145
Independent expenditures 189–192
Initiation fees 68
Injunctive relief 152
In-kind contributions 190
Insurance
    group coverage, tax issues 408–415
    incorporation status effects 18
    liability 81, 84, 87–91, 119, 123
    meeting cancellation insurance 119,
        122–123
    product liability 137, 139, 143–146
Internal Revenue Code (see Taxation)
Internal Revenue Service (IRS) (see also
        Taxation)
    records available to 72–73

J

Joint purchasing (see Group buying and
        selling)
Joint research (see Research)
Justice Department
    antitrust enforcement 357–358
        Business Review Letters 360
    on exhibit space availability at trade
        shows 126–127
    on joint research 303–305, 311–312
    on membership restrictions 224–225
    on professional credentialing 332,
        333
    records available to 74, 77

L

Labeling (see Product certification)
Labor Department 73
Labor relations 5
    joint employer collective
        bargaining 147–155
    tax issues 426–427
Laboratories
    accreditation 333
    product testing 287
Landrum-Griffin Act 149, 150

Lawyers
    advertising by 245
    minimum fee schedules 245, 332
Legal contracts (see Contracts)
Legal counsel 22
    activities summary 99–106
    antitrust advice 350–351, 357
    conflict of interest 103–104
    fees 104
    meetings, role in 110, 114
    multiple association management 97
Liability (see also Product liability)
    antitrust liability, Hydrolevel
        doctrine 14, 82, 294–299, 349
    insurance 81, 84, 87–91, 119, 123
    for labor law violations 148, 149
    officers and directors 80–86
    PAC treasurers 167
    subsidiaries of associations 433–435
Libel 134, 314, 317
Licensing (see also Credentialing) 331
Lobbying
    federal contract or grant funds
        for 209–211
    registration requirements 204–208,
        342, 345
    by scientific and educational
        organizations 454–460
    tax issues 425, 450–453
Lodging expenses 438
Longshore industry 147

M

Magnuson-Moss Act 358
Mailing lists 135
Management
    multiple management 95–98
    policy manuals 32–34
Management and Budget, Office of
        (OMB)
    on federal contract and grant funds
        used for lobbying 209–211
    on standards-setting 279
Manual of policies and procedures
    content and purpose 21, 32–34
    political action committees 164
Maple Flooring Mfrs. Assn. v. U.S. 14,
        253
Maritime shipping industry 153
Marketing (see also Group buying and
        selling) 4
Meals expenses 438
Meetings
    antitrust compliance 110, 215–218
    arrangement and conduct of 109–111
    cancellation insurance 119, 122–123
    facilities arrangement 119–124
    minutes 110, 112–115

About the Author

Jerald A. Jacobs, partner and Head of the Association Department of the law firm of Jenner & Block in Washington, D.C., and Chicago, has extensive experience in the legal affairs of associations. He is the editor of *Association Issues* published by the American Society of Association Executives and a contributor to it. Mr. Jacobs served for three years as Chairman of ASAE's Government Affairs Committee. He is Chairman of an ASAE section for association legal counsel.

Mr. Jacobs has written and lectured widely on antitrust law, as well as trade and professional association matters for the Practising Law Institute, the Chamber of Commerce of the United States, the Antitrust Law Section of the American Bar Association, and the American Society of Association Executives.

Jerald Jacobs holds undergraduate and law degrees from Georgetown University and is a member of the District of Columbia, Illinois, and Supreme Court bars, as well as the American Bar Association, Antitrust Section, the Federal Bar Association, and the National Health Lawyers Association.